www.wadsworth.com

www.wadsworth.com is the World Wide Web site for Thomson Wadsworth and is your direct source to dozens of online resources.

At *www.wadsworth.com* you can find out about supplements, demonstration software, and student resources. You can also send email to many of our authors and preview new publications and exciting new technologies.

www.wadsworth.com
Changing the way the world learns®

Explorations in Cultural Competence

Explorations in Cultural Competence

Journeys to the Four Directions

Hilary N. Weaver
State University of New York at Buffalo

THOMSON

BROOKS/COLE

Australia • Canada • Mexico • Singapore • Spain
United Kingdom • United States

Executive Editor: *Lisa Gebo*
Assistant Editor: *Alma Dea Michelena*
Editorial Assistant: *Sheila Walsh*
Marketing Manager: *Caroline Concilla*
Marketing Assistant: *Mary Ho*
Advertising Project Manager: *Tami Strang*
Project Manager, Editorial Production: *Rita Jaramillo*
Art Director: *Vernon Boes*
Print/Media Buyer: *Emma Claydon*

Permissions Editor: *Stephanie Lee*
Production Service: *Mary Deeg, Buuji, Inc.*
Copy Editor: *Robin Gold*
Cover Designer: *Laurie Albrecht*
Cover Image: *Getty Images, Digital Vision*
Cover Printer: *Transcon-Louiseville*
Compositor: *Buuji, Inc.*
Printer: *Transcon-Louiseville*

For more information about our products, contact us at:
Thomson Learning Academic Resource Center
1-800-423-0563

For permission to use material from this text or product, submit a request online at
http://www.thomsonrights.com.

Any additional questions about permissions can be submitted by email to
thomsonrights@thomson.com.

Library of Congress Control Number: 2003116121

ISBN-13: 978-0-534-64148-1
ISBN-10: 0-534-64148-2

Thomson Brooks/Cole
10 Davis Drive
Belmont, CA 94002
USA

Asia
Thomson Learning
5 Shenton Way #01-01
UIC Building
Singapore 068808

Australia/New Zealand
Thomson Learning
102 Dodds Street
Southbank, Victoria 3006
Australia

Canada
Nelson
1120 Birchmount Road
Toronto, Ontario M1K 5G4
Canada

Europe/Middle East/Africa
Thomson Learning
High Holborn House
50/51 Bedford Row
London WC1R 4LR
United Kingdom

Latin America
Thomson Learning
Seneca, 53
Colonia Polanco
11560 Mexico D.F.
Mexico

Spain/Portugal
Paraninfo
Calle/Magallanes, 25
28015 Madrid, Spain

Brief Contents

Contents

PART 2 | THEORETICAL FOUNDATIONS

CHAPTER 11

Arab Americans   236

CHAPTER 12

Immigrants and Refugees   263

PART 4 | LOOKING TOWARD THE FUTURE

WK5

Preface

There have always been some helping professionals who deliberately and thoughtfully integrated issues related to cultural diversity into their work, but only recently has cultural competence
become a common topic at conferences and in social science literature. Indeed, as helping professionals developed a growing awareness of the importance of cultural competence, this awareness has
been transformed into both a professional mandate and an ethical
imperative. Now that the need for cultural competence has
received widespread recognition, practitioners and educators are
faced with questions of how to move in that direction. In particular, the literature of the helping professions is filled with calls for
professionals to apply culturally appropriate knowledge, skills,
and values/attitudes in their work with clients. The next questions
to be answered are what knowledge, what skills, and what
values/attitudes are likely to result in culturally competent work
with different cultural groups? Helping professionals must also be
able to apply the principles of cultural competence to all levels of
practice, not just to clinical interactions with clients. Helping professionals must become actively involved in influencing agencies,
policies, and communities to respond to the needs of many different types of clients.

This book provides guidance for helping professionals as they strive for cultural competence. The goal of this work is to present the reader with the context for the contemporary discussions of cultural competence, provide background information on several of the major cultural populations in the United States, and help the reader think about how the helping professions as well as individual practitioners can strive for cultural competence.

Just as helping professionals are not technicians who perform rote tasks with little discretion or judgment, a text on cultural competence cannot serve as a "how-to" manual with explicit instructions for handling every conceivable scenario related to cultural diversity. Rather, this book is designed to provide useful information and to stimulate thinking about often-difficult and value-laden issues. Professional judgment and self-reflection must always be part of the process of working with clients from any cultural background.

This book begins with an overview of the status of contemporary scholarship on cultural competence and the history that brought us to this point. Although the central focus, particularly in the historical discussion, is on social work with diverse clients, other professions have traveled parallel paths and encountered similar interactions. Part One presents readers with a historical context for understanding contemporary issues related to working with culturally diverse clientele.

Part Two presents the reader with a theoretical and conceptual context. Chapters address theories of cultural identity, self-reflection, and how professionals can strive for cultural competence. Exercises are included at the end of each chapter in this section.

Part Three gives an overview of select cultural groups in the United States, including specific information on culturally competent work with these populations at both micro and macro levels. The populations covered are Native Americans, African Americans, Latinos, Asian Americans, Pacific Islanders, Jewish Americans, Arab Americans, and immigrants and refugees. Case examples are used to illustrate the principles of culturally competent helping with these populations. Each chapter in this section concludes with exercises that can be used in the classroom or for external assignments. Additional resources are suggested for readers who would like to know more about the populations discussed.

Part Four concludes the book with reflections on the future of cultural competence. In particular, discussions focus on how helping professionals can shape their professions and society in ways that increase respect for diversity.

This book is the result of both a professional and personal journey. Personally, growing up as a person of color in a predominantly White area of Eastern Washington State left many questions of cultural identity submerged and unexamined. Pursuing social work education in regions where I was exposed to significantly more diversity raised parallel questions of my own cultural identity and how that identity could fit in a profession with strong roots in Anglo traditions. This book is ultimately the result of my own inquiries and search for balance as a social worker whose profession has often been perceived as hostile, uncaring, and culturally incompetent with my own cultural group, the Lakota. It is my hope that this book will be a useful tool for other helping professionals as they strive to find a comfortable balance between their chosen profession, the needs of the clients they serve, and who they, themselves, are as cultural beings.

This book is far from an individual endeavor. I own a great debt to my family who gave me the support and nurturance that made this project possible; particularly my husband Joseph, daughter Iris, and son Wanblee. The book has been shaped and refined with the input of several readers: Janice Adams, Indiana Weslyan University; Frederica H. Barrow, University of South Florida; Mary Brainerd, Elms College; Barbara A. Candales, Central Connecticut State University; Alice Chornesky, New Mexico State University; Edwin Gonzales-Santin, Arizona State University, and Mike Jacobsen, Southwest Missouri State University. I owe a significant debt to Janine Hunt-Jackson, Linda Schlicting Ray, and Warren Skye who gave me meticulous and detailed feedback and helped me to present my ideas in clear and meaningful ways. I also owe a debt to countless others who are unaware of their influences on me, including the members of the American Indian Alaska Native Social Work Educators' Association and the various colleagues who have supported me throughout my career. I would also like to acknowledge the helping professionals and scholars who paved the way for contemporary discussions of cultural competence. I know I stand on the shoulders of many who have come before me, and I hope to serve as a platform for later scholars who will further develop this important line of work.

Explorations in Cultural Competence

Introduction

The quest for cultural competence as currently articulated in the helping professions is of relatively recent origin, yet, ideas about respecting diversity are long standing. For example, the medicine wheel, an image prominent in some Native American cultures, has many meanings including depicting the importance of diversity. The medicine wheel consists of a circle divided into quadrants that are black, red, yellow, and white. Lakota teachings tell of a world populated by different types of people, originating in different areas or directions. The four sacred colors are associated with four types of people (indigenous people of the Americas, Africans, Europeans, and Asians) coming from four different parts of the world. All kinds of people (represented by the four colors) are equal and are necessary for the world to be in balance.

The values integral to the medicine wheel are at the heart of striving for cultural competence. This ancient conceptualization of diversity provides a meaningful starting point for a contemporary examination of diversity in the helping process. To provide culturally competent services to clients from a variety of backgrounds, helping professionals will find they need to take a journey of learning to the Four Directions. In that spirit, this text provides information about people from the different "directions" that now reside in the United States.

In today's world, helping professionals are increasingly likely to encounter clients from backgrounds different than their own.

Although it isn't possible for a helping professional to know everything about all cultures, this book provides the reader with some background information and ideas about how to think about cultural diversity and maximize cultural competence.

Cultural differences between social workers and their clients can have a major impact on the helping relationship. A client's cultural background may influence what is defined as a problem, how he or she goes about seeking help, and what interventions and solutions are seen as desirable. Likewise, social workers bring their own cultural backgrounds as well as their professional backgrounds to the helping relationship, and this may influence how they approach their clients.

Cultural competence is integrally connected to professional competence; without it, a helping professional is incompetent (Coleman, 1998). Cultural competence is critical to shaping quality social work practice at the micro, mezzo, and macro levels. Although some social workers anticipate only working with one type of client, the extraordinary diversity in U.S. society makes this highly unlikely. Diversity grows as immigrants and refugees continue to arrive in the United States from all over the world. Social workers must be prepared to work with clients from many different cultural backgrounds. Cultural competence requires helping professionals to bring a sense of social justice as well as clinical skills to their work.

The importance of cultural competence has been recognized by the largest, most prominent social work organizations in the United States including the National Association of Social Workers (NASW) and the Council on Social Work Education (CSWE). The Code of Ethics of NASW states that cultural competence with diverse populations is an ethical imperative (NASW, 1999). In addition, social work education programs are required by CSWE to incorporate material on culturally diverse populations in the curriculum to maintain accreditation (CSWE, 2000).

The term *culture* is used in different ways by different authors. Sometimes it is applied broadly to a variety of distinct groups including ethnic groups, gay, lesbian, transgendered, and transsexual people, and people with disabilities. In other contexts, *culture* is used only with particular ethnic groups. In this text, *culture* is used to refer to factors such as the values, beliefs, and worldviews often associated with people who share a common ethnic heritage. These distinct values and beliefs often become important factors in the helping relationship.

The term *cultural competence* is frequently used in social work today. This concept is based on the premise that social services should be provided in ways that respect the cultural context and values of clients (Green, 1999). Developing cultural competence is an ongoing process (Sue & Sue, 1990). A social worker can always learn more about working with clients from diverse cultural groups.

The social work profession has gone through a number of theoretical shifts before arriving at the current emphasis on cultural competence. In the 1950s and 1960s, many social work proponents of equal treatment for all people advocated for a colorblind approach. For example, sometimes agencies were urged to end programs that reflected practices of segregation and move forward with colorblind approaches such as those encouraging transracial adoption (Collmeyer, 1995; Fricke, 1965; Polier, 1960; Young, 1968). It was thought that treating people equally was a fair and just approach to service provision.

It became clear, however, that a colorblind approach ignores culture, a significant and vital part of the identity of many clients. To ignore culture may lead to ineffective service provision rather than to the equitable treatment social workers seek to provide. In the 1970s and 1980s, social workers began to abandon the colorblind approach in favor of a stance valuing cultural sensitivity (e.g., Funnye, 1970). With this approach, it became important for social workers to recognize that cultural differences exist. Social workers were urged to develop a basic understanding of different cultural groups to serve their clients more effectively. Likewise, there was a growing emphasis on the importance of self-awareness and reflection in cross-cultural practice.

In recent years, the emphasis has moved from cultural sensitivity to cultural competence (Green, 1999). Cultural competence is the logical successor to cultural sensitivity. Although sensitivity is important, the culturally competent practitioner takes an additional step to integrate sensitivity with skills. This action component leads to more effective practice. Most scholars who study culturally competent helping practices (see, for example, Campinha-Bacote, 2001; Sue & Sue, 1990) agree that cultural competence consists of a blend of knowledge about diverse populations, values and attitudes including self-awareness and a genuine valuing of diversity, and high quality social work skills.

The theoretical knowledge base on working with culturally diverse clients has expanded rapidly in recent years. This area is now attracting the attention of researchers who are beginning to empirically test theoretical concepts and practice wisdom about cultural competence (see for example Applewhite, 1998; Weaver, 1999). A logical next step is to develop operational definitions of cultural competence with different populations. This would involve identifying *what* knowledge, *what* values and attitudes, and *what* skills are important to be culturally competent with particular populations.

Keep in mind that culture, as the term is used throughout this text, is simply one layer of a client's identity. In addition to having values, beliefs, and worldviews associated with a particular ethnic group, other factors such as religion, gender, sexual orientation, and class can be influential in a person's identity. It is impossible to know simply by observation what factors are most important in an individual's identity. A social worker who assumes that culture is the most significant component of a client's identity may miss the fact that another component such as religion or gender is equally or more important. This book focuses primarily on culture as a factor in identity while recognizing the validity of many other factors. By focusing on this one element, it is possible to spend more time and do the topic more justice than if an attempt was made to include five or six different factors in identity.

The names that people use to label themselves both reflect and reinforce a sense of cultural identity. It is important that social workers strive to use terminology that respects the wishes of clients but it is often difficult to know which terms are considered most appropriate. Preferences for cultural labels have changed over time. The once-common term *Oriental* has now largely been replaced by *Asian*. Likewise, the term *Negro,* used in the social work literature through the 1960s, has been replaced by *Black* or *African American.* Terms like *Hispanic, Latino,* and *Chicano* have all been used to refer to people whose families originated in areas colonized by the Spanish Empire, but these labels may carry different connotations for different people. In a similar vein, *American Indian, Native American, indigenous,* and *First Nations* people are terms that have all been used to describe the original inhabitants of the Americas. Although common usage of such terms has changed over the years, the terms that people use to describe themselves can also be a matter of personal preference. In this book, I use the terms that are generally considered respectful at this time, but the reader should be advised that these may not be the terms preferred by some clients.

No one term is "right" for all members of a cultural group. Preference of terms may be shaped by age, region, and politics as well as other factors. When in doubt, social workers should ask clients about their preferred labels. This is an important way of communicating respect as part of the engaging process. Also, it is not unusual for members of one family to choose different labels to describe their cultural identity. For instance, within one indigenous family it would not be unusual for the father to identify as Sioux, the mother as Oglala, one child as Lakota, and another as a First Nations person. Exploring the different meanings these labels hold for members of this family can provide important information as part of the assessment process.

The purpose of this book is to present and synthesize material on cultural groups in a way that is accessible and useful for social workers and other helping professionals. Part One analyzes how the social work profession stands in relation to culturally competent practice and presents an historical overview of how we have come to this position. Part Two explores what culture is, how it influences various aspects of life, and why this can be a sensitive topic to discuss honestly. The text will guide the reader to become more self-reflective and able to examine his or her own biases and how these influence interactions with clients. Part Three presents information on various groups, or peoples from the Four Directions, while emphasizing intragroup diversity. This section addresses common stereotypes about cultural groups and helps social work students to get past stereotypical perceptions and be more effective in helping their clients. Further readings are suggested on different populations. The text concludes with a discussion of how culturally competent social workers can use their skills to enhance the profession and society. Explorations in cultural competence can be seen as journeys to the Four Directions. In that vein, this text can serve as a road map.

References

Applewhite, S. L. (1998). Culturally competent practice with elderly Latinos. *Journal of Gerontological Social Work, 30*(1/2), 1–15.

Campinha-Bacote, J. (2001). A model of practice to address cultural competence in rehabilitation nursing. *Rehabilitation Nursing, 26*(1), 8–11.

Coleman, H. L. K. (1998). General and multicultural counseling competency: Apples and oranges? *Journal of Multicultural Counseling and Development, 26*, 147–156.

Collmeyer, P. M. (1995). From "Operation Brown Baby" to "Opportunity": The placement of children of color at the Boys and Girls Aid Society of Oregon. *Child Welfare, 74*(1), 242–263.

Council on Social Work Education. (2000). http://www.cswe.org

Fricke, H. (1965). Interracial adoption: The little revolution. *Social Work, 10*(3), 92–97.

Funnye, C. (1970). The militant Black social worker and the urban hustle. *Social Work, 15*(2), 5–12.

Green, J. W. (1999). *Cultural Awareness in the Human Services: A Multi-Ethnic Approach*. Boston: Allyn & Bacon.

National Association of Social Workers (NASW). (1999). *Code of Ethics of the National Association of Social Workers*. Washington, DC: National Association of Social Workers.

Polier, J. W. (1960). Attitudes and contradictions in our culture. *Child Welfare, 39*(9), 1–7.

Sue, D. W., & Sue, D. (1990). *Counseling the Culturally Different*. New York: Wiley.

Weaver, H. N. (1999). Indigenous people and the social work profession: Defining culturally competent services. *Social Work, 44*(3), 217–225.

Young, W. M., Jr. (1968). Tell it like it is. *Social Casework, 49*(4), 207–212.

CHAPTER | # Social Work History and Cultural Diversity

The social work profession has a mandate to work with disadvantaged and disenfranchised populations. This often means that social workers find themselves working with ethnic minorities. This important mandate has been part of the social work profession from its beginnings. The traditions established in the social work profession's formative years have had a lasting influence. Many of our values, beliefs, and practices are directly related to these early helping efforts.

A historical review of the social work profession provides a foundation for understanding contemporary issues. This history reveals both successful innovations and problematic areas in need of change. Understanding social work history is particularly important when working with diverse populations. Although a number of authors have conducted thoughtful explorations of how early social workers worked with specific culturally diverse populations (e.g., Collmeyer, 1995; Iglehart & Becerra, 1995, 1996; Kogut, 1972; Peebles-Wilkins, 1995; Platt & Chandler, 1988), this history is not widely known. The study of social welfare history has not gained much recognition in its own right. Historians who do research in this area are found in a variety of fields from women's studies, to immigration studies, to family studies (Chambers, 1992). Thus, those who seek to learn from the history of the social work profession must take additional steps in their quest. As social workers strive for cultural competence today, it is helpful to review the strengths and weaknesses of their predecessors.

Philosophically, the profession of social work has always condemned prejudice and discrimination. Unfortunately, social workers have not always lived up to these ideals (Golden, 1965; Iglehart & Becerra, 1996). Social agencies gain their sanction, legitimacy, recognition, and funding from the larger society, so they are subject to society's biases (Iglehart & Becerra, 1996). Even in the 1950s and 1960s, segregated services existed, and some social workers avoided confrontations and fights against social injustice (Golden, 1965; Iglehart & Becerra, 1996; Simons, 1956; Sytz, 1957). Because some people of color viewed social workers as part of the problem rather than part of the solution, minority communities rarely embraced social workers to champion their causes (Iglehart & Becerra, 1996).

Throughout the history of the social work profession, the needs of some types of clients have been made priorities over others. A distinction was frequently made between those who deserved help and those who did not. Services primarily targeted the worthy poor, those who were seen as poor through no fault of their own and who could be rescued through the moral example of upper-class friendly visitors (Iglehart & Becerra, 1996). Early agencies and service providers also made distinctions about how they would serve people based on their race or ethnicity. Sometimes agency policies reflected thinly veiled racism. These policies also reinforced class structures and failed to respond to the needs of different cultural groups (Iglehart & Becerra, 1996).

Ethnic minority social workers saw many doors within the profession as closed to them. Exclusionary practices existed in social agencies despite policies with nondiscrimination statements. Likewise, many social workers of color did not feel that the National Association of Social Workers (NASW) addressed their needs or concerns and went on to found organizations such as the National Association of Black Social Workers and Trabajadores de la Raza, both formed in 1969 (Iglehart & Becerra, 1996).

Throughout the history of the social work profession, there has been tension between its stated ideals and day-to-day realities. That tension can clearly be seen in a review of social work practice with diverse populations. Social work, itself, is a very diverse profession made up of people from many different backgrounds and viewpoints. Some social workers advocated for social justice and respect for cultural diversity, but others have not seen these as important issues.

Social workers often differ in background from the clients they serve. Friction sometimes results when social workers are perceived as outsiders trying to impose their views and values on culturally different clients and their communities. Sometimes the clients' or communities' views of problems and the need for change vary from those of social workers, thus leading to tension between client/community self-actualization and social work goals.

Another tension-inducing force that must be recognized is that of institutionalized racism. This insidious force exists throughout society. Social work agencies, policies, and associations are not immune. To live up to their ideals of social justice and respect for cultural diversity, social workers are in a position in which they must question themselves and their own institutions. This is a precarious position for helping professionals to be in: to challenge the very entities that guide their work and employ them.

A review of the history of social work with diverse populations can help illuminate current challenges as helping professionals strive for culturally competent practice. Reviewing the actions and policies of the past reveals both positive role models and mistakes that provide foundations for learning. This chapter will present an overview of the history of social work with European immigrants, Native Americans, African Americans, Latinos, and Asian Americans. It will shed light on the sort of work done with some populations while illuminating large service gaps that existed with other groups.

THE EVOLUTION OF SOCIAL WORK

It is difficult to truly know the experiences of early social work clients. Although there is a fair amount of documentation of the lives of the vulnerable populations that social workers served, these records have been generated by what Chambers (1992) refers to as the guardian classes: those who were in charge of schools, orphanages, agencies, and asylums. These records document the lives of clients from the perspectives of people who often differed from them in class and culture. The information available on early services is also more likely to give information about administrators and programs (Chambers, 1992). Despite these limitations, it is possible to glean some information about clients from what is known about early social workers and their agencies.

The roots of the social work profession are often traced to two main types of agencies: Settlement houses and Charity Organization Societies. These two types of agencies reflect different orientations about the people they served and the root causes of social problems. These philosophies were distinct but not mutually exclusive. Charity Organization Society workers often saw problems as residing within the individual and, thus, individuals had the means to overcome their problems. Settlement house workers tended to define problems as existing in the environment; however, they did see part of their goal as assisting immigrants to adapt to life in America (Iglehart & Becerra, 1996). Settlement houses took on a major role in serving new immigrants, so a review of their services is particularly relevant to the current state of social work with diverse populations.

Although different philosophies initially guided the work of settlement houses and Charity Organization Societies, differences also existed among settlement houses. An analysis of the policies and practices of major settlements in Chicago, New York City, and Boston reveals they were guided by a variety of attitudes and philosophies, from veiled racism to egalitarianism (Kogut, 1972). Settlement houses familiar with serving European immigrants were faced with new challenges as more African Americans moved north into urban areas. Many settlement workers believed the difficulties facing African Americans could be overcome with individuals' hard work and initiative, but others, such as Jane Addams at Hull House in Chicago, believed the problems facing this population, including economic and political discrimination and racial segregation, far exceeded the difficulties faced by European immigrants. Despite this understanding, Addams and her colleagues did not push for integration but, rather, encouraged segregated settlement houses, founded by African Americans, serving African Americans (Popple & Leighninger, 1990).

Many changes have happened since settlement houses and Charity Organization Societies initiated the birth of the social work profession. The last hundred years have seen monumental developments in the professionalism of social work including the development of educational standards and a system of accreditation administered by the Council on Social Work Education. Many of these developments have been positive, but the professionalization of social work has largely devalued ethnic agencies (Iglehart & Becerra, 1996). With professionalization came a greater emphasis on individual change. This conflicted with the perception of many communities of color that external forces contribute significantly to the plight of individuals.

As the field of social work grew to emphasize professionalization, the philosophies of Charity Organization Societies and settlement houses converged with an emphasis on individual change and personal responsibility (Iglehart & Becerra, 1996). The rising influence of psychoanalysis in the 1920s and 1930s encouraged a narrow definition of social work that de-emphasized social action and change. This shift took the profession farther away from goals emphasized by communities of color, such as fighting for equal rights in education, employment, and housing.

All cultural groups have indigenous ways of helping that often meet many of the needs of their communities. Although many of these ways of helping may not be readily visible to people outside those communities, they often still exist as vital and important ways of helping and healing. Formal social agencies should also be available to provide help to people in need. Because mainstream social agencies often excluded or did not adequately address the needs of diverse populations, ethnic communities often developed their own mechanisms for helping people. Most cultural communities developed mutual aid endeavors that were sometimes formalized in social agencies. Ethnic agencies have played a significant role in closing service gaps, appreciating ethnicity, and using an empowerment model of practice, yet these agencies have been virtually ignored by the social work profession. Mutual aid has continued to be an important source of services in ethnic minority communities, even after government agencies expanded service delivery to include these populations (Iglehart & Becerra, 1996).

Examining the history of social work with diverse groups can shed light on the relationships between contemporary social workers and culturally diverse clients. In part, because of the philosophies of the day and in part because of geographic factors, early social work agencies had more involvement with some cultural groups than with others. Early social workers had significantly more involvement with European immigrants than with populations of color. Among populations of color, early social workers had much more involvement with African Americans than with other groups. Accordingly, this level of involvement is reflected in the following discussion.

SERVICES FOR EUROPEAN IMMIGRANTS: A HISTORICAL PERSPECTIVE

The development of settlement houses coincided with a significant wave of immigration from Europe and a strong American belief in social progress. At the end of the 19th century and beginning of the 20th century, the United States experienced its greatest influx of European immigrants (Popple & Leighninger, 1990). The mid-1890s through World War I, known as the Progressive Era, was seen as a time of social advancement and progress in the United States; yet, clearly, it was a more positive time for some groups than for others. Early settlement houses, still in their formative period, were confronted with questions about their roles in working with these new national minorities (Kogut, 1972). Settlement houses developed a variety of responses to new immigrants who often came from southern and Eastern Europe and who were perceived as different from earlier European immigrants in literacy, skills, and appearance.

The dramatic change in immigration patterns during the Progressive Era led to strong anti-immigrant sentiments. In part, these sentiments were based on fears about losing jobs to new immigrants. Fears were also fueled by beliefs that "American" values and ways of life would be overwhelmed and lost in the rising tide of culturally diverse immigrants. Those of White Anglo Saxon stock who were born in the United States often viewed themselves as superior to the new immigrants who came from countries like Poland, Italy, Russia, and Greece (Iglehart & Becerra, 1995). Sometimes settlement house philosophies and actions mirrored the xenophobia and assimilationist attitudes of the larger society whereas other settlements such as Hull House in Chicago led the way in thinking about a pluralistic society (Popple & Leighninger, 1990).

The new wave of immigrants faced harsh discrimination in housing and employment. As a response, Catholic and Jewish immigrants often developed their own schools and institutions. Some Americans viewed this as separatism, which further fueled the view that these new immigrants were troublemakers unwilling to fit into the American way of life (Iglehart & Becerra, 1995).

The Progressive Era was a difficult time for European immigrants. Overcrowded urban tenements led to disease and death. Unsafe working conditions also posed major hazards. Children were especially susceptible to the hazards of unsanitary living conditions and the abuses of child labor. Some children became homeless and some became involved in delinquent behavior (Iglehart & Becerra, 1995).

Violence against foreign-born people was particularly acute during economic recessions in 1910–11, 1914–15, and just after World War I. Nativism, racism, and bitter competition for jobs fueled violence. The Ku Klux Klan was reinvigorated at this time with its campaigns of terror against those perceived as anything other than all-American. In addition to targeting African Americans, the Klan targeted Catholics and Jews (Iglehart & Becerra, 1995).

Charity Organization Societies and settlement houses were both involved in the Americanization of European immigrants (Iglehart & Becerra, 1995). Americanization, a major assimilationist doctrine of the Progressive Era, suggested that the problems of the new immigrants would be of short duration as they took on the values and behaviors of middle-class Americans. Early social workers responded to the social issues of their day, but still were influenced by the society they lived in. An examination of early social workers reveals a complex mixture of reactions and philosophies not only within the profession as a whole but also within individual social workers. Many helping professionals participated in a reform movement tainted by racism and nativism, but they also displayed an interest in and sympathy for minorities (Kogut, 1972).

From their beginning in 1886, settlement houses were associated with a tradition of social reform. The emphasis placed on the individual by social welfare institutions in general was tempered by a neighborhood and group focus, although philosophies of settlement leaders varied widely and some were hardly distinguishable from their counterparts, the Charity Organization Societies (Kogut, 1972). Hull House in Chicago appears to have had one of the most supportive responses to new immigrants, but not all Settlement houses respected new immigrants and their cultures. "In telling the social work history, a few major settlement houses are singled out to exemplify settlement house work. The history that involved anti-immigration sentiment, belief in the individual as the cause of his or her plight in life, the role of Americanization in settlement house work, and the social control aspects of this work is frequently minimized or ignored" (Iglehart & Becerra, 1995, p. 118).

SERVICES FOR NATIVE AMERICANS: A HISTORICAL PERSPECTIVE

Early social workers and social service agencies had minimal involvement with Native Americans. At the time the social work profession was developing in the late 1800s, many Native people, particularly in the Western United States, continued to live in their traditional territories or on reservation lands reserved by treaty or set aside for them by the federal government. Few Native Americans lived in urban Eastern areas where the seeds of what would become social work had begun to grow.

The federal government has a unique relationship with Native Americans. Native Nations existed as sovereign entities before contact with Europeans and are recognized as such in the U.S. Constitution and through treaties and other agreements with the United States. When treaties were negotiated, agreements were made between the United States and various Native Nations. The Native Nations made concessions such as giving up land while reserving lands for their use. The federal government also agreed to make payments that were sometimes monetary and sometimes in-kind. In-kind payments the federal government agreed to make under treaty arrangements included providing food, clothing, blankets, educational services, and health services. Although many of these goods and services are similar to those provided by social agencies, the goods and services that Native Americans received at this time were not a form of charity but, rather, were payments for treaty obligations. The United States has broken many treaties, but legally they remain in force and require compliance (Morris, 1992).

As U.S. policy toward Native Nations developed in the late 1800s, many Native people were considered by the federal government and its representatives to be incompetent and thus wards of the federal government. Paternalistic policies developed through U.S. Supreme Court decisions and acts of Congress created a trust responsibility in which the federal government assumed a unique responsibility for the welfare of Native Americans. More than a century of paternalistic policies has created a tangled web of dependency that makes it extraordinarily difficult for contemporary Native people and Native Nations to develop and operate their own social services.

Because of their historic relationship with the federal government, Native Nations have been subject to significant governmental intrusion in the arena of social welfare. As part of an assimilation campaign promulgated by the federal government, beginning in the late 1800s, it became U.S. social policy to remove Native American children from their families and communities and educate them in distant boarding schools. In these schools, children were forbidden to speak their languages, practice their religions, or practice any of their cultural traditions. These schools had a devastating impact, resulting in a contemporary legacy of child abuse and neglect, substance abuse, and mental health problems (Brave Heart-Jordan & DeBruyn, 1995; Morrisette, 1994; Weaver & White, 1999).

The dependency created by paternalistic policies and the family disruption caused by the boarding schools have made Native communities vulnerable to a host of social problems, thus leading to ongoing government intrusion and social work involvement. By the 1970s, 25 to 35% of Native children were being raised outside of their families, with 85% of those in substitute care being placed in non-Native homes or facilities (Mannes, 1995). The vast numbers of children being raised away from their cultural traditions threatened cultural continuity and the very future of Native Nations (Weaver & White, 1999). Throughout the 20th century, social workers were heavily involved in the removal of Native children and their frequent placement with non-Native families through organizations like the Bureau of Indian Affairs and the Child Welfare League of America (George, 1997). Social workers' contribution to the cultural destruction of Native communities has left a bitter taste for many contemporary Native people.

The ongoing provision of social and health services guaranteed by the federal government to Native Americans has sometimes resulted in devastating betrayals of trust. Rather than helping, at times services have been destructive. During the 1960s and 1970s, 25 to 50% of all Native women between the ages of 15 and 44 were sterilized under the auspices of the federally run Indian Health Service, often without their knowledge or consent (Lawrence, 2000). Sometimes women were coerced or threatened with the loss of their welfare benefits or their children if they did not consent to tubal ligation or hysterectomy (Lawrence, 2000; Torpy, 2000).

Social workers were directly involved in removing Native children from their homes and communities as well as the sterilization of Native American women. These factors have led to an ongoing climate of mistrust of helping services offered under auspices of government agencies or any agency associated with the dominant society.

SERVICES FOR AFRICAN AMERICANS: A HISTORICAL PERSPECTIVE

Many African Americans have their roots in the economic system that enslaved Africans and brought them to the United States in the 16th to 19th centuries. As slaves, these people received limited basic necessities like food and shelter but little else. Emancipation raised the question of who would take responsibility for dependent African Americans, particularly orphaned children (Peebles-Wilkins, 1995). From 1865 to 1872, the federal government operated the Freedman's Bureau, the first federal social welfare program (other than veteran's benefits) in the United States. (Popple & Leighninger, 1990; Weaver, 1992). This organization took major strides in promoting education for the newly freed slaves but was less successful in meeting its objective of promoting economic self-sufficiency. The Freedman's Bureau was short lived in its operation. When it closed in 1872, major service gaps remained in African American communities.

The segregation that developed and was institutionalized after the Civil War included vastly different treatment and services for African Americans than for people of European origin. Young African American children have historically been jailed or sent to reform schools, even when their behavior was not delinquent, because communities have been slow to respond with needed foster care services (Peebles-Wilkins, 1995). Likewise, other education, health, and recreational services have been sorely lacking.

During the Progressive Era, African American children were excluded from White-operated orphanages in Chicago. Likewise in Virginia, services existed for delinquent White boys, but none existed for African American boys who were confined to jails, penitentiaries, stockades, or chain gangs (Iglehart & Becerra, 1996). Even 75 years after this practice became illegal in Virginia, many African American children under age 15 were still being jailed (Peebles-Wilkins, 1995). Historical exclusion of African Americans from health and educational systems has led many to have less knowledge of, and trust in, formal care systems, thus perpetuating their continuing exclusion (American Psychiatric Association, 1994).

Settlement Houses and Charity Organization Societies

Settlement houses were slow to develop services for African Americans, in part because many African Americans still lived in rural southern areas and in part because of overt prejudice or institutional racism that led social workers to pay little attention to this population (Popple & Leighninger, 1990). Settlements generally responded in one of five ways to the influx of African Americans to northern urban areas: (1) provide services, (2) develop separate, segregated services, (3) refuse to serve African Americans, (4) close rather than serve African Americans, or (5) relocate to areas without African Americans (Iglehart & Becerra, 1996).

A few settlements welcomed African American clients or developed branches in African American neighborhoods. In 1909, W. E. B. Du Bois' volume, *Efforts for Social Betterment Among Negro Americans,* noted a number of settlements that served African Americans, most of which had both White and African American staff. Settlements that opened separate facilities for African Americans included the Women's Federation of Elmira, New York, Henry Street Settlement in New York City, College Settlement in Philadelphia, and the South End House in Boston. Even those settlements that served African American communities usually had all or primarily White boards; thus, African Americans had little influence over their policies or practices (Iglehart & Becerra, 1995).

Most settlements, however, were slow to accommodate, much less welcome African Americans. Kingsley House in Philadelphia, Central Presbyterian Chapel and Settlement House in Kansas City, Missouri, the Neighborhood House of Ft. Worth, Texas, and Friendship House in Washington, D.C., all excluded African Americans. Eli Bates House in Chicago chose to close rather than admit African Americans. One New York settlement substantially increased its membership fee to discourage African Americans from joining, and Christamore settlement in Indianapolis and Marcy Center of Chicago decided to move rather than integrate (Iglehart & Becerra, 1995).

Americanization, a major function of most settlement houses, was not a relevant goal for African Americans who already were Americans, grounded in U.S. values, beliefs, and culture. Thus, settlement houses were at a loss for what to do with this population (Iglehart & Becerra, 1995). Some settlement houses took the patronizing and moralistic perspective that African Americans were in need of uplifting. Even at Hull House in Chicago, Jane Addams stated that African Americans were in the early stages of their development (Iglehart & Becerra, 1995).

> The discriminatory practices that existed outside the settlement house found their way inside the settlement house. In addition, the creation of separate facilities to serve African-American populations was a perpetuation of the prevailing belief that races should be segregated. As with other services, segregation meant less—less service, less attention, less advocacy—for this group. The reform arm of the nascent social work profession was handcuffed by the pervasive racism that dominated the external polity and external economy, as well as by the

racism that permeated the internal polity and internal economy of the settlement houses. (Iglehart & Becerra, 1995, p. 124)

Although settlement houses had more contact with African Americans than other agencies of their time, Charity Organization Societies also provided some services to this population. In fact, African Americans were the only population of color found in significant numbers in areas served by Charity Organization Societies (Iglehart & Becerra, 1995). Although African Americans received little ongoing benefit from Charity Organization Society services or support of social reform measures such as housing code enforcement or labor legislation, Charity Organization Societies did conduct investigations and publish reports on the conditions of African Americans. Some Charity Organization Societies also trained African American friendly visitors to work within African American communities. Charity Organization Society workers often displayed paternalistic and patronizing views of this population. Such views were seen as sympathetic rather than racist. The Charity Organization Society focus on changing the individual was at odds with the reform focus of many African Americans, which viewed social problems as the result of oppressive laws and social policies that kept people in poverty (Iglehart & Becerra, 1995). These different ways of viewing the world alienated many African Americans from service delivery systems during the Progressive era (Iglehart & Becerra, 1996).

The Development of Mutual Aid

Mutual aid efforts developed in African American communities because of a history of exclusion, segregation, and differential treatment (Iglehart & Becerra, 1996; Peebles-Wilkins, 1995). Churches became a significant source of mutual aid and social service provision in African American communities because of their primacy for many African Americans and their role as safe, central meeting places (Iglehart & Becerra, 1996). As Du Bois reported in 1907, the strength of the African American church is directly linked to African social institutions and thus it serves as the hub of African American economic, educational, and social activity (Du Bois, 1907/1969). Eventually the social needs of African American communities exceeded what churches were able to provide, thus voluntary organizations such as service organizations, fraternities, and social clubs were formed (Iglehart & Becerra, 1996).

Early efforts at social services in African American communities emphasized collective responsibility and self-development as well as external community involvement and interracial cooperation. In addition, these services emphasized the development of personal and racial pride through programs that preserved cultural heritage and promoted social justice (Peebles-Wilkins, 1995). Many forms of mutual aid and what Du Bois (1907/1969) called cooperative benevolence existed in African American communities. He documented 75 to 100 homes and orphanages, 40 hospitals, and numerous societies run primarily by African Americans, for African Americans, in the late 1800s and early 1900s. During this period, African American women began to develop services to meet the needs of children and youth. Services for children were closely linked to a philosophy of uplifting the race espoused by organizations such as the National Association of Colored Women (Peebles-Wilkins, 1995).

Examples of the fruitful efforts of African American women abound as the foundation for contemporary social services in African American communities. Carrie Steele, a maid in the Atlanta Terminal Railroad Station, began caring for children she found abandoned in the station. Initially she took them home with her at night and back to the station during the day where they played while she worked. In 1888, after a successful community fundraising effort, she opened her own orphanage. By 1923, she began receiving United Way support and the home exists today as the Carrie Steele-Pitts Home, serving 100 neglected, abused, abandoned, or orphaned children of all cultural backgrounds (Peebles-Wilkins, 1995). Service gaps also existed in other areas throughout the country. In Kansas City, Missouri, the Community Chest would not serve African Americans so when girls were released from the orphanage at age 12, they were automatically sent to the state institution for delinquents until they turned 17. This practice ended in 1934 when the Colored Big Sister Association began home-finding efforts that culminated in developing their own residential facility (Peebles-Wilkins, 1995).

Although private efforts of African American women in the late 19th and early 20th centuries led to the formation of a number of schools and orphanages serving African American children, differential treatment persisted and many youth, including children as young as 8 years old, were sentenced to jail (Peebles-Wilkins, 1995). As cases like this gained media attention, White philanthropists began to join with African American leaders to raise funds and develop more appropriate services and agencies. These private services for children began to decline as institutionalized social welfare increased after the Great Depression and broader governmental alternatives became available after World War II (Peebles-Wilkins, 1995).

The Professionalization of African American Social Work

Like their White colleagues, some African Americans advocated for the professionalization of social work. From its founding in 1911, the National Urban League considered itself a social work organization and pushed for educated African Americans to join its staff. E. Franklin Frazier, a sociologist by training, became the director of the Atlanta School of Social Work in 1922, the first African American school of social work (Platt & Chandler, 1988).

Frazier was an activist who published articles criticizing racism. His writing is one of the few examples of content on African Americans found in social work journals and conferences in the 1920s. Although African American social workers were involved in substantial service provision, research, and activism with African American clients and communities, mainstream social work publications paid little attention to this population (Platt & Chandler, 1988).

Social Work Agencies and Civil Rights

Some social workers and social agencies championed the cause of civil rights in the 1950s and 1960s, but most were not at the forefront of this movement. Some social work organizations were slow to respond to calls for integration and equal treatment of African Americans. In some areas, social agencies set quotas for the maximum number of African American clients they would accept for fear they would become "Negro agencies" (Jackson, 1957), and social work conferences were sometimes segregated (Platt & Chandler, 1988).

Not all social workers resisted involvement in civil rights struggles. Some social workers called for their colleagues to take a more proactive role in striving to serve African Americans. One social worker in 1960 made a connection between involvement in civil rights and increased service utilization:

> If the social agencies were to desert their posture of benevolent neutrality in the civil rights field and were to take more forceful action on some of the civil rights issues such as housing, employment, and education—and, further, if this were to become known in the Negro community—the utilization of agency services by this group might tend to increase, for the agencies would then be regarded as interested friends and protagonists rather than as ambivalent preservers of the *status quo*. With those who might say that this is merely conjecture, one must agree. But the advantages to the agencies and to the social work profession would be great, and all they stand to lose is their timidity. (Manning, 1960, p. 13, emphasis in original)

Likewise, some African American social workers called for their colleagues to get more involved with social justice and to reject social work theories that were colorblind and viewed the social environment and responses to that environment as the same for Whites and African Americans. Contemporary social work theories were critiqued as irrelevant, and the call was sounded for new theories to be developed that were not necessarily based on social work's European heritage (Funnye, 1970).

SERVICES FOR LATINOS: A HISTORICAL PERSPECTIVE

Mexican Americans are the largest Latino group and the first to reside in what is now the United States in significant numbers. Some Mexican Americans trace their ancestry to people who resided in the Southwest before Mexico ceded it to the United States in 1848 under the Treaty of Guadelupe Hidalgo. Others came as immigrants to the United States in the early 1900s because of U.S. economic expansion and Mexican political instability.

During its formative years, the profession of social work had minimal involvement with Latino populations. Mexican Americans resided primarily in the West whereas the majority of settlement houses and Charity Organization Societies originated in the East. Puerto Ricans, the second largest Latino group, currently reside in the Northeast in large numbers, but at the turn of the 20th century, few lived on the mainland. Likewise, other Latino groups immigrated to the United States in significant numbers after the profession of social work was well established. A few settlements reported serving some Latino clients, but they offered primarily religious teachings and did little to address economic and political issues (Iglehart & Becerra, 1995).

Self-help efforts developed to fill the service gaps left by social service agencies. Mutual aid efforts in Latino communities often emphasized uplifting of the group and decreasing their outsider status, thereby leading to more social acceptance and social justice (Iglehart & Becerra, 1995).

Mexicans developed mutual aid societies or *mutualistas* before the U.S. annexation of much of Mexico in 1848. These organizations sponsored cultural events, issued funeral insurance, served as credit unions, published newspapers, and opened libraries. After annexation, these organizations also focused on activism and rejection of assimilation (Marquez & Jennings, 2000). Mexican Americans also developed labor unions and civil rights organizations in response to struggles with oppression. Beginning in the mid-1960s Mexican American community organizations and university groups became revitalized with a sense of cultural pride, advocacy, and in some cases a desire for separatism and return of U.S. land that had once been part of Mexico (Marquez & Jennings, 2000). Although social workers had minimal involvement in these grassroots efforts, the emphasis on mutual aid and social justice parallel primary social work values.

Puerto Ricans have also participated in social movements to advocate for worker rights, human rights, and educational opportunities. For example, the Puerto Rican studies movement fought to make education more accessible and led to development of a group of educated Puerto Ricans who could help shape policies that affect this population (Marquez & Jennings, 2000). In addition to participating with other groups in social movements, Puerto Ricans are faced with struggles regarding the status of Puerto Rico. Various constituents within the Puerto Rican population have favored options as different as statehood and complete independence for the island of Puerto Rico.

SERVICES FOR ASIAN AMERICANS: A HISTORICAL PERSPECTIVE

Like many Latino groups, most Asian American groups arrived after social work was well established as a profession, thus, early social agencies had little or no involvement with Asian clients. The Chinese were the first to arrive in the United States in significant numbers. They did arrive during social work's formative years, but they settled primarily in the West, an area with few settlement houses or Charity Organization Societies. The Japanese were the next Asian group to arrive in the United States, and they tended to settle in the West.

Mutual aid was the primary assistance available to Asians in the United States. Early Chinese communities were closed systems that focused on meeting all the needs of their group. Segregation and anti-Asian violence led the

Chinese to cluster in ethnic enclaves. The isolation of Chinese communities led to the perception that they could take care of themselves. Voluntary Chinese associations were often controlled by the merchant class that supported them (Iglehart & Becerra, 1995). Early communities were primarily made up of male laborers; thus, issues of women and children did not need attention (Green, 1999).

Early Japanese immigrants had similar experiences to their Chinese counterparts. Mutual aid associations tended to form around economic issues. Communities were cohesive and developed internal mechanisms for serving the needs of their members (Iglehart & Becerra, 1995).

Only one Chinese settlement is listed in the *Handbook of Settlements* published in 1911. The True Sunshine Mission was located in San Francisco's Chinatown. Its work focused on Americanization rather than social reform, perhaps in part because of strong anti-Chinese sentiments that dominated much of the West. Although the Chinatown Rescue Settlement and Recreation Room existed in New York City, its work targeted young women of European origin who lived with Chinese and American men in the Chinatown area (Iglehart & Becerra, 1995).

The biases apparent in the relationship between social agencies and other clients of color also extended to Asian Americans. In 1901, the superintendent of the Boys and Girls Aid Society of Oregon strongly disapproved of the placement of a White infant with a Chinese family. The child was forcibly removed by police who kicked in the door of the family home and removed her. Meanwhile, that same agency reported having little difficulty finding adoptive homes for Asian children and 65% were adopted by White families (Collmeyer, 1995).

REFLECTIONS ON THE HISTORY OF SOCIAL WORK WITH DIVERSE GROUPS

During its first decades, professional social work was dominated by settlement houses and Charity Organization Societies. Both shared a philosophy of assimilation and Americanization, although some settlement houses also concerned themselves with social reform and macro-level issues. Although generalizations such as these can be used to summarize early social work, it is important to remember that social workers and social agencies have never represented one monolithic viewpoint. In fact, some social workers were on the cutting edge of the movement for social reform and social justice, whereas others had paternalistic or bigoted perspectives that inhibited their ability or willingness to serve diverse populations. Many took positions somewhere in between these extremes.

By the 1950s, the social work profession was well established and seven groups joined to form the National Association of Social Workers. A review of articles published in the major social work journals in the late 1950s through early 1970s reveals a lot about the actions and perceptions of social workers of that day. For the United States, this was a time of struggle for civil rights. The civil rights movement of the 1950s and 1960s served as a major impetus for disenfranchised client groups to demand relevant services (Sue et al., 1998). Issues of race, culture, and diversity were highly visible and hotly debated. In the late 1950s, the civil rights movement, in particular the Supreme Court decision to integrate schools in *Brown v. Board of Education*, spawned a few articles on racial and cultural issues in the journal *Social Work*. Topics included desegregation (Simons, 1956; Sytz, 1957), understanding racial problems (Jackson, 1957), infusing cultural issues in casework (Fantl, 1958; Meir, 1959), minorities in school settings (Landes, 1959), and immigration (Bernard, 1959).

Some social workers in the 1950s called on their colleagues to become involved in civil rights issues as a professional responsibility. As one social worker stated in 1957, "Building community understanding of racial problems and their amelioration is currently one of social work's most perplexing tasks. It is a chore that should be done, but is often shirked; a problem tickled but not tackled; an obligation assumed, but not fulfilled" (Jackson, 1957, p. 9). However eloquent, voices raised on behalf of civil rights were often tarnished by the era they lived in. Writing often continued to be paternalistic toward people of color. Although a few strong voices were raised in earlier decades, the social work literature gave minimal attention to people of color until the late 1960s.

The social work literature of the 1960s focusing on people of color falls into two distinct categories: social activism and clinical implications. As social activists, a number of social workers discussed the timely topic of integration. Some supported integration wholeheartedly (e.g., Funnye & Shiffman, 1967; Young, 1967), but others expressed the view that integration worsened ghetto conditions and urged that separate institutions were important as a base for developing political power and ethnic identity (e.g., Piven & Cloward, 1967). Freedom rides were discussed as a way of mobilizing for social change (Olds, 1963). Articles of a more clinical nature focused on issues like exploring racial anger in the social work relationship (Gochros, 1966), the breakdown of the African American family (Herzog, 1966), and countertransference of White workers with African American clients (Bloch, 1968).

Early articles on integrating culture in the helping process take an important step in recognizing that helping methods may need modification to be effective with diverse populations. Some articles (e.g., Fantl, 1958), however, are marred with a paternalistic perspective when discussing people who cannot comprehend how they can be helped by casework and are ignorant of what is expected of them because of cultural differences or their newcomer status. Some social workers felt that when clients of different cultural backgrounds approached agencies steeped in the dominant culture this could indicate they desire help with acculturation. One article reported, "The caseworker has the delicate task of balancing awareness of the client's differing standards, goals, and values against the possibility that he is mutely reaching out for help in becoming more similar to those who represent the dominant culture" (Meier, 1959, p. 16). Another social work author stated that recognizing cultural differences is a prerequisite to being able to "redirect minority thinking and ambitions" (Landes, 1959, p. 95). Clearly, a part of social work was still grounded in the tradition of Americanization and assimilation.

A number of social workers believed their profession did not go far enough in advocating for clients from oppressed groups. In part, this led to the creation of groups like the National Association of Black Social Workers. They chastised colleagues for ignoring civil rights issues and discriminatory policies and practices (Iglehart & Becerra, 1995) and expressing little professional concern with issues of cultural diversity (Kolodny, 1969). Some social workers, no doubt echoing the concerns of others, expressed fears and seem to have been part of a backlash response to the Civil Rights and Black Power movements. The article, "'Crow Jim': Implications for social work" (Simmons, 1963) expresses fears of reverse discrimination and African American prejudice against Whites. Simmons believes social workers must work to stop oppression, not because it is the right thing to do, but as a means of reducing its aftermath, Black rage.

In addition to focusing on societal change, social workers wrote that they must get their own houses in order. They pointed out the disparity between the values professed by social workers and the practices of social agencies. Agencies, themselves, required integration. Concerns were expressed about unequal facilities, unequal use of facilities, lack of minority representation on boards, differential treatment of staff, and services limited to one group (Golden, 1965). By the late 1960s, the critical voices of African American social workers were regularly heard in the social work literature. Marie Simmons Saunders (1969) wrote as an impassioned African American social worker trying to help White social workers understand the dynamics of the ghetto with the ultimate goal of eliminating hostility and the ghetto itself.

Some critics of social work claimed that social welfare institutions served as colonial influences in communities of color. Miller (1969) compared the role of social work to other colonizing entities: "The modern colonialist ministers to the underdeveloped rather than the primitive—to the deprived rather than the despised. Most pernicious of all, he looks to the future with hope; through charity and patient instruction his charges will be brought into today with strength and vigor and the real equality that comes from competitive viability" (p. 67). Miller notes that the stance taken by the social work profession is sincere, but, in fact, social welfare institutions and social workers approach African Americans from a paternalistic, deficit perspective. "Social work's unique contribution to the ideology of the White man's burden could be called *clinicalism*. It is founded on a presumption of damage—that is, as a result of the sad and brutal history of the Negro people the individual member of that race is likely to have been psychologically injured. The nature of the damage is seen as multifaceted" (Miller, 1969, p. 70, emphasis in original).

Whitney Young, a prominent African American social worker and civil rights leader, called for social workers to stop trying to be "little psychiatrists" and to get more involved in urban renewal, antipoverty programs, and social reform. He called for social workers to confront stereotypes of African Americans as violent militants and to approach African American clients from a strengths perspective. He expressed concern that social workers' low expectations of African American clients result in self-fulfilling prophecies (Young, 1968). Other African American social workers echoed Young's concerns and called for African American social workers to influence the profession, both by research and practice. African American social workers were encouraged to be strong advocates and to avoid cooptation into large-scale government projects that promised hope but in reality were little more than diversionary urban repair (Funnye, 1970).

A historical review reveals that social welfare has taken an ambivalent position wavering between support for the melting pot and cultural pluralism (Miller, 1969). Social workers, whether on the cutting edge of social reform or steeped in bigoted philosophies, are all influenced by the times they live in. In hindsight, it is easy to see that even reform-minded activists sometimes held patronizing views of their clients. Perhaps, in the decades to come, readers will have similar reflections on the current dialogue on cultural competence. Contemporary social workers can learn from their predecessors and select positive role models while trying to avoid the pitfalls of paternalistic practices grounded in their own cultural biases.

References

American Psychiatric Association. (1994). *Ethnic Minority Elderly: A Task Force Report of the American Psychiatric Association.* Washington DC: American Psychiatric Association.

Bernard, W. S. (1959). American immigration policy in the era of the dispossessed. *Social Work, 4*(1), 66–73.

Bloch, J. B. (1968). The White workers and the Negro client in psychotherapy. *Social Work, 13*(2), 36–42.

Brave Heart-Jordan, M., & DeBruyn, L. (1995). So she may walk in balance: Integrating the impact of historical trauma in the treatment of American Indian women. In J. Adelman & G. Enguidanos (Eds.), *Racism in the Lives of Women: Testimony, Theory, and Guides to Antiracist Practice.* New York: Haworth Press, 345–368.

Chambers, C. (1992). "Uphill all the way": Reflections on the course and study of welfare history. *Social Service Review, 66*(4), 492–504.

Collmeyer, P. M. (1995). From "Operation Brown Baby" to "Opportunity": The placement of children of color at the Boys and Girls Aid Society of Oregon. *Child Welfare, 74*(1), 242–263.

Du Bois, W. E. B. (1907/1969). *Economic Cooperation Among Negro Americans.* Atlanta: Atlanta University Press.

Du Bois, W. E. B. (1909/1969). *Efforts for Social Betterment Among Negro Americans.* Atlanta: Atlanta University Press.

Fantl, B. (1958). Integrating psychological, social, and cultural factors in assertive casework. *Social Work, 3*(4), 30–37.

Funnye, C. (1970). The militant Black social worker and the urban hustle. *Social Work, 15*(2), 5–12.

Funnye, C., & Shiffman, R. (1967). The imperative of deghettoization: An answer to Piven and Cloward. *Social Work, 12*(2).

George, L. J. (1997). Why the need for the Indian Child Welfare Act? *Journal of Multicultural Social Work, 5*(3/4), 165–175.

Gochros, J. S. (1966). Recognition and use of anger in Negro clients. *Social Work, 11*(1), 28–34.

Golden, J. (1965). Desegregation of social agencies in the South. *Social Work, 10*(1), 58–67.

Green, J. W. (1999). *Cultural Awareness in the Human Services: A Multi-Ethnic Approach.* Englewood Cliffs, NJ: Prentice-Hall.

Herzog, E. (1966). Is there a "breakdown" of the Negro family? *Social Work, 11*(1), 3–9.

Iglehart, A., & Becerra, R. M. (1995). *Social Services and the Ethnic Community.* Boston: Allyn & Bacon.

Iglehart, A., & Becerra, R. M. (1996). Social work and the ethnic agency: A history of neglect. *Journal of Multicultural Social Work, 4*(1), 1–20.

Jackson, N. C. (1957). Building community understanding of racial problems. *Social Work, 2*(3), 9–15.

Kogut, A. (1972). The settlements and ethnicity: 1890–1914. *Social Work, 17*(3), 22–31.

Kolodny, R. L. (1969). Ethnic cleavages in the United States: An historical reminder to social workers. *Social Work, 14*(1), 13–23.

Landes, R. (1959). Minority groups and school social work. *Social Work, 4*(3), 91–97.

Lawrence, J. (2000). The Indian Health Service and the sterilization of Native American women. *American Indian Quarterly, 24*(3), 400–423.

Mannes, M. (1995). Factors and events leading to the passage of the Indian Child Welfare Act. *Child Welfare, 74*(1), 264–282.

Manning, S. W. (1960). Cultural and value factors affecting the Negro's use of agency services. *Social Work, 5*(4), 3–13.

Marquez, B., & Jennings, J. (2000). Representation of other means: Mexican American and Puerto Rican social movement organization. *Political Science and Politics, 33*(3), 541–546.

Meier, E. G. (1959). Social and cultural factors in casework diagnosis. *Social Work, 4*(3), 15–26.

Miller, H. (1969). Social work in the Black ghetto: The new colonialism. *Social Work, 14*(3), 65–76.

Morris, G. T. (1992). International law and politics: Toward a right of self-determination for indigenous peoples. In M. A. Jaimes, (ed.), *The State of Native America: Genocide, Colonization, and Resistance.* Boston: South End Press, 55–86.

Morrisette, P. J. (1994). The holocaust of First Nations people. *Contemporary Family Therapy, 16*(5), 381–392.

Olds, V. M. (1963). Freedom Rides: A social movement as an aspect of social change. *Social Work, 8*(3), 16–23.

Peebles-Wilkins, W. (1995). Janie Porter Barrett and the Virginia Industrial School for Colored Girls: Community response to the needs of African American children. *Child Welfare, 74*(1), 143–161.

Piven, F. F., & Cloward, R. A. (1967). The case against urban desegregation. *Social Work, 12*(1), 12–21.

Platt, T., & Chandler, S. (1988). Constant struggle: E. Franklin Frazier and Black social work in the 1920s. *Social Work, 33*(4), 293–297.

Popple, P. R., & Leighninger, L. H. (1990). *Social Work, Social Welfare, and American Society.* Boston: Allyn & Bacon.

Saunders, M. S. (1969). The ghetto: Some perceptions of a Black social worker. *Social Work, 14*(4), 84–88.

Simmons, L. S. (1963). "Crow Jim": Implications for social work. *Social Work, 8*(3), 24–30.

Simons, S. M. (1956). Desegregation and integration in social work. *Social Work, 1*(4), 20–25.

Sue, D. W., Carter, R. T., Casas, J. M., Fouad, N. A., Ivey, A. E., Jensen, M., LaFromboise, T., Manese, J. E., Ponterotto, J. G., & Vazquez-Natall, E. (1998). *Multicultural Counseling Competencies: Individual and Organizational Development.* Thousand Oaks: Sage.

Sytz, F. (1957). Desegregation: One view from the Deep South. *Social Work, 2*(3), 3–8.

Torpy, S. J. (2000). Native American women and coerced sterilization: On the trail of tears in the 1970s. *American Indian Culture and Research Journal, 24*(2), 1–22.

Weaver, H. N. (1992). African Americans and social work: An overview of the Antebellum through Progressive eras. *Journal of Multicultural Social Work, 2*(4), 91–102.

Weaver, H. N., & White, B. J. (1999). Protecting the future of indigenous children and nations: An examination of the Indian Child Welfare Act. *Journal of Health and Social Policy, 10*(4), 35–50.

Young, W. M., Jr. (1967). The case for urban integration. *Social Work, 12*(3), 12–17.

Young, W. M., Jr. (1968). Tell it like it is. *Social Casework, 49*(4), 207–212.

Cultural Identity

CHAPTER

Theories and Implications

This chapter reviews the influence of culture, key terms, and major theories of cultural identity. Flexible and multidimensional aspects of identity are reviewed as well as how theory informs social work practice and the influences of culture on specific values and help seeking behaviors.

THE INFLUENCE OF CULTURE

Culture has a significant influence on an individual's values, beliefs, and worldview. Cultural groups exert influence over their own members as well as those from other cultures (Orlandi, 1992). "Culture is so basic to human experience that it cannot be separated from humanness or from personality: there is no such thing as a basic, pre-cultural or 'blue print' human being" (Swinomish Tribal Mental Health Project, 1991, p. 103).

Put another way, "culture lies at the very heart of what it means to be human . . . Objectivity is impossible since our understanding of the social world is inevitably filtered through the parochial worldviews that we inherit . . . from the culture into which we were born" (Angel & Williams, 2000, p. 27). Culture represents a way of life that binds people together through language, nationality, values, beliefs, and practices that are considered appropriate and desirable. Culture guides thinking and shapes behavior (Applewhite, 1998).

Nonmaterial elements of culture are what unify ethnic groups. It is not the readily apparent surface similarities and differences that are important. What are most meaningful are the dynamic forces that give groups coherence, uniqueness, and unity within their own diversity. These more meaningful elements are not easily discernable and recognized. Understanding these intangible elements of culture is important in building productive social work relationships (Butler, 1992).

Culture influences the choices people make in their lives. For example, culture is one of several factors that influence physical activity and thus health status. A study on the impact of culture on physical activity of older (40+) African American and Native American women explored connections between lifestyle and cardiovascular disease. For the Native American women, dancing at ceremonies was an important source of cultural pride as well as physical activity; however, a lack of recreational facilities on reservations limited other types of exercise (Henderson & Ainsworth, 2000).

African American women noted the difficulties of being the only people of color at activities like swimming. Often others would make disparaging remarks such as "you think you're White?" These comments were made simply because African American women were participating in an activity considered unusual for someone from their background. The African American women also noted that those who had hair with a texture similar to European Americans were more free to exercise. For those with more nappy or kinky hair, exercise often conflicted with their ability to maintain hairstyles that met societal standards of beauty (Henderson & Ainsworth, 2000).

Both African American and Native American women stated they had limited free time for exercise because their days were filled with work responsibilities (Henderson & Ainsworth, 2000). The conflict between work and exercise (perceived as a leisure activity) illustrates how issues of class are intertwined with issues of culture. Economic pressures led these women to focus their energy almost exclusively on work, leaving little time for health-promoting exercise.

Culture is likely to influence what is identified as a problem, perspectives on potential remedies, and ideas about desired solutions. Cultural differences lead to different beliefs about cause and effect (Mason, Benjamin & Lewis, 1996). Views on the causes of problems influence symptom patterns as well as the types of treatments that are effective. Culture also influences how symptoms are expressed (Marsella & Yamada, 2000; Rodriguez, 1996; Swinomish Tribal Mental Health Project, 1991). Who experiences various health and social problems, where and how they are identified and treated, and the effectiveness of interventions are also influenced by culture (Abe-Kim & Takeuchi, 1996).

Because culture has such a powerful shaping influence on behavior, social workers need to develop an understanding of what culture means in their clients' lives. Understanding how clients experience their cultures can help social workers be more effective in their work. In recent decades, social scientists from various disciplines have moved toward conceptual and methodological frameworks that view cultural factors as playing a major role in the onset, expression, and outcome of mental disorders. Thus, previous assumptions that psychopathology was universal in nature were rejected (Marsella & Yamada, 2000).

THE USE OF KEY TERMS

The field of social work has borrowed, and continues to borrow, knowledge from a number of related disciplines. Social workers then shape and integrate this knowledge into their practice. In particular, the profession of social work has borrowed extensively from psychology, sociology, and medicine. Social work also owes a debt to the field of anthropology, which is especially relevant with the growing emphasis on cultural competence. Social workers have focused on culture as an important element in their work in recent decades, but culture has been a primary focus of anthropology since its inception. Social workers still have much to learn from anthropologists as social workers try to integrate theories about cultural identity into their work.

The terms *race, culture,* and *ethnicity* are used inconsistently throughout the social science literature. Different authors use these terms in different ways, thus obscuring their meanings. For example, the term *race* is quite common in social science literature; however, anthropologists have long argued there is no such thing as race or distinct categories of people grounded in biology (Green, 1999).

The terms *ethnicity* and *culture* are frequently used interchangeably, and it is often difficult to distinguish one from the other. Even in the *Social Work Dictionary* (Barker, 1999), the definitions for race, ethnicity, and culture each contain these terms, which play a part in making distinctions vague. In fact, many authors use the term they prefer without making any clear distinctions. Even James Green, an anthropologist who wrote a well-known textbook for social workers on cross-cultural practice, has shifted from emphasizing the term *ethnicity* in his first and second editions to primarily using the term *culture* in the third edition (Green, 1999).

For purposes of this book, the term *culture* is used to reflect the values, beliefs, and worldviews of different groups of people. This term is seen as preferable because it shifts the emphasis away from the purported biological connotations associated with *race* and *ethnicity*. *Culture* also de-emphasizes fixed traits as characteristic of different types of people. The terms *race* and *ethnicity* are used in this book primarily when they occur in quotations or descriptions of content taken from other works. In these instances, the choice of terms used by other authors is preserved. Likewise, the terms *theory* and *model*, though having distinct meanings, are often used inconsistently in social science literature. *Theory* more adequately describes much of the content in this chapter; however, the term *model* is used when that is the term more consistently associated with a particular concept (e.g., the Orthogonal Model of Cultural Identification).

In reviewing theories about cultural identity, it is important to remember that culture is not the only aspect of identity. An individual's identity is composed of many different layers such as age, class, gender, level of ability, and national origin. All these layers are important in making someone who he or she is. The social worker must identify which of these elements is most influential for a particular client in a particular situation.

Some authors use the term *culture* to identify various layers of identity (e.g., deaf culture, gay culture). Although these different facets of identity are equally important, it can be confusing to refer to each of them as culture. When a term is used to represent different but related entities, the term itself becomes less clear and meaningful. Although different layers or facets of identity do influence worldview and behaviors, in this text, the term *culture* is reserved for values, beliefs, and worldviews associated with members of particular ethnic or religious groups. The influence of other facets of identity is considered along with cultural influences.

THEORETICAL FOUNDATIONS

Theories of Assimilation and the American Melting Pot

For centuries, theories have been proposed to explain what happens when different types of people come into contact with each other. Most of these early theories are linear and hierarchical. In other words, they proposed a simple relationship in which one culture was seen as less desirable than the other and members of the less desirable group would assimilate or give up their old cultural values and beliefs to blend in and adopt the values and beliefs of the other group. At the very least, people were expected to acculturate (become competent participants in the majority culture while remaining identifiable as members of a minority culture) (LaFromboise, Coleman, & Gerton, 1993). Cultural change was generally seen as happening only in one direction; the less desirable cultural group would conform.

Assimilation theory assumes that absorption into the dominant culture is desirable. Culturally distinct individuals who do not assimilate experience alienation and isolation. The maintenance of cultural traditions is believed to be stressful and lead to marginality (LaFromboise et al., 1993). Early theories on racial mixing espoused a deficit perspective and tended to view individuals who maintained minority cultural traditions as caught between two worlds. As a result, such individuals would experience social and psychological problems (Kahn & Denmon, 1997). Social workers have taken important strides in discarding deficit approaches throughout their work and, thus, should recognize the limitations of linear, hierarchical theories of assimilation.

In the United States, where people from many different cultural groups have come into contact with each other over an extended period of time, it was theorized that culturally distinct individuals would give up their distinctiveness as they went through the "Melting Pot." They would then become generic

Americans; that is, a cultural ideal based on Western European norms and values that came to characterize the dominant society in the United States. This blending of cultures, whether through assimilation or acculturation, has often been far from a benign process. Indeed, acculturation for Native Americans has served as a euphemism for cultural genocide (Green, 1999).

Although social scientists have long discredited the Melting Pot theory, it still functions as a popular ideology. People are often described as more or less assimilated or acculturated, referring to the extent to which they are presumed to have given up their cultural uniqueness. Assimilation is often measured by language ability or food preferences with those who have retained culturally based characteristics falling at the "traditional" end of the scale and those who appear to have entirely given up their ethnic lifestyle characterized as "assimilated" (Green, 1999). Many contemporary cultural assessment tools used by helping professionals are still built on these faulty theoretical foundations.

The Melting Pot theory's assumption that assimilation would result in a new, singular national social identity has not been realized. The newer, related theory of cultural pluralism, sometimes referred to as the Salad Bowl or Tossed Salad approach, proposes that individuals will retain some cultural distinctiveness. This theory, however, still shares many characteristics with the Melting Pot theory. "While it postulates a happier future where everyone 'celebrates' his or her ethnicity without hindrance, it still pigeonholes—separating the lettuce from the celery from the olives—as though ethnic identities are fixed, permanent assemblages of traits. It does not understand ethnicity as a matter of perspectives, shifting and changing with time" (Green, 1999, p. 21).

Bicultural, Multicultural, and Nondeficit Theories

Early theories such as the Melting Pot theory viewed cultural differences as deficits to be overcome. In response, anthropologists began to pose nondeficit theories and acknowledge that being grounded in more than one culture can be beneficial. Bicultural individuals can participate in mainstream culture and be involved in culturally distinct groups. They have the ability to move, as the situation dictates, between different cultural realities (Green, 1999; LaFromboise et al., 1993).

The term *bicultural* was once used to depict individuals with a cultural identity at some median point on a linear continuum between assimilation and traditionalism; however, this simplistic view has been questioned by many social scientists in recent decades. People who have strong connections to more than one culture are more accurately represented by the related but more dynamic concept of situational ethnic identity or code switching. Individuals who are grounded in more than one culture have the skills to act within different cultural norms depending on their context. In other words, they are not halfway between traditional and assimilated/acculturated on a linear scale. Rather, they are able to change their behaviors and adapt to different cultural contexts as they choose.

Contemporary theories of bicultural identification such as the Alternation Model (LaFromboise et al., 1993) propose an independent and bidirectional relationship between cultures rather than a linear and unidirectional relationship. The Alternation Model does not assume a hierarchical relationship between different cultures and views bicultural identification from an additive rather than a deficit perspective. In other words, the Alternation Model does not assume that someone would progress from a "lesser" culture to a "more advanced" one. All cultures are equally valid and exposure to more than one culture can be a strength rather than a liability.

Helping professionals from the Tri-Ethnic Center for Prevention Research have taken an important step in developing an Orthogonal Model of Cultural Identification. In the Orthogonal Model, identification with any culture can be a source of personal and social strength. *Orthogonal*, a term usually associated with statistics, is used to identify the independent nature of different cultures. For instance, an individual can identify with both Pueblo and Mexican American cultures. Because he or she identifies with one does not in any way limit his or her ability to identify with the other. Cultural attitudes and behaviors are linked strongly to identification with that culture and weakly, if at all, to identification with other cultures, so it is necessary to assess identification with any culture independently of identification with other cultures. The Orthogonal Model posits that transition from one cultural belief system to another does not necessarily explain cultural identity in an adequate manner (Oetting & Beauvais, 1991).

The Existence of American Culture

Even though assimilationist theories have long been challenged, many people have lost some of the cultural traditions of their ancestors and see themselves primarily or solely as American. Most people from other countries would agree that there are values and behaviors that characterize many Americans. From the outside looking in, they are able to identify a distinct American culture. American or dominant society values are rooted in the traditions of early immigrants from Western Europe. The cultural values of these early immigrants have been transformed from their earlier state into a new cultural value system. One guide for international students coming to universities in the United States identifies 13 characteristic American values: (1) personal control over the environment, (2) change, (3) time and its control, (4) equality and egalitarianism, (5) individualism and privacy, (6) self-help, (7) competition and free enterprise, (8) future orientation, (9) action and work orientation, (10) informality, (11) directness, openness, and honesty, (12) practicality and efficiency, and (13) materialism and acquisitiveness (Kohls, 1984). The guide lists these characteristics in an attempt to be useful and promote understanding, but it is easy to see how any list of characteristics can reinforce stereotypes.

As in other cultures, individual Americans subscribe to American values to a greater or lesser extent depending on factors such as class, gender, ethnicity, and context. The fact that many Americans also see themselves as belonging to other cultural groups (e.g., Chinese American, African American, Puerto Rican) illustrates that cultural identity can be multidimensional. Indeed, people from the same background can experience cultural identity very differently. For example, one Puerto Rican person may identify as American rather than as Puerto Rican or Latino whereas another views himself or herself exclusively as Puerto Rican.

Identity Development

Early theories of identity formation such as those posed by Erik Erikson were originally contextualized within the White experience (Cunningham, 1997). These and other previously held beliefs about development that have been relied on for years are now subject to challenge (Miehls, 2001). Cultural identity is likely to be a significant part of self-concept for people from subjugated groups. Studies of Mexican Americans and African Americans have found that current theories of identity and self-concept need revision. In particular, models of ego identity such as Erikson's model tend to ignore the impact of racism on affected groups, yet psychological reactions to racism significantly influence aspects of self-concept (Miville, Koonce, Darlington, & Whitlock, 2000). Cultural identity is developed through a process of socialization. The dynamic interplay between people and their environment shapes their sense of themselves as cultural beings (Orlandi, 1992). Children learn from their parents and others around them what it means to be a member of a particular cultural group. The way that parents feel about themselves is transmitted to children as they gain a sense of self-worth and their own identities. Likewise, the ways that family, community, and society feel about a particular cultural group are learned and often internalized by children (Cunningham, 1997). Thus, children from groups that are stereotyped and devalued may internalize negative self-images. Parents from communities of color often strive to give children strong positive cultural identities despite negative societal messages. Role models are important in maintaining a healthy sense of self (Cunningham, 1997).

Racial socialization, the teachings of parents raising children in a hostile and discriminatory environment, promotes racial identity. For example, African American parents prepare children to maintain positive self-concepts in a hostile environment by teaching them coping mechanisms for when they are judged and devalued (Thomas, 1999). Identity is influenced by covert and overt racism. Social injustice leads to frustrations between American ideals and reality, thus leading to feelings of powerlessness to influence the environment. This can lead to either a deprecated character with a sense of worthlessness or a transcendent character that seeks to overcome environmental adversity (Miller, 1999). Personal identity is deeply connected to cultural identity. When people are taught to devalue their culture, they devalue themselves. Racial socialization and identity protect urban African American youth from the harmful effects of discriminatory environments and promote academic achievement (Miller, 1999).

Color and phenotype influence identity formation. For example, racial identity development is different for light-skinned African Americans than for Whites or African Americans with darker skin. Light-skinned African Americans often experience rejection from their own community as well as prejudice from the dominant society, thus influencing their sense of self (Cunningham, 1997).

Learning about differences is a normal developmental process. Young children initially categorize others based on physical appearance, particularly skin color, and then by other phenotypical characteristics. After age eight they begin to understand the sociopolitical aspects of race (Thomas, 1999).

Racial identity development is a process by which people of color overcome society's negative images of themselves and develop an identity rooted in the sociopolitical experiences of their group (Kohatsu, Dulay, Lam, & Concepcion, 2000; Phelps, Taylor, & Gerard, 2001). The literature on racial identity theory highlights five primary elements: (1) everyone belongs to one or more groups (race, gender, etc.), (2) membership in a group influences worldview, (3) the United States is a race-centered society, (4) a racist social environment influences the process of identity development, and (5) as a person establishes social interactions with people of diverse racial groups, he or she solidifies a sense of self as a member of a particular group (Pack-Brown, 1999).

Many different theories of racial identity and biracial identity have been proposed, including some specific to particular groups, most commonly African Americans. Models have also been proposed to raise the awareness of White Americans of their own sense of racial identity.

Many White Americans do not perceive themselves as having a cultural identity, particularly if they or their families are not recent immigrants. They may see themselves as simply Americans because they do not stand out as a culturally distinct minority. Racial identity development is different for Whites because of the impact of the privileges ascribed to them in American society (Miehls, 2001). They have not had to reflect on oppression and inequality the way people of color have. Most White Americans perceive the United States to be a country of equal opportunity for all in housing, education, and jobs, but most people of color perceive a separate and unequal America (Kohatsu et al., 2000).

Some theorists suggest that White helping professionals should become more conscious of their own cultural or racial identity as a critical part of becoming culturally competent. An individualistic worldview, common among White Americans, can be an impediment to White racial identity development and understanding cultures that emphasize collectivism (Croteau, 1999). In learning about racial identity, the primary developmental issue for Whites is the abandonment of entitlement (Pack-Brown, 1999).

Transactional versus Categorical Models

Many descriptions of different cultural groups in the social work literature use the shorthand approach of providing a list of cultural traits. For example, such a list might note that Chinese Americans tend to have hierarchical, patriarchal family structures, value the elderly, and avoid confrontations or displays of disrespect. These statements contain some truth, but they fail to reflect the rich diversity among Chinese Americans and are likely to promote stereotypes if not viewed flexibly and within a context.

The sort of shorthand just noted results in a categorical approach to cultural difference. The subtlety and pervasiveness of categorical thinking throughout American society is profound. The categorical approach to understanding culture is imposed by those with more power on those with less, thereby fostering stereotypes (Green, 1999). This approach categorizes individuals according to a predetermined list of traits. People are measured according to the degree to which they conform to a standardized, stereotypical expectation. Not all people, however, fit neatly into these categories. For example, a social worker who encounters a Native American client with an advanced degree in mathematics, who sent her two children to Stanford, and works as a software engineer for NASA, might assume that the client had given up or lost her Native American culture and assimilated into the dominant society. In fact, this background information reveals nothing about the client's cultural identity. In the mind of a categorical thinker, "the presence of a software-designing Native American client does not challenge the validity of the categorical approach; rather, the categorizer redefines her to fit preconceived ideas about ethnicity. This kind of pigeonholing seems obviously misguided, especially in this example, but it is surprising how often it occurs, even in social service settings" (Green, 1999, p. 19). The result of categorical thinking is to shape the person being categorized rather than to adjust the categories. In this example, the ultimate conclusion is that the categorization scheme can't be wrong, so the client must not be a culturally authentic Native American.

A transactional view of cultural diversity is more appropriate than is a categorical approach. In this view, "ethnicity resides in the boundaries between distinctive cultural communities" (Green, 1999, p. 24). In other words, difference exists between people rather than someone in the minority or with less power simply being different from someone with the power to set the norm. Cultural values are also dynamic and shifting rather than being set beliefs or ideals (Kavanaugh, Absalom, Beil, & Schliessmann, 1999). Culture does not consist of rigid guiding principles or latent structures that dictate behavior. Instead, culture is a set of flexible and changing cognitive options that individuals and groups can choose from in striving for specific goals (Angel & Williams, 2000).

It is not possible to fully understand how people experience their cultures simply by knowing their ethnic heritage. People vary in the extent to which they espouse the traditions and practices of a particular group. Some people are strongly grounded in their cultures but others are not (Marsella & Yamada, 2000). Thus, it is important to understand how each person experiences his or her own culture.

The Role of Power Inherent in Theories of Cultural Identity

Although not often made explicit, power is a dynamic inherent in the various theories of cultural identity. The expectation that people assimilate into the dominant society is a reflection of the power associated with that society and the relative lack of power of those expected to assimilate. Even though newer theories seek to avoid the hierarchical nature of their predecessors, the role of power is rarely made explicit. In a society that continues to be stratified, it is important for social workers to actively question how power dynamics affect the lives of their clients from various cultural backgrounds.

THE FLEXIBLE NATURE OF CULTURE

Given that culture is not simply a composite of fixed attributes, it becomes clear that how individuals see themselves as cultural beings can change. Although people behave as if ethnicity is an objective fact, reports of ethnicity vary during a person's lifetime. A study of Roman Catholics of European descent revealed that participants changed how they reported their ethnicity at different points in their lives (Waters, 1990). Identification with a particular culture may vary depending on social factors and life experiences. How others perceive someone's culture and ethnicity also shapes how people experience their cultural identities. For example, a child who is taunted and shunned because of his or her skin color is likely to internalize a negative image of himself or herself and cultural group. This negative image may in turn lead to reluctance to partake in cultural activities.

In today's world, there is considerable interaction between cultures and how they influence each other. It is not uncommon for people to deliberately adopt explanatory frameworks from other cultures. For example, a middle-class White American may adopt principles and beliefs about the mind and body from Chinese medicine (Angel & Williams, 2000). Thus, there can be some level of choice involved in consciously accepting a belief system.

How people experience their own identities may vary from how others see them. This insider's perspective on culture is known as *emic* whereas the perspective of an outsider is known as *etic*. Just as empathy is developed through trying to understand what someone is feeling from his or her perspective, understanding someone's experience as a cultural being requires listening to and learning from the client about his or her subjective perspectives.

It can be difficult to know what cultural group or groups people feel connected to, especially when they have mixed heritage. Observation of phenotypical features often results in identifying people differently than they would identify themselves. Allowing people to self-identify can help validate their identity rather than impose an identity on them. This also avoids the imposition of power inherent in a social worker labeling or mislabeling a client. The experiences of people must be documented through their eyes rather than through the lens of ethnocentrism (Kahn & Denmon, 1997).

There are an estimated 600,000 to 6,000,000 people of multiracial ancestry in the United States (Kahn & Denmon, 1997), yet limited attention has been paid to issues of how people of mixed heritage experience their cultural identity. Although significant literature suggests that separate races do not in fact exist (e.g., Green, 1999; Omi & Winant, 2001), the socially constructed categories often referred to as races have reinforced shared experiences and beliefs. People who do not see themselves as fitting into a particular category in this paradigm may view themselves as multiracial (Kahn & Denmon, 1997).

Cultures continually change and grow, much like an individual's experience of his or her culture can shift. It is important to dismiss the belief that culture is a single variable. Cultures are constantly changing as a result of interactions with others (Cuellar, 2000). For example, Native American cultures have adapted to new influences while maintaining core values. The Native Nations of the Great Plains region are often associated with the use of horses, yet, today many Native people neither own nor ride horses. This does not make them any less culturally Native, though their daily activities have changed. In fact, the Plains Nations had no horses before their introduction by Spanish explorers but adapted quickly to this change. The introduction of horses changed many aspects of daily life including methods of hunting and styles of headdresses. Likewise, the advent of modern technologies has brought changes and cultural adaptations to indigenous cultures although core values persist. Today many tribal governments make extensive use of the Internet and have their own Web sites. Use of contemporary technologies does not necessarily compromise the values and traditions of Native Nations.

MULTIPLE LAYERS OF IDENTITY

The flexible nature of culture is highlighted when individuals have ties to more than one ethnic or national group. People of mixed heritage may identify with one, none, or multiple parts of their heritage. The identity of individuals is also likely to vary because of factors such as class, sexuality, gender (Kahn & Denmon, 1997), and generation (McCallion, Janicki, & Grant-Griffin, 1997). It is important to understand not only how someone experiences his or her own culture but also the interactive influence of various factors in an individual's identity.

Many different elements go into making people who they are. Culture is just one of these elements, and it may or may not be the most influential factor in someone's identity. All people participate in multiple identities at the same time, such as being members of both professional and religious groups (Angel & Williams, 2000).

More scholarship is needed on the intersections between different aspects of identity such as class and culture. What we think of as culture is confounded with social stratification. Aspects of culture are intertwined with political and economic realities. For example, different cultural groups experience different health outcomes, so helping professionals must examine the complex interactions between different facets of identity rather than simply attributing these differences to culture. Health is influenced by factors such as gender, class, and age as well as by culture. The power differentials between groups influence access to services and help-seeking behavior (Angel & Williams, 2000).

It is often difficult to sort out the influences of different aspects of identity. For example, race is closely related to socioeconomic status, and socioeconomic differences between racial groups play a major role in accounting for health variations. This raises the question, do health disparities exist because of class or race? In fact, although the two factors are inextricably linked, racial differences persist in health status after controlling for socioeconomic status (Williams & Rucker, 1996).

HOW THEORY INFORMS SOCIAL WORK PRACTICE

Although social workers may not be consciously aware of it, theory and beliefs about cultural identity shape social work practice. The Melting Pot theory, in which culturally distinct individuals were expected to shed their cultures and blend into the dominant society, was reflected in the practices of early agencies like settlement houses and Charity Organization Societies. Many social workers took on the role of helping immigrants adjust to life in the United States and become assimilated. These social workers believed this goal was appropriate and that assimilation would ultimately benefit individuals as well as American society.

Even when the Melting Pot theory was largely discredited, most social workers did not recognize culture as fluid and changing. Early literature emphasizing cultural sensitivity often urged social workers to become knowledgeable about different populations. Many lists of cultural traits were published to assist social workers in their quest for cultural knowledge. Despite cautions about diversity within cultural groups, these lists encouraged a categorical approach to working with clients.

Cultures are complex and cannot be adequately represented by simple, linear models. In recognition of this, scholars have encouraged helping professionals to adopt approaches such as Transactional (Green, 1999), Alternation (LaFromboise et al., 1993), or Orthogonal Models (Oetting & Beauvais, 1991). Despite these recommendations, many social workers continue to do little to incorporate cultural variables in their work in a meaningful way (Green, 1999). The literature is filled with current examples of practice, research, and theory that have yet to adequately move beyond categorical thinking, such as assessment tools that continue to be developed based on linear models of identity.

Theory and research on practice with culturally diverse populations is an active and growing body of scholarship. Scholars within a variety of helping disciplines are turning their attention to this important area. Culture is not a simple entity and, as such, it requires the development of more sophisticated explanatory frameworks. As they have in the past, social workers will need to review and borrow knowledge from other disciplines as well as generate social work–specific knowledge about how best to work with culturally diverse clients.

THE INFLUENCE OF CULTURE ON SPECIFIC VALUES

Many different values are influenced by culture. The values discussed here are likely to be particularly meaningful in understanding clients and in cultivating productive social work relationships. These values include independence and interdependence; defining success and priorities; raising children; gender roles and sexuality, perceptions of physical and mental differences; and beliefs about equality and inequality. These values are all interrelated with other layers of identity such as gender, class, and sexual orientation.

Independence and Interdependence

Issues of dependence and independence are integral to the social work process. They are at the heart of the social work value of empowerment (i.e., having clients as partners in the work rather than "doing for" clients). American society also has strong values that favor independence and encourage individuality rather than emphasize the group.

Professional and societal values about independence may conflict with the value systems of clients who come from cultures that emphasize interdependence and group cohesiveness. For example, the Western priority placed on individuality may conflict with traditional values that emphasize the importance of the group when decisions must be made about the level of family involvement in critical medical decisions (Martinez, 2000).

Professionals' and clients' differing views about independence and interdependence can lead to misinterpretations of each other's perspectives. Ester Ruiz Rodriguez, a nurse educator, remembers how as a young girl her mother told her that White women did not take good care of their young children. From her perspective, White mothers encouraged children to emulate inappropriate adult ways such as demanding to be heard and asking questions. To a traditional Mexican mother, it appeared that White mothers did not allow children to be children (Rodriguez, 1996). The Mexican and White women each had culturally grounded beliefs about the most appropriate ways to raise children. This illustrates how perceptions can clash when people come from different cultural backgrounds.

Defining Success and Setting Priorities

How success is defined and priorities are set is largely influenced by culture. American society tends to value financial accomplishments, accumulation of possessions, and education as hallmarks of success. This is at odds with cultures that view success in terms of wisdom and experience. In the dominant American society, setting priorities and defining success are clearly mingled with ideas about class. In other cultures, however, people are likely to see themselves as successful if they have achieved their goals, regardless of whether financial success is a priority. In group-oriented cultures, success is often measured by the actions of family members, particularly children. Actions of family members can either reflect well on, or shame, the family. A successful person is one whose family behaves well according to a particular cultural standard.

Cultures are constantly changing (Orlandi, 1992). Thus, it comes as no surprise that culturally grounded definitions of success also change over time. Likewise, cultures are influenced by other cultural groups. For instance, in recent decades when federal policy focused on assimilation, Native Americans who followed a traditional indigenous lifestyle were often perceived by both non-Natives and other Native Americans as backwards and unsuccessful. Today, however, for many Native Americans, success is associated with the attainment of traditional skills and knowledge while still being able to function within the larger society. Someone with limited income may be seen as rich in cultural or spiritual resources (Fleming, 1992).

Raising Children

The definition of family differs across cultures (Mason et al., 1996). Some people define the boundaries of a family as a married couple and their children, but others define families to include grandparents, aunts, uncles, cousins, and others who are not related by blood but play significant roles within the family.

The way that children are raised is often a clear example of the cultural values and beliefs of their parents. Values about who has the primary caregiving role or whether that role is shared among two or more people is influenced by culture. In some cultures, grandparents, older siblings, or other relatives take on significant caregiving responsibilities. Although culture plays a major role in child-rearing, other factors can be meaningful as well. For example, family income will have an impact on whether a parent is able to remain home to care for a child or whether child-care arrangements must be made to enable a parent to work.

Children are raised with values and expectations that are often strongly grounded in their cultures. Beliefs about whether children should be assertive or submissive and whether they should act independently or cooperatively are often culturally based. Whether children approach adults, particularly elders and other authority figures, from an egalitarian stance, or with respect and deference may also be culturally determined.

Styles of discipline are influenced by culture. Physical punishment is viewed as acceptable and appropriate by some cultural groups whereas others view this as abusive. Likewise, some see reasoning with children and granting or taking away privileges as effective, but others view it as an abdication of parental responsibility. Indirect communication is often used as a traditional method of teaching and disciplining children in many Native American cultures. Rather than being explicitly told not to do something, children may hear a story about the negative consequences of behavior. For example, to teach a child to be wary of wandering away from the family yard, a parent may tell a story of a child who wandered away and became lost and frightened. This form of guidance has been effective for generations, but people from cultures that value more direct communication and physical intervention often misunderstand and believe this represents a lack of caring, and even neglect.

Human beings go through a variety of stages in their lives such as infancy, childhood, adulthood, and aging. How different parts of the lifecycle are perceived, and the roles associated with them, are largely culturally determined. What people are taught as children often communicates the expectations, roles, and behaviors they are to fulfill throughout their lifetimes. Culturally based norms about children's responsibilities for elderly parents have a significant impact on the well-being of elderly people in declining health. Cultural norms may also encourage nonfamily members in the community to take on caregiving roles. This can be particularly important for elderly people who are widowed or never married (Angel & Angel, 1995).

Some cultures, notably Asian and Native American cultures, place high esteem on aging. People in the later stages of life are revered for their knowledge and are often included in major decisions. On the other hand, the dominant society in the United States has a more youth-oriented culture in which physical agility is valued.

Gender Roles and Sexuality

Gender roles also reflect cultural expectations. Whether roles are egalitarian or hierarchical is a function of culture. What is expected of men and women in their respective roles (e.g., who is expected to earn income, who is expected to discipline children, who is expected to take the initiative in setting a date or establishing a relationship) are all influenced by cultural values.

Often the roles and interactions between men and women are discussed within a context in which heterosexuality is the presumed norm. In fact, gay and lesbian identities are intertwined with cultural expectations as people define how they interact with a variety of people. For example, some Native American societies traditionally, and in contemporary times, recognize at least six gender styles: men, women, not-women (those who are biologically male but assume female roles), not-men (those who are biologically female but assume male roles), lesbians, and gays. Not-women and not-men are typically identified in childhood and have a spiritual calling and special place in society (Brown, 1997). It is often difficult to distinguish between lifestyles dictated by gender roles and those shaped by sexuality.

Cultures influence views about what is normal and what is abnormal. For example, in most traditional Native American cultures, sexuality and gender roles are seen as a natural part of creation. All different statuses are sacred, whether they are heterosexual or homosexual, female or male. "If the Great Spirit chose to create alternative sexualities or gender roles, who was bold enough to oppose such power? In contrast, the Judeo-Christian tradition honors the male and female roles within the scope of heterosexuality, but alternative sexuality is regarded as sinful and outside of God's plan. Consequently G[ay] A[merican] I[ndians] have a much more benevolent and understanding tradition from which to assert their identity and reaffirm their sacred being" (Champagne, 1997, p. xviii). Although Judeo-Christian teachings focus on the sanctity of heterosexuality, this does not prohibit some branches of Jewish and Christian faiths or their individual members from showing tolerance and respect for differing sexualities.

Culture shapes the explanatory framework for sexuality and gender roles. Likewise, it influences what place gay and lesbian individuals play in society and whether they are accepted or rejected. Some limited research has examined interactions between sexuality and cultural layers of identity, yet research studies have usually had small samples of gays and lesbians of color. The research that does exist identifies two parallel processes of identity formation that occur simultaneously, one for cultural identity and the other for sexual identity (Walters, 1997). The interactions of these layers of identity need closer examination.

Perceptions of Physical and Mental Differences

There is tremendous variation in people's physical and mental abilities. At some point, these differences become categorized as abilities versus disabilities. Culture can influence whether or not someone is viewed as disabled. Likewise, there are culturally distinct perspectives on illness and health (Mason et al., 1996). Culture also influences beliefs about the origin and meaning of physical and mental differences. Someone who has an IQ below what is considered normal intelligence may be perceived as a gift from God, perhaps having a special place or function within society. On the other hand, some cultures at times have perceived individuals who have significant physical or psychological differences to be associated with evil forces.

The treatment of people who are physically or mentally disabled by their communities and caregivers is closely related to culturally determined values about dependence and independence. A qualitative study of African American, Chinese American, Haitian American, Latino, Korean American, and Native American caregivers of developmentally disabled individuals found cultural differences in how families cared for their disabled members. Differences were identified in a number of areas including the following: (1) how disability is perceived, (2) who is in the family, (3) who provides care, (4) how family decisions are made, (5) what family members expect of each other, (6) what supports families receive from friends and communities, (7) cultural values important to family members, (8) family willingness to accept outside services,

(9) family's first language, and (10) family's concerns about service providers (McCallion et al., 1997). Whether a group is individualistic or community oriented is likely to influence the level of support that disabled individuals and their caregivers receive. Even within a particular culture, views of ability/disability change over time. For instance, passage of the Americans with Disabilities Act (passed in 1990) reflects a growing awareness in the United States of the rights of disabled individuals to participate in all aspects of society as fully as possible.

Equality and Inequality

Culture also influences ideas about equality and inequality, and egalitarianism and hierarchical structures. Culturally influenced beliefs include ideas about whether people are equal or whether there are important status differences based on factors such as age, gender, and occupation. Such distinctions are often represented in class and caste structures. In some cultures, such as tribal groups from India, clear distinctions are recognized among people. These distinctions are present at birth and make up a caste system in which some people are considered inherently superior and others inferior. This caste system dictates a variety of behaviors including who has privileges in society and what type of people fill certain occupations.

In the dominant society of the United States, it is often professed that all people are equal or at least have an equal chance at success. Although different classes associated with income, level of education, and career achievement clearly exist, theoretically, social mobility allows anyone to shift class affiliations. In reality, class is intertwined with other factors such as race. Social mobility is not a simple task.

Poverty is a risk factor for many social and health problems (Rodriguez, 1996). Certain cultural groups are more likely to experience poverty, so it becomes difficult if not impossible to determine whether culture or class is the most relevant factor in identifying risks for various social and health problems. Inequalities of power and privilege are because of sociocultural factors such as race and class (Henderson & Ainsworth, 2000). These layers of identity are strongly interconnected.

HELP-SEEKING BEHAVIORS

Culture influences what types of help people seek (e.g., professional counseling, spiritual guidance) and how they behave once they have obtained help. An understanding of differential help-seeking behavior is important in outreach to various groups and engaging them in the helping process. In particular, it is important for social workers to understand how time is perceived and how people communicate to engage clients from diverse cultural groups effectively.

Time is perceived differently across cultures (Mason et al., 1996). Social workers may be frustrated with expectations that clients arrive for appointments at a designated time. When clients are late for appointments, social workers may assume they are resistant or do not consider the appointment important. In fact, clients may have a different interpretation. Latino and Native American cultures tend to emphasize interpersonal interactions rather than governing actions by a predesignated time. As Native American elders often say, it is time for an event to begin when all the appropriate people are present. In this conceptualization, it is impossible to not be "on time" because it cannot be "time" until all key people have arrived. This sense of time is often in direct conflict with service providers who schedule appointments based on a dominant society perspective. When possible, such potential conflicts can be resolved by social workers having designated drop-in hours rather than specific appointments (e.g., the social worker will be available from 1:00 to 4:30 on Tuesday and Thursday afternoons to meet with clients).

Communication patterns, greeting behavior, and social etiquette vary across cultures (Mason et al., 1996). Knowledge of these different patterns can be important in engaging clients. Communication patterns also have ongoing importance throughout the social work relationship. These patterns include verbal behavior (e.g., when someone speaks or is silent) and nonverbal behavior (e.g., eye contact). Most social workers expect clients to participate in a verbally active manner during sessions. This often includes significant disclosure and a willingness to talk about problems. Levels of disclosure vary across cultures. In the dominant society, there is often the belief that talking about things is healthy. Families of color, however, may not share openly for cultural or sociopolitical reasons such as fear of bias and racism (Mason et al., 1996). Racial mistrust limits disclosure and engagement (Kohatsu et al., 2000). Some clients also have cultural norms that limit self-disclosure. For example, many Chinese clients are reluctant to talk about personal matters with someone outside the family. Likewise, a Navajo client, when asked how family members feel about a particular subject, may be reluctant to answer because it is considered culturally inappropriate to answer on behalf of someone else in many Native American cultures.

It is important for social workers to recognize that some cultures, particularly those of Native American people, often use silence as a part of communication (Weaver, 1999). This silence should not be misinterpreted as resistance or anger; rather, it should be allowed to continue as long as the client needs to process, translate, or reflect on information.

Nonverbal communication, such as eye contact, also varies across cultures. In the dominant society culture, eye contact is seen as the norm and a sign that someone is attentive, but eye contact is viewed as disrespectful in some Latino, Native American, and Asian cultures. A Puerto Rican child is likely to avert his or her eyes when speaking to teachers or social workers. Both teachers and social workers are perceived as having higher status than the child because of their professional standing and age. Thus, to show respect, a child is likely to avoid eye contact. To make eye contact, particularly for an extended period, can be viewed as confrontational and disrespectful. A social worker who is unaware of this norm may misinterpret this type of nonverbal communication.

CONCLUSION

Culture influences values, beliefs, behaviors, and the way people view the world. Therefore, understanding cultural dynamics is necessary to understand many of the things that people do and the ways that they think. Cultural understanding will not only help social workers recruit and engage with clients from diverse backgrounds, it will enable them to choose more appropriate goals and interventions to facilitate the work.

Exercises

Exercise #1: Reflecting on independence and interdependence
Review a case plan for a client including all goals and objectives. This can be for a client that you are working with or a case example provided by an instructor. As you read the plan, think about how values of independence or interdependence may be implicit in the goals and objectives. Analyze how these values fit with the client's cultural norms and values, the norms and values of the social work profession, and the norms and values of American society. Identify any potential conflicts or areas of compatibility.

Exercise #2: Applying a categorical approach
Using a categorical approach, develop a list of traits that are commonly associated with your own cultural group. How might a social worker using a categorical approach work with someone from this group? How might a social worker using a transactional approach work with the same client?

Exercise #3: Examining culturally based views of social issues
Choose one of the following issues: mild mental retardation, dating at age 12, schizophrenia, unwed parenthood, or another issue that interests you. Choose a culture such as Mien, Croatian, Dominican, Comanche, African American, or Filipino. Conduct a thorough literature search to identify how your chosen issue is perceived within that particular culture. Compare how this issue is typically viewed by helping professionals in the United States.

References

Abe-Kim, J. S., & Takeuchi, D. T. (1996). Cultural competence and quality of care: Issues for mental health service delivery in managed care. *Clinical Psychology: Science and Practice, 3*(4), 273–295.

Angel, R. J., & Angel, J. L. (1995). Mental and physical comorbidity among the elderly: The role of culture and social class. In D. K. Padgett (ed.), *Handbook on Ethnicity, Aging, and Mental Health*, Westport, CT: Greenwood Press, 47–70.

Angel, R. J., & Williams, K. (2000). Cultural models of health and illness. In I. Cuellar & F. A. Paniagua, *Handbook of Multicultural Mental Health*. San Diego: Academic Press, 25–44.

Applewhite, S. L. (1998). Culturally competent practice with elderly

Latinos. *Journal of Gerontological Social Work, 30*(1/2), 1–15.

Barker, R. L. (1999). *The Social Work Dictionary.* Washington DC: National Association of Social Workers Press.

Brown, L. B. (1997). Women and men, not-men and not-women, lesbians and gays: American Indian gender style alternatives. In L. B. Brown, *Two Spirit People: American Indian Lesbian Women and Gay Men.* Binghamton, NY: Haworth Press, 5–20.

Butler, J. P. (1992). Of kindred minds: The ties that bind. In M. A. Orlandi, R. Weston, & L. G. Epstein (Eds.) *Cultural Competence for Evaluators: A Guide for Alcohol and Other Drug Abuse Prevention Practitioners Working with Ethnic/Racial Communities.* Rockville, MD: Office of Substance Abuse Prevention, U.S. Department of Health and Human Services, 23–54.

Champagne, D. (1997). Preface: Sharing the gift of sacred being. In L. B. Brown, *Two Spirit People: American Indian Lesbian Women and Gay Men.* Binghamton, NY: Haworth Press, xiii–xxiv.

Croteau, J. M. (1999). One struggle through individualism: Toward an antiracist white racial identity. *Journal of Counseling and Development, 77*(1), 30–32.

Cuellar, I. (2000). Acculturation and mental health: Ecological transactional relations of adjustment. In I. Cuellar & F. A. Paniagua, *Handbook of Multicultural Mental Health.* San Diego: Academic Press. P. 45–62.

Cunningham, J. L. (1997). Colored existence: Racial identity formation in light-skinned Blacks. *Smith College Studies in Social Work, 67*(3), 375–400.

Fleming, C. M. (1992). American Indians and Alaska Natives: Changing societies past and present. In M. A. Orlandi, R. Weston, & L. G. Epstein (Eds.) *Cultural Competence for Evaluators: A Guide for Alcohol and other Drug Abuse Prevention Practitioners Working with Ethnic/Racial Communities.* Rockville, MD: Office of Substance Abuse Prevention, U.S. Department of Health and Human Services, 147–171.

Green, J. W. (1999). *Cultural Awareness in the Human Services: A Multi-Ethnic Approach.* Englewood Cliffs, NJ: Prentice-Hall.

Henderson, K. A., & Ainsworth, B. E. (2000). Sociocultural perspectives on physical activity in the lives of older African American and American Indian women: A cross cultural activity participation study. *Women and Health, 31*(1), 1–20.

Kahn, J. S. & Denmon, J. (1997). An examination of social science literature pertaining to multiracial identity: A historical perspective. *Journal of Multicultural Social Work, 6*(1/2), 117–137.

Kavanaugh, K., Absalom, K., Beil, W., & Schliessmann, L. (1999). Connecting and becoming culturally competent: A Lakota example. *Advances in Nursing Science, 21*(3), 9–31.

Kohatsu, E. L., Dulay, M., Lam, C., & Concepcion, W. (2000). Using racial identity theory to explore racial mistrust and interracial contact among Asian Americans. *Journal of Counseling and Development, 78*(3), 334–342.

Kohls, L.R. (1984). *The Values Americans Live By.* Washington, DC: Meridian House International.

LaFromboise, T., Coleman, H., & Gerton, J. (1993). Psychological impact of biculturalism: Evidence and theory. *Psychological Bulletin, 114,* 395–412.

Marsella, A. J., & Yamada, A. M. (2000). Culture and mental health: An introduction and overview of foundations, concepts, and issues. In I. Cuellar & Paniagua, F. A. *Handbook of Multicultural Mental Health*. San Diego: Academic Press, 3–22.

Martinez, C., Jr. (2000). Conducting the cross-cultural interview. In I. Cuellar & F. A. Paniagua, *Handbook of Multicultural Mental Health*. San Diego: Academic Press, 311–323.

Mason, J. L., Benjamin, M. P., & Lewis, S. A. (1996). The cultural competence model: Implications for child and family mental health services. In C. A. Heflinger & C. T. Nixon (eds.) *Families and the Mental Health System for Children and Adolescents: Policies, Services and Research*. Thousand Oaks: Sage, 165–190.

McCallion, P. Janicki, M., & Grant-Griffin, L. (1997). Exploring the impact of culture and acculturation on older families caregiving for persons with developmental disabilities. *Family Relations*, 46(4), 347–357.

Miehls, D. (2001). The interface of racial identity development with identity complexity in clinical social work student practitioners. *Clinical Social Work Journal*, 29(3), 229–244.

Miller, D. B. (1999). Racial socialization and racial identity: Can they promote resiliency for African American adolescents? *Adolescence, 34*(135), 493–501.

Miville, M. L., Koonce, D., Darlington, P., & Whitlock, B. (2000). Exploring the relationships between racial/cultural identity and ego identity among African Americans and Mexican Americans. *Journal of Multicultural Counseling and Development, 28*(4), 208–224

Oetting, E. R., & Beauvais, F. (1991). Orthogonal cultural identification theory: The cultural identification of minority adolescents. *International Journal of the Addictions, 25*(5A & 6A), 655–685.

Omi, M., & Winant, H. (2001). Racial formations. In P. S. Rothenberg, *Race, Class, and Gender in the United States*. New York: Worth, 11–20.

Orlandi, M. A. (1992). The challenge of evaluating community-based prevention programs: a cross-cultural perspective. In M. A. Orlandi, R. Weston, & L. G. Epstein (Eds.) *Cultural Competence for Evaluators: a Guide for Alcohol and other Drug Abuse Prevention Practitioners Working with Ethnic/Racial Communities*. Rockville, MD: Office of Substance Abuse Prevention, U.S. Department of Health and Human Services, 1–22.

Pack-Brown, S. P. (1999). Racism and White counselor training: Influence of White racial identity theory and research. *Journal of Counseling and Development*, 77(1), 87–92.

Phelps, R. E., Taylor, J. D., & Gerard, P. A. (2001). Cultural mistrust, ethnic identity, racial identity, and self-esteem among ethnically diverse Black university students. *Journal of Counseling and Development*, 79(2), 209–216.

Rodriguez, E. R. (1996). The sociocultural context of stress and depression in Hispanics. In S. Torres (Ed.), *Hispanic Voices: Hispanic Health Educators Speak Out*. New York: National League for Nursing Press, 143–158.

Swinomish Tribal Mental Health Project. (1991). *A Gathering of Wisdoms, Tribal Mental Health: a Cultural Perspective*. LaConner, WA: Swinomish Tribal Community.

Thomas, A. (1999). Racism, racial identity, and racial socialization: a personal reflection. *Journal of Counseling and Development*, 77(1), 35–37.

Waters, M. C. (1990). *Ethnic Options: Choosing Identities in America.* Berkeley: University of California Press.

Walters, K. L. (1997). Urban lesbian and gay American Indian identity: Implications for mental health service delivery. In L. B. Brown, *Two Spirit People: American Indian Lesbian Women and Gay Men.* Binghamton, NY: Haworth Press. 43–65.

Weaver, H. N. (1999). Indigenous people and the social work profession: Defining culturally competent services. *Social Work, 44*(3), 217–225.

Williams, D. R., & Rucker, T. (1996). Socioeconomic status and the health of racial minority populations. In P. M. Kato & T. Mann (eds.) *Handbook of Diversity Issues in Health Psychology,* New York: Plenum Press, p. 407–423.

Self-Reflection and Beyond

*The Challenges of Examining
Cultural Diversity Honestly*

To strive for cultural competence in social work practice and a greater respect for diversity in general, it is critical to have honest discussions about diversity. True honesty requires significant vulnerability. The stated ideals and values of the social work profession embrace diversity, yet history, as discussed in the first chapter, shows social workers have often fallen short of this goal. It is helpful to examine the barriers that stand in the way of implementing social work practice based on respect for diversity. Respecting diversity in the social work relationship must be grounded in respect for diversity in other aspects of life. The two areas are inextricably intertwined.

EXPLORING UNCOMFORTABLE AREAS

An honest, in-depth discussion of diversity requires conscious efforts at self-reflection. The terms *diversity* and *different* both describe a relationship between two or more entities. Examining cultural differences raises the question, different from whom? Often, differences have been framed from a majority-minority perspective. The power dynamics inherent in this perspective place the "minority" in the position of being different, while the "majority" is in the position of setting the standard or being the norm. In fact, it is just as true that the majority is different from the minority as vice versa. Diversity exists when two or more people differ from each other, not because one or more differ

from the dominant society or some Eurocentric ideal. To recognize that someone who is different has characteristics that are valuable and legitimate, an individual is in a position of questioning his or her sense of self-worth. If this causes
discomfort, that individual may resort to a defensive stance of rejecting the
value of the other.

The topics of cultural diversity and cultural competence are politically
charged and trigger a range of emotional responses derived from an individual's memory and experiences with diversity (Pope-Davis, Liu, Toporek, &
Brittan-Powell, 2001). Culture is much more than simply wearing a certain
hairstyle or type of clothing. Some people act differently than others, not
because they have been excluded, but because they feel their way is better
(Green, 1999). There is a tendency toward ethnocentrism inherent in all people. Once people begin to consciously examine their own ethnocentrism, they
may be afraid of appearing racist or revealing a lack of knowledge and experience with diverse populations (Sevig & Etzkorn, 2001).

Self-reflection is a key value in social work practice. Social workers have
long recognized that this is a critical component of working effectively with
diverse populations. In its first year of publication, the journal *Social Work*
contained a passionate article on integration that emphasized social workers
must "examine our own anxieties and fears from which prejudices stem"
(Simons, 1956, p. 24). Examining anxieties and fears can be an unsettling
process. As part of this endeavor, social workers need to admit to themselves
that they have stereotypes or negative views of certain types of people.

Developing cultural competence requires that individuals explore areas
where they may feel uncomfortable or unsafe (Kavanaugh, Absalom, Beil, &
Schliessmann, 1999). Admitting prejudices and confronting fears and biases,
in part, requires letting go of a self-image as a competent, unbiased professional. Striving for true cultural competence requires that an individual shift
his or her worldview, change the way he or she understands the world, and
alter his or her feelings about self in relation to others (Toporek & Reza,
2001). These changes require a shift in power dynamics from the ethnocentric
position of viewing his or her own perspective as good and others as not as
good to a position in which the two positions are not hierarchically ordered
but are merely different. Such a shift in thinking changes the social worker's
own place in the scheme of things and requires significant changes in institutional practices (Pope-Davis et al., 2001). Enlightened consciousness often
requires a radical restructuring of entrenched belief systems and ethnocentrism
(McPhatter, 1997). Whereas some people may have limited insight into their
own biases or are unwilling to be nonjudgmental of people who differ from
themselves, this process of honest self-examination, recognition of and letting
go of biases is crucial for helping professionals.

Sometimes, people experience difference as threatening and respond with
emotions such as fear and anger. This type of emotional reaction can also be
expressed in the social work relationship. It is important to recognize that
anger is likely to emerge in cross-cultural work (Abernathy, 1995). Clients
from disenfranchised groups paired with social workers who are perceived to

represent the oppressive forces of the dominant society may experience anger and resentment and be reluctant to trust these professionals. Likewise, when a client and social worker come from groups that have some historical or contemporary animosity (e.g., Arabs and Jews, Koreans and African Americans) negative emotions may block effective work unless these feelings are openly acknowledged and explored.

Examining Feelings about Difference

Three types of responses typically occur when people are first required to approach learning about and incorporating cultural information in their work. One reaction involves naively embracing diversity without understanding it in any depth. This response can also involve feelings of guilt (Sanchez-Hucles, 2000). People who respond in this way may feel some responsibility for past transgressions perpetrated by members of their group against others; for instance, White Americans may feel guilty for atrocities perpetrated against Native Americans.

A second response occurs when helping professionals express the attitude that they want to help those who are less fortunate. This attitude is grounded in paternalism. Later, they may recognize their arrogance and shift to a focus on empowering people to help themselves (Kavanaugh et al., 1999).

A third response to being presented with diversity content involves resentment and anger. People who respond this way may believe that oppression and bigotry are historical phenomena perpetrated by others and accept no responsibility for injustice. The importance of diversity is rejected, and incorporating such content is viewed as meaningless and an intrusive burden. The reluctance of some social workers to incorporate issues of diversity in their practices is a long-standing concern. As recognized three decades ago, some faculty, students, and even educational institutions themselves may feel threatened by a mandate to incorporate cultural diversity as a key element in practice (Turner, 1972).

Anger may be a common feeling for both clients and helpers in cross-cultural relationships. Clients may feel angry for being viewed as inferior and helpers from the dominant society may be angry for being viewed as racist. Anger can be important and legitimate as an emotional response but it is imperative that helpers control it and keep appropriate boundaries with their clients (Abernathy, 1995).

OVERCOMING BIAS

Ethnocentrism and Prejudice

It is impossible to discuss culture objectively because everyone is immersed in his or her own culture (Angel & Williams, 2000). Ethnocentrism is the natural tendency of people to view reality from their own cultural perspective and to believe that perspective is the most appropriate. This belief—that the way they see the world is "normal," and that others are abnormal, strange, or inferior—can create oppressive situations (Abrums & Leppa, 2001; Marsella & Yamada, 2000). Prejudice is closely related to ethnocentrism. When people hold negative attitudes toward members of other cultural groups, this creates a psychological distance between the prejudiced person and the target of prejudice. This distance makes it difficult to overcome biases and develop understandings among diverse people (Stephan & Finlay, 1999).

It is possible, however, to actively seek to reduce ethnocentrism and prejudice. This requires people to shift their thinking and take the stance that their beliefs, values, and ways of doing things are not the only or the best way. Prejudice is not inevitable. Indeed, beliefs and ideologies can be changed and empathy for different types of people can be increased (Levy, 1999; Stephan & Finlay, 1999). Using empathy to narrow the psychological distance between prejudiced people and those they are prejudiced against can improve intergroup relations.

Significant research has examined the foundations of prejudice. Both ideology and cognitive development influence levels of prejudice, stereotyping, and discrimination (Levy, 1999). Cognitive-developmental theories, based on the work of Piaget, posit that children's attitudes about gender and race are influenced by their acquisition of cognitive skills. Thus, as children mature and develop more skills, they show a decline in prejudice. These age-related changes are based on acquisition of specific cognitive skills such as the ability to classify others on multiple dimensions, the ability to take on differing perspectives, and the ability to see similarities between different groups, and to see differences within the same group. Likewise, adults who exhibit lower levels of stereotyping see others as having a variety of complex attributes and are able to perceive more overlap between different groups of people (Levy, 1999).

People are not always consciously aware of the ideologies that guide their lives. Thus, insight training may be helpful in changing stereotypes. Successful interventions to combat stereotyping include teaching people to see differences between members of the same group, teaching people to classify others on multiple dimensions (e.g., gender, occupation), and pointing out differences between beliefs and behaviors (Levy, 1999). Interventions that increase empathy can be effective in increasing prosocial behavior and reducing prejudice (Stephan & Finlay, 1999).

The Impact of Prejudice

Stereotypes develop when people have limited knowledge of each other. When one group with greater socioeconomic power holds stereotypes about a group with less power, the stereotypes held by the more powerful group often become justifications for oppression and discrimination (Swinomish Tribal Mental Health Project, 1991).

For more than a century, African American scholars have written about the crippling impact of racism, including how it can lead to self-questioning, self-disparagement, lowering of ideals, and failure as a self-fulfilling prophecy among targets of bigotry. A powerful collection of short stories, *The Souls of Black Folk* (Du Bois, 1990) articulately describes the impact of racism on African Americans. Few people, however, raise the question, what does prejudice do to the souls of White folk? Likewise, does prejudice constrain and limit the freedom of racists as it does those who experience racism? (Pratkanis & Turner, 1999).

Frederick Douglass, a former enslaved African American, discussed the impact of slavery and racism on Whites. From his perspective, slave owners were no more immoral than anyone else but the act of participating in the institution of slavery transformed them into cruel and evil people so they could justify their roles in this practice. People continued to practice slavery even though it was widely agreed that it was wrong and immoral. This led to cognitive dissonance and hypocrisy; Christians who loved democracy yet participated in an institution that undermined their ideals (Pratkanis & Turner, 1999). Indeed, people that display significant prejudice can subscribe to egalitarian beliefs. In this type of "ambivalent racism," they can show sympathy for disadvantaged groups while believing that such groups are failing to take advantage of opportunities to change their social standing (Levy, 1999).

The few studies that look at the mental health implications of prejudice consistently identify correlations between prejudice and poor mental health status including depression, psychopathology, and schizophrenia. Prejudice, including scapegoating of an outgroup, requires a distortion of reality and conformity to rigid dichotomized thinking (Pratkanis & Turner, 1999). It is important to ask,

> What happens to the souls of White folk when they accept the myth of White supremacy and use race as an excuse for their problems? In a nutshell, the identity of such White folks becomes transformed, so that all psychological energy must be directed at maintaining the excuse for one's shortcomings and for preserving the myth of racial superiority. If the excuse fails, all is lost. The myth of White supremacy can result in some short-term positive feelings: a sense of power and strength along with immediate satisfaction that one is superior. However, maintaining the myth is not without its psychological costs. (Pratkanis & Turner, 1999, p. 799)

Bias in the Helping Professions

The helping professions, along with service delivery systems, are culture-bound or grounded within certain belief and value systems (Sue et al., 1998; Wohl, 1995). Helping practices are grounded in specific cultural and historical contexts that are shaped by the values of practitioners and the clients for which they are designed. For example, the social work profession values empowering clients to act on their own behalf: thus, many social work interventions are tailored to this end. Most measurement tools have been developed in the context of Western science. As a result, these tests are culture-specific and only truly accurate for English-speaking people with a Eurocentric worldview (Dana, 1995). Likewise, psychotherapy is shaped primarily by White, middle-class practitioners. The belief that this framework is universally valid has been increasingly challenged in recent decades (Wohl, 1995).

Ethnocentrism is present in the helping professions as well as in society as a whole. Helping professionals who use their power to impose their own beliefs about the nature and treatment of problems on their clients without concern for possible bias are acting from a basis of ethnocentrism (Marsella & Yamada, 2000). The process of critical self-reflection must extend to examining professional as well as individual belief systems and behaviors.

> Realities, including our scientific realities, are all culturally constructed. Knowledge in psychiatry and the social sciences is culturally relative, and as such, it is ethnocentric and biased. What passes for truth is, in fact, a function of who holds the power. Those who are in power (e.g., Western psychiatry) have the "privilege" of determining what is acceptable, and those who are not, are marginalized in their opinion and influence. This is not a pleasant reality for many, but it is an accurate portrayal of the situation. (Marsella & Yamada, 2000, p. 7)

Most contemporary theories that form the foundation of the helping professions are grounded in European American middle-class cultures and assumptions about human behavior and well-being. Until recent decades, it was assumed by most helping professionals that theories and models apply to all clients equally, across cultures. Eurocentric values that pervade interventions include an emphasis on talking as a way to resolve psychological problems, intrapsychic causes of problems, the value of sharing intimate feelings and thoughts with a helping professional, and separation and autonomy from the family. Variations from these values are considered pathological, and clients who do not espouse these same values and norms have often been labeled resistant (Lee & Ramirez, 2000).

The social work knowledge base contains major weaknesses and gaps. For example, the contributions of people of color to the social welfare system are rarely acknowledged. Mainstream developmental theories created by Freud, Erikson, Kohlberg, and others provide only limited conceptualizations of normal life-course development that describe women and culturally different people as deficient. "Theorists who described normal adult development as career attainment, heterosexual marriage, childbearing, and managing a household exclude the developmental experiences of a substantial number of people" (McPhatter, 1997, p. 266).

It can be unsettling for helping professionals to recognize that the foundations of professional knowledge are steeped in ethnocentrism. "It is difficult for professionals to work within a context that questions the validity of their decisions and that suggests that 'truths' may be little more than relativistic assumptions supported by data that are themselves questionable" (Marsella & Yamada, 2000, p. 7). Yet, this is precisely the type of critical self-examination that is needed to begin to identify and prevent the replication of institutionalized biases.

Until recently, helping professionals viewed culture as ancillary to the basic helping process. Culturally different clients were viewed from a deficit perspective (i.e., as lacking necessary education and sophistication to benefit from many therapies). This often led to a "blaming the victim" mentality in which people were seen as the cause of their own problems. The responsibility rested with the client to learn to adapt to Western-based therapeutic techniques. Only in recent years has there been a shift from a "client as problem" orientation to a "helper as problem" orientation in which professionals' insensitivity, biases, and prejudices are recognized as barriers to successful helping (Lee & Ramirez, 2000).

The helping professions as practiced in the United States have developed with an implicit assumption that the human condition is governed by universal principles that apply equally to all clients regardless of culture, gender, or class. Euro-American values form the foundation for the helping professions including values of secularism, individualism, and egalitarianism. As a result, helping practices tend to associate healthy functioning with autonomy and independence. There is an implicit and sometimes explicit belief that clients can and should master and control their own lives. There is also an emphasis on self-awareness and personal growth as goals of the therapeutic process (Sue et al., 1998). These values are culture-bound and do not necessarily apply equally to all clients. When helping professionals and researchers fail to recognize cultural factors, they ultimately contribute to the demise of cultures and the reduction of diversity (Marsella & Yamada, 2000).

RESPECTING DIVERSITY

Diversity in Daily Life

There are many ways to demonstrate respect for cultural differences, both in day-to-day interactions and within the social work relationship. One important way to show respect is to begin to avoid assumptions by taking time to deliberately think before speaking or acting. Assumptions may be stereotypical or based on what is known about past experiences, and this "knowledge" often does not translate in cross-cultural situations.

It is more appropriate to ask rather than to make an assumption. Asking communicates respect through a desire to understand the other person and his or her life experiences. If a social worker is unsure how to pronounce an unfamiliar name or does not know if someone would prefer to be called by a surname rather than a first name, it is appropriate to ask. A similar situation arises when someone encounters a person with a disability and perceives that person may need some assistance. It would be inappropriate to assume that (1) the person with a disability is automatically in need of help, or (2) would prefer to act independently. Asking whether that person would like some assistance is preferable to acting on assumptions about dependence and independence.

Striving for empathy is a deliberate process. Although it is not possible for anyone to be completely immersed in another's feelings or experiences, it is possible to take a moment to reflect on how everyone's perspective is subjective. A social worker can take the time to reflect on how others may experience a situation and ask what might it be like to be in their shoes. For instance, when meeting a newly arrived refugee from Sri Lanka, someone might reflect on the following: What might it be like to have escaped from a bombing that killed three members of your family? What might it be like to not know who to trust and to live in fear of the police and military? What might it be like to be separated from your spouse for two years and not know if he or she is safe or even still alive? Although most Americans have not experienced the same events as a refugee, it is possible to empathize with feelings of loss, fear, and uncertainty. Taking time for these deliberate reflections and expressions of empathy are ways to communicate respect for someone in a different situation.

In cross-cultural situations, the other person's values or behaviors may seem not only unfamiliar but strange and perhaps threatening. Taking time to reflect and think about what might be positive about the value or behavior is another way of communicating respect. When learning that Orthodox Jews, Muslims, and Native American Longhouse practitioners have separate places for men and women during many ceremonies and rituals, some Americans might initially perceive that this is unfair and wrong. Before judging, it is helpful to learn more about the reasons for these practices and why people of these faiths view such separations as positive and appropriate.

Likewise, upon reflection, it will become clear that some people from other cultures perceive American values and perspectives as odd or threatening. Sometimes cultural misunderstandings turn into distorted, twisted views of people from different cultures or belief systems. For example, someone unfamiliar with certain Christian practices might be quite disturbed to hear that some Christians drink blood and eat flesh. This apparent act of cannibalism is, in fact, a sacred ritual of communion—something very positive from an insider's perspective. During this ritual, believers experience spiritual renewal through wine or juice and bread that has been transformed into the blood and flesh of their Christ. Unfamiliarity with such practices can lead to distorted perceptions.

Demonstrating Respect in the Social Work Relationship

Incorporating respect in the social work relationship needs to happen on multiple levels. Showing respect begins in very basic ways in the early phases of the work and continues throughout its duration. The way the client is greeted can help him or her feel comfortable. In the United States, it is common to greet someone with a handshake, but this is not a comfortable greeting for everyone. A woman from an Orthodox Jewish background may feel uncomfortable when a male social worker reaches out to shake her hand. Likewise, many Native Americans have a handshake that consists of a gentle touch and may be taken aback by an overly firm grip.

Having some knowledge of the client's background before the first meeting will give some tentative guidelines about what types of greetings might be perceived as comfortable. Even with background knowledge, however, social workers will still occasionally make mistakes. A good social worker is not one who doesn't make mistakes. Rather, a good social worker is one who recognizes mistakes and is able to learn from them (Shulman, 1999). It is important to watch the client's reaction to any offered greeting to determine his or her level of comfort. Not everyone is comfortable with physical touch as part of an initial greeting. For those who are comfortable with physical contact, the type of touch is likely to vary. Recognizing that the social worker's preferred form of greeting is not universal is a good beginning toward demonstrating respect for differences throughout the social work relationship.

Another basic way of communicating respect is by learning the proper pronunciation of a client's name. This may be a challenge when a name is composed of letter combinations and sounds that are unfamiliar to the social worker. Although the social worker may struggle at first, making the effort to learn a client's name is an essential way of showing respect. Social workers should never take the initiative to shorten or anglicize a client's name. For instance, a client named Manuranjan should not be called Manu and a client named Jose should not be called Joe, just for the social worker's convenience. It is also important to keep in mind that some clients are not comfortable being called by their first names, and this preference should be respected. Interviews can begin by determining which language the interview needs to be conducted in. Asking the client's preference is an important start if both the client and helper speak more than one language (Martinez, 2000).

Scheduling appointments according to the client's needs and preferences is another tangible way of communicating respect. Most agencies have schedules that automatically work around major Christian holidays like Christmas and Easter. In fact, the Christian tradition of Sunday being the day of rest is so institutionalized in the United States that many agencies are closed on this day, yet Saturday is the Jewish Sabbath, and Friday is the Muslim day of rest. Many significant holidays do not even appear on most calendars. For example, Midwinter is a nine-day period of ceremonies central to the Longhouse traditions of the Haudenosaunee (or Six Nations) indigenous people in the Northeastern United States and Southeastern Canada. Midwinter is at a slightly different time each year based on lunar phases rather than on the Roman calendar. Social workers should be aware that scheduling appointments with clients during this time or during other ceremonial times raises potential conflicts for clients who follow these traditions.

Likewise, social workers need to be sensitive to the fact that certain times of day may be inappropriate for scheduling appointments for some clients. Jewish holidays begin at sundown. Scheduling a late afternoon appointment on the day a holiday begins might make it difficult for a Jewish client to both keep the appointment and celebrate the holiday. Likewise, traditional Muslims pray at several points throughout the day. Social workers should be flexible in scheduling appointments as a way of respecting clients' cultural and spiritual needs.

It is not possible for a social worker to know how to pronounce every client's name, be aware of every client's holidays or spiritual needs, and know everything about greeting clients in a culturally appropriate way. The most important thing is for the social worker to recognize that his or her ways are not universal and should not be imposed on clients. Social workers should always be open to learning and incorporating new knowledge in their work.

Reading or workshops can raise awareness about cultural issues. Most importantly, social workers need to be open to learning from their clients. After all, the client is in the best position to tell the social worker how to pronounce a name, how he or she is comfortable being greeted, and cultural issues around scheduling appointments. Showing an interest in learning from the client about the best way to meet his or her needs is central to communicating respect. These small tangible ways of respecting the client set the stage for the often-challenging tasks of showing respect for the client's culture and values throughout the work.

On a deeper level, helping professionals can show respect for clients by seeking and valuing their input in all areas of the case including identifying problems, setting goals, and identifying solutions. People from different cultures may see aspects of the world in fundamentally different ways, so it is not surprising that a social worker and client from different backgrounds may have different perceptions of the nature and cause of a problem. Inquiring about the client's perception of the problem should be a basic aspect of the problem identification and assessment phase. This includes asking the client his or her beliefs about what the problem is, what has caused it, what makes it better or worse, and what the ultimate solution should be. Having knowledge of the client's culture is important in the engaging process, although it is also important for the helper to be willing to learn from the client. Successful engagement involves establishing a level of compatibility (in areas such as the perception of problems, goals, and tasks) and trust (Tsang & Bogo, 1997). Likewise, the social worker reflects on these same questions within the context of professional knowledge about human behavior and social problems, informed by both theory and research.

Helping professionals who do not actively incorporate the client's perspective in their work are likely to be ineffective. The poignant true story of a Hmong refugee family trying to cope with the vast cultural divide between their own worldview and that of the American medical establishment depicted in the best selling book, *The Spirit Catches You and You Fall Down: A Hmong Child, Her American Doctors, and the Collision of Two Cultures* (Fadiman, 1997), clearly illustrates this point. In this story, the family experiences struggles with various helping professionals regarding the care of their young daughter who has a severe form of epilepsy. Only after years of struggles and repeated cultural misunderstandings does a social worker take the time to ask the family how they see the problem. This simple question opens the door to significant new information and begins to illuminate some major barriers to culturally competent care for the child. If the question had been asked years earlier, it might have made a significant difference in the quality of care.

The social worker and client may often have different views of the nature and cause of a problem. For example, in the case of the Hmong family just described, the family saw the problem as the soul being frightened away from the body, thus requiring spiritual intervention. The helping professionals, on the other hand, saw the problem as a disease to be managed medically. Although differing perspectives may exist, it is important that the professional and client come to a compatible understanding and agree on appropriate goals. The social worker and client may never come to full agreement about the cause of the problem. This can be all right as long as they agree on areas for work. In the case just illustrated, although the family and professionals have vastly different perspectives on the cause of the problem, they can probably come to an agreement on minimizing future seizures as a reasonable goal. It is important that clients have input into setting goals or they are unlikely to subscribe to them.

There are many different ways to work on goals. It is important that the client and social worker reach an agreement about how best to achieve their mutually agreed-upon goals. In fact, multiple ways of striving for goals may reinforce each other. An Arapaho client struggling to achieve a goal of maintaining sobriety may value traditional approaches as well as western-based counseling. The client may attend Native American Church ceremonies in addition to outpatient counseling as different but equally meaningful ways to reach the goal.

CULTURAL RELATIVISM

Biases and ethnocentrism have been well documented in the helping professions. Cultural differences have typically been equated with deviancy and pathology (Sue et al., 1998). Helping professionals need to consciously strive to be nonjudgmental and keep an open mind. This includes understanding and validating value systems and behaviors that differ from one's own (Kavanaugh et al., 1999). In an attempt to reject ethnocentrism and be responsive to the needs of diverse people, all major helping professions have recognized the need for cultural competence and have taken steps to achieve that goal. By deliberately trying to shift away from ethnocentrism, helping professionals are, to a greater or lesser degree, espousing positions of cultural relativism.

According to the *Social Work Dictionary*, cultural relativism is "the view that specific norms or rituals can be understood accurately only in the context of a culture's goals, social history, and environmental demands" (Barker, 1999, p. 114). Cultural relativism, a view grounded in the concept of respect for diversity, implies that all cultures and cultural practices are equally valid.

Carried to extremes, however, cultural relativism poses ethical dilemmas for helping professionals. For example, culture has a major influence on how children are raised, thus influencing styles of discipline. Social workers employed in the field of child protection are often faced with difficult decisions when they work with families from cultures that espouse physical discipline. The distinction between culturally sanctioned discipline and abuse is not always clear. What is considered appropriate in one cultural context is not necessarily appropriate in another. Child welfare institutions grounded in the standards of the Western-based dominant society may find themselves in conflict with the child-rearing practices of clients from a variety of cultures.

Many helping professionals who generally take a position of cultural relativism as part of culturally competent practice draw the line when faced with the practice of female genital mutilation (FGM) practiced in some African and Arab societies. The practice of excising the clitoris (equivalent to castration) is illegal in the United States, but it is still conducted in secret in some communities. Although variations on this practice exist, generally it involves cutting out the clitoris of a young girl and sewing her vagina virtually shut leaving only a small hole for menstrual flow. This practice is designed to make the girl more attractive to a future husband and assure him of her virginity. The procedure not only reduces her sexual feeling but also makes the girl highly vulnerable to infection, scarring, ongoing pain, and tearing with intercourse, pregnancy, and childbirth. Although some practitioners of FGM see it as a crucial part of their cultural traditions, most helping professionals do not accept this practice as a part of respecting a client's culture. There are, however, other areas where cultural practices that conflict with U.S. laws or dominant society norms may not be so clearly rejected.

There are no easy guidelines for determining what should be respected as cultural practices and where social workers should draw the line. It is important to remember that even though culture is an important element in understanding clients, it is not the only thing that must be considered. Before making judgments, social workers should consider whether a response to a client is grounded in ethnocentrism, either their own or that of the profession. There may be times when social workers cannot support cultural practices that threaten someone's well-being.

SELF-AWARENESS AND REFLECTION

As the transactional approach to understanding diversity makes clear, differences exist *between* people, and not within an individual. Therefore, learning about someone else's values, behaviors, and worldview requires reflection on one's own. Integral shifts in values are associated with changes in cultural competence (Kavanaugh et al., 1999). Likewise, understanding the dynamics of oppression is key in cultural competence (McPhatter, 1997).

The push for cultural competence comes partly from a recognition that culture is an integral part of who a client is (Vinson & Neimeyer, 2000). It makes sense that culture is a major shaping force in helpers' identities as well. Helping professionals are products of their own cultures and environments. They must be cognizant of their own worldviews and aware that they may react to client behaviors based on their own experiences (Hargrow, 2001; Kwan, 2001). Indeed, helping professionals who consciously examine their own cultural identities are likely to demonstrate greater cultural competence (Pack-Brown, 1999; Vinson & Neimeyer, 2000). A cultural genogram can help a social worker examine how his or her own culture may influence interactions with clients from similar and different cultural backgrounds (Imber-Black, 1997).

Coming from a position of privilege (i.e., White middle class) often does not necessitate an examination of power, status, or racial identity (Miehls, 2001). Thus, this type of self-examination may be new for social workers from the dominant society and may create tension and anxiety. Given that people have multiple facets of their identities, it can be helpful for White people to explore aspects in which they are in the minority to help them empathize with the oppression experienced by people of color (Croteau, 1999).

Cultural encounters and immersion experiences are good ways to increase self-awareness and consciousness of one's own cultural identity. In turn, such experiences increase cultural competence (Allen, 1998; Holland & Courtney, 1998; Kavanaugh et al., 1999). Helping professionals can seek out cross-cultural experiences that help develop a balanced view of different kinds of people. In the quest for cultural competence, professionals can seek the help of a cultural guide or member of a particular group, read literature written by members of different groups, and attend cultural events, meetings, and community forums. As part of these learning experiences, professionals can begin to reflect on their feelings and reactions (Sue et al., 1998).

In one example of a cultural immersion project, non-Native nurses took part in a participatory research project with Lakota people on the Pine Ridge reservation in South Dakota. Through this immersion experience they began to realize how what they "know" is skewed by assumptions, stereotypes, and biases (Kavanaugh et al., 1999). As one nurse stated, "I have come to recognize that—although I always thought I had empathy for people who were oppressed in some way—I never really let myself look deeply into their lives. I never let them inside me. I think I was so afraid of seeing the sadness that I looked the other way. What I missed, however, was all the joy and happiness too, the sense of family, community, and tradition" (Kavanaugh et al., 1999, p. 19).

CONCLUSION

Discussing diversity in depth in an honest manner can be a challenge. This type of exploration involves social workers questioning their own sense of right and wrong. It also involves challenging established power structures and positions of comfort. It involves going out on a limb into unexplored territory.

Honest self-reflection is a necessary component of developing cultural competence. This includes critiquing individual ethnocentrism as well as ethnocentrism inherent in the helping professions. Taking these steps may heighten the social worker's feelings of vulnerability, yet this can establish an important example for helping clients to take similar risks in exploring their own feelings and behaviors.

Cultural relativism can be an important component of cultural competence, but it does have limits. When making culturally competent decisions, a social worker must actively question whether the goals and interventions that he or she is planning incorporate the client's belief systems and values. When interventions do not fully incorporate the client's perspectives, the social worker should critically examine whether the client's cultural practices are being excluded simply because of ethnocentrism or whether compelling reasons, such as protecting someone's safety, justify going against a client's beliefs.

Exercises

Exercise #1: Reflecting on anxieties

For decades, social work leaders have urged all social workers to examine their own anxieties and fears. Take a few moments to reflect and identify one or two things that make you anxious about working with a particular type of client. Write each item on a separate piece of paper. The instructor collects all the pieces of paper and mixes them together. The class divides into small groups and each group is given several pieces of paper at random. Each group reviews each item and discusses the following points: (1) What might be the source of the anxiety? (2) If a social worker feels this way, how might it influence his or her ability to work with a client from this background? (3) How might a social worker strive to overcome this anxiety?

Exercise #2: The merits and drawbacks of cultural relativism

Discuss the following case example in small groups: You have been assigned to assess a Puerto Rican family charged with child abuse. One form of discipline they use with their five- and seven-year-old children is to have them kneel on uncooked grains of rice for 20 to 30 minutes at a time while facing the corner with their hands on their heads. How will you determine if this culturally based form of discipline is acceptable? What ethical problems does cultural relativism raise in this case? Is it possible for culturally based values and practices to be bad? Where do we draw the line between cultural relativism and ethnocentrism?

Exercise #3: Checking the facts

Choose a cultural group that you aren't very familiar with. Write down two or three things that you have heard about the group. For example, "I've heard that Gypsies are secretive and travel around a lot. They don't trust many people and tend to keep to themselves." Turn these statements in to your instructor or put them away safely where you won't be tempted to change what you have written. Next, investigate literature, the Internet, and community resources to determine whether your beliefs about this population are factual, distorted, or perhaps altogether wrong. Be sure to consult some sources written from insider perspectives and not just what others say about this group. Write a short reflection paper examining the similarities and discrepancies between your original statements and what you have learned about the group through your research.

References

Abernathy, A. D. (1995). Managing racial anger: A critical skill in cultural competence. *Journal of Multicultural Counseling and Development, 23,* 96–102.

Abrums, M. E., & Leppa, C. (2001). Beyond cultural competence: Teaching about race, gender, class, and sexual orientation. *Journal of Nursing Education, 40*(6), 270–275.

Allen, J. (1998). Personality assessment with American Indians and Alaska Natives: Instrument considerations and service delivery style. *Journal of Personality Assessment, 70*(1), 17–42.

Angel, R. J., & Williams, K. (2000). Cultural models of health and illness. In I. Cuellar & F. A. Paniagua, *Handbook of Multicultural Mental Health*. San Diego: Academic Press, 25–44.

Barker, R. L. (1999). *The Social Work Dictionary*. Washington DC: National Association of Social Workers Press.

Croteau, J. M. (1999). One struggle through individualism: Toward an antiracist white racial identity. *Journal of Counseling and Development, 77*(1), 30–32.

Dana, R. H. (1995). Impact of the use of standard psychological assessment on the diagnosis and treatment of ethnic minorities. In J. F. Aponte, R. Young Rivers, & J. Wohl (Eds.), *Psychological Intervention and Cultural Diversity*. Boston: Allyn & Bacon, 57–73.

Du Bois, W. E. B. (1990). *The Souls of Black Folk*. New York: Random House.

Fadiman, A. (1997). *The Spirit Catches You and You Fall Down: A Hmong Child, Her American Doctors, and the Collision of Two Cultures*. New York: Farrar, Straus, & Giroux.

Green, J. W. (1999). *Cultural awareness in the human services: A Multi-Ethnic Approach*. Englewood Cliffs, NJ: Prentice Hall.

Hargrow, A. M. (2001). Racial identity development: The case of Mr. X, an African American. *Journal of Mental Health Counseling, 23*(3), 222–237.

Holland, L., & Courtney, R. (1998). Increasing cultural competence with the Latino community. *Journal of Mental Health Nursing, 15*(1), 45–53.

Imber-Black, E. (1997). Developing cultural competence: Contributions from recent family therapy literature. *American Journal of Psychotherapy, 51*(4), 607–610.

Kavanaugh, K., Absalom, K., Beil, W., & Schliessmann, L. (1999). Connecting and becoming culturally competent: A Lakota example. *Advances in Nursing Science, 21*(3), 9–31.

Kolodny, R. L. (1969). Ethnic cleavages in the United States: An historical reminder to social workers. *Social Work, 14*(1), 13–23.

Kwan, K. K. (2001). Models of racial and ethnic identity development: Delineation of practice implications. *Journal of Mental Health Counseling, 23*(3), 269–277.

Lee, R. M., & Ramirez, M., III. (2000). The history, current status, and future of multicultural psychotherapy. In I. Cuellar & F. A. Paniagua, *Handbook of Multicultural Mental Health*. San Diego: Academic Press, 279–310.

Levy, S. R. (1999). Reducing prejudice: Lessons from social-cognitive factors underlying perceiver differences in prejudice. *Journal of Social Issues, 55*(4), 745–765.

Marsella, A. J., & Yamada, A. M. (2000). Culture and mental health: An introduction and overview of foundations, concepts, and issues. In I. Cuellar & Paniagua, F. A. *Handbook of Multicultural Mental Health*. San Diego: Academic Press, 3–22.

Martinez, C., Jr. (2000). Conducting the cross-cultural interview. In I. Cuellar & F. A. Paniagua, *Handbook of Multicultural Mental Health*. San Diego: Academic Press, 311–323.

McPhatter, A. R. (1997). Cultural competence in child welfare: What is it? How do we achieve it? What happens without it? *Child Welfare, 76*(1), 255–279.

Miehls, D. (2001). The interface of racial identity development with identity complexity in clinical social work student practitioners. *Clinical Social Work Journal, 29*(3), 229–244.

Pack-Brown, S. P. (1999). Racism and White counselor training: Influence of White racial identity theory and research. *Journal of Counseling and Development, 77*(1), 87–92.

Pope-Davis, D. B., Liu, W. M., Toporek, R. L., & Brittan-Powell, C. S. (2001). What's missing from multicultural competency research: Review, introspection, and recommendations. *Cultural Diversity and Ethnic Minority Psychology, 7*(2), 121–138.

Pratkanis, A. R., & Turner, M. E. (1999). The significance of Affirmative Action for the souls of White folk: Further implications of a helping model. *Journal of Social Issues, 55*(4), 787–922.

Sanchez-Hucles, J. (2000). *The First Session with African Americans: A Step-by-Step Guide.* San Francisco: Jossey-Bass.

Sevig, T., & Etzkorn, J. (2001). Transformative training: A year-long multicultural counseling seminar for graduate students. *Journal of Multicultural Counseling and Development, 29*(1), 57–72.

Shulman, L. (1999). *The Skills of Helping Individuals, Families, Groups, and Communities.* Itasca, IL: F. E. Peacock.

Simons, S. M. (1956). Desegregation and integration in social work. *Social Work, 1*(4), 20–25.

Stephan, W. G., & Finlay, K. (1999). The role of empathy in improving intergroup relations. *Journal of Social Issues, 55*(4), 729–744.

Sue, D. W., Carter, R. T., Casas, J. M., Fouad, N. A., Ivey, A. E., Jensen, M., LaFromboise, T., Manese, J. E., Ponterotto, J. G., & Vazquez-Natall, E. (1998). *Multicultural Counseling Competencies: Individual and Organizational Development.* Thousand Oaks, CA: Sage.

Swinomish Tribal Mental Health Project. (1991). *A Gathering of Wisdoms, Tribal Mental Health: A Cultural Perspective.* LaConner, WA: Swinomish Tribal Community.

Toporek, R. L., & Reza, J. V. (2001). Context as a critical dimension of multicultural counseling: Articulating personal, professional, and institutional competence. *Journal of Multicultural Counseling and Development, 29*(1), 13–30.

Tsang, A. K. T., & Bogo, M. (1997). Engaging with clients cross-culturally: Towards developing research-based practice. *Journal of Multicultural Social Work, 6*(3/4), 73–91.

Turner, J. B. (1972). Education for practice with minorities. *Social Work, 17*(3), 112–118.

Vinson, T. S., & Neimeyer, G. J. (2000). The relationship between racial identity development and multicultural counseling competency. *Journal of Multicultural Counseling and Development, 28*(3), 177–192.

Wohl, J. (1995). Traditional individual psychotherapy and ethnic minorities. In J. F. Aponte, R. Young Rivers, & J. Wohl (Eds.), *Psychological Intervention and Cultural Diversity.* Boston: Allyn & Bacon, 74–91.

Striving for Cultural Competence

A number of related and overlapping definitions of cultural competence exist, yet the lack of a single working definition continues to hinder advancing this imperative (Sue et al., 1998). The *Social Work Dictionary* (Barker, 1999) does not even list the term *cultural competence* or the sometimes-interchangeable term *multicultural counseling competence*; however, it does include many related terms. Although there is consensus that cultural competence is important and should be monitored, there is no agreement about what it means or how to measure it (Switzer, Scholle, Johnson, & Kelleher, 1998). Indeed, cultural competence "has become a buzz phrase in dire need of elucidation if we are to move beyond fragmented approaches that have characterized previous efforts" (McPhatter, 1997, p. 256). To complicate matters, the need for cultural competence has been recognized at a time when other, potentially conflicting trends, such as managed care, are emerging.

The goal of cultural competence is to transform helping professionals and make their work more relevant to diverse populations (Pope-Davis, Liu, Toporek, & Brittan-Powell, 2001). Cultural competence begins with recognizing the similar and distinct values, norms, customs, history, and institutions of various groups (Poole, 1998). One of the most noted scholars working in this area, Derald Sue, a psychologist, defines multicultural counseling competence as a helping professional having an awareness of his or her own assumptions, values, and biases; understanding the worldview of culturally distinct clients; being able to develop appropriate intervention strategies and techniques; being able to define a multiculturally competent organization; and understanding how organizational and institutional forces can enhance or negate the development of multicultural competence (Sue et al., 1998). This definition is particularly important in that it includes the context for service delivery in addition to the micro-level focus emphasized by many scholars. Consideration of the context for practice is crucial given that problems attributed to cultural insensitivity are often caused by incongruence between helping systems and various cultures, including assessment instruments, clinicians' practices, and policies in programs and systems (Abe-Kim & Takeuchi, 1996).

Some scholars have examined the relationship between cultural competence and general counseling competence. Coleman (1998) has found these two concepts to be so interconnected that they may be inseparable. Other scholars, however, have postulated that multicultural counseling competencies, although strongly related to general counseling competence, are competencies of a higher order, requiring more specific and sophisticated knowledge and skills that can be developed only after sound basic counseling competence is established (Fuertes, Bartolomeo, & Nichols, 2001).

Cultural competence is a continuous process of striving to provide services effectively within the client's cultural context. It is an ongoing process rather than an outcome (Campinha-Bacote, 2001; Fahrenwald, Boysen, Fischer, & Maurer, 2001). Although there is no single definition, there is general agreement on many of the key components of cultural competence. This chapter reviews key aspects of cultural competence, barriers to cultural competence, specific models, measurement issues, and moving cultural competence beyond the micro level.

KEY ASPECTS OF CULTURAL COMPETENCE

The Layers of Identity

In striving for cultural competence, it is important to recognize that considerable diversity exists within cultural groups and to embrace the complexity of the intersections between the layers of identity such as culture, gender, sexual orientation, religion, class, disability, national origin, and age (Kavanaugh, Absalom, Beil, & Schliessmann, 1999; Sevig & Etzkorn, 2001). Culturally appropriate services must go beyond incorporating client belief systems, spiritual practices, extended family relationships and child-rearing patterns and be grounded directly in the cultural base of the clients being served (Swinomish Tribal Mental Health Project, 1991). Cultural competence means identifying the most meaningful aspects of a client's identity in a particular case situation and factoring that information into all aspects of the work.

Assessing Cultural Identity

It is important to avoid applying information about a client's cultural background in a stereotypical manner. Cultural information should not be seen as a rigid template but, rather, as a lens to be adjusted with different clients or discarded if exceptions are found (Boyd-Franklin, Aleman, Jean-Gilles, & Lewis, 1995). Indeed, behavior is a composite of universal characteristics, cultural characteristics, and individual characteristics. Helping professionals must decipher how these three forces influence clients' behaviors as part of developing culturally competent services (Yoshioka, 1999). When including culture in the assessment, it is not necessary to have information on every aspect of culture. Rather, helping professionals need to identify major beliefs and behaviors as they influence the problem or setting (Mattson, 2000).

An assessment of any client should be done with consideration for the client's cultural norms. Ideas that appear to be delusional such as beliefs about witchcraft and sorcery may be commonly held beliefs in some cultures (Lukoff & Lu, 1999). It is important to differentiate between pathology and spiritual beliefs in a cross-cultural assessment. how is this due w/out bias?

Scholars are still in the process of developing meaningful ways to assess cultural identity. Only recently has a section on culture-bound disorders been included in the *Diagnostic and Statistical Manual (DSM)*, largely because of pressure from minority professionals and others who recognize the importance of culture (Marsella & Yamada, 2000). Modification of existing tests to make them culturally appropriate, or creation of new culturally specific measures, is a necessary part of cultural competence (Dana, 1995). In the 1980s and 1990s, many scales were developed to measure cultural identity (Kahn & Denmon, 1997). Most of these assessment tools conceptualize culture on a continuum from assimilated to traditional. The theoretical foundations upon which these tools are built lag behind current perspectives that discard linear models of culture, thus making the usefulness of these tools questionable.

The Interaction of Knowledge, Skills, and Values/Attitudes

Although different scholars conceptualize cultural competence somewhat differently, many recognize knowledge, skills, and values/attitudes as its major components and use this as an organizing framework. The values/attitudes dimension of cultural competence is sometimes known by other names including beliefs or awareness (Hong, Garcia, & Soriano, 2000). These primary components of cultural competence were identified by Turner as early as 1972, yet it has taken the helping professions decades to further develop this concept.

These components are highly interactive and all are necessary in the quest for cultural competence. It is possible to be knowledgeable about cultures without changing behavior or affect (Toporek & Reza, 2001). Specific content about diverse groups (knowledge) is important, but cognitive learning must be supplemented with affective cultural sensitivity that requires helpers to have meaningful cross-cultural experiences (Imber-Black, 1997). Skills must be built on a solid foundation of knowledge and enlightened consciousness (McPhatter, 1997). Ongoing, active development of the components of cultural competence is required (McPhatter, 1997; Toporek & Reza, 2001). True cognitive, affective, and behavioral change must go beyond the counseling relationship and permeate the helping professional's life.

Steady progress has been made in identifying multicultural counseling competencies in the broad areas of attitude, knowledge, and skill. Sue and a variety of his colleagues conceptualized 11 specific competencies in the early 1980s. By the late 1990s, the list was expanded to 34 competencies. Each competency was considered in light of counselor beliefs and attitudes, counselor knowledge, and counselor skills (Fuertes, Bartolomeo, & Nichols, 2001). Theory and development of instruments to measure cultural competence have progressed steadily, but empirical research in this area is still scant (Fuertes et al., 2001).

A Strengths-Based, Holistic Approach

Culturally competent professionals must approach their work with a non-judgmental attitude and a respect for differences. Developing deep relationships and truly learning about clients before moving into problem solving helps promote a strengths-based focus in the helping relationship (Kavanaugh et al., 1999). When approaching work from a perspective of wellness, discussions about clients' coping strategies may reveal information about networks of natural helpers and indigenous healing practices (Mason, Benjamin, & Lewis, 1996).

A holistic assessment that includes mind, body, and spirit is important in developing an understanding of how people protect health, prevent illness, and restore health (Mattson, 2000). Exploring different facets of a client's well-being helps the practitioner more fully understand the client. Cultural competence must include an awareness of religious and spiritual practices. Treatment can be enhanced by understanding spiritual beliefs, participation in religious rituals, and affiliation with a religious community. Spirituality is also helpful in coping with depression, controlling pain, and fighting disease (Lukoff & Lu, 1999).

Power Dynamics

Cultural competence must include recognition of power dynamics, especially for clients who are visibly distinct such as African Americans, Native Americans, Asian Americans, and Latinos. Social work with people of color is inextricably linked with social justice. It is important to go beyond an understanding of cultural values to establish a firm understanding of how social, political, and economic structures interact with diverse people to analyze, understand, and address complex social problems. This broader understanding of a social context, including structural inequalities, discrimination, and one's own place in relation to individual and institutional bias, is integral to developing cultural competence (Abrums & Leppa, 2001; Padilla, 1996; Sevig & Etzkorn, 2001; Sue et al., 1998).

Cultural competence requires critical thinking about issues of power and oppression (Flannery & Ward, 1999). Social workers need to understand how different forms of bias, including institutionalized oppression, affect their clients (Hargrow, 2001; Sevig & Etzkorn, 2001). Helping professionals must be comfortable with race, and they must understand the history of oppression to be culturally competent. Discussions of racial issues may be appropriate in the first session (Hargrow, 2001). Culturally competent helpers must also be equipped to deal with the anger that is an inherent by-product of racism (Abernathy, 1995).

Understanding the dynamics of power and oppression can also be relevant to working with clients who feel threatened by the growing cultural diversity in the United States. Abernathy, an African American helping professional, presents an example from her practice in which a White male being seen for depression after job loss lashed out at her because he believed that special treatment was being given to African Americans, thus, depriving him of job opportunities. Abernathy allowed the client to express his racially laden anger without reacting defensively. She then explored the source of his anger and his underlying feelings and perceptions, and assisted him in controlling his rage. A focus of the work was challenging his distorted perception of himself and African Americans and helping him to express feelings other than anger (Abernathy, 1995).

Respect

Showing respect for clients whose values, beliefs, traditions, and behaviors differ from those of the social worker is a key component of cultural competence. Respecting culturally diverse clients is particularly important, given that many come from groups that have experienced decades of oppression and cultural imposition by members of the dominant society (Kavanaugh et al., 1999).

Increased awareness of cultural identity promotes recognition of both intragroup and intergroup diversity. Recognizing and acknowledging that the diversity within a group is as great as between people of that group and outsiders is an important part of learning and establishing a connection with clients (Kavanaugh et al., 1999). Such awareness is key to showing respect and is exemplified by using clients' preferred names, languages, and credible, comfortable, culture-specific etiquette for service delivery. Failure to recognize cultural differences may lead to frustrations, misunderstandings, defensive reactions, and underutilization of services (Dana, 1998).

Respect includes taking time to learn about the client and his or her situation rather than making assumptions. Helping professionals should avoid premature displays of empathy. A helper who claims to understand the client's perspectives without first getting to know him or her may be perceived as acting on stereotypes (Abernathy, 1995).

Self-Awareness

Self-awareness is important for helping professionals, both as individuals and as members of professions. It is important for the helping professional to understand himself or herself as a cultural being and the impact this may have on the helping relationship (Sue et al., 1998). Cultural competence begins with the helping professional's honest self-assessment of how he or she works with culturally different clients (McPhatter, 1997). In cross-cultural interviews, it is particularly important to constantly reflect on feelings, perceptions, and responses to the client. It is important for helping professionals to be alert for stereotypes and biases they may have (Martinez, 2000).

The European worldview, as expressed through language, can promote racism, political exploitation, individuality, and private property. Words and phrases have powerful and specific connotations. Culture-bound views embedded in the choice of words become apparent when contrasted with other options. For example, did Columbus discover or invade America? What constitutes a victory rather than a massacre? Rebellions or revolutions? Equality or conformity? Black pride or separatism? Illegitimate babies or babies? Racism can be found in social work jargon, and this in turn influences social policies and practice. Terms such as *cultural lag, culturally disadvantaged,* and *culturally deprived* are culture-bound. Social workers must reflect on the connotations of these terms and how they shape work with clients (Burgest, 1973).

The Ongoing Process of Cultural Learning

Greater cross-cultural life experiences leads to greater multicultural competence (Diaz-Lazaro & Cohen, 2001). Cross-cultural contact reduces negative attitudes toward members of culturally different groups. This contact must be supplemented with a cognitive component to maximize cultural competence. Service learning can help move beyond cultural awareness to competence. This type of community-based learning combines academic study with service, thus, increasing awareness of cultural differences and the need to take action against oppression. Community-based learning and other forms of direct contact with different types of people are humanizing and participatory ways of learning (Baines, 2000; Fahrenwald et al., 2001; Flannery & Ward, 1999; Manese, Wu, & Nepomuceno, 2001).

Having direct contact with people from different cultural backgrounds can bring about meaningful change in helping professionals. Tyrone Baines, an employee of the Kellog Foundation, poignantly describes the transformation he experienced as he learned more about Native Americans through direct contact. Initially, Baines watched as representatives of funding sources like himself delivered presentations to Native Americans that were received courteously but weren't meaningful. Not wanting to replicate this problem, he sought to improve his cultural competence by spending time with Native Americans in daily activities. Baines went to meals, fitness centers, and nightclubs, but most of all he listened to Native American people. He learned about listening circles, elders, the Four Directions, the relationships among living things, and the circular nature of the world. What he learned through these simple interactions led him to modify all his subsequent work with Native Americans, including acknowledging the wisdom of the elders, speaking in a less direct, linear manner, and showing respect for indigenous methods of evaluation (Baines, 2000).

BARRIERS TO CULTURAL COMPETENCE

[handwritten margin notes: Also-less commonly employed; force; Jang; credits]

Although the need for cultural competence has long been recognized, a number of barriers exist to realizing this important value, including the attitudes of helping professionals, differences in belief systems, cost containment mechanisms, ethnocentric theoretical frameworks that guide helping practices, and limited incorporation of cultural dynamics in the curricula of helping professions. Some of these barriers exist on the micro level within helping professionals or in the relationship between professionals and clients. For example, sometimes helping professionals trivialize cultural competence as a form of political correctness, thereby limiting the examination of complex cultural issues (Poole, 1998). The term *politically correct* is used to denigrate people with progressive beliefs on issues of race, gender, sexual orientation, and various marginalized groups.

Another barrier to culturally competent services occurs when significant differences exist between social workers' and clients' belief systems. The larger the difference between belief systems, the more difficult it is to meet clients' needs. Culturally competent care should match a client's perception of the problem and meet his or her expectations for treatment (Mattson, 2000).

Barriers to cultural competence also exist in various systems and policies. For instance, cost-containment mechanisms that control supply and demand, utilization management, and gatekeeping processes may interfere with the delivery of culturally competent services. A service provider may be highly skilled in providing culturally competent services, but the intervention may be undermined by case managers or utilization reviewers who do not understand the cultural aspects of the work (Abe-Kim & Takeuchi, 1996).

Part of cultural competence includes understanding the barriers to care faced by many clients. This may include barriers created unknowingly and unnecessarily by service providers and care systems that have a limited understanding of culturally diverse clients (Holland & Courtney, 1998). Sometimes the theoretical frameworks that guide service provision create barriers to cultural competence. For example, improvements in medical care and technology have reinforced a clinical philosophy of treating a disease rather than a complex human being. Ignorance of cultural issues raises barriers to care, thereby reinforcing health disparities between different groups of people (Donini-Lenhoff, 2001).

MODELS OF CULTURAL COMPETENCE

A number of different models of cultural competence have emerged, including the Child and Adolescent Service System Program (CASSP) model. This model encourages: (1) valuing diversity as a strength in clients, agency staff, administration, board membership, and volunteers, (2) conducting a cultural self-assessment so that professionals and agencies become aware of their cultural blind spots; for example, do the agencies' expectations about time orientation and level of disclosure conflict with client norms?, (3) understanding the dynamics of difference, for example, is there strain because of historic mistrust or different communication styles when people of different cultures interact?, (4) incorporating cultural knowledge, and (5) modifying direct service approaches or agency administration to adapt to diversity (Mason et al., 1996).

Another social work scholar among the first to propose a model of ethnic or cultural competence was J. S. Gallegos. His model proposes that people of color share a history of oppression based primarily on color and cultural differences from the dominant society, the ancestral roots of people of color are grounded in non-Western traditions, and the experiences of these groups are characterized by sociocultural dissonance. To gain insight and develop appropriate interventions for clients of color, helping professionals need to acknowledge (1) that there is often dissonance between the dual perspective that people of color have from their immediate environment and the larger society; (2) that help-seeking behavior is influenced by culture; and (3) that empowerment is central to ethnic or cultural competence (Gallegos, 1982).

In the early 1980s, Sue and his colleagues in psychology became leaders in calling for cultural competence (Lee & Ramirez, 2000). They developed a model that focuses on social justice as well as clinical considerations and is applicable at individual, institutional, and societal levels. In their conceptualization, multiculturalism and multicultural counseling encompass many forms of diversity including class, gender, and sexual orientation as well as ethnicity. Multiculturalism values pluralism, and although it respects other positions, it is not value neutral. Rather, multiculturalism requires an activist stance and a commitment to changing societal conditions that inhibit equal access and opportunities. As applied in the helping professions, multiculturalism requires that helping professionals be aware of their own assumptions, biases, and values, understand the worldviews of their clients, and develop culturally appropriate intervention strategies and techniques (Sue et al., 1998).

Toporek and Reza (2001) built on the work of Sue and colleagues in developing an expanded model of multicultural competence that includes personal, professional, and institutional contexts. The Multicultural Counseling Competency Assessment and Planning Model (MCCAP) integrates self-assessment and strategic planning. Cognitive, affective, and behavioral change are necessary for competence. Helping professionals must change personally, professionally, and institutionally.

The nursing profession has been on the cutting edge of recognizing the need for cultural competence. Some of the earliest work in this area was done by Madeleine Leininger, a nurse trained in anthropology (see for example Leininger, 1988, 1991). Josepha Campinha-Bacote, another nurse who writes prolifically on cultural competence, proposed a model of cultural competence involving five intersecting areas: (1) cultural awareness, including being respectful, appreciative and sensitive to clients' cultures as well as examining the professional's own biases; (2) cultural knowledge, including gathering information to develop an understanding of clients' worldviews; (3) cultural encounters, including cross-cultural interactions that lead to knowledge; (4) cultural skill, including the ability to collect relevant cultural data and accurately conduct culturally specific assessments; and (5) cultural desire, including the motivation to engage in the process of becoming culturally competent (2001).

MEASURING CULTURAL COMPETENCE

Thus far, recommendations for cultural competence have been based on theories about cultural match and fit rather than on empirical evidence. No rigorous research has been conducted on the efficacy of treatment for any ethnic minority population (Sue, 1998). It is important to move beyond the early stages of knowledge building and practice wisdom to generate empirical knowledge about cross-cultural practice and its effectiveness (Tsang & Bogo, 1997). This has not happened yet, partly because it is difficult to measure cultural competence when models are still being built and refined.

Some professionals believe that matching, the process of pairing clients and helping professionals from the same cultural background, will lead to culturally competent services because, presumably, both share cultural knowledge and belief systems. Studies on matching have produced inconsistent results about whether clients view competency in the same way as helpers (Pope-Davis et. al., 2001; Sawyer et al., 1995). Some empirical support has been found to support the claim that ethnic and cognitive matching is important in cultural competence as measured by lower premature termination rates, more sessions, or better treatment outcomes. Matching, however, is neither a necessary nor sufficient criterion for a positive treatment outcome (Sue, 1998). Matching has been suggested as a way of increasing cultural competence, but this is often impractical.

A number of instruments have been developed to measure counselor cultural competence, including the Cross-Cultural Counseling Inventory—Revised, the Multicultural Counseling Awareness Scale—Form B, the Multicultural Counseling Inventory, and the Multicultural Awareness-Knowledge-Skills Survey. Tools have also been developed to assess multicultural competence training including the Multicultural Competency Checklist and the Multicultural Environmental Inventory (Fuertes et al., 2001; Vinson & Neimeyer, 2000). Many of these instruments are based on the knowledge, skills, and awareness components specified by Sue and colleagues.

Nine components of care have been empirically associated with positive mental health outcomes for minority clients. These can be summarized as representing respect for differences, easy access to care, community and family involvement and consist of the following: (1) shared culture; (2) shared language; (3) agency located in clients' community; (4) flexible hours and appointments; (5) provision of or referral to social, economic, legal, and medical services; (6) family involvement; (7) brief interventions; (8) referral to spiritual advisors or traditional healers; and (9) involving clients in determining, evaluating, and publicizing services (Switzer, Scholle, Johnson, & Kelleher, 1998).

Cultural competence is attained when clients from diverse backgrounds perceive that care is delivered in ways that respect cultural beliefs and attitudes (Switzer et al., 1998). In other words, the client should be the ultimate judge of the helping professional's cultural competence. Unfortunately, this is rarely the case. Few measures assess clients' perceptions of counselors' cultural competence (Fuertes et al., 2001; Pope-Davis et al., 2001). Measurement of the cultural competence of agencies and practitioners is often done through self-reports of helping professionals or observer assessment. When data is gathered from within an agency, there is pressure to overestimate cultural competence. There may also be a lack of congruence between agency/helper reports and clients' perceptions (Pope-Davis et al., 2001; Switzer et al., 1998).

Process and outcome indices of counseling must also be compared with multicultural counseling competencies (Fuertes et al., 2001). The Client Cultural Competence Inventory focuses on client perceptions. This instrument has (1) low susceptibility to social desirability bias; (2) an ability to assess attitudes about therapists, providers, and plans; and, (3) a focus on clients (Switzer et al., 1998). The Cross-Cultural Counseling Inventory—Revised, which currently measures cultural competence as perceived by supervisors, could easily be modified for client feedback. However, it is necessary to consider how cultural variables such as a respect for authority may influence clients' evaluation of helping professionals' cultural competence (Fuertes et al., 2001). Clients may be reluctant to give negative evaluations out of respect for helping professionals as authority figures.

TAKING CULTURAL COMPETENCE BEYOND THE MICRO LEVEL

Cultural competence must be carried out beyond the micro level to encompass policies, theory building, instrument development, and administration of social agencies. Cultural competence is also necessary in all community-level interventions. Likewise, it is a critical element in research and education for helping professions. Indeed, all helping professionals, regardless of their practice area or level of intervention, must be culturally competent to be effective, ethical professionals.

Policies

It is a mistake to assume that policies are culturally neutral. Such an assumption replicates earlier efforts to achieve colorblindness that have proven ineffective. In fact, policies are often monocultural in nature and serve as impediments to multiculturalism (Sue et al., 1998).

Some policies target particular cultural groups. For instance, the Indian Child Welfare Act (enacted in 1978) was designed to remedy the large numbers of indigenous children placed in fostercare or adoption in non-Native homes and thus applies only to this population. This policy was based, in part, on an understanding of the meaning of children to Native American peoples and their importance in the continuity of indigenous cultures. On the other hand, the refugee resettlement policies of the late 1970s and early 1980s, though targeting large groups of Southeast Asian refugees that arrived in the United States in the wake of the Vietnam War, ignored many of the cultural characteristics of these groups. Most of these refugees came from strong *history* extended family networks that served as important sources of emotional and tangible support. Resettlement policies, however, placed these refugees as nuclear families in communities scattered across the country. This undermined the potential for mutual support and eventually resulted in secondary migrations as families did whatever they could to reunite their members.

Other policies do not target specific groups but may have a differential impact on varied populations. For instance, welfare reform applies to recipients regardless of cultural background but may have different meanings for clients from cultures that emphasize a woman's responsibility to stay home and care for children, rather than participate in the workforce. Policy makers need to consider the impact that policies have on different populations. If the cultural context is considered during policy making, resulting policies are likely to be more culturally congruent and ultimately more effective.

Theories and Standardized Assessment Instruments

Theories and instruments such as assessment tools are not culturally neutral. Personality conceptualizations are usually based on Euro-American theories, particularly psychoanalytic theories that posit a human development process that has not been documented to be universal. These theories have failed to demonstrate cross-cultural construct validity. In other words, they are not based on psychological universals.

> In a multicultural society, there may be no acceptable reasons for continued use of standard tests predicated exclusively on Eurocentric assumptions and outdated test construction methodologies. Similarly, an exclusive commitment to empirical rationales for deprivation of personality constructs or psychopathological conditions may not permit an adequate investigation of cultural dimensions. Nonetheless, vested interests in the psychometric establishment continue to be persuasive arbiters of assessment training contents, choice of validation technologies by researchers, and use of particular tests by practitioners. (Dana, 1998, p. 9)

Helping professionals are faced with the challenge of incorporating culture in theoretical stances and in the tools they use. This can be done either by creating new, culturally based theories and instruments or by modifying existing ones. For instance, it may be possible to modify Eurocentric techniques like psychotherapy to make them more appropriate for different types of clients (Wohl, 1995). Likewise, instruments need to be modified to ensure that the questions are understood and meaningful within the cultural context of the client. Revision or translation of standardized assessments, however, raises issues of construct validity and usefulness within a specific cultural context. Likewise, modifying standardized instruments or even being flexible with how they are applied raises the need to reestablish validity and reliability. Modifying standardized tests is likely to remain more common than development of culture-specific instruments (Dana, 1998). Modification of existing tools is perceived to be easier and less of a departure from current practices.

Social Agencies

Social agencies must make a commitment to incorporate the principles of cultural competence throughout their policies and structures, not just in direct practice with clients. Institutional biases and practices found in social agencies often reflect those of the larger society (Sue et al., 1998). For example, the physical setup of the agency waiting area and the way clients are greeted on arrival (perhaps with a clipboard filled with forms to be completed) reflect practices in the dominant society and may be considered cold and unfriendly by some clients. Likewise, it is important that services be offered with recognition of the impact of environmental stresses such as discrimination and oppression. These stresses are experienced differently by different groups of people. Programs that use a colorblind approach and treat all people equally are not culturally competent (Mason et al., 1996).

Culturally competent services may well be the most cost-effective as well as clinically effective way to serve clients (Pumariega, 1996). When cultural competence is not infused into every aspect of service delivery, its importance is likely to be minimized, used only as a marketing tool, or relegated to political correctness (Mason et al., 1996). As part of increasing and demonstrating cultural competence, agencies can co-sponsor events that celebrate cultural diversity and strengths. Agency staff members can assess their cultural blind spots and participate in antibias training (Mason et al., 1996). This will better equip them to provide appropriate and meaningful services. Administrators should make training available to staff and set the expectation that staff members will participate in ongoing learning throughout their careers.

Program structure and services must be consistent with cultural values (Swinomish Tribal Mental Health Project, 1991). Agencies can participate in a self-assessment process that includes reflecting on the people in their catchment area, who they actually serve (including within and between group differences), and barriers to service delivery (Mason et al., 1996). For decades, some social workers have recognized the need for agencies to be responsive to diverse clients. In discussing improved services to African Americans, Pettit (1960) emphasized that agencies should examine their reception, intake, service procedures, and philosophy. These factors are all likely to affect how well clients are served. Regional and class differences should also be considered in targeting services to clientele.

Several models have been developed to assess the cultural competence of agencies. Prominent models include those developed by Cross, Bazron, Dennis, and Issacs, (1989; cited in Hong et al., 2000) and Sue et al. (1998). The models and measurement instruments that focus on agency cultural competence fall into two types: (1) awareness, sensitivity, and skills of direct practice workers, and enhancing these through staff development and training; and (2) structure, management, and policies of the organization as responsive to needs of culturally diverse clients. Before agencies can deliver services in a culturally competent manner, administrators and service providers must become aware of their own organizational culture and accept divergent cultural orientations. Only within this context can cultural sensitivity and knowledge be integrated into competent practice (Matthews, 1996).

The cultural competence continuum developed by Cross and colleagues (1989, cited in Hong et al., 2000) is a tool that can be used to assess cultural proficiency in both individuals and institutions. This paradigm consists of six positions along a continuum: cultural destructiveness, cultural incapacity, cultural blindness, cultural precompetence, cultural competence, and cultural proficiency (Hong et al., 2000). Kim, McLeod, and Shantzis (1992) have built on the Cross model and have applied it, with slight modifications, to evaluate the cultural competence of agencies serving Asian Americans with alcohol and drug problems.

Sue et al. (1998) identify the following characteristics associated with culturally competent and inclusive organizations: (1) a commitment to cultural competence from top levels; (2) an operationalized written policy, mission, or vision statement of multiculturalism; (3) a multicultural and diversity action plan; (4) an empowered subordinate or multicultural oversight team; (5) active solicitation of feedback from employee groups and accountability for cultural competence built into the system; (6) infusion of cultural competence into evaluation criteria; (7) mentoring and support networks for minority employees; (8) encouragement of coalition building and networking among minorities and women; (9) a systematic, long-term commitment to educating the entire workforce; and (10) a view of the organization as a reflection of the larger community.

Community Interventions

Cultural competence is a necessary component of macro-level work, yet the theory and practice in this area is considerably less developed than cultural competence on a micro level. Historically, social workers have alienated clients of color by ignoring macro-level issues. This needs to change. Social workers need to go beyond viewing the social environment as simply a context for understanding the client. They must actively consider the environment as a target of change when oppression, institutional biases, and lack of response to clients' basic needs are identified as problems. Helping professionals who ignore macro issues severely limit their ability to be effective with culturally diverse clients (McPhatter, 1997).

Ethnic communities must be involved in all levels of planning and service implementation (Flannery & Ward, 1999). Often interventions are initiated on behalf of, rather than in partnership with, communities. Such one-sided interventions are likely to foster resentment and be doomed to fail. Social workers, in partnership with communities, have the opportunity to bring about mean-ingful change. For example, in one urban area with many small, scattered grassroots and professional efforts to provide services to immigrants and refugees, lack of service coordination and duplication of effort hindered attempts to provide services to newcomers. Helping professionals were instru-mental in building a coalition of service providers, immigrants, and refugees to network with each other, identify strengths and service gaps, and develop coordinated advocacy efforts.

Research

Like other aspects of social work, research requires cultural competence. Research and practice should be mutually reinforcing. Researchers can learn from practitioners how to incorporate culture for effective engaging and implementation. For many projects in communities of color, researchers will need to demonstrate cultural competence to gain access. Likewise, research with diverse populations is needed to inform culturally competent practice. Practice wisdom has been important thus far in developing theories and mod-els. Empirical evidence can aid in further developing knowledge about the spe-cific dimensions of cultural competence with various populations.

Researchers need to establish trust with culturally diverse communities and help them move beyond their fears of exploitation (Weaver, 1997). Many culturally diverse communities resist being the subjects of study because of experiences of prejudice and mistreatment. Fears and suspicions about research studies remain high including the fear that probing into cultural issues may unleash unhealthy racist prejudices leading to renewed discrimination. This type of concern has led to efforts to eliminate questions about race in gov-ernmental surveys (American Psychiatric Association, 1994).

Culturally specific knowledge can be helpful in defining the problem for study, identifying research questions, and formulating hypotheses (Weaver, 1997). Learning about the culture of the population involved in the project needs to be standard in planning a research project (Rogler, 1989).

Choice of a research design for service evaluation can be a significant issue with culturally diverse groups (Pumariega, 1996). Using a culturally congru-ent methodology will maximize the project's likelihood of success. For exam-ple, in Native American cultures where personal interaction is highly valued, sending a survey through the mail may be less effective than interviews con-ducted by trusted members of the community (Weaver, 1997). Once data is collected, the cultural context must be considered as part of its interpretation (Landrine & Klonoff, 1992; Rogler, 1989).

Developmental research, an inductive approach that is one of the few methodologies specific to design and development of social and behavioral interventions, is helpful for developing culturally appropriate interventions. This type of research can be important in designing an intervention prototype, going through a reiterative process of testing and refinement, and evaluating intervention effectiveness. The intervention is grounded in ongoing work between the social worker and client and, as such, reflects the needs, circumstances, and concerns of the client group. The substantive content of the intervention and its underlying assumptions must be considered. This is more meaningful than simply changing language or examples (Yoshioka, 1999).

Helping Professions and Their Training Programs

Helping professionals must recognize how their values, beliefs, and behaviors interact with those of diverse clients and take steps to move beyond ethnocentrism. Helping professions have begun this process, yet still have far to go. Recognition that cultural issues had not been explicitly acknowledged in the American Psychological Association code led to its revision in 1992; however, the Code does not distinguish cultural competence from sensitivity, recognize emic measures, or discuss inclusion of acculturation measures and useful moderator variables (Dana, 1998). Likewise, the National Association of Social Workers Code of Ethics (1999) has become more explicit about cultural competence as an ethical imperative. The difficulty, however, is how to move beyond words to ensure that statements on the importance of diversity become guiding principles to change the behaviors of all members of the helping professions. This significant shift in values does not come easily.

Much has been written in the last two decades on incorporating cultural content in professional training. Innovative techniques and exercises have been developed for use, both in and outside the classroom. Implementation of such teaching strategies, however, requires diligence. Cultural competence is more than adding cultural content to an existing course. It requires transformation of content, pedagogy, and organizational structures (Flannery & Ward, 1999). To bring about real change in the cultural competence of future helping professionals, instructors must change their thinking and the way they approach diversity in the classroom.

Higher education curricula must be transformed. This requires challenging the fundamental paradigms of education. Students must move beyond organizational walls and go out into culturally diverse communities (Flannery & Ward, 1999). Community service can be integrated with academic study as part of community-based learning (Fahrenwald et al., 2001; Flannery & Ward, 1999; Kavanaugh et al., 1999; Manese et al., 2001). Only through comprehensive, well-planned efforts can cultural and professional competence be achieved.

CONCLUSION

Cultural competence is an evolving concept. Even though the need to include cultural dimensions in the helping professions has been recognized for decades, the process of operationalizing this principle has been slow. Much of what is currently known about cultural competence is based on practice wisdom. The years of experience of social workers and other helping professionals who are concerned about this area is a valuable starting point for advancing practice. Only recently have researchers begun to develop an empirical dimension to the state of current knowledge. At the same time, scholars have been involved in developing theories and models of cultural competence.

Clearly, practice wisdom, theories, models, and empirical evidence are all crucial aspects of the knowledge base on cultural competence. Many of these aspects are still being developed, so we do not yet have a full picture of the specific components of cultural competence. In future decades, as knowledge increases, this concept will be more fully elucidated and understood.

Exercises

Exercise #1: Recognizing your own beliefs and behaviors

Individually, answer the following questions, based on the work of Kwan (2001), about your beliefs and behaviors as a social worker. Discuss your answers with a partner or in a small group. Use these questions to identify how your beliefs may influence your work with clients.

a. What do you consider to be normal social worker and client behavior during work together?
b. If group goals conflict with the client's individual needs or desires, how can these conflicts be resolved?
c. At what age should a young person leave his or her parents and live independently?
d. What strategies do you use to include clients' support systems in your work?
e. Describe an instance when you intervened to change a system to fit the client's needs rather than requiring the client to change to fit the system.

Exercise #2: Cultural learning through poetry

Reading poetry can be an important tool for increasing cross-cultural understanding. Poetry reveals significant information about diverse groups in their own words. This can help social workers develop an understanding of the meaning of cultural identity and oppression (Holman, 1996). Read some poetry by an author from a cultural group that you know little about (for example, a selection from the book of poetry, *The Shock of Arrival* by Meena Alexander about Asian Indian immigrants). You may also choose to read a poem about multicultural identity (for example, the poem "Child of the Americas" by Aurora Levins Morales). Write a brief essay describing what the poetry reveals about the cultural group you have chosen.

Exercise #3: Self-reflection through cultural immersion

Choose a cultural community that you are unfamiliar with and do a mini cultural immersion experience in which you spend at least an hour on someone else's "turf." Make sure that you enter with respect as someone genuinely interested in learning cultural information so you can become a better helping professional. Places that you may choose to go include a synagogue, Hindu festival, Korean Methodist church, botanica in a Puerto Rican neighborhood, a Native American pow wow, and an African American church. You can take a friend with you who is knowledgeable about the culture, if you choose. Write a brief paper describing your experiences, including the following: (1) how you felt in this unfamiliar environment, (2) how you were received, and (3) what cultural information you learned during this experience (e.g., did you see something that gave you insight into gender roles or the place of elders and children in this culture?). Self-reflection during this experience is the primary focus of the paper.

References

Abe-Kim, J. S., & Takeuchi, D. T. (1996). Cultural competence and quality of care: Issues for mental health service delivery in managed care. *Clinical Psychology: Science and Practice, 3*(4), 273–295.

Abernathy, A. D. (1995). Managing racial anger: A critical skill in cultural competence. *Journal of Multicultural Counseling and Development, 23,* 96–102.

Abrums, M. E., & Leppa, C. (2001). Beyond cultural competence: Teaching about race, gender, class, and sexual orientation. *Journal of Nursing Education, 40*(6), 270–275.

Alexander, M. (1996). *The Shock of Arrival.* Boston: South End Press.

American Psychiatric Association. (1994). *Ethnic Minority Elderly: A Task Force Report Of the American Psychiatric Association.* Washington DC: American Psychiatric Association.

Baines, T. (2000). Improving cultural competence face to face. *Tribal College, 512*(1), 21.

Barker, R. L. (1998). *The Social Work Dictionary.* Washington, DC: National Association of Social Workers Press.

Boyd-Franklin, N., Aleman, J., Jean-Gilles, M. M., & Lewis, S. Y. (1995). Cultural sensitivity and cultural competence: African-American, Latino, and Haitian families with HIV/AIDS. In N. Boyd-Franklin, G. L. Steiner, &

M. G. Boland (Eds.) *Children, Families, and HIV/AIDS: Psychosocial and Therapeutic Issues.* New York: Guilford Press, 53–77.

Burgest, D. R. (1973). Racism in everyday speech and social work jargon. *Social Work, 18*(4), 20–25.

Campinha-Bacote, J. (2001). A model of practice to address cultural competence in rehabilitation nursing. *Rehabilitation Nursing, 26*(1), 8–11.

Coleman, H. L. K. (1998). General and multicultural counseling competency: Apples and oranges? *Journal of Multicultural Counseling and Development, 26,* 147–156.

Dana, R. H. (1995). Impact of the use of standard psychological assessment on the diagnosis and treatment of ethnic minorities. In J. F. Aponte, R. Young Rivers, & J. Wohl (Eds.), *Psychological Interventions and Cultural Diversity.* Boston: Allyn & Bacon, 57–73.

Dana, R. H. (1998). Cultural identity assessment of culturally diverse groups: 1997. *Journal of Personality Assessment, 70*(1), 1–16.

Diaz-Lazaro, D. M., & Cohen, B. B. (2001). Cross-cultural contact in counseling training. *Journal of Multicultural Counseling and Development, 29*(1), 41–56.

Donini-Lenhoff, F. (2001), Health: Cultural competence in the health professions: Insuring a uniform standard of care. *Hispanic Outlook in Higher Education, 7*(7), 22–25.

Fahrenwald, N. L., Boysen, R., Fischer, C., & Maurer, R. (2001). Developing cultural competence in the baccalaureate nursing student: A population-based project with the Hutterites. *Journal of Transcultural Nursing, 12*(1), 48–55.

Flannery, D., & Ward, K. (1999). Service learning: A vehicle for developing cultural competence in health education. *American Journal of Health Behavior, 23*(5), 323–331.

Fuertes, J. N., Bartolomeo, M., & Nichols, C. M. (2001). Future research directions in the study of counselor multicultural competency. *Journal of Multicultural Counseling and Development, 29*(1), 3–12.

Gallegos, J. S. (1982). The ethnic competence model for social work education. In B. W. white (Ed.), *Color in a White Society*. Silver Spring, MD: National Association of Social Workers Press.

Hargrow, A. M. (2001). Racial identity development: The case of Mr. X, an African American. *Journal of Mental Health Counseling, 23*(3), 222–237.

Holland, L., & Courtney, R. (1998). Increasing cultural competence with the Latino community. *Journal of Community Health Nursing, 15*(1), 45–53.

Holman, W. D. (1996). In their words: Mainland Puerto Rican poetry, grounded theory, and the generation of culturally sensitive social work knowledge. *Journal of Multicultural Social Work, 4*(3), 69–79.

Hong, G. K., Garcia, M., & Soriano, M. (2000). Responding to the challenge: Preparing mental health professionals for the new millennium. In I. Cuellar & F. A. Paniagua (Eds.), *Handbook of Multicultural Mental Health*. San Diego: Academic Press, 455–476.

Imber-Black, E. (1997). Developing cultural competence: Contributions from recent family therapy literature. *American Journal of Psychotherapy, 51*(4), 607–610.

Kahn, J. S., & Denmon, J. (1997). An examination of social science literature pertaining to multiracial identity: A historical perspective. *Journal of Multicultural Social Work, 6*(1/2), 117–137.

Kavanaugh, K., Absalom, K., Beil, W., & Schliessmann, L. (1999). Connecting and becoming culturally competent: A Lakota example. *Advances in Nursing Science, 21*(3), 9–31.

Kim, S., McLeod, J. H., & Shantzis, C. (1992). Cultural competence for evaluators working with Asian-American communities: Some practical considerations. In M. A. Orlandi, R. Weston, & L. G. Epstein (Eds.) *Cultural Competence for Evaluators: A Guide for Alcohol and other Drug Abuse Prevention Practitioners Working with Ethnic/Racial Communities*. Rockville, MD: Office of Substance Abuse Prevention, U. S. Department of Health and Human Services. 203–260.

Kwan, K. K. (2001). Models of racial and ethnic identity development: Delineation of practice implications. *Journal of Mental Health Counseling, 23*(3), 269–277.

Landrine, H., & Klonoff, E. A. (1992). Culture and health-related schemas: A review and proposal for interdisciplinary integration. *Health Psychology, 11*(4), 267–276.

Lee, R. M., & Ramirez, M., III. (2000). The history, current status, and future of multicultural psychotherapy. In I. Cuellar & F. A. Paniagua (Eds.), *Handbook of Multicultural Mental Health*. San Diego: Academic Press, 279–310.

Leininger, M. M. (1988). Leininger's theory of nursing: Cultural care, diversity and universality. *Nursing Science Quarterly, 1*(4), 152–160.

Leininger, M. M. (1991). *Culture Care Diversity and Universality: A Theory of*

Nursing. New York: National League for Nursing Press.

Lukoff, D., & Lu, F. G. (1999). Cultural competence includes religious and spiritual issues in clinical practice. *Psychiatric Annals, 29*(8), 469–472.

Manese, J. E., Wu, J. T., & Nepomuceno, C. A. (2001). The effect of training on multicultural counseling competencies: An exploratory study over a ten-year period. *Journal of Multicultural Counseling and Development, 29*(1), 31–40.

Marsella, A. J., & Yamada, A. M. (2000). Culture and mental health: An introduction and overview of foundations, concepts, and issues. In I. Cuellar & F. A. Paniagua (Eds.). *Handbook of Multicultural Mental Health*. San Diego: Academic Press, 3–22.

Martinez, C., Jr. (2000). Conducting the cross-cultural interview. In I. Cuellar & F. A. Paniagua (Eds.), *Handbook of Multicultural Mental Health*. San Diego: Academic Press, 311–323.

Mason, J. L., Benjamin, M. P., & Lewis, S. A. (1996). The cultural competence model: Implications for child and family mental health services. In C. A. Heflinger & C. T. Nixon (Eds.), *Families and the mental health system for children and adolescents: Policies, services and research*. Thousand Oaks, CA: Sage, 165–190.

Matthews, L. (1996). Culturally competent models in human service organizations. *Journal of Multicultural Social Work, 4*(4), 131–135.

Mattson, S. (2000). Striving for cultural competence: Providing care for the changing face of the U. S. *AWHONN Lifelines, 4*(3), 49–52.

McPhatter, A. R. (1997). Cultural competence in child welfare: What is it? How do we achieve it? What happens without it? *Child Welfare, 76*(1), 255–279.

Morales, A. L. (2001). Child of the Americas. In P. S. Rothenberg (Ed.), Race,

Class, and *Gender in the United States*. New York: Worth, 660–661.

National Association of Social Workers. (1999). *Code of Ethics of the National Association of Social Workers*. Washington, DC: National Association of Social Workers.

Padilla, Y. (1996). Incorporating social science concepts in the analysis of ethnic issues in social work: The case of Latinos. *Journal of Multicultural Social Work, 4*(3), 1–12.

Pettit, L. (1960). Some observations on the Negro culture in the United States. *Social Work, 5*(3), 104–109.

Poole, D. L. (1998). Politically correct or culturally competent? *Health and Social Work, 23*(3), 163–166.

Pope-Davis, D. B., Liu, W. M., Toporek, R. L., & Brittan-Powell, C. S. (2001). What's missing from multicultural competency research: Review, introspection, and recommendations. *Cultural Diversity and Ethnic Minority Psychology, 7*(2), 121–138.

Pumariega, A. J. (1996). Culturally competent outcome evaluation in systems of care for children's mental health. *Journal of Child and Family Studies, 5*(4), 389–397.

Rogler, L. H. (1989). The meaning of culturally sensitive research in mental health. *American Journal of Psychiatry, 146*(3), 296–303.

Sawyer, L., Regev, H., Proctor, S., Nelson, M., Messias, D., Barnes, D., & Meleis, A. I. (1995). Matching versus cultural competence in research: Methodological considerations. *Research on Nursing and Health, 18*, 557–567.

Sevig, T., & Etzkorn, J. (2001). Transformative training: A year-long multicultural counseling seminar for graduate students. *Journal of Multicultural Counseling and Development, 29*(1), 57–72.

Sue, D. W., Carter, R. T., Casas, J. M., Fouad, N. A., Ivey, A. E., Jensen, M.,

LaFromboise, T., Manese, J. E., Ponterotto, J. G., & Vazquez-Natall, E. (1998). *Multicultural Counseling Competencies: Individual and Organizational Development.* Thousand Oaks, CA: Sage.

Sue, S. (1998). In search of cultural competence in psychotherapy and counseling. *American Psychologist, 53*(4), 440–448.

Swinomish Tribal Mental Health Project. (1991). *A Gathering of Wisdoms, Tribal Mental Health: A Cultural Perspective.* LaConner, WA: Swinomish Tribal Community.

Switzer, G. E., Scholle, S. H., Johnson, B. A., & Kelleher, K. J. (1998). The Client Cultural Competence Inventory: An instrument for assessing cultural competence in behavioral managed care organizations. *Journal of Child and Family Studies, 7*(4), 483–491.

Toporek, R. L., & Reza, J. V. (2001). Context as a critical dimension of multicultural counseling: Articulating personal, professional, and institutional competence. *Journal of Multicultural Counseling and Development, 29*(1), 13–30.

Tsang, A. K. T., & Bogo, M. (1997). Engaging with clients cross-culturally: Towards developing research-based practice. *Journal of Multicultural Social Work, 6*(3/4), 73–91.

Turner, J. B. (1972). Education for practice with minorities. *Social Work, 17*(3), 112–118.

Vinson, T. S., & Neimeyer, G. J. (2000). The relationship between racial identity development and multicultural counseling competency. *Journal of Multicultural Counseling and Development, 28*(3), 177–192.

Weaver, H. N. (1997). The challenges of research in Native American communities: Incorporating principles of cultural competence. *Journal of Social Service Research, 23*(2), 1–15.

Wohl, J. (1995). Traditional individual psychotherapy and ethnic minorities. In J. F. Aponte, R. Young Rivers, & J. Wohl (Eds.), *Psychological Interventions and Cultural Diversity.* Boston: Allyn & Bacon, 74–91.

Yoshioka, M. R. (1999). The use of developmental research methods to design culturally competent intervention. *Journal of Multicultural Social Work, 7*(3/4), 113–128.

Native Americans

Many social workers never expect to encounter a Native American client. Native people are often perceived as relics of a distant past who live on isolated reservations in a few regions of the country. In fact, Native Americans are a growing population that resides across the country in urban, suburban, and rural settings. Social workers who do not expect to see Native clients may fail to recognize that some of their clients are indeed Native Americans.

At the time of the 2000 census, there were 4.1 million Native Americans (including Alaska Natives). This accounts for 1.5% of the U.S. population. Of these, 2.5 million people (.9% of the population) identified as solely Native American, and 1.6 million (.6% of the population) identified as a mixture of Native American and some other group. In 1990, there were 2 million Native Americans, equaling .8% of the population. The 2000 data for those who identify solely as Native American represents a 26% increase over the 1990 figure, and the data on Native Americans of mixed heritage represents a 110% increase over the 1990 figure[1] (Ogunwole, 2002).

Forty-three percent of Native Americans live in the West, 31% in the South, 17% in the Midwest, and 9% in the Northeast United

---

[1]In 1990, the census did not allow people to designate more than one racial or ethnic group. Therefore, precise comparisons between 1990 and 2000 census figures are not possible, making it difficult to determine how much the Native American population has grown.

States. More than half of the Native population lives in 10 states, with the largest populations being in California (627,562) and Oklahoma (391,949). The cities with the largest Native populations are New York City (87,241) and Los Angeles (53,092). The largest Native Nations or tribes are the Cherokee (729,533), Navajo (298,197), Sioux (261,632), Chippewa (255,576), Latin American Indian (180,940), and Choctaw (142,123).[2] The largest group of Alaska Natives is the Eskimo (54,761) (Ogunwole, 2002).

There are many different definitions of a Native American. Each Native Nation (also known as a tribe) has its own criteria for membership. These criteria are often based on the amount of Native ancestry someone has (blood quantum). There is extensive intermarriage between Native Americans and non-Natives or among Native Americans from different nations, thus raising the question of the identity of their offspring. Some Native Nations are matrilineal and only consider someone to be a tribal member if that person's mother is a member of that nation. Others are patrilineal and trace descent only through the father. Still others accept members with Native heritage through either their mother or father. When a Native person is formally considered a member or citizen of a Native Nation, that person is listed on the tribal roles and is considered enrolled. Being enrolled allows access to a variety of tribal entitlements such as payments based on treaties or social services offered under tribal auspices. Enrollment confers other rights such as the ability to vote in tribal elections and the right to own land on a particular reservation.

Although Native Nations set criteria for enrollment, competing definitions also exist of who is a Native American. The federal government has its own definitions that are typically based on blood quantum. Different federal programs use different definitions for Native Americans in their eligibility requirements. The U.S. census uses the terms *American Indian* and *Alaska Native*, defined as "a person having origins in any of the original peoples of North and South America (including Central America), and who maintain tribal affiliation or community attachment" (U.S. Census Bureau, 2001). This definition is based primarily on social roles and does not consider blood quantum.

Many different terms are used to refer to the original inhabitants of the Americas including *Native American, American Indian, indigenous, First Nations People, Native,* and *Indian.* There is no consensus about which term is most appropriate, although many people have strong preferences. These terms are often used interchangeably, but *American Indian* and *Indian* have somewhat narrow meanings and exclude many but not all of the indigenous people of Alaska. The term *Native American* is broader and includes Alaska Natives as well as indigenous people found in the continental United States. The term *Native American* may also include indigenous people from other

---

[2]The categories used by the census do not necessarily coincide with the labels used by many indigenous people. For example, the term *Sioux*, considered outdated and even offensive by some indigenous people, is used by the census to represent a combined grouping of Lakota, Dakota, and Nakota people, and the census term *Latin American Indian* is a conglomerate of tribal groupings.

parts of the United States and its territories, such as Native Hawaiians, Samoans, and Guamanians. The terms *indigenous* and *Native,* though sometimes used in a narrow sense, can be used for original inhabitants of any area. For instance, these terms may refer to the original inhabitants of New Zealand (Maori) or the original inhabitants of Scandinavia (Sami). *First Nations People,* a common term for the original inhabitants of Canada, has gained some popularity among Native people in the United States. This term is often linked to a strong sense of sovereignty and political awareness. Although seen by many younger people as a positive term, it is not widely used by elders and may be unfamiliar to many non-Native people. Given the lack of precision in these terms, it is often best to use the most specific term possible. For instance, when referring to someone from the Hopi Nation, it may be most appropriate to use the term *Hopi* rather than any of the broader terms. Many indigenous people identify primarily with their nation (e.g., Seneca) or clan (e.g., Beaver, a network of extended families within the Seneca) rather than with an umbrella label like Native American or American Indian. The terms *Native, Native American, First Nations,* and *indigenous* are used interchangeably here when use of more specific terms is not possible.

This chapter gives an overview of social work with First Nations people. The significant diversity within and among Native Nations sets the context for discussion. The chapter also presents information on knowledge, skills, and values/attitudes necessary for cultural competence, and presents issues for cultural competence on micro and macro levels.

KNOWLEDGE FOR CULTURAL COMPETENCE

A qualitative study designed to operationalize the elements of cultural competence with Native Americans found that helping professionals need to be knowledgeable in four areas: diversity, history, culture, and contemporary realities (Weaver, 1999b). Diversity is an overarching concept. The history, culture, and contemporary realities of indigenous people vary, both within and among nations.

Diversity

More than 500 distinct Native Nations exist within the boundaries of what is now the United States. Some of these nations straddle the borders with Canada and Mexico. Indigenous nations never shared a single social structure, value system, religion, or language. Although there are some commonalities among indigenous groups within a particular region, there is considerable diversity among and within Native Nations. Understanding this diversity is key to culturally competent social work practice with First Nations people.

The diversity among Native peoples makes it difficult to gather accurate, generalizable information (McNeil, Porter, Zvolensky, Chaney, & Kee, 2000). Generalizations often lead to stereotypes. When working with Native clients, it is important to know which Native Nations they are affiliated with because information about one group (e.g., Chickasaw) may not be applicable to another (e.g., Blackfeet). The diversity across indigenous groups presents challenges to researchers. It is often difficult to recruit adequate numbers of different groups of Native people for meaningful intertribal comparisons. Thus, the usefulness of research as a guideline for practice is limited.

Likewise, the diversity among Native Nations presents challenges for practitioners. For example, variables tentatively associated with violence, such as male restrictiveness, male authority, and socioeconomic stress, vary widely across Native groups. Whether an indigenous client is from a matrilineal or patrilineal nation has far-reaching implications for the community context of domestic violence (Hamby, 2000).

There are also intertribal differences in help-seeking behavior. For example, military veterans from the Northern Plains and the Southwest differ significantly in their use of Western-based services and traditional healing options for mental and emotional problems (Manson, 2000). Likewise, helping professionals developing alcohol prevention programs must consider the heterogeneity of First Nations people. Comprehensive, community-based approaches must be shaped by local culture (Moran & May, 1995).

Some Native Americans live on reservations but others do not. Researchers have long been interested in exploring differences between reservation dwellers and their urban counterparts. A study commissioned by the Administration on Aging found most elders only have a grade school education although urban elders were more likely than their reservation counterparts to have a high school degree (29% compared with 17% of reservation dwellers). Elders on reservations appear to have a higher risk of social isolation, even though extended family members are more available in reservation environments. Generally, urban elders have better mental and physical health. Needs are high and service utilization is low for both groups, but urban elders are more likely to seek help from agencies (John, 1991).

Native Americans differ in many variables including income and education. Native people also differ in their level of knowledge and adherence to cultural traditions. Even among elders on reservations, there is a wide range of values and behaviors. Some are very knowledgeable and grounded in traditional ways but others are not (Kavanaugh, Absalom, Beil, & Schliessmann, 1999).

History

Many social problems result from centuries of forced change (Fleming, 1992). Administrators and service providers must be knowledgeable of the history of various Native American groups to develop effective services in indigenous communities (Swinomish Tribal Mental Health Project, 1991).

It is important to understand and to validate a Native client's sense of history. Often, helping professionals do not know the history of indigenous groups and are surprised to learn that what they have been taught about history and even pre-history is quite different from the perspective of many First

Nations people. For example, non-Native people have often been taught that Native Americans are not actually indigenous but were early migrants across the Bering Strait from Asia. There is substantial conflict between the Bering Strait theory of immigration and creation stories of First Nations people that tell of migrations across physical and spiritual dimensions (Fleming, 1992).

Loss of Children One of the most painful aspects in the history of Native Nations is the loss of their children, first to government-sponsored or government-sanctioned boarding schools, and subsequently to fostercare and adoption. After the U.S. Civil War, it became federal policy to remove children, often forcibly, from their families and communities. They were placed in boarding schools, often far from their homes, where they were taught Christianity and vocational skills to assimilate and "civilize" them. In these schools, children were forbidden to speak their languages and practice their spiritual traditions. Physical, emotional, and sexual abuse were common.

The impact of forced acculturation in boarding schools has left a lasting legacy (Fleming, 1992). Boarding schools led to loss of indigenous languages as well as to high rates of depression, illness, and death. Many children taken to boarding schools became ashamed of their cultural heritage and disowned the values and lifestyles of their families. Others assumed dysfunctional behaviors and exhibited symptoms such as rebelliousness, distrust, withdrawal, and depression. If former boarding school residents returned to their tribal communities, they often had difficulty fitting into a way of life they no longer completely understood. Lack of indigenous role models during childhood severely stunted their social and emotional development as Native American people. In adulthood, many of these children developed severe problems such as alcoholism, depression, or violent behavior (Swinomish Tribal Mental Health Project, 1991).

The boarding school era was a time of child removal and assimilationist social policies. The subsequent era of Native American adoptions continued in the same vein (George, 1997). Many First Nations children were taken from their families, ostensibly on charges of neglect and the belief they would be better off with White families than living in poverty on reservations under the influence of their "savage" parents. For example, the Boys and Girls Aid Society of Oregon, the largest adoption agency in that state, found many adoptive homes for Native children with White families. Between 1944 and 1977, 94 percent of Native children in this agency were adopted by non-Native families (Collmeyer, 1995). Loss of children was equated with loss of a future. If children were raised outside Native cultural traditions, there could be no cultural continuity and, thus, Native people would cease to exist as distinct cultural entities. "Adoption represented a spiritual death and rupture in the social fabric of the tribe that could never be repaired" (George, 1997, p. 171).

Alienation of indigenous children from their families and communities through boarding schools, fostercare, and adoption has led to significant cultural loss. As a result of these experiences, many Native people have lost their ability to speak their indigenous languages. Native people who cannot speak their languages often feel a deep sense of loss, shame, guilt, sadness, and anger (Swinomish Tribal Mental Health Project, 1991). Loss of language and cultural traditions often caused a rift between those who retained cultural knowledge and those who did not. Many children who returned from the schools or who were raised in White families were unable to communicate with their grandparents and older community members who continued to speak only their traditional languages.

The removal of Native children also disrupted the transmission of parenting skills across generations. Children raised in an institutional setting were without positive role models when they became parents themselves. The extensive physical, emotional, and sexual abuse common in the boarding schools left this new generation of parents with dysfunctional and often brutal ways of interacting with their children (Morrisette, 1994; Weaver & White, 1999).

Suppression of Spirituality   The history of indigenous people in the United States is filled with examples of spiritual oppression and denial of religious freedom. Misunderstandings and ethnocentric assumptions led to active persecution of indigenous spiritual practices. In the late 1800s, many indigenous religions and ceremonies such as the Sun Dance and the Potlatch were outlawed, despite the fact that this is in direct opposition to freedom of religion promised in the U.S. Constitution. The suppression of indigenous spirituality, in turn, led to practices going underground and the loss of some traditional knowledge (Swinomish Tribal Mental Health Project, 1991).

Alcohol and Disease as Tools of Cultural Destruction   Alcohol played a significant role in the history of indigenous and non-indigenous interactions. Most Native Nations had no contact with alcohol until Europeans introduced it as a trade item. Only a few nations in the Southwest developed forms of wine and beer. When alcohol was used before White contact, it involved controlled, supervised use in ritualized occasions, and did not involve excessive drunkenness (Abbott, 1996).

European colonizers used alcohol as a tool of conquest and cultural destruction (Maracle, 1993; Swinomish Tribal Mental Health Project, 1991). Fur traders and frontiersmen paid for Native goods using alcohol. Native people were encouraged to drink heavily and become intoxicated. Alcohol has been implicated as being used to swindle Native people and take their land.

Disease has also been implicated as a tool of conquest. Historically, population loss from disease decimated Native populations far more than did overt acts of war. Native people had no immunities to diseases common in Europe and thus died in large numbers when exposed to illnesses such as smallpox. As this lack of immunity became apparent to European and later American military commanders, they began to deliberately spread disease among indigenous people as a way of weakening their foes, thus clearing the land for European settlement (Stiffarm & Lane, 1992).

Growing European and European-American Domination   During the early history of interactions between European nations and Native Nations, treaties were made to govern how these groups would interact. Treaties designated rights and lands to be retained by First Nations people and those to be given up in exchange for various types of payments. Treaties were subsequently made between the U.S. federal government and Native Nations. According to the U.S. Constitution, treaties are the supreme law of the land.

At the time of original contact between European colonists and First Nations people, the Native Nations held more power. That changed as European immigrants became more numerous. As the balance of power shifted, the new Americans were able to violate treaties with minimal fear of repercussions. They forced one-sided treaty agreements on Native Nations with diminishing power. Even though the federal government has violated all treaties, they continue to govern many modern day interactions between First Nations People and the United States (Clinton, Newton & Price, 1991).

At times, the United States used military force to remove Native people from land set aside for them. History contains many examples of these forced removals. The most famous were the Trail of Tears, in which the Cherokee were forced to leave their traditional lands in the Southeastern United States and walk 1,500 miles to Oklahoma, and the Longest Walk, in which 9,000 Navajo were forced to walk 300 miles to be imprisoned at Bosque Redondo (Stiffarm & Lane, 1992). Forced marches and subsequent confinement often led to the death of large segments of indigenous populations.

Culture

First Nations people come from many different cultures. Some Native people follow traditional indigenous beliefs and values whereas others do not. It is important to keep in mind the cultural diversity among First Nations people, yet some common cultural elements are found in many Native traditions. These include a fluid sense of time, spirituality, emphasis on the group over the individual, and respect.

Time   Most Native cultures have a fluid sense of time. Many Native people view being "ruled by the clock" as unnatural and unhealthy. Rigidly following the dictates of a clock diminishes natural life rhythms and destroys the quality of human interactions and relationships (Swinomish Tribal Mental Health Project, 1991). When viewed from a deficit perspective, this fluid sense of time is interpreted as chronic lateness, laziness, lack of caring, and disrespect. The indigenous concept of time, however, is much more person-centered than is the Western concept. Native people are likely to take time to interact with others rather than stating they have no time for them and rushing off to appointments. It can be challenging for social workers to accommodate this fluid sense of time within a restrictive agency context. If possible, being available for a block of time (drop-in hours) may be more effective than scheduling specific appointment times.

Spirituality   Spirituality plays an important role in maintaining and restoring health in Native cultures. Disease is perceived as lack of balance or harmony with the Creator and nature, thus requiring both material and spiritual remedies. A study of Native elders found that faith and frequency of prayer were strongly correlated with mental health and other aspects of social functioning (Meisenhelder & Chandler, 2000).

In contrast to dominant society views, indigenous people view spiritual, mental, physical, and social aspects of their lives as connected and continuously interacting. Indigenous spirituality goes beyond a belief system to incorporate guidelines for behavior. It is a spiritual necessity to live a balanced life in harmony with all other beings. To be out of balance or to deny the interconnectedness of all creation risks the well-being of individuals, families, and communities. For traditional Native Americans, spirituality is a part of every aspect of life including worldview, relationships, health and illness, healing, and ways of grieving (Swinomish Tribal Mental Health Project, 1991).

Many First Nations people experience the eagerness of non-indigenous people to discuss and participate in Native spiritual practices as intrusive and rude. Non-Native helping professionals need to respect the private nature of many indigenous spiritual beliefs and practices (Swinomish Tribal Mental Health Project, 1991). Past exploitation, distortion, and laws that have prohibited indigenous spiritual traditions have left Native people protective of their spiritual practices and reluctant to share information with outsiders.

Social workers can learn basic information on cultural and spiritual practices outside the context of the social work relationship. In this way, they can avoid exploiting the client. Reading and viewing videos can provide this background information without overstepping boundaries. In particular, a recent PBS video, *In the Light of Reverence,* can be useful for understanding the importance of sacred traditions and the reluctance of many Native people to share this information.

Primacy of the Group   A sense of identity is rooted in group membership. Native people often refer to themselves as members of the Native community, regardless of their geographic location. Many Native Americans identify first with their nation or tribe and second with a clan or society to which they belong. Some express fear that knowledge of, or identification with, non-Native culture is equivalent to loss of indigenous culture (Fleming, 1992).

Social cooperation is often valued over independent decision making. The wishes and plans of individuals must be balanced along with the needs of family and community members (Swinomish Tribal Mental Health Project, 1991). This emphasis on the group leads to strong mutual support networks. The well-being of the group is paramount.

Social control is often maintained through indirect mechanisms such as gossip, shaming, withdrawal of approval, humor, and teasing (Swinomish Tribal Mental Health Services, 1991). These methods are often used to teach children what behaviors are expected of them and reinforce the behavioral expectations of all community members. Likewise, adults who behave outside community norms are likely to experience teasing, shaming, and gossip.

Respect   Respect is emphasized in all social interactions. There are appropriate ways to communicate respectfully with others, including limiting eye contact and not interrupting someone who is speaking. People are accorded respect for the different roles they fulfill within a community. Elders are respected for their knowledge and wisdom, children are respected as the future of Native Nations, and leaders are respected for their willingness to sacrifice their own needs on behalf of First Nations communities.

Respect is a key value in all interactions, yet displays of respect often conflict with dominant society values. For example, at home Native American children learn to listen respectfully without asking questions. In school, they are confronted with a very different set of expectations and requirements for success, thus leaving them confused and unable to succeed in one or both environments (Swinomish Tribal Mental Health Project, 1991).

Contemporary Realities

Many Americans think of Native people primarily within a historical context and fail to recognize that Native cultures are still vital, even though many ways of life have changed. Romantic notions of Native Americans wearing beads and feathers perpetuate the idea of indigenous cultures as monolithic and static. Because few people have in-depth contact with Native Americans, these romantic notions go unchallenged (Fleming, 1992).

Understanding the contemporary realities of Native people involves understanding the context of federal policies that significantly affect Native people, the dynamics of tribal governments that continue to function with some sovereignty while subsumed under federal authority, social problems and their relationship to a legacy of colonialism, and the strengths and vitality that have withstood centuries of oppression.

The Context of Federal Policies   Because of their unique relationship with the federal government, Native people are subject to intrusion by many federal bureaucracies. Native people have federal policies and regulations that apply solely to them. The federal government still treats Native people as its wards, and, as such, it often holds and manages money for both Native Nations and individual Native people. In this role as guardian, the federal government also has the power to sue entities such as states on behalf of Native people when they are treated unjustly (e.g., illegal seizing of land).

One of the most important areas of involvement in the lives of Native people, especially relevant to social workers, is the Indian Child Welfare Act (ICWA). ICWA is a federal law and thus does not apply to indigenous people from Native Nations that are not federally recognized or are located outside the United States (e.g., the Shinnecock of New York State that only have state recognition). Thus, some states have passed similar legislation to extend comparable protection to indigenous people within their borders that are not covered under ICWA. Washington state has a tribal–state agreement that goes beyond ICWA to extend services to Canadian Natives and members of nonfederally recognized tribes in Washington state (Bending, 1997). New York state has a similar law (Weaver & White, 1999).

The Indian Child Welfare Act was passed in response to the large numbers of Native American children being raised by non-Native families, either through fostercare or adoption. Under ICWA, Native Nations have the right to assume jurisdiction over fostercare and adoption proceedings involving their children. A social agency involved in fostercare or adoption proceedings for a Native American child must notify the child's nation. That nation has the right to handle the case itself if it chooses. Another critical provision of ICWA states that cultural continuity is in the best interest of the child. When Native American children are placed in fostercare or for adoption, the following order must be followed: (1) placement with the extended family, (2) placement with a family from the same Native Nation, (3) placement with any Native American family, then (4) placement with any qualified family (Barsh, 1996). A social worker who has a case covered by ICWA must contact the child's nation immediately. The nation has the right to handle the case itself, work with a non-Native social service department on the case, or relinquish the case entirely to a non-Native social service department. The provisions of ICWA are not diminished by subsequent legislation. For example, the Multiethnic Placement Act, designed to remove barriers to transracial placements, and the Adoption and Safe Families Act, designed to reduce the time children spend in fostercare, specifically state they do not apply to cases covered by ICWA.

Contemporary Tribal Governments   Native Nations have retained sovereignty that allows them to continue to operate their own governments. Although Native Nations are subject to federal laws and oversight, they are not subject to state laws unless this right is specifically granted by the federal government or Native Nations themselves. Today most Native Nations have an elected government, often led by a tribal president and tribal council. Many have law enforcement and social service systems in place that serve their members. As a result of the Indian Reorganization Act of 1934, many Native Nations have constitutions modeled on those of states; however, a few nations continue to function with traditional leaders such as chiefs and clan mothers. Still others have an official, elected government but retain vestiges of traditional forms of governance.

Today, many tribal governments are striving for culturally appropriate economic development and self sufficiency after generations of federal domination and imposed dependency. Because Native Nations retain vestiges of sovereignty, each has a right to determine which types of economic development best meet its needs. Tribal revitalization is a way to overcome the legacy of historical tragedies and keep identity and language alive. This means cultural renaissance in contemporary terms, not returning to a way of life of past centuries, often referred to as going back to the blanket (Fleming, 1992). Often, however, members of Native Nations are divided over economic development opportunities such as casinos, tourism, and exploitation of natural resources. What some Native people see as positive sources of income others view as devastating compromises to cultural and spiritual integrity.

Social and Health Problems   Native Americans experience a variety of health and social problems, many as a direct result of colonization and dependency created by the federal government. For example, the cycle of neglect and subsequent removal of children and disruption of families is a lasting consequence of the boarding schools (Swinomish Tribal Mental Health Project, 1991). The social science literature on Native people suggests that they suffer disproportionately from a variety of problems including diabetes (Gilliland, Mahler, Hunt, & Davis, 1999; Kavanaugh et al., 1999), tuberculosis, suicide, alcohol-related problems (Kavanaugh et al., 1999), mental health problems (Narduzzi, 1994), and rapidly increasing incidence of, and mortality from, cardiovascular disease, cancer, and other chronic diseases (Gilliland et al., 1999). Native Americans are overrepresented in the homeless veteran population (by at least 19%), and they exhibit more severe alcohol problems (40% more than Whites) but fewer psychiatric problems than other homeless veterans (Kasprow & Rosenheck, 1998).

Probably the most widely known and stereotyped social problem of Native communities is that of alcohol dependence. Alcohol takes a disproportionate toll in Native American communities, resulting in a higher rate of alcohol-related deaths than in the general population (Moran & May, 1995). There is significant diversity in alcohol use among First Nations groups and within groups based on age and gender. For example, although stereotypes lead many to believe that all Native people are heavy drinkers, the Navajo abstain at twice the rate of the U.S. population. Among Native people in general, abstinence is particularly common among those middle-aged and older. The disparity between Native Americans and the general population of the United States is greatest among younger groups. Native American youth use alcohol earlier, with more frequency, in greater amounts, and with more negative consequences than do non-Natives. Alcohol has negative consequences for both males and females but is frequently a bigger problem for males (Moran & May, 1995). A study of Native American adolescents in the Northwest found that Native males attribute their drinking to heredity and fate. Native females were more likely to attribute their drinking to environmental events like problems at home (Sage & Burns, 1993).

Native people experience high rates of violence and trauma. Injury morbidity and mortality far exceed other groups. A study conducted at a trauma center in Seattle, Washington, found high injury rates, including a high proportion of intentional injuries (e.g., suicide, homicide), and a significant proportion of injuries among the homeless. Alcohol plays a major role in injuries among Native Americans (more than three-fourths of those injured were legally intoxicated). Risk for injury is increased by poverty, unemployment, and inadequate education that lead to homelessness and substance abuse (Sugarman & Grossman, 1996).

Interpreting the Research   Statistics on Native people must be interpreted cautiously. Misclassification of Native Americans in studies is a major problem that limits data quality (Weaver, 1999c). For example, some data in the Northwest underestimates the number of Native people by one-third (Sugarman & Grossman, 1996).

Some research now disputes the high rates of social and health problems alleged among First Nations people. For instance, although empirical evidence is limited, scholars often suggest that higher rates of psychopathology exist among Native people than their non-Native peers (McNeil et al., 2000); yet a study of depression and conduct disorder in Native and non-Native children found no difference in parent and child self-ratings of conduct disorders. Non-Native teachers, however, rated the Native children higher on conduct disorders, possibly because of negative bias resulting from cultural distance. All children rated themselves higher on depression than did the adults rating them (Dion, Gotowiec, & Beiser, 1998).

Cultural Loss   Even though some First Nations people have successfully retained their traditions, cultural loss is perceived to be a major threat in many Native communities. "Historical theft of Indian lands, outlawing of Indian spiritual practices, the massive removal of Indian children from their families, and the introduction of alcohol have all contributed to cultural loss, and have made it difficult for young people to develop a healthy cultural identity. Many native languages have been lost. The imposition of non-Indian values has weakened traditional Indian culture and thereby jeopardized individual psychological health" (Swinomish Tribal Mental Health Project, 1991, p. 43).

Loss of cultural identity and negative self-images contribute to mental health problems and are problems in and of themselves. Psychological well-being cannot be maintained without a sense of cultural vitality. Lack of a strong, positive cultural identity puts people at risk for depression, alcohol abuse, and destructive behaviors (Swinomish Tribal Mental Health Project, 1991).

Continuity and Strengths   Native communities continue to exist as distinct cultural entities with many strengths. Even when federal policies interrupted values transmission, wisdom, beliefs, and practices are strengths that have survived (Long & Curry, 1998). Communities are striving to revitalize traditions through programs that teach language and culture. Many youth now participate in kindergarten or grade school immersion programs that teach language. The importance of the group reinforces socially acceptable behaviors and emphasizes the value of learning traditions (Swinomish Tribal Mental Health Project, 1991).

First Nations people of all ages are seeking and reclaiming cultural knowledge and traditions. A study of Native women (predominantly Oneida) revealed they handle multiple roles through integration and balance of traditional and contemporary feminine strengths in a positive, culturally consistent manner. Healing the spirit is done through returning to traditions to reclaim the self (Napholz, 2000).

Native communities, especially on tribal lands, are becoming more assertive in their resistance to exploitation. For example, many Native communities have begun to restrict researchers' access because of past problems. Currently, there is heightened suspicion of researchers, particularly from the dominant society. Access to Native communities may be restricted or denied by tribal governments (Beauvais & Trimble, 1992; McNeil et al., 2000). Informal gatekeepers may restrict access for various projects and research for the protection of the community (Beauvais & Trimble, 1992).

SKILLS FOR CULTURAL COMPETENCE

A survey of Native American helping professionals identified that both general skills and containment skills are important in delivering culturally competent services to Native Americans (Weaver, 1999b). Although the skills themselves can be generic, the guiding frameworks within which the skills are applied (i.e., theories that guide interventions in particular situations or with certain types of clients) are far from neutral. Social work theories and practices often have a Eurocentric bias and are ineffective with Native American people (Bending, 1997).

Engaging

Social workers should try to recognize and set aside the stereotypes they hold about Native Americans. Most research has overemphasized and given credibility to selected negative beliefs about Native Americans. The continued focus on alarming rates of self-destructive behavior promotes an image of the drunken, suicidal Native American. It is important to have balanced treatment that explores strengths, resilience, and contributions (Fleming, 1992). Social workers must strive to overcome stereotypes so they see their clients as individuals and can engage them as such.

Engaging Native American clients may be a lengthy process. Establishing trust may be difficult and involve testing the social worker's commitment. There is a connection between engaging individual clients and establishing trust in the Native American community. For example, some social agencies in rural Alaska ask staff to participate in events in the Native community. As Native community members see helping professionals at these events, they begin to understand that these professionals have an ongoing commitment to serving the Native community and are not detached individuals who only interact with Native people in a hierarchical relationship during a 9–5 job. Helping professionals who establish a presence in Native communities encourage Native people to feel comfortable seeking services. Helping professionals may feel awkward about learning about Native cultures and not wish to intrude or be voyeuristic. Events that are likely to be open to the public such festivals and pow wows are good opportunities to learn through observation and listening. Social agencies like the American Indian Community House in

New York City regularly publish newsletters with announcements of events and protocols for visitors. Events such as ceremonies are generally closed to the public and would not be publicly announced.

Assessing

Assessments of Native American clients must consider indigenous cultural norms. Examination of the cultural context allows the helping professional to judge how a client's behaviors fit within a range of what is typical. Helping professionals need to take the time to explore the client's perception of the problem or situation.

Indigenous concepts of health and illness differ considerably from non-Native diagnostic categories such as those in the *Diagnostic and Statistical Manual (DSM)*. Constructs such as depression, as operationalized through Western psychiatric conceptualizations, are not necessarily meaningful in an indigenous context. The lack of equivalence between indigenous expressions of illness and Western psychiatric disorders makes culturally appropriate assessments challenging (Allen, 1998; Swinomish Tribal Mental Health Project, 1991). Recent changes in the *DSM* have taken an important step in acknowledging culture's role in shaping symptom expression and the course of mental illnesses (Manson, 2000); however, additional changes are needed to adequately address cultural identity and cultural elements in the therapeutic relationship for Native American youth (Novins et al., 1997).

 Using Western criteria in assessing First Nations clients is inappropriate and can be a form of institutional racism. Indeed, applying the diagnostic criteria that fit members of one culture to assess members of another culture is cultural imperialism (Swinomish Tribal Mental Health Project, 1991). Forcing the problems of Native clients into Western categories can distort their true nature.

Although many standardized assessment tools have been developed to explore issues such as depression, self-esteem, suicidality, and alcohol dependence, most of these tools have not been developed or modified for use with Native Americans. The universal applicability of standardized tools is questionable (Allen, 1998); therefore, social workers who use such tools should do so with caution. Where Native American assessment tools exist, those designed for specific tribal groups are usually nonexistent or do not have established validity or conceptual equivalence (Allen, 1998). One exception to this is the tribally specific and carefully tested Zuni Life Skills Development Curriculum (LaFromboise & Howard-Pitney, 1995).

Many assessment tools, developed specifically for use with Native Americans, attempt to measure cultural identity. See for example, the work of Young, Lujan, and Dixon (1998); Garrett and Pichette (2000); and Zimmermann, Ramirez-Valles, Washienko, Walter, and Dyer (1996). Many of these cultural assessment instruments, however, conceptualize culture along a linear continuum, thus failing to account for the complexities of cultural identity. The Orthogonal Model of Cultural Identity and its measurement scale, though not developed exclusively for Native American youth, has been used extensively and successfully with this population. This tool assesses identification with one culture independently from others, thus allowing for identification with more than one culture (Oetting & Beauvais, 1991; Weaver, 1996).

Another tool that measures cultural identity, the Urban American Indian Identity model and scale, expands on earlier models of identity. This model contains four stages (internalization, marginalization, externalization, and actualization) that tap into the identity development process from internalized oppression and group deprecation to positive integrated self and group identity. This model considers identity as formed within the context of self, group, environment, and a historical relationship with the dominant society. The model predicts depression, self-esteem, and other psychological wellness (Walters, 1997).

Other assessment tools have been developed or modified to measure Native American clients on a variety of variables. For example, the Native American Cultural Involvement and Detachment Anxiety Questionnaire was developed with tribal college students to measure anxiety about social involvement with Native Americans, cultural knowledge, economic issues, and social involvement with the majority culture (McNeil et al., 2000). Another assessment instrument, the Center for Epidemiological Studies Depression Scale, appears to be capable of identifying depression in some populations of Native elders, as long as a higher cut-off point is used to avoid mislabeling people as depressed (Curyto, Chapleski, Lichtenberg, Hodges, Kaczynski, & Sobeck, 1998). Likewise, an instrument has been developed to measure knowledge, attitudes, and behaviors regarding physical activity and diet for Native youth in grades 3 through 5 (Stevens et al., 1999).

Intervening

Culturally competent service delivery begins with a strong grounding in general helping skills such as listening and problem solving. Listening in a cross-cultural context can be challenging since the helping professional may have expectations about what the client is likely to say, based on his or her own cultural context.

Containment skills are a particular set of skills useful with many types of clients and particularly important when working with Native American clients because of cultural communication norms. Containment skills are those in which the social worker refrains from speaking too quickly or too much, thus promoting productive silence (Shulman, 1999). By displaying patience and allowing the session to proceed at a comfortable pace, significant material will often emerge.

One helping professional describes the importance of listening in her work with Native Americans of the Great Plains region:

> As a nurse I am used to listening, to gathering a history to make an assessment and coming to a diagnosis. But in truly listening to Lakota people, one is usually led—often in a round-about way—to a deeper, more significant issue. If we fail to listen until they finish speaking, we never really get to hear the real thoughts

or concerns. While we are used to being fast and as efficient as possible, Lakota see this as a lack of interest in them and as an insincere attempt to help them. I must spend time, settle into a chair, and be very present to be trusted. (Kavanaugh, et al., 1999, p. 20)

Non-Natives often misinterpret periods of silence that can be common among First Nations people. For many Native people, "the non-verbal aspects of conversation are often regarded as more important than the words exchanged. Often, much is left unsaid. Many Indian people are highly skilled at 'reading between the lines': they pick up on nuances of tone, gesture and glance. Often Indian people can exchange a great deal of information in a very few words" (Swinomish Tribal Mental Health Project, 1991, p. 189).

Resisting the temptation to be verbally assertive in conducting the social work interview is often the most productive approach with Native American clients. Likewise, it can be helpful for social workers to consciously monitor their nonverbal behavior to ensure they are not being physically assertive in ways that may inhibit the interview. Avoiding eye contact can be a way of respecting privacy. The firmness typical of American handshakes may be mis-construed for aggressiveness and lead to negative impressions. First Nations people often express negative feelings subtly. Feelings may be shut down because of prior experiences of trauma and deprivation (Swinomish Tribal Mental Health Project, 1991).

Social work skills must be integrated into interventions in culturally appropriate ways. One of the few empirically validated approaches to work-ing effectively with Native Americans involves culturally grounded behav-ioral approaches to preventing poor dietary practices, tobacco, and other substance misuse (Schinke, 1996). Culturally grounded approaches include using elders to teach about traditional foods and tobacco use as a ceremonial rather than recreational practice. This culturally based information is used to encourage behavior change.

Another important area for work with Native Americans is in acknowl-edging and addressing issues of grief and loss, both related to historical trauma and to contemporary social problems. Many Native people have experienced significant losses and trauma that need to be grieved and mourned. Traditions provide important ways for dealing with grief and loss that are important in maintaining mental health (Swinomish Tribal Mental Health Project, 1991). Social workers such as Yellow Horse Brave Heart are leading the way in devel-oping culturally appropriate clinical interventions to address these critical needs. (See for example, Brave Heart-Jordan & DeBruyn, 1995; Weaver & Yellow Horse Brave Heart, 1999).

Networking with indigenous helpers such as medicine men and women is important for helping professionals. Social workers can form cooperative relationships with indigenous healers that include mutual referrals and col-laboration in helping some clients. Forging links with traditional healers can be critical in providing mental health services (Swinomish Tribal Mental Health Project, 1991).

Conducting culturally appropriate interventions is challenging in and of itself and has become even more complicated by outside constraints such as managed care. The length of time needed to truly establish trust as a foundation for a sound working relationship may no longer be possible in some settings. The helping relationship is likely to be significantly impaired when a culture that values time in social conversation and establishing relationships is faced with managed care and similar time-limited ways of helping (Abe-Kim & Takeuchi, 1996; Kavanaugh et al., 1999).

Helping professionals need to be aware of indigenous communication norms. Disclosure in the therapeutic context may be difficult. Individuals who refrain from talking may be seen as resistant or unwilling to work. Native clients may use indirect communication to share intimate information. This may be misunderstood if it appears the client is discussing someone else or a hypothetical situation. Stating "I" messages directly conflicts with the value of humility and may be a barrier to treatment for some First Nations clients (Wing, Crow, & Thompson, 1995).

The factors that predict mental health difficulties in the general population of elders do not always predict difficulties for Native elders. In fact, income, education, and social support are not good predictors of mental health status for Native elders, and physical health and coping are predictors for both Natives and non-Natives. Significant differences between men and women, and urban and reservation populations, influence the strength of predictors of mental health in Native American elders (Narduzzi, 1994).

Conflicts between traditional beliefs and practices and Western models of care result in barriers to service. Focus groups of Native elders and young women in Oregon explored traditional beliefs and their relationship to prenatal care. The study found a breakdown in transmission of traditional health beliefs because of federal assimilation policies and the death of elders. Traditional care was often not available and Western care was perceived as culturally inappropriate and hostile, thus leaving many without services (Long & Curry, 1998).

Many Native people still seek traditional forms of healing for social and health problems. Western and traditional care may be complementary, with different types of care sought for different maladies. A study of Native military veterans in the Southwest and Northern Plains found that 16 percent reported using traditional healing. The Southwestern sample used traditional healing more often, possibly because this was more available to them than was Western medical care (Gurley et al., 2001).

Culturally competent interventions with Native American clients should incorporate the use of containment skills such as listening, patience, and silence. The needs of clients should guide the work rather than the social worker's preference for particular models or methods. Respect for culturally based beliefs, values, and behaviors must also be an integral part of choosing and implementing interventions.

VALUES/ATTITUDES FOR CULTURAL COMPETENCE

A survey of Native American helping professionals identified four major values or attitudes associated with culturally competent services for Native Americans: (1) helper wellness and self-awareness, (2) humility and willingness to learn, (3) respect, open-mindedness, and a nonjudgmental attitude, and (4) social justice (Weaver, 1999b). Although in part, these values are already present in helping professionals and are often what led them to these professions in the first place, these values and attitudes can also be cultivated and enhanced.

The work of social workers and other helping professionals can be very stressful. Helping professionals are often confronted with difficult situations such as removing a child from an abusive family, reaching out to mentally ill people living on the streets, and helping a client heal after the death of a loved one. In particular, the multiproblem situations experienced by many Native American clients can seem overwhelming. To effectively assist clients, helping professionals must be aware of their own feelings and reactions.

Social workers who fail to recognize and take care of their own needs are likely to experience compassion fatigue, become less effective in their work, and may ultimately suffer physical and emotional symptoms themselves. The self-awareness component, critical in the helping professions, can help professionals recognize their own needs, biases, and reactions to certain types of clients. Supervision is an important venue to assist helping professionals to deal with stress that accumulates in day-to-day work. Helping professionals can look to other sources to replenish their energy and emotions. Such sources may include physical exercise, spending time in a peaceful, secluded mountain setting, getting a massage, or participating in spiritual activities or prayer. To be effective helpers, it is important that helping professionals have balance in their own lives.

In a quest for balance and wholeness, some new age religions have turned to Native American spirituality. Native Americans often experience this as exploitation. Helping professionals who experience their own spiritual hunger have sometimes hoped to meet these needs through Native American clients by asking them about spiritual practices and indigenous belief systems. Clearly, the social work relationship exists to meet the needs of clients, not the needs of professionals. Although it is important for helping professionals to meet their own needs, this must be done outside of the social work relationship. To place these expectations on clients is unethical.

It is important to be open to learning from clients. Professionals who think they must know it all hold themselves to an impossible standard. This attitude reinforces the hierarchical status difference between clients and helping professionals. Approaching the helping relationship with humility and recognizing there are many things the professional does not know, leaves the door open for learning.

Humility can be reinforced by deliberately entering cross-cultural situations to learn to empathize with cultural minority groups. Cross-cultural encounters in minority communities allow people from the dominant society to experience what it is like to not understand the cultural context, including expected behavior. As cultural outsiders, they may not understand all the jokes and may be regarded with uncertainty or suspicion (Hamby, 2000). Helping professionals can identify cross-cultural learning situations like pow wows or Native American community events through indigenous publications and Web sites.

Social workers will often find that clients have different beliefs, values, and behaviors than they do. How the social worker responds to these differences is crucial. A century ago, early social workers saw themselves as role models and encouraged clients to conform to their standards. This is no longer done consciously, but helping professionals who do not reflect on value differences and approach them with respect may still replicate these value-laden practices.

Most helping professionals today would agree it is important to show respect for clients and their beliefs, but keeping an open mind and being non-judgmental can be difficult tasks. Helping professions need to move beyond simply agreeing to be respectful to actually demonstrating respect for differences in their practice. Respect can be demonstrated through actively listening to clients' concerns and values and choosing interventions accordingly.

Oppression and discrimination faced by many Native Americans are much more than just artifacts of a distant past. Many contemporary problems faced by First Nations people originate in society or in the relationship between indigenous people and the federal government. Counseling, concrete services, and other direct practice approaches can be important in alleviating the symptoms of many social ills, but the exclusive use of such approaches is like putting a bandage on a problem that requires surgery.

Advocacy and activism have been part of the social work repertoire since its beginning. Social workers have long recognized the importance of going from "case to cause." In other words, the problems of one client are often experienced by many and may require macro-level solutions. If a Native American family approaches an agency in need of food, it is important to provide food, but this is often not a solution to the problem. In fact, poverty is a major problem in many Native communities, with reservations consistently constituting some of the poorest areas of the country. It is important to look at the root causes of hunger and poverty in First Nations communities, such as few job opportunities, lack of transportation in isolated areas, and centuries of federal policies that systematically destroyed traditional Native economies and created ongoing dependency on federal programs.

CASE EXAMPLE

Lorena and George White are an elderly Shoshone couple living in Boise, Idaho. They were referred to the Goodman Family Services Agency by their minister for assistance in processing paperwork for the Home Energy Assistance Program (HEAP). Bruno Smith, their assigned caseworker, met with them in his office. He assisted them with the paperwork and inquired about other concrete service needs such as meal preparation and housekeeping services. He allowed plenty of time in his appointment with them and didn't rush them when they were slow responding to his questions. After the initial appointment, he called them to make sure their service needs were being met through the referrals he initiated. Bruno scheduled a home visit after two weeks to assess their living situation and see if they had additional needs before closing the case. During this meeting, they mentioned their son recently had his leg amputated because of diabetes and he was having difficulty adjusting to this loss. They asked if Bruno might be able to help.

In this case, knowledge, skills, and values/attitudes helped facilitate the work in several areas:

- Knowledge of the mistrust that Native Americans often feel for service providers led Bruno to take extra time in establishing a relationship.
- Knowledge about culturally based communication norms helped Bruno to allow silence during the interview and maximize his use of containment skills.
- By not rushing Lorena and George in the interviews, Bruno helped them feel comfortable and relaxed. This led to their concerns emerging naturally.
- Bruno took time to reflect on his feelings and beliefs about Native American clients in general and Native elders in particular. He had heard that Native people had an earth-centered spirituality and was surprised that this couple was referred by an Episcopal minister. Bruno vowed to keep an open mind and try to monitor his own stereotypes so they would not influence the work.
- Native American clients often feel more comfortable trusting helping professionals with minor or concrete issues before raising more emotional or difficult problems. Bruno's competent handling of Lorena and George's need for concrete services, along with his thorough follow-up and cultivation of the relationship, led to a preliminary trust that resulted in the identification of other needs. If Bruno continues to address this family's needs in a culturally competent manner, he and his agency are likely to develop a good reputation that will lead to other Native clients seeking services.

CULTURAL COMPETENCE IN SOCIAL POLICIES

The unique relationship between the federal government and Native Americans has led to significant policy regulation in virtually all aspects of Native American life. For example, the allotment policy, also known as the Dawes Act, destroyed the collective ownership of Native lands and declared unallotted land surplus, leading to the loss of more than 100 million acres or two-thirds of all reservation land between 1887 and 1934 (Churchill & Morris, 1992). Likewise, policies have threatened the economic base of Native Nations. For example, the federal government intervened with traditional

Diné subsistence when it issued an edict that the Diné's sheep were to be taken away for fear of overgrazing. Relocation policies of the 1950s shaped where Native people should live by promising jobs in urban areas. Termination policies, also originating in the 1950s, legislated away the very existence of whole Native Nations. The current policies of federal recognition still dictate who the federal government acknowledges to be a Native American. Policies also affect Native Americans by governing what services and funding are available for social and health programs.

Little quality research is available, thus leaving policy makers and program planners with no empirical information to use (Narduzzi, 1994). The majority of federal policies have been unilateral with little meaningful input from Native people. One exception to this rule is the Indian Child Welfare Act of 1978. The law was crafted with significant input from Native people, including indigenous helping professionals. Although implementation of this policy has been hindered by inadequate funding and training (Bending, 1997), it is a significant piece of legislation that differs from all other social welfare legislation. It applies only to First Nations people, and it clearly identifies cultural continuity as in the best interest of the child.

Policy makers need to be knowledgeable about First Nations cultures so they can develop and implement culturally congruent policies. Input from First Nations people can help ensure that policies are appropriate and effective. In the past, federal policies have had a predominantly destructive impact on indigenous cultures. Culturally competent policy makers have the potential to develop meaningful programs and regulations that encourage First Nations' self-sufficiency and eliminate federal paternalism.

CULTURAL COMPETENCE IN SOCIAL AGENCIES

Indigenous values do not easily blend with mainstream mental health expectations and requirements. This is particularly a problem in record keeping, staff roles, and diagnosis. Funding authorities must recognize the need for flexibility and innovation, or bureaucratic requirements may inadvertently stifle culturally appropriate programs (Swinomish Tribal Mental Health Project, 1991).

Social service programs run by Native Nations often have more fluid program structures, less defined and more flexible boundaries, and more complex client–provider role relationships than do their non-Native counterparts (Swinomish Tribal Mental Health Project, 1991). Although outsiders may view these programs as unprofessional, they serve an important function in meeting the needs of First Nations people.

Just like individual practitioners, agencies need to reflect on their work and how their services invite or inhibit Native American clients. Agency administrators and boards of directors need to ask themselves critical questions about how they incorporate the principles of cultural competence in every aspect of service delivery and agency governance. Self-awareness must lead to behavior change in the struggle for cultural competence.

COMMUNITY INTERVENTIONS

Many social problems have their roots in the relationship between Native Americans and the larger society, and thus require macro-level analysis and change. Social workers can use advocacy and community organizing skills to begin to address these large scale needs.

Helping professionals can use their skills to assist Native communities to conduct needs assessments to plan meaningful services (Weaver, 1999a). Through such assessments, service providers can begin to recognize gaps in, and duplication of services. A community-based needs assessment can also serve as a catalyst for coalition building.

Indigenous social workers have become adept at using macro-level social work skills to bring about important change in, and on behalf of, First Nations communities. For example, Wilma Mankiller, a Cherokee BSW, used her skills to bring plumbing and sanitation services to the people of the Cherokee Nation before going on to become her nation's first female Principal Chief. Likewise, Ada Deer, a Menominee MSW, used her advocacy skills to help overturn the federal termination of her nation before being appointed Director of the Bureau of Indian Affairs, Assistant Secretary of the Interior. These notable women have set excellent examples of how helping professionals can use macro-level skills to bring about important change.

The voices of Native people need to be respected and incorporated in research and program planning. Researchers often adhere to scientific ethics but disregard local ethics (Piquemal, 2001). Many Native people believe this leads to misappropriated knowledge: knowledge that has been acquired under the pretense of helping the Native community but that ultimately does not provide any benefits. Informed consent has different meanings in cross-cultural situations. Consent must be an ongoing process of renegotiation. Data must come back to the Native community.

Images of Native Americans continue to promote stereotypes and influence Native youth to see themselves in negative ways as blood-thirsty savages, pitiful drunks, or mystics lost in a modern world they can't understand. Use of Native American names and images in mascots and advertising, such as the Washington Redskins football team or Crazy Horse malt liquor, is a form of discrimination. Many Native people condemn the use of these types of images as demeaning and hurtful. Using the names of other cultural groups would not be tolerated. These images assault self-esteem. Self-image is clearly linked to other social problems such as violence and substance abuse (Hatfield, 2000).

CONCLUSION

Native Americans are a diverse population with a long history of government regulation and subsequent mistrust of helping professionals. Mistrust is a natural outcome of a legacy of racism, cultural imperialism, and cultural incompetence. Cultural competence begins with understanding the impact of historical and contemporary losses and how these coexist with strengths and resilience that facilitate survival in a context of colonization.

Helping professionals must strive for cultural competence at all levels of practice including direct services, program planning, and policy development. Only through culturally competent work at all levels of helping can we begin to truly alleviate the extensive social and health problems effecting First Nations people.

Exercises

Exercise #1: Examining local service provision to Native Americans

Identify the major Native American groups in your area including their approximate numbers and location. Contact three major social service agencies that serve these areas. Find out how many Native clients they serve each year and what type of services they provide to this population. Based on these inquiries, make some tentative conclusions about how well the needs of the Native American community are being met by these agencies. Discuss your tentative findings and begin to make hypotheses about what these agencies are doing that may make them hospitable or inhospitable to local Native Americans. Make recommendations for improvement.

Exercise #2: Applying the Indian Child Welfare Act

Reflect on the following case example: Janie Singer from Santa Clara Pueblo has recently been reported for child abuse of her three young children. The charges have been verified, and you need to make foster care arrangements for the children. Does the Indian Child Welfare Act apply in this case? If so, what steps do you need to take?

Exercise #3: Experiential learning activities in Native American communities

Attend a pow wow, social, or other Native American gathering or festival that is open to the public. What can you learn about communication norms and social etiquette from this experience? How can you apply what you have learned in a social work setting?

Additional Resources

Bachman, R. (1992). *Death and Violence on the Reservation*. New York: Auburn House. This book gives an excellent overview of the extent of violence in Native American communities. The author uses statistics on arrests, imprisonment, and mortality to present a side of Native American life that is unfamiliar to most non-Native people. Helping professionals can use this information to become better informed about the social environment of many Native people then go beyond these statistics to apply a strengths perspective in their work.

In the White Man's Image. (1992). American Experience Series. Public Broadcasting Service. This video recounts the historical development of the boarding school system with a particular focus on Carlisle, one of the first and most famous Native American boarding schools. First person accounts and commentary by historians are presented. The video includes "before and after" pictures taken of Native American children when they first arrived at the school and after their traditional clothes were taken away and their hair was cut and styled to illustrate how they were remade "in the white man's image."

Jaimes, M. A. (1992). *The State of Native America: Genocide, Colonization, and Resistance.* Boston: South End Press. This edited book provides key information on laws, policies, and historical developments that have influenced contemporary Native Americans. Topics covered include the political nature of early indigenous population estimates, issues of sovereignty in a colonial context, and rights to natural resources. This information provides important contextual information for helping professionals and identifies numerous issues in need of advocacy.

Maracle, B. (1993). *Crazywater: Native Voices on Addiction and Recovery.* Toronto: Penguin Books. This book provides numerous personal stories of indigenous people and their encounters with alcohol. These narratives clearly depict a diversity of experiences including a variety of therapeutic solutions. While these narratives are taken from the Canadian context, the book provides useful insights into indigenous struggles with addiction for helping professionals in both the United States and Canada.

Ogunwole, S. U. (2002). *The American Indian and Alaska Native Population: 2000.* U.S. Bureau of the Census. This brief narrative provides an accessible overview of U.S. census material on Native Americans. The material includes information on residential patterns, age, education, and other demographic information. The size of various Native populations and changing demographic patterns are identified.

References

Abbott, P. J. (1996). American Indian and Alaska Native aboriginal use of alcohol in the United States. *American Indian and Alaska Native Mental Health Research, 7*(2), 1–13.

Abe-Kim, J. S., & Takeuchi, D. T. (1996). Cultural competence and quality of care: Issues for mental health service delivery in managed care. *Clinical Psychology: Science and Practice, 3*(4), 273–295.

Allen, J. (1998). Personality assessment with American Indians and Alaska Natives: Instrument considerations and service delivery style. *Journal of Personality Assessment, 70*(1), 17–42.

Barsh, R. L. (1996). The Indian Child Welfare Act of 1978: A critical analysis. In J. R. Wunder, *Recent Legal Issues for American Indians, 1968 to the Present.* New York: Garland, 219–268.

Beauvais, F., & Trimble, J. E. (1992). The role of the researcher in evaluating American Indian alcohol and other drug abuse prevention programs. In M. A. Orlandi, R. Weston, & L. G. Epstein (Eds.) *Cultural Competence for Evaluators: A Guide for Alcohol and other Drug Abuse Prevention Practitioners Working with Ethnic and Racial Communities.* Rockville, MD: Office of Substance Abuse Prevention, U.S. Department of Health and Human Services. 147–171.

Bending, R. L. (1997). Training child welfare workers to meet the requirements of the Indian Child Welfare Act. *Journal of Multicultural Social Work, 5*(3/4), 151–164.

Brave Heart-Jordan, M., & DeBruyn, L. (1995). So she may walk in balance: Integrating the impact of historical trauma in the treatment of American Indian women. In J. Adelman & G.

Enguidanos (Eds.), *Racism in the lives of Women: Testimony, Theory, and Guides to Antiracist Practice.* New York: Haworth Press, 345–368.

Churchill, W., & Morris, G. T. (1992). Key Indian laws and cases. In M. A. Jaimes (Ed.), *The State of Native America: Genocide, Colonization, and Resistance.* Boston: South End Press, 13–21.

Clinton, R. N., Newton, N. J., & Price, M. E. (1991). *American Indian Law: Cases and Materials.* Charlottesville, VA: Michie Company.

Collmeyer, P. M. (1995). From "Operation Brown Baby" to "Opportunity": The placement of children of color at the Boys and Girls Aid Society of Oregon. *Child Welfare, 74*(1), 242–263.

Curyto, K. J., Chapleski, E. E., Lichtenberg, P. A., Hodges, E., Kaczynski, R., & Sobeck, J. (1998). Prevalence and prediction of depression in American Indian elderly. *Clinical Gerontologist, 18*(3), 19–37.

Dion, R., Gotowiec, A., & Beiser, M. (1998). Depression and conduct disorder in Native and non-Native children. *Journal of the American Academy of Child and Adolescent Psychiatry, 37*(7), 736–742.

Fleming, C. M. (1992). American Indians and Alaska Natives: Changing societies past and present. In M. A. Orlandi, R. Weston, & L. G. Epstein (Eds.), *Cultural Competence for Evaluators: A Guide for Alcohol and other Drug Abuse Prevention Practitioners Working with Ethnic/Racial Communities.* Rockville, MD: Office of Substance Abuse Prevention, U.S. Department of Health and Human Services, 147–171.

Garrett, M. T., & Pichette, E. F. (2000). Red as an apple: Native American acculturation and counseling with or without reservation. *Journal of Counseling and Development, 78*, 3–13.

George, L. J. (1997). Why the need for the Indian Child Welfare Act? *Journal of Multicultural Social Work, 5*(3/4), 165–175.

Gilliland, F. D., Mahler, R., Hunt, W. C., & Davis, S. M. (1999). Preventive health care among rural American Indians in New Mexico. *Preventive Medicine, 28*(2), 194–202.

Gurley, D., Novins, D. K., Jones, M. C., Beals, J., Shore, J. H., & Manson, S. M. (2001). Comparative use of biomedical services and traditional healing options by American Indian veterans. *Psychiatric Services, 52*(1), 68–74.

Hamby, S. L. (2000). The importance of community in a feminist analysis of domestic violence among American Indians. *American Journal of Community Psychology, 28*(5), 649–672.

Hatfield, D. L. (2000). The stereotyping of Native Americans. *The Humanist, 60*(5), 43–45.

John, R. (1991). *Defining and Meeting the Needs of Native American Elders: Applied Research on their Current Status, Social Service Needs, and Support Network Operation.* Lawrence: University of Kansas.

Kavanaugh, K., Absalom, K., Beil, W., & Schliessmann, L. (1999). Connecting and becoming culturally competent: A Lakota example. *Advances in Nursing Science, 21*(3), 9–31.

Kasprow, W. J., & Rosenheck, R. (1998). Substance use and psychiatric problems of homeless Native American veterans. *Psychiatric Services, 49*(3), 345–350.

LaFromboise, T., & Howard-Pitney, B. (1995). Zuni Life Skills Development Curriculum: Description and evaluation of a suicide prevention program. *Journal of Counseling Psychology*, 42(4), 479–486.

Long, C. R., & Curry, M. A. (1998). Living in two worlds: Native American women and prenatal care. *Health Care for Women International*, 19(3), 205–215.

Manson, S. M. (2000). Mental health services for American Indians and Alaska Natives: Need, use, and barriers to effective care. *Canadian Journal of Psychiatry*, 45(7), 617–626.

Maracle, B. (1993). *Crazywater: Native Voices on Addiction and Recovery*. Toronto: Penguin Books.

McNeil, D. W., Porter, C. A., Zvolensky, M. J., Chaney, J. M., & Kee, M. (2000). Assessment of culturally related anxiety in American Indians and Alaska Natives. *Behavior Therapy*, 31(2), 301–325.

Meisenhelder, J. B., & Chandler, E. N. (2000). Faith, prayer, and health outcomes in elderly Native Americans. *Clinical Nursing Research*, 9(2), 191–203.

Moran, J. R., & May, P. A. (1995). American Indians. In J. Philleo & F. L. Brisbane (Eds.), *Cultural Competence for Social Workers: A Guide for Alcohol and other Drug Abuse Prevention Professionals Working with Ethnic/Racial Communities*. Center for Substance Abuse Prevention, 3–39.

Morrisette, P. J. (1994). The holocaust of First Nations people. *Contemporary Family Therapy*, 16(5), 381–392.

Napholz, L. (2000). Balancing multiple roles among a group of urban midlife American Indian working women. *Health Care for Women International*, 21(4), 255–266.

Narduzzi, J. L. (1994). *Mental Health among Elderly Native Americans*. New York: Garland.

Novins, D. K., Bechtold, D. W., Sack, W. H., Thompson, J., Carter, D. R., & Manson, S. M. (1997). The *DSM-IV* outline for cultural formulations: A critical demonstration with American Indian children. *Journal of the American Academy of Child and Adolescent Psychiatry*, 36(9), 1244–1252.

Oetting, E. R., & Beauvais, F. (1991). Orthogonal cultural identification theory: The cultural identification of minority adolescents. *International Journal of the Addictions*, 25(5A & 6A), 655–685.

Ogunwole, S. U. (2002). *The American Indian and Alaska Native Population: 2000*. U.S. Bureau of theCensus.http://www.census.gov/population/www/cen2000/briefs.html

Piquemal, N. (2001). Free and informed consent in research involving Native American communities. *American Indian Culture and Research Journal*, 25(1), 65–79.

Sage, G. P., & Burns, G. L. (1993). Attributional antecedents of alcohol use in American Indian and Euroamerican adolescents. *American Indian and Alaska Native Mental Health Research*, 5(2), 46–53.

Schinke, S. (1996). Behavioral approaches to illness prevention for Native Americans. In P. M. Kato & T. Mann (Eds.), *Handbook of Diversity Issues in Health Psychology*, New York: Plenum Press, 367–387.

Shulman, L. (1999). *The Skills of Helping Individuals Families, Groups, and Communities*. Itasca, IL: F. E. Peacock.

Stevens, J., Cornell, C. E., Story, M., French, S. A., Levin, S., Becenti, A., Gittelsohn, J., Going, S. B., & Reid, R. (1999). Development of a questionnaire to assess knowledge, attitudes, and behaviors in American Indian children. American *Journal of Clinical Nutrition, 69*(4), 773s-781s.

Stiffarm, L. A., & Lane, P., Jr. (1992). The demography of Native North America: A Question of American Indian survival. In M. A. Jaimes (Ed.), *The State of Native America: Genocide, Colonization, and Resistance.* Boston: South End Press, 23–53.

Sugarman, J. R., & Grossman, D. C. (1996). Trauma among American Indians in an urban county. *Public Health Reports, 111*(4), 321–327.

Swinomish Tribal Mental Health Project. (1991). *A Gathering of Wisdoms, Tribal Mental Health: A Cultural Perspective.* LaConner, WA: Swinomish Tribal Community.

U.S. Census Bureau. (2001). Current Population Survey. http://www.census.gov

Walters, K. L. (1997). Urban lesbian and gay American Indian identity: Implications for mental health service delivery. In L. B. Brown, *Two Spirit People: American Indian Lesbian Women and Gay Men.* Binghamton, NY: Haworth Press, 43–65.

Weaver, H. N. (1996). Social work with American Indian youth using the orthogonal model of cultural identification. *Families in Society: The Journal of Contemporary Human Services, 77*(2), 98–107.

Weaver, H. N. (1999a). Assessing the needs of Native American communities: A Northeastern example. *Evaluation and Program Planning: An International Journal, 22*(2), 155–161.

Weaver, H. N. (1999b). Indigenous people and the social work profession: Defining culturally competent services. *Social Work, 44*(3), 217–225.

Weaver, H. N. (1999c). Through indigenous eyes: A Native American perspective on the HIV epidemic. *Health and Social Work, 24*(1), 27–34.

Weaver, H. N., & Yellow Horse Brave Heart, M. (1999). Examining two facets of American Indian identity: Exposure to other cultures and the influence of historical trauma. *Journal of Human Behavior in the Social Environment, 2*(1/2), 19–33.

Weaver, H. N., & White, B. J. (1999). Protecting the future of indigenous children and nations: An examination of the Indian Child Welfare Act. *Journal of Health and Social Policy, 10*(4), 35–50.

Wing, D. M., Crow, S. S., & Thompson, T. (1995). An ethnonursing study of Muscogee (Creek) Indians and effective health care practices for treating alcohol abuse. *Family Community Health, 18*(2), 52–64.

Young, Y. K., Lujan, P., & Dixon, L. D. (1998). I can walk both ways. *Human Communication Research, 25*(2), 252–275.

Zimmermann, M. A., Ramirez-Valles, J., Washienko, K. M., Walter, B., & Dyer, S. (1996). The development of a measure of enculturation for Native American youth. *American Journal of Community Psychology, 24*(2), 295–310.

CHAPTER **6**

African Americans

African Americans constitute one of the largest populations of color in the United States; only recently have their numbers been equaled by the faster growing Latino group. Many African Americans are descendants of enslaved West Africans brought to the United States and Caribbean islands in the 18th and early 19th centuries. Through the practice of slavery, there was an attempt to eradicate the values and traditions of these people who came from a variety of tribal backgrounds. Even though some cultural traditions were lost, others, influenced by life in the United States, merged into a distinct African American culture.

In the Americas, extensive racial mixing took place between West Africans, Europeans, and indigenous populations. The enslaved Africans were considered property by European and American slave-holders and it was common for White men to have sexual contact with African women. This led to the birth of many children of mixed heritage. Likewise, the lives of Africans and indigenous people intersected. Some slaves fled plantations and sought shelter with Native Americans, often being adopted by or marrying into Native families. A number of Native American Nations have historically had significant intermixing with Africans, such as the Seminole, Shinnecock, Pequot, and Narraganset Nations.

The African American population continues to grow but at a slower pace than some other groups. According to the 1990 census, 30 million people self-identified as African American (12.1% of the population). In 2000, 34.7 million identified exclusively as African American (12.3% of the population), a growth rate of 15.6%. An additional 1.8 million stated they were African American and another ethnicity (.6% of the population), a growth rate of 21.5%[1] (McKinnon, 2001). Although many African Americans have ancestors that have lived in the United States for centuries, new immigrants continue to arrive from Africa and the Caribbean. According to the 2000 census, 2,221,000 African Americans were foreign-born, with 860,000 of these being naturalized citizens (U.S. Census Bureau, 2001).

Most African Americans (54%) live in the South, 19% in the Midwest, 18% in the Northeast, and 10% in the West (McKinnon, 2001). African Americans tend to be an urban population, with 53.1% living in central cities. They are a fairly young population with 32.4% being under age 18 compared with 26.4% of the general population and 23.5% of Whites. Of those African Americans over age 25, 35.2% have high school degrees compared with 33.1% of the U.S. population and 34.1% of Whites. African Americans experience a disproportionate amount of poverty with 23.6% living below the poverty level, compared with 7.7% of Whites. Poverty varies significantly according to age and is most likely to be a problem experienced by children and the elderly. Poverty affects 33.1% of African Americans under age 18 compared with 9.4% of Whites. In addition, 22.7% of African Americans over age 65 live below the poverty line, compared with 7.6% of Whites. Women are poorer than men across all age groups (U.S. Census Bureau, 2001).

As a historically stigmatized minority group, African Americans have had little choice as to what they were called. Slaves were categorized according to the amount of African heritage they were presumed to possess. Thus, someone who was thought to be half African and half White was categorized as mulatto, someone who was one-quarter African was considered a quadroon, and someone who was one-eighth African was considered an octoroon. In reality, these classifications were never precise. Sometimes these labels were used for Native Americans, regardless of whether they had African heritage (Brooks, 1998). Terms that presume to reduce people to categories based on fractions of heritage are not only imprecise and outdated; they are also highly offensive.

Other labels for the descendants of West Africans have been used, although some have faded from usage. The terms *Negro* (Spanish for black) and *colored*, in common use through the 1950s, are now largely rejected as derogatory. The label *Black* was once considered offensive, but was reclaimed by many people of African heritage. This reclamation is illustrated by slogans such as "Black is Beautiful" and "Black Power." In the 1960s, displays of cultural pride led many people of color to exercise their right to determine their own preference of terms. As the Black Pride movement invoked a sense of connection/reconnection to African heritage, some people began to use the terms *Afro-American* and *African American*. The terms *Black* and *African American* are both still commonly used. An individual's choice of the terms *Black* or

---

[1]In 1990, the census did not allow people to designate more than one racial or ethnic group. Therefore, precise comparisons between 1990 and 2000 census figures are not possible, making it difficult to determine how much the African American population has grown.

African American is linked to how he or she views identity. The choice of terms also gives insight into conceptual and contemporary links with African/African American history and African consciousness (Lindsey, 1998). In this text, the term *African American* is used to reflect the blending of cultural roots that exist within this population. Other terms are used to indicate people of African heritage who are not American or have cultural roots in the Caribbean (e.g., Haitians).

This chapter provides an overview of social work with African American people. The significant diversity that exists within and among African Americans and others of African descent sets the context for discussion. The chapter also presents information on knowledge, skills, and values/attitudes necessary for cultural competence, and presents issues for cultural competence on micro and macro levels.

KNOWLEDGE FOR CULTURAL COMPETENCE

The knowledge needed for culturally competent social work with African Americans can be divided into four broad areas: diversity, history, culture, and contemporary realities. Diversity serves as an overarching concept. The history, culture, and contemporary realities of African Americans vary according to factors such as national origin, gender, class, and sexual orientation.

Diversity

African Americans are a diverse group united by the common legacy of African descent and a history of oppression and institutionalized discrimination that has shaped their cultural identity. Other layers of identity such as class, gender, and sexuality present significant diversity among African Americans. For example, women and men may experience their lives and aspects of African American culture in varied ways, leading to gender-based differences in racial identity (Wilson & Constantine, 1999).

African Americans also vary in sexual orientation. Like members of other cultural groups, some are heterosexual, some are homosexual, some are bisexual, and some are transgendered. Despite this diversity, homophobic attitudes are common among African Americans. Even though African Americans, themselves, are a stigmatized minority, they can at least attain heterosexual privilege. Some African Americans believe that those who are homosexual or bisexual further stigmatize African Americans as a whole, thus making them appear more pathological. That African American women outnumber African American men also fuels homophobia, as a gay lifestyle further reduces the population of available males. Some African Americans use Christian teachings and the AIDS epidemic to justify prejudices against homosexual and bisexual people (Greene, 2000; Sanchez-Hucles, 2000). On the other hand, some gay African Americans have attained high status positions such as choir director in the church. Although the congregation knows these individuals are gay, this is not discussed, and they are accepted despite intolerant rhetoric about homosexuality in general. Although clearly not all African Americans are homophobic, homophobia remains a significant presence in many African American communities.

African Americans as a group are often perceived as a stigmatized caste, yet internal class distinctions also exist. As a population, African Americans are disproportionately poor but many individuals are middle-class and some are affluent. Indeed, class differences may be particularly relevant between African American helping professionals and clients. Class differences may impede engagement and mutual understanding when clients and helping professionals come from very different socioeconomic realities (Jordan, Bogat, & Smith, 2001).

Not all people of African heritage in the United States are the descendants of slaves brought to the United States centuries ago. Some come from the Caribbean. Distinct cultures evolved on these islands where, although they were enslaved, the majority of the population was of African descent (Brent & Callwood, 1993). Some are more recent immigrants from a variety of African countries. A study of cultural mistrust, ethnic identity, racial identity, and self-esteem found significant differences between Africans, African Americans, and West Indians/Caribbeans on all variables but self-esteem. These differences exist because of different life experiences and historical perspectives (Phelps, Taylor, & Gerard, 2001).

Increasing numbers of people from the Caribbean, often known as West Indians, have immigrated to the United States. The greatest number of first- and second-generation West Indians in the United States reside in Brooklyn, New York. In particular, many come from the Caribbean islands of Jamaica, Barbados, Trinidad, Tobago, Antigua, and St. Croix (Thrasher & Anderson, 1988). English is the primary language of many Caribbean people of African descent (with the notable exception of Haitians), but linguistic forms vary from standard British English to Creole dialects (Brent & Callwood, 1993). Most Caribbean people come to the United States seeking employment and educational opportunities to establish a better life for themselves and their families. Typically, one adult immigrates to the United States, establishes economic security, then sends money home to support the family members until they can come to the United States (Boyd-Franklin, Aleman, Jean-Gilles, & Lewis, 1995; Thrasher & Anderson, 1988).

Haitians are one of the largest groups of Caribbeans of African descent in the United States. Haitians arrived in the United States in three distinct waves. In the 1950s, educated members of the upper class fled the harsh regime of Papa Doc Duvalier. They were followed in the 1960s by middle-class immigrants and in the mid-1970s by unskilled, uneducated urban immigrants (Boyd-Franklin et al., 1995). Haitian clients often face language barriers in the United States. Some service providers assume they are likely to speak French, but Haitian clients speak Haitian Creole. Haitians in the United States often face stigma, discrimination, and stereotypical associations with HIV/AIDS. They may also experience stress associated with tenuous or no legal status and fears of being returned to Haiti. These factors may lead them to avoid contact with health and social service agencies (Boyd-Franklin et al., 1995).

Some West Indians maintain a belief system that incorporates West African deities. In addition to Westernized medical and social services, some Haitians and other West Indians seek help from indigenous healers known as Obeah men or women (Brent & Callwood, 1993) or from indigenous healers such as root doctors (Campinha-Bacote, 1992). The syncretic belief system known as Voodoo is often parodied in film and fiction, yet this remains an important and viable belief system for some people from the Caribbean (Campinha-Bacote, 1992).

Social scientists and helping professionals have paid little attention to the needs of African immigrants (Kamya, 1997). Once in the United States, host communities rarely distinguish between African immigrants and African Americans, yet they may see themselves as Black, immigrants, or as members of distinct cultural or tribal groups. African immigrants may experience double invisibility because of their race and national origin. Tension between African Americans and African immigrants is exacerbated by myths about immigrants and their supposed preferential treatment, thus creating mutual suspicion and exploitation (Kamya, 1997).

History

The history of African Americans reflects a struggle against oppression and domination by White America (Gordon, 1998). This history begins with involuntary immigration and servitude. Even those who came to the United States later by their own choice are influenced by the pervasive legacy of slavery that dictates much of the ongoing interactions of African Americans as a minority of color within a predominantly White society.

History presents the context for understanding contemporary interactions and behaviors. For example, knowledge of slavery informs an understanding of African Americans' distinctive form of humor, in which tragedy is transformed into comedy and absurdity. Humor was a way to express anger and rage that was part of the slave experience. This humor, often found in folktales, protest hymns, and self-deprecation, has roots in West Africa. Today the expression of anger through humor is used to display feelings about historical and continuing injustice (Gordon, 1998).

Residential patterns of contemporary African Americans are linked to historical occupational patterns. Many African Americans continue to reside in the southern United States because most slaves were brought to work on plantations in the South. Subsequent Northern migration is also linked to the economic base of American society (Butler, 1992). Thus, industrialization led many African Americans to migrate to cities in the North in search of jobs.

The historical exclusion of African Americans from many mainstream social and educational institutions led to the development of specific African American social agencies, educational institutions, and approaches to helping. African Americans "share a history of encountering barriers to appropriate services. This history includes African Americans being overlooked, overmedicated, offered group rather than individual treatment, and pathologized based on racial, gender, and class considerations" (Sanchez-Hucles, 2000, p. 3).

E. Franklin Frazier was one of the first to apply an African American perspective to social work. Frazier was the second director of the Atlanta School of Social Work, the first social work program specifically designed to serve African Americans. His writing focused on the impact of slavery on African American families. He emphasized scientific methods in the study and alleviation of social problems, advocated for African American business cooperatives, and offered an analysis and critique of racism (Schiele, 1999).

Traditional African ways of life were threatened and distorted by oppression yet threads of cultural continuity remain.

> Despite insults to their humanity; psychological disorientation; and the social, cultural, and environmental displacement experienced during their early years in America and after, African Americans have managed to defy the forms of enslavement (both physical and psychological) and have attested in every media and form to their resiliency as a people and to the tenacity of their cultural heritage. Old patterns have persisted; some have been reinterpreted; others have been syncretized and adapted to fit the environment. Through it all and at each stage of development a consistent mode of thought has prevailed. (Butler, 1992, p. 25)

Culture

While some early African American scholars believed slavery decimated African values (Schiele, 1999), this view has largely been discarded, and Afrocentric paradigms have been proposed for understanding contemporary African Americans. It is often difficult to separate cultural factors from other influences. In fact, traits and behaviors connected to African cultures are confounded with behaviors derived from the need to manage racism and sexism of the dominant society (Gavazzi, Alford, & McHenry, 1996; Greene, 2000; L. Robinson, 2000). The legacy of slavery and continuing assaults on personhood necessitate survival strategies. It is often difficult to distinguish these strategies from African American culture (Grace, 1992).

Cultural influences of African Americans must be considered without minimizing individual differences or stereotyping (Kane, 2000). It is important to recognize that racial identity attitudes are not fixed, but change during a lifetime (L. Robinson, 2000; Wilson & Constantine, 1999). Cross (1991) analyzed and synthesized studies of African American identity from the 1930s to the 1960s and proposed a model of Nigrescence, or the process of becoming Black. This model delineates stages of African American identity from a self-deprecating racial identity to acceptance of an African American identity. These stages involve development and change, but an underlying theme of continuity persists throughout the stages. Cross's model has been widely used in the United States (Wilson & Constantine, 1999) and applied in England (L. Robinson, 2000).

Cultural Identity and Resilience   Many African Americans take pride in their cultural heritage (Mosely-Howard & Evans, 2000). Having a strong African American identity is associated with resilience and protective factors including self-esteem, attitudes about substance abuse, and social functioning (Miller & MacIntosh, 1999; Resnicow, Soler, Braithwaite, Ben Selassie, & Smith, 1999). Cultural pride is associated with positive personality development and social behaviors. Negative attitudes toward Whites are not related to cultural pride and are associated with less optimal functioning (Resnicow et al., 1999). Likewise, a study of African Caribbean youth in England found a positive relationship between self-esteem and racial identity (L. Robinson, 2000).

Adaptive social functioning requires the ability to live in two worlds (Miller & MacIntosh, 1999). African Americans go through a process of multicultural socialization: they are exposed to majority culture, minority status, and African American culture within a mainstream environment (Mosely-Howard & Evans, 2000; Stevens, 1997). Parents strive to protect children from racism and oppression and help them develop bicultural competence (Greene, 2000; Leslie, 1998; Miller & MacIntosh, 1999; Mosely-Howard & Evans, 2000; Stevens, 1997).

Family Structures   African Americans tend to have extended family kinship networks (Kane, 2000). Intergenerational relationships are fundamental for transmitting values and expectations (Butler, 1992). The extended family is a source of strength and cultural pride.

Egalitarian, adaptable family roles and strong coping skills are typical of African American families (Butler, 1992; Kane, 2000). Kinship ties control all community relationships (Butler, 1992). Role flexibility is common; extended family members and non-relatives, especially older women, often take on parenting roles (Boyd-Franklin et al., 1995; Mosley-Howard & Evans, 2000). An emphasis is placed on raising children with a solid, stable sense of self. Children are raised to respect and maintain connections with extended family members and elders. A study of African American college students found they perceive their family of origin to give strong support to both autonomy and intimacy. Family dynamics were primarily positive (Kane, 2000).

Values   Although antithetical stereotypes persist, African Americans typically have a strong education and work ethic (Green, 1999; Kane, 2000; Mosley-Howard & Evans, 2000). Education is often valued, but sometimes African Americans are suspicious of educated African Americans who may be over-identified with White institutions and ideologies (Jordan et al., 2001). Demeanor and communication styles of African Americans are often distinctive. Gestures, intonations, and expressions may be more important than actual words (Jordan et al., 2001). Research has found that adolescent girls participate in loud boisterous behavior in a style that is culturally grounded. This may reinforce stereotypes and conflict with acceptable school behavior

(Stevens, 1997). Communication styles can differ by class. Those who are educated in mainstream institutions may be trained to speak without emotion as part of a professional demeanor.

Connection to others is highly valued and self-identity is defined by membership in the group. A shift away from the collective good toward individual attainments found among some African Americans erodes the cultural foundation and quality of life (Butler, 1992).

Spirituality   Spirituality is an important coping mechanism in everyday life and a source of strength in times of trouble (Boyd-Franklin et al., 1995; Carter, 1999; Haight, 1998; Kane, 2000; Mosley-Howard & Evans, 2000; T. L. Robinson, 2000; Schiele, 1996). For many African Americans, spirituality is expressed through connection to Christian denominations. The church is the heart of African American communities and serves as a refuge that reinforces a sense of self and self-esteem when other institutions exclude African Americans (Butler, 1992). The church plays a central role in civil rights struggles and in the development of political leaders (Carter, 1999).

The church and African American community are highly integrated. Approximately 70% of African Americans are affiliated with a church. The church is a vital part of natural helping networks. Even those with no formal church affiliation may seek help from ministers in times of need (Carter, 1999). The church also serves as a place of spiritual and racial socialization for African American children, which in turn fosters resilience. For example, telling stories from the Bible can be a teaching and socialization tool to help children understand how to cope with adversity (Butler, 1992; Haight, 1998).

Understanding the importance of the church in African American communities can lead social workers to schedule more collaborative activities in church facilities (Carter, 1999). Churches can be platforms for outreach to prospective clients, support systems for clients in need, and partners in planning and implementing services.

Not all African Americans experience the influence of the church in equally positive ways. The church can be a source of support, but the atmosphere of compulsory heterosexuality can be alienating (Greene, 2000). In addition, although the church is a dominant force in African American communities, not all African American spirituality is expressed through Christianity. Indigenous African spiritual beliefs are often meaningful for African immigrants. In traditional African thinking, an emphasis is placed on the community, spirituality, and nature as part of self-esteem and well-being. Indigenous spiritual beliefs continue to be a shaping force in the lives of many Africans who have embraced major Western and Eastern religions (Kamya, 1997).

Some people of African descent participate in spiritual traditions that blend indigenous and Christian beliefs. For example, some Haitians participate in syncretic religions such as Voodoo and seek assistance from folk healers instead of, or in addition to, help from medical or social agencies. This belief system shapes how clients view their situations (Boyd-Franklin et al.,

1995). In addition, the Nation of Islam serves as an important spiritual center for many African Americans. Its teachings include a focus on discipline, a drug-free lifestyle, and anti-gang messages.

Africentrism/Afrocentrism   In recent decades, some African Americans have explored traditional African concepts and beliefs as a way to find meaning in their lives. This paradigm, known as Africentrism or Afrocentrism, has gained popularity and is most visible in the celebration of the African American centered holiday, Kwanzaa. The principles of Africentrism have also been incorporated into theories and social programs tailored to the needs of African Americans.

Africentric thought posits that African Americans, to some degree, have retained African notions of collectivism including kinship bonds beyond the biological family. Africentrism links values and patterns such as spirituality, role flexibility, mutual aid, and an integrated, rather than dichotomized, view of life that emphasizes balance rather than divisions such as material/spiritual and male/female to West African cultures. The degree to which an individual adheres to these values is critical in understanding African Americans (Mosley-Howard & Evans, 2000).

In the Africentric perspective, Africa is the center of the development of human life, not on the fringes of the Western experience. This perspective emphasizes the values of inclusiveness, interdependence, and connection with nature and the collective unconscious (Gavazzi et al., 1996; Harvey & Rauch, 1997) and spirituality (Harvey & Rauch, 1997; Schiele, 1996). The Africentric worldview is based on the guiding principles of Umoja (unity), Kujichagulia (self-determination), Ujima (collective work and responsibility), Ujamaa (cooperative economics), Nia (purpose), Kuumba (creativity), and Imani (faith) (Butler, 1992; Gavazzi et al., 1996; Harvey & Rauch, 1997).

Africentric theory posits that (1) aspects of European American social work practice are inappropriate for African Americans; (2) systematic efforts to destroy African culture have been harmful; and (3) an African ethos is central to the ability to survive racism. Societal denigration of all things African has fostered self-hatred and destructiveness among African Americans. Hence, a consciousness about racism is important in Africentric social work (Harvey & Rauch, 1997). Family systems theory and Africentric world views are valuable frameworks for examining the experiences of African Americans (Mosley-Howard & Evans, 2000). Social workers may find an Africentric paradigm applicable in work with a variety of clients because it calls attention to oppression and spirituality (Schiele, 1996).

Contemporary Issues

Social workers need to understand contemporary issues facing African Americans. Although individual African Americans have different life experiences and concerns, common issues include the context of oppression, family issues, children in substitute care, violence, and poverty. Many of these concerns could be considered struggles; however, the coping strategies that African Americans have developed to survive these challenges can be viewed as strengths.

The Context of Oppression The African American experience is shaped by a larger society that continues to denigrate and oppress. Oppression causes trauma and anxiety. Racism can take many forms including day-to-day discrimination and the trauma of invisibility (e.g., being ignored when next in line, unable to get a cab, being referred to in derogatory ways as if not there). These day-to-day experiences of invisibility are a source of stress, anxiety, depression, frustration, and anger. Paradoxically, African Americans also experience hypervisibility. They may be followed in stores by security agents, see others cross the street or exit an elevator to avoid contact, and be asked for multiple forms of identification to make a purchase with a credit card or check. The potential for racial discrimination in addition to the everyday ups and downs in life can be overwhelming (Sanchez-Hucles, 2000).

Many African Americans experience multiple levels of oppression associated with class, gender, and sexuality (Greene, 2000). An African American woman is likely to have two strikes against her as she tries to earn an adequate income to support her family because African Americans tend to earn less money than Whites and women tend to earn less money than men. Likewise, oppression is compounded for African Americans with disabilities. Microaggressions associated with being invisible in American society are often daily occurrences for an African American in a wheelchair who is ignored or presumed incompetent.

The African American world is parallel and sometimes counter to mainstream culture because of deep social disequilibrium and nonacceptance. African Americans find themselves in a hostile environment shaped by social injustice, societal inconsistency, and personal impotency. These forces have a destructive impact on the personality and result in either deprecated or transcendent behavior (Butler, 1992). Many social problems such as substance abuse result from racism and discrimination (Grace, 1992).

The development of African American children occurs within a societal context that is negligent at best and virulently racist at worst. Racism has a detrimental effect on development. White teachers often have biased expectations for African American students. This racism contributes to children's feelings of inferiority and nonacceptance, which, in turn, limits their motivation to succeed in school (Haight, 1998). A child who repeatedly receives the message he or she is not intellectually capable of going to college will often internalize this belief and not even try to realize this dream.

Class, gender, sexuality, and culture are intertwined forces. African American young men often live within a societal context of racism, unemployment, and poverty. Understanding African American manhood involves understanding how race, class, and gender intersect with power (Price, 1999). Likewise, it is important to understand the individual and collective impact of historical and contemporary racism on identity formation in African American women (T. L. Robinson, 2000). African American women are rewarded for embracing and imitating White ideals of female attractiveness, but ultimately they are doomed to failure. According to these standards, they must eradicate ethnic characteristics to be feminine and attractive. These messages are destructive to self-worth (Greene, 1997, 2000). Integrating aspects of African cultures can be a way for African American women to maintain psychological health. At the same time, they must integrate and mitigate the influences of the dominant culture, thus creating adaptive responses to racism.

The convergence of racism, sexism, and heterosexism is apparent in the lives of lesbian and bisexual African American women. In working with these women, social workers must understand the impact of the dominant society, African American culture, and relationships with family, community, and partners. It is also important to understand the complex ways individuals construct an identity based on components of culture, gender, and sexual orientation. Rigid gender-role stereotypes restrict the range of acceptable behaviors, and racism denigrates African Americans. Thus, multiple levels of oppression are created and must be addressed in the helping relationship (Greene, 2000).

Gender and racial oppression cannot be neatly separated. Stereotypes of lesbians as masculinized women intersect with stereotypes of African American women as strong, independent, and castrating to the detriment of African American men. Racism, sexism, and heterosexism intersect in the view that African American women are to blame for problems in their families and that families headed by men in which women are subordinate are the solution (Greene, 1997).

Family Issues   African American families have often been depicted from a deficit perspective. Early studies typically examined families' marital and parental status and emphasized legal and biological ties, thus missing the strengths of families that do not fit these narrow guidelines (Mosley-Howard & Evans, 2000). A family does not necessarily have to be bound by biological or legal ties such as marriage to provide a nurturing environment. While problems do exist in some African American families, evidence exists that African Americans access substantial strengths and resources from extended families and communities. A qualitative study examined resilience in 10 African American single mothers in urban areas characterized by poverty, drugs, and crime. The academic term "resilience" was replaced by the phrase "making it," which the women defined as the ongoing process of achieving goals under risky circumstances. This was done through appreciating resources and successes, reframing stressors in motivating ways, and finding and using resources to cope with stressors (Brodsky, 1999).

Extended family members are often called on for support. Increasing numbers of African American children live with their grandparents. Almost 30% of grandmothers and 14% of grandfathers report having primary responsibility for raising a grandchild for at least six months (Fuller-Thomson & Minkler, 2000). Parenting through the extended family can be traced back to West

African family structures, but much of today's caregiving is in response to crises such as mothers' incarceration, HIV/AIDS, and substance abuse.

The network of women offering support in their extended families can be an important resource, yet the strength of this network may be drained by families with debilitating drug use and diseases such as HIV/AIDS. Grandparent caregivers may have their own stressors such as adverse physical and mental health outcomes that effect caregiving. One-half of grandparent caregivers live below the poverty line and may become overwhelmed by care-giving responsibilities unless additional supports and resources are available to them. Service providers can play an important role in providing support ser-vices to these caregivers (Boyd-Franklin et al., 1995; Fuller-Thomson & Minkler, 2000).

A study that examined five different African American family constella-tions with 634 adolescents found many fathers who do not live with their chil-dren are still involved in their lives. This contradicts stereotypes about absent African American fathers. The results also challenge the belief that living with single mothers adversely affects the psychosocial development of youth. Family structure was not related to problem behaviors or psychological dis-tress (Salem, Zimmerman, & Notaro, 1998).

Empirical evidence increasingly challenges stereotypes of African American families as pathological. Indeed, they are often resourceful and cre-ative in their use of strengths. Given the abundant stressors in the environ-ment, these strengths and resources may become depleted. Social workers can play a role in enhancing and bolstering existing strengths and in making resources more accessible.

Children in Substitute Care   African American youth are disproportion-ately represented in substitute care such as the foster care system (Brissett-Chapman, 1997; Brown & Bailey-Etta, 1997; Gavazzi et al., 1996; Lawrence-Webb, 1997; McRoy, Oglesby, & Grape, 1997). Factors accounting for growing out-of-home placement include parental drug use, poverty, and increased reporting of abuse and neglect. Poverty is the greatest predictor of child removal (McRoy et al., 1997). Social, political, and economic forces, especially the economic impact of deindustrialization and subsequent loss of jobs in African American communities, contribute to high rates of substitute care. A history of discrimination and economic marginality has left African Americans vulnerable to economic changes. This has led to a sharp decline in a stable working class and fewer jobs for youth. Urban areas that are unable to absorb large numbers of disadvantaged people become destablized (Brown & Bailey-Etta, 1997).

Increasingly, the demographic profile of children in care includes children of color, yet most adoption agency workers are White females (McRoy et al., 1997). African American children enter the system in increased numbers, remain in the system longer, receive fewer in-home support services, and have more undesirable experiences than White children. Although policies have sought to minimize time in substitute care, many African American children remain in bureaucratic systems that are not culturally responsive or that lack appropriate resources to assist them and their families (Brown & Bailey-Etta, 1997). Private and public agencies have displayed a reluctance to use specialized minority programs, although such programs are more likely to be able to keep children within their cultural context (McRoy et al., 1997).

There are more White than African American adoptive families, but it is a myth that African American families are unwilling to adopt. When family composition, age, and income are controlled, African American families adopt at five times the rate of Whites. Many are screened out of the process but are willing to adopt if obstacles are removed. Agency fees, inflexible standards, institutional racism, and lack of minority staff members are primary obstacles to adoption for African American families (McRoy et al., 1997). More culturally competent policies and minority staff doing outreach are needed.

Exposure to Violence   African Americans are subject to disproportionate arrest rates, victimization, and risk factors for violence (Williams, Stiffman, & O'Neal, 1998). Understanding the lives of African American clients involves acknowledging that their world is not as safe as that of many other Americans. Each day, regardless of class, they live at higher risk of assault, rape, and murder than White Americans do. All African Americans are vulnerable to these problems, however, those in lower income brackets may be at increased risk (Sanchez-Hucles, 2000). Encounters with law enforcement officials are often negative. Being stopped by police without cause leads to feelings of frustration, rage, powerlessness, and depression.

A violent social environment has clear implications for mental health. A study of 89 mother-child dyads living in a moderate to high violence urban area revealed that children who were more depressed had higher daily stress and were more likely to have been abused. Additionally their mothers were less educated, more depressed, and often had a history of domestic abuse (Johnson & Kliewer, 1999).

Inner-city African American youth are exposed to a steady onslaught of violence that shapes, rather than interrupts their development, psychological functioning, and well-being. Violence has always been in their lives and is characterized by chronicity, proximity, human causation, and lethality (Tolleson, 1997). A study of 684 youth ages 14 to 17 in St. Louis examined environmental and behavioral risk factors as predictors of involvement in violence. Environmental risk factors such as exposure to violence, deteriorated school environment, negative peer environment, traumatic experiences, and behavioral risk factors of alcohol and drug use accounted for 40% of the variance. In particular, environmental risks were stronger predictors of involvement in violence for males (Williams et al., 1998). In addition to the risk factors experienced by African American young men, other barriers to resilience include lack of insurance, and agencies and practitioners that are perceived to manifest racism, classism, and cultural insensitivity (Harvey & Rauch, 1997). A study of incarcerated inner-city gang members revealed that perpetration of violence is a psychological adaptation to the trauma of unremitting violence. A gang member "vaccinates himself against the trauma incurred by the fantasy of his own impending obliteration" by perpetrating violence (Tolleson, 1997, p. 417). The stereotype of the inner-city male as a violent gang member is created by trauma, and is not a cultural characteristic.

Poverty   The urban context of poor families is marked by a street culture that is directly related to poverty and is a result of victimization. Street culture erodes the strengths of African American culture (Wright & Anderson, 1998). However, not all African Americans living in poverty participate in this street culture. Risk factors are only part of the story and should not obscure factors that promote resilience. A study of low-income African American sixth grade students explored their thoughts and feelings about the future and found them to be optimistic and realistic (McCabe & Barnett, 2000).

A study of the academic and psychosocial adjustment of 6- to-9-year-old African American children of single mothers in the rural South found that self-esteem was linked to family routines and the quality of the mother-child relationship. Lack of financial resources was associated with depressive symptoms and low self-esteem of mothers (Brody & Flor, 1997). Changing the environment to produce economic security can be an important way to enhance psychosocial outcomes.

SKILLS FOR CULTURAL COMPETENCE

A wide variety of social work skills are applicable to working with African Americans. For example, skills such as listening and empathy are important with any client, but listening and empathizing in cross-cultural situations require extra effort for maximum effectiveness. Validation is also important. Recognizing and labeling the clients' strengths can be particularly important with African American clients. Validating clients' competence, sometimes referred to as "giving gifts" within an African American context, is often reciprocated with "gifts" such as client disclosure and deeper engagement (Stevenson & Renard, 1993).

Engaging

It is important to recognize obstacles to successful engagement including barriers grounded in historical facts and those rooted in contemporary practices. African American clients may be suspicious of therapy and other forms of help because of centuries of racism and the ensuing belief that family matters should be handled privately (Boyd-Franklin et al., 1995). Successful engaging involves getting past the stigma against counseling evident in many African American communities (T. L. Robinson, 2000).

Mistrust of helping professionals and researchers developed as a result of negative experiences. For example, midnight raids looking for men in the homes of African American women on public assistance led many to view social workers as punitive, rather than as a source of help. Culturally biased assessment of school children has led to stigma and labeling rather than helpful services. Such past problems have led many African Americans to feel exposed, stigmatized, discriminated against, and dehumanized by helping professionals (Jordan et al., 2001). In light of this, helping professionals must take additional time to deliberately focus on engaging.

Demonstrations of knowledge and skill are only meaningful after a relationship is established (Jordan et al., 2001). Using the formal form of address (Miss, Mr., Mrs., Dr.) is recommended in the beginning. This will help counteract the history of disrespect in which adults were often referred to as boy, girl, or by their first names (Sanchez-Hucles, 2000). Interpersonal aspects are crucial in engaging African American clients. Personal attributes of the helping professional are considered, as clients determine how much to disclose and make themselves vulnerable.

The physical set-up of the agency communicates how clients are perceived and whether it is likely to be a comfortable setting for them. The reception area can have art work, magazines, and music that depict a variety of people including African Americans. Interpersonal contact such as a friendly greeting and warm-up time in the interview for the client and social worker to gradually approach sensitive content are important in establishing a climate of trust and respect (Sanchez-Hucles, 2000).

Helping professionals need to communicate a willingness to explore issues of importance to clients. While some social workers may be uncomfortable with discussions of spirituality, creating space for exploration of spiritual issues is important. A survey of African immigrants identified a preference for helping professionals who show interest in spiritual well-being (Kamya, 1997).

In conducting outreach in African American communities, it is important to establish connections with key community members. Status is not just conferred by degrees and titles. Failure to solicit support from the eldest or most experienced community residents or people in an agency may result in project failure (Jordan et al., 2001).

Assessing

Assessment of African Americans is often based on dominant society expectations and norms. This leads to identifying deficits, rather than simply differences. Culture must be considered as part of the assessment to avoid viewing African American families from a deficit perspective (Brissett-Chapman, 1997). When cultural influences on behavior are not considered, inappropriate assessments and interventions may result. For example, youth who behave in a culturally appropriate, boisterous manner may be viewed as loud, out of control, and perhaps aggressive. Social workers' stereotypes may inadvertently influence assessments and interventions. For example, African American elderly may be overdiagnosed with schizophrenia and dementia partly because of stereotyping and nontraditional means of presenting complaints such as hallucinations and delusions that commonly accompany depression (American Psychiatric Association, 1994). Stereotypes of African American fathers not living with their children and not being involved in their lives may lead social workers to exclude the possibility that fathers are resources and can be included in family interventions (Salem et al., 1998).

Recognizing oppression and the ways it can be internalized can be important parts of the work. However, a primary focus on oppression and disadvantage risks proceeding from a deficit perspective. A sole focus on internalized oppression and victimization neglects what African Americans affirm as positive about their identity as African Americans and as Americans. Negative and positive racial self-valuations may coexist (Stevens, 1997). In moving beyond a deficit perspective, it is important to identify how coping mechanisms have been developed within the context of a racist society. High arrest rates and problems with the criminal justice system lead to fears, frustrations, anger, and impotence (Sanchez-Hucles, 2000). These feelings may be manifested as a justifiable paranoia (Kane, 2000).

A culturally competent assessment for African Americans must include an examination of the societal context (Williams et al., 1998). For example, the identities of young African American men are strongly associated with "race, class, and gender relations of power. To ignore the power relations and these different contexts would be to dismiss not only the barriers and penalties that they encounter but the possibilities they have to shape their own lives in productive and generative ways" (Price, 1999, p. 260). The analysis of social context and awareness of oppression inherent in feminist therapy may be helpful when integrated with a cultural component (Greene, 1997).

Nonverbal behavior must be considered in conducting an assessment. Gestures, intonations, and expressions give important information beyond clients' words (Jordan et al., 2001). Nonverbal behavior, like verbal information, must be interpreted within a cultural context to be meaningful.

Using standardized assessment tools based on dominant society norms has led to tracking minorities in school systems, thus disproportionately placing them in special needs classrooms and vocational tracks. Some scholars (e.g., Lindsey, 1998) are vocal opponents of using standardized assessment instruments with African American clients and believe this invariably leads to culturally incompetent assessments. Alternatives to using current standardized instruments include devising culture-specific norms for existing instruments or creating new instruments with an Africentric foundation.

A number of measurement tools have been developed to assess cultural identity in African Americans. These measures include the Belief Systems Analysis Scale (Montgomery, Fine, & James-Myers, 1990, cited in Lindsey, 1998), the African Self-Consciousness Scale (Stokes, Murray, Peacock, & Kaiser, 1994, cited in Lindsey, 1998), and the African American Acculturation Scale (Landrine & Klonoff, 1994, cited in Lindsey, 1998). Culturally specific assessment tools have also been created to assess a variety of concepts. *The Handbook of Tests and Measurements for Black Populations* (Jones, 1996, cited in Lindsey, 1998) includes more than 100 tests and measures that consider African American history, characteristics, behaviors, and needs. Some of these tools measure basic concepts such as stress and self-esteem whereas others are unique to African Americans and measure issues such as perceived racism, coping with racism, and African American identity development.

Intervening

Societal or macro level change is clearly needed, but many social work interventions can also be helpful on an individual, or micro level. For example, youth violence can be reduced through skills training and interventions that decrease alcohol and drug use (Williams et al., 1998). Individual strategies can complement efforts at macro-level change. Collaborative strategies that include community input can also be meaningful for African Americans. Professionals must cultivate relationships with family and kinship networks. It is important to make use of indigenous resources such as church, educational, and social institutions (Brissett-Chapman, 1997).

Strengths-based and competency-based approaches are important in working with African Americans. Practice models need to tap into personal and cultural strengths while avoiding support for pathologizing, blaming, shaming, and disempowering behaviors. Competency approaches begin with concern for, and understanding of, the sociopolitical context of clients' behaviors (Wright & Anderson, 1998). Helping professionals can validate clients' accurate perceptions of discrimination and bias and the affect of these on their lives (Greene, 1997).

Empowerment and healing can be promoted by affirming the moral worth of African Americans. Validation is critical and initiates a healing process (Leslie, 1998). Empowerment includes helping disadvantaged people recognize structural factors in society such as oppression, injustice, and discrimination. Belief in a just world is often associated with resilience and reliance on God. Helping professionals should be cautious about challenging clients' sense of a just world or control over events as this may be disempowering and immobilizing (Littrell & Beck, 1999).

Interventions may involve supporting existing resource networks. For example, grandmothers and other extended family caregivers often display great strength caring for children, but they may become overburdened and need help from formal service systems. They may experience role overload, and their needs may be overlooked by service providers (Boyd-Franklin et al., 1995).

Stories such as Brer Rabbit are used by some African American women to teach their children. Although mischievous, some of Brer Rabbit's tricks affirm the group and show cleverness and forethought. Although women who tell these stories may not be explicitly knowledgeable of African values, an African ethos is reflected in these stories through (1) rejecting the concept of sin/intrinsic evil, (2) admiration for traits of Brer Rabbit that affirm group connectedness, and (3) thinking highly of clever tricks similar to African characters' exploits. Promotion of traditional storytelling can help clients connect with their culture. There is an African American folktale for almost every circumstance. These can be used in a variety of therapeutic and educational ways to help solve problems in social living. Listeners can identify with the intelligence of characters such as Brer Rabbit. An emphasis on this non-elitist concept of intelligence can be empowering in a low-income community (Leslie, 1998).

Skills in problem conceptualization, problem solving, grant writing, data collection, analysis, and presentation of results can be valuable contributions in communities with few resources (Jordan et al., 2001). Social workers can use these skills to become allies and resources in African American communities.

Given a societal context where oppression is often present, social workers need skills in recognizing and addressing injustice. The social environment often exacerbates problems; thus, skills for assessing and modifying the environment become particularly important. Advocacy is an important skill in helping clients who are disenfranchised.

Social workers need skills in empowering clients to develop their own confidence and skills. Empowerment begins with developing a working partnership in which clients' strengths are acknowledged as crucial to bringing about change. A strengths perspective is important in allowing the social worker to recognize and point out the strengths and resources inherent in clients and their environments.

VALUES/ATTITUDES FOR CULTURAL COMPETENCE

Helping professionals must examine their own value systems and the impact of their values on their abilities to maintain empathetic therapeutic relationships. The process of self-examination includes scrutinizing feelings and motivations for working with oppressed clients (Greene, 1997). Social workers who become overwhelmed by feelings of guilt for possessing privileges in a society that oppresses African Americans cannot fully assess African Americans and empower them to identify and use their strengths. Guilt can be a natural reaction, but social workers must get past the guilt to help clients move toward positive change.

Social workers must examine their own culturally influenced beliefs about clients' behaviors to see alternative explanations (Leslie, 1998). For example, stereotypes about African American men abandoning their children may lead social workers to miss complex reasons that inhibit these fathers' participation. Social workers may also be blind to different ways African American men are present in their children's lives.

Helping professionals must be aware of how they are influenced by their own sociopolitical backgrounds (Wright & Anderson, 1998). Social workers can analyze their own position of privilege or disadvantage, and explore their feelings about this position in relation to clients (Greene, 1997). It is easier for privileged Whites to believe that society is fair and just, than it is for African Americans who experience oppression and injustice on a regular basis. Privilege consists of unearned assets available to some and not others. In American society, privilege is highest for White, heterosexual, financially secure, young, and able-bodied men. People with privilege often do not take the time to recognize this status or to examine why they are in a desirable category relative to others (Sanchez-Hucles, 2000). People who have privilege are able to take it for granted, but those without privilege constantly experience their lack of status. Social workers must be aware that bias permeates theoretical orientations (Greene, 1997). Not all models, theories, and interventions apply equally to all people. Social workers should question the origin of the tools and theories they use in their work and insure that those they choose are an appropriate fit for African American clients.

Core social work values and practices such as client self-determination, empowerment, and social justice fit well in practice with African Americans (Stevens, 1998). It is important that social workers take a strong stance of social justice and acknowledge societal oppression. Social workers who value self-determination and empowerment can validate and support African American clients in struggles against oppression.

CASE EXAMPLE

Barb McIntosh, the school social worker, was notified by a teacher that Ramona Jones was at risk of failing the fifth grade because of low reading comprehension and disruptive classroom behavior. Barb made a home visit to gain a fuller understanding of Ramona and her family. Ramona and her two younger siblings are being raised by their grandmother. They are active members of the Baptist church. Barb conducted a strengths-based assessment and found that Ramona's father sees his children once or twice a month and is himself receiving counseling for substance abuse recovery at a local African American social service center. In Barb's assessment, Ramona's environment has some strengths (e.g., her caring grandmother, support from the church, some relationship with her father), but she could benefit from strengthening ties to environmental resources. In particular, Barb believed Ramona's school problems would substantially improve if she received tutoring in reading and developed a stronger connection to her father. Barb learned that the African American center where Ramona's father receives services has a strong family component where the children, their father, and grandmother can participate in activities together. Barb also identified a college volunteer program through the Baptist church where Ramona can receive mentoring and tutoring in reading.

In this case, culturally competent knowledge, skills, and values/attitudes helped facilitate the work in several areas:

- A strengths-based perspective guided Barb to look for ways Ramona's father was in her life and strengthen these connections, rather than assume that he played no meaningful roles.
- Barb's knowledge of culturally appropriate resources in the environment led her to explore service referrals through the church (where the family already had connections) and the African American social service center (which her father had already found to be a culturally congruent agency).
- Barb's knowledge that self-esteem in African American youth is often linked to cultural identity also reinforced her belief that services rendered through a culturally specific agency are likely to reinforce self-esteem and identity, thus decreasing acting out behaviors in school.
- A culturally competent, strengths-based assessment and intervention plan will explore Ramona's connection to other relatives and community members (e.g., her mother, fictive kin) and other elements in her environment

(e.g., clubs and organizations) and will identify those which can serve as resources.

- Rather than approaching the case from a deficit perspective, Barb searched for appropriate community-based resources; this approach is grounded in Barb's values about strengths and empowerment. In this case, Barb demonstrates skills in identifying appropriate resources, making referrals, and following up to ensure the referrals are successful in meeting Ramona's needs.

CULTURAL COMPETENCE IN SOCIAL POLICIES

Many social policies either have been ineffective in African American communities or have had a negative impact. Often policies and programs intervene at an individual level as if families live in a vacuum. This neglects resources and stressors at community and societal levels (Brodsky, 1999).

Aid to Families with Dependent Children (AFDC) provides an example of a policy both differentially applied and with negative consequences for African Americans. From the beginning, the AFDC program contained racial biases in rules about suitability of homes. Likewise, state discretion in programs led to application of different eligibility standards for African Americans, particularly in southern states. Before 1955, most southern African American families were arbitrarily denied welfare benefits. In Louisiana in 1960, 23,000 children and their mothers were expelled from AFDC because the mothers had a child outside of marriage. Similar mass expulsions happened in other states. Expulsions for "unsuitability" were overwhelmingly applied to African Americans (Lawrence-Webb, 1997).

In response to negative publicity, the Fleming Rule, named for President Eisenhower's Secretary of Health Education and Welfare, was passed to address arbitrary home suitability policies. This rule stated that if a home was deemed unsuitable, the state must provide due process protections for families and provide services, thus leading to the joining of services and cash payments. The result, however, was that instead of denying benefits because of morality, children were often removed for neglect, resulting in many African American children in substitute care. "The Fleming Rule has had a profound effect on the modern United States child welfare system. Little did Secretary Fleming know the significance and far-reaching implications of a ruling that was intended to protect children. Instead, the ruling was used in an oppressive manner that proved to be detrimental to the very children whom he was attempting to protect" (Lawrence-Webb, 1997, p. 23).

Given the large proportion of African American children in care, foster-care and adoption policies have a significant impact on African American communities. Project Opportunity was designed to recruit families for transracial adoption of African American children as a partial solution to the need to find permanent homes. This project initially received support within the African American community and from prominent civil rights activists like Whitney

Young. As transracial adoptions grew in number, however, many African American social workers began to speak out against this practice on the grounds that African American children must learn survival skills for living in a racist society that can only come from African American parents. The National Association of Black Social Workers took the controversial position that it would be preferable for African American children to remain in foster homes and institutions rather than be adopted by White families (Collmeyer, 1995). Federal laws and policies have not supported this position.

Currently, state and federal laws are shifting away from restrictions on transracial adoptions. For example, Texas law prohibits foster placement decisions based on assumptions that a same-race placement is preferable. Likewise, an employee who removes a child from a transracial foster placement to seek or make a same-race placement is subject to dismissal (McRoy et al., 1997). On the federal level, the Multiethnic Placement Act (passed in 1994) has similar goals but is less restrictive. This act prohibits any agency receiving federal funds from denying placement solely because of race, but does allow consideration of cultural, ethnic, or racial background to meet the needs of the child. This act also requires diligent recruitment efforts of foster and adoptive parents that reflect the backgrounds of children in care (McRoy et al., 1997). Despite initial attempts to allow consideration of cultural background in making placements, this was essentially an unfunded mandate. Later tightening of the Multiethnic Placement Act that restricted consideration of race or ethnicity in placements generated outrage and charges of genocide by the National Association of Black Social Workers.

Policies can be developed to support African American families willing to adopt children with special needs. Permanency planning in two-parent families can be elusive for African American children who are vulnerable (e.g., learning disabilities, oppositional social behavior). A 10-year study of family and child functioning in two-parent adoptive families with developmentally vulnerable infants and toddlers found that these families demonstrated family cohesion and adaptability. Modest income families were able to provide a setting with connectedness, bonding, and flexibility for at-risk children (Hoopes, Alexander, Silver, Ober, & Kirby, 1997). These findings contradict stereotypes of pathology. Adoption was a satisfying experience, even when some young males had behavior problems. Risk factors were overcome by positive family characteristics.

Although past policies have often had an undesirable impact, it doesn't need to be that way. Policies can capitalize on natural networks within communities and stimulate empowerment (Carter, 1999). Policy makers can recognize and incorporate the extended family structures found among African Americans into their policies while providing needed support so these natural structures do not become overwhelmed. For example, kinship care is common and culturally congruent for African Americans but should not be viewed as a low-cost alternative to out-of-home care. These families are often poor and in need of services themselves. Currently, African American children in kinship care receive fewer services than do those in nonrelative care and less than

White children in kinship care (Brown & Bailey-Etta, 1997). Policies that provide support to caregivers can cultivate and enhance these important resources. Policy makers can also recognize the important role played by the church and develop policies to support and expand programs in this venue.

Policy makers can seek input from key people in African American communities. Helping professionals can convene stakeholders, and convey policy recommendations to power brokers that result in long-term positive outcomes for African American communities (Jordan et al., 2001).

CULTURAL COMPETENCE IN SOCIAL AGENCIES

Social agencies have not always considered the cultural norms of clients. For example, bureaucratic red tape, the length of the adoption process, and the reluctance of some adoptive applicants to share personal information with the agency were identified by African American adoptive families as reasons why some African Americans may be reluctant to become adoptive parents (Collmeyer, 1995). Agency administrators can streamline bureaucratic processes and paperwork to be more welcoming to African American clients. They can also ensure that personal information collected from clients is directly related to their service needs and that the relevance and importance of this information is clearly explained.

Some agencies have been founded specifically to serve African American clients. However, African American agencies are chronically underfunded, understaffed, and overtaxed by community needs. Financial instability and inadequate personnel often lead these agencies to function in crisis mode (Jordan et al., 2001). African American community agencies can benefit from various types of support including funding and training. They should be recognized for the contribution they make to providing culturally appropriate services.

Including a cultural component is critical in programs designed to help youth in fostercare develop independent living skills. Establishing cultural identity is integral to an adolescent's ability to develop other aspects of identity related to occupation, ideology, and interpersonal relationships. In Ohio, where foster care is approximately 60% African American, the Office of Child Care and Family Services developed a culturally specific rites-of-passage program to build cultural identity through didactic and experiential activities. Program leaders instill cultural pride and self-esteem by teaching African centered principles and values (Gavazzi et al., 1996). This cultural pride, in turn, is designed to increase self-sufficiency of the youth and enhance the impact of life-skills training. This particular program focuses on males and uses the Africentric Self Knowledge for Independent Living curriculum.

Agencies such as Project Hustle in Dallas-Fort Worth, Texas, that focus on keeping African American children with African American families, have developed intensive and creative outreach strategies, mentoring programs, quick and responsive feedback mechanisms and hold meetings in targeted areas (McRoy et al., 1997). A similar program, One Church One Child, founded in 1980, encourages African American churches around the nation to identify their members who are able and willing to adopt African American children. Individualized home studies and flexible scheduling are key components of services (McRoy et al., 1997).

In another example, the Institute of Black Parenting (IBP), founded in 1976 as the service and research component of the Association of Black Social Workers of Greater Los Angeles, uses the Effective Black Parenting curriculum to deliver culturally competent recruitment and retention efforts. IBP practices offer a flexibility not often found in other agencies. Evening hours are common and interactions with prospective families focus on education rather than investigation. All staff members receive specific training in cultural competency. Helping professionals follow up with applicants within 72 hours of the orientation meeting to demystify the process and promote retention (McRoy et al., 1997).

Program planners can incorporate dimensions of African American culture in agency services. Using an Afrocentric framework for services can foster self-esteem and survival skills in youth (Gavazzi et al., 1996). Spirituality and collectivity are important aspects of Afrocentric programming for African American males involved in the juvenile justice system. Reinforcement of identity helps create self-esteem to cope in society, thus curbing negative behaviors (Harvey & Coleman, 1997). Nonprofit agencies can develop rites of passage programs to reestablish a sense of dignity, self-worth, spirituality, and community for African American youth.

A number of successful, culturally grounded programs have been affected by changing policy mandates. Funding for IBP and similar culturally grounded programs has been curtailed because of implementation of federal laws such as the Multiethnic Placement Act that support transracial placement. Specialized minority adoption programs around the country are declining because of funding threats for programs that advocate same race adoptions (McRoy et al., 1997).

COMMUNITY INTERVENTIONS

In the past, divergent views and values of professionals and communities have hindered collaboration. Epistemological differences exist such as discrepancies over different ways of knowing. The values, goals, and needs of the community may differ from those of professionals, thus leading to conflict, antagonistic attitudes, and deliberate sabotage of projects. Some of this friction is grounded in class differences between professionals and community members (Jordan et al., 2001).

Research and interventions that gather data are sometimes viewed with suspicion in African American communities. Many past projects have had a deficit focus and were designed to explore pathology. Some study participants have been deceived and damaged (Gavazzi et al., 1996; Jordan et al., 2001). Projects like the infamous Tuskegee experiment, in which researchers observed the progress of untreated syphilis in African American men who believed they were receiving help, have generated significant mistrust. Research that doesn't benefit communities is experienced as external domination and control. African American professionals struggle with these issues as do White researchers. Projects must be shaped by community needs, not by the priorities of funding sources or professionals (Jordan et al., 2001).

Professionals must work to establish trust with communities to develop meaningful collaborations. This includes becoming knowledgeable about the unique history and resources of specific communities and taking an active role in promoting interagency cooperation (Jordan et al., 2001). When working with church-based groups, social workers can begin meetings with a prayer or hymn to enhance the cultural relevance of interventions and increase rapport between community members and community organizers (Carter, 1999).

Projects need to have an infrastructure for continuance. They must promote autonomy, not dependence on continued professional involvement. Community residents can be trained in assessment, evaluation, and intervention skills to create new resources in the community. This promotes empowerment. Community projects have the potential to improve infrastructure by providing training and services not otherwise available in low-income communities (Jordan et al., 2001).

Social workers can take the lead in initiating an honest dialogue on race. The contribution that social workers make when they attend hearings on racial issues at national, state, and local forums can be very meaningful. Social workers can take a proactive stance and help build a climate that makes racial hatred impossible (Carter, 1999). Research can examine issues such as how racism and stereotypes about African Americans affects the experiences of African immigrants (Kamya, 1997).

Helping professionals can promote economic development, including government intervention, and address the climate that allows hate to occur. This can involve political and economic empowerment. Grantsmanship skills can be used to aid communities in acquiring funds and creative financing can be developed to address issues of racism. Helping professionals can turn media attention to these issues (Carter, 1999).

The mid-1990s saw a rise in church burnings, particularly in the South. Church arson brings memories of bombings, burnings, and destructive acts common in the 1950s and 1960s. Such terrorist activities strike at the heart of the African American community, destroying a major source of support in communities with few resources for rebuilding. At such times of disempowerment, community members may turn to community organizers for assistance (Carter, 1999). Social workers have not played an active role in addressing church burnings, but the profession is in a good position to mobilize community strengths as part of empowerment practice.

Social workers can help develop comprehensive violence prevention strategies that target environmental change (Williams et al., 1998). Social workers can participate in and facilitate community-based responses to hate crimes. Networking with key people such as ministers, local government officials, parishioners, safety officials, community volunteers, and corporations from effected communities can lead to coalition building and crucial changes. A unified message that acts of hatred will not be condoned is politically empowering to members of effected African American churches and communities as a whole (Carter, 1999).

Environment is a strong predictor of violence in African American youth, so macro-level change leading to improved school environments must happen. Gender-specific environmental change can be an important prevention strategy. Decreasing family instability may be helpful for females and a more positive peer environment may be helpful for reducing violence in males. Because witnessing or experiencing violence breeds violence, a decrease in violence is likely to have significant, ongoing benefits (Williams et al., 1998).

Constructive dialogue is the key to meaningful professional collaborations in the African American community. Effective collaboration can lead to resource mobilization and building of capital through education, training, and empowering at individual and organizational levels (Jordan et al., 2001).

CONCLUSION

African Americans are a diverse population that includes the descendants of enslaved West Africans, Caribbean immigrants, and recent African immigrants. Historic and contemporary oppression based on skin color is often compounded by oppression based on gender, class, sexuality, and immigration status. Social workers must recognize their own experiences with privilege and disenfranchisement as part of delivering culturally competent services. Likewise, social workers and policy makers can learn a lot from the work done by African Americans in their own communities to promote resilience and social justice. Macro-level changes designed to confront oppressive societal structures are key to bringing about change in the lives of African American clients.

Exercises

Exercise #1: Incorporating census data in culturally competent planning

Review recent census data for your region. Basic census data can be accessed through the U.S. Census Bureau Web site: http://www.census.gov. Write a brief overview of African Americans describing their numbers, age, education, occupations, and where they live. Describe how program planners could use this information to enhance services for this population.

Exercise #2: Understanding and alleviating tension among groups of African heritage

Reflect on the following case example: As a social worker in a community agency, you have noticed increasing tension between U.S.-born and Caribbean-born youth of African descent. This tension has been manifested in verbal harassment, physical altercations, and in graffiti throughout the community. How would you develop an understanding of the factors underlying this tension and develop a community-wide prevention program to eliminate future problems?

Exercise #3: Reflecting on privilege and disenfranchisement

Reflect on the ways you experience privilege and disenfranchisement in your life. How do your own experiences influence your ability to empathize and effectively work with African American clients?

Additional Resources

A Question of Color. (1992). Film Two Production. This provocative video examines issues of color among African Americans. Interviews with a wide variety of African Americans are used to highlight how this issue affects both individuals and communities. The video raises a subject that is powerful yet rarely explicitly examined. The material presented aids helping professionals in understanding the impact of skin color and phenotype on self-esteem and cultural identity.

McKinnon, J. (2001). *The Black Population: 2000.* U.S. Census Bureau. This report provides a concise overview of African Americans in the U.S. Information includes size and location of the population as well as information on age, education, occupation, and other demographic information.

Schiele, J. H. (2000). *Human Services and the Afrocentric Paradigm.* New York: Haworth Press. This book describes the Afrocentric paradigm and how it can be integrated in the helping process. Schiele, one of the most noted scholars on the Afrocentric paradigm, articulates both commonalities and differences between this and other approaches to helping.

Stark, E. (1993). The myth of Black violence. *Social Work, 38*(4), 485–490. This article examines the statistical evidence for claims of extensive violence in African American communities. Statistics are critiqued and the role of stereotypes in perpetuating images of violence and criminal activities in African American communities are examined. This article assists helping professionals think critically about the issue of violence and African Americans and to approach this subject from a strengths rather than a deficit perspective.

References

American Psychiatric Association. (1994). *Ethnic Minority Elderly: A Task Force Report of the American Psychiatric Association.* Washington DC: American Psychiatric Association.

Boyd-Franklin, N., Aleman, J., Jean-Gilles, M. M., & Lewis, S. Y. (1995). Cultural sensitivity and cultural competence: African-American, Latino, and Haitian families with HIV/AIDS. In N. Boyd-Franklin, G. L. Steiner, & M. G. Boland (Eds.) *Children, Families, and HIV/AIDS: Psychosocial and Therapeutic Issues.* New York: Guilford Press, 53–77.

Brent, J. E., & Callwood, G. B. (1993). Culturally relevant psychiatric care: The West Indian as a client. *Journal of Black Psychology, 19*(3), 290–302.

Brissett-Chapman, S. (1997). Child protection risk assessment and African American children: Cultural ramifications for families and communities. *Child Welfare, 76*(1), 45–63.

Brodsky, A. E. (1999). "Making it": The components and process of resilience among urban, African-American, single mothers. *American Journal of Orthopsychiatry, 69*(2), 148–160.

Brody, G. H., & Flor, D. L. (1997). Maternal psychological functioning, family processes, and child adjustment in rural, single parent, African American families. *Developmental Psychology, 33*(6), 1000–1011.

Brooks, J. F. (1998). Confounding the color line: Indian-Black relations in historical and anthropological perspective. *American Indian Quarterly, 22*(1/2), 125–133.

Brown, A. W., & Bailey-Etta, B. (1997). An out-of-home care system in crisis: Implications for African American children in the child welfare system. *Child Welfare, 76*(1), 65–83.

Butler, J. P. (1992). Of kindred minds: The ties that bind. In M. A. Orlandi, R. Weston, & L. G. Epstein (Eds.) *Cultural Competence for Evaluators: A Guide for Alcohol and other Drug Abuse Prevention Practitioners Working with Ethnic/Racial Communities.* Rockville, MD: Office of Substance Abuse Prevention, U.S. Department of Health and Human Services. 23–54.

Campinha-Bacote, J. (1992). Voodoo illness. *Perspectives in Psychiatric Care, 28*(1), 11–17.

Carter, C. S. (1999). Church burning in African American communities: Implications for empowerment practice. *Social Work, 44*(1), 62–68.

Collmeyer, P. M. (1995). From "Operation Brown Baby" to "Opportunity": The placement of children of color at the Boys and Girls Aid Society of Oregon. *Child Welfare, 74*(1), 242–263.

Cross, W. E. (1991). Shades of Black: Diversity in African American Identity. Philadelphia: Temple University Press.

Fuller-Thomson, E., & Minkler, M., (2000). African American grandparents raising grandchildren: A national profile of demographic and health characteristics. *Health and Social Work, 25*(2), 109–126.

Gavazzi, S. M., Alford, K. A., & McHenry, P. C. (1996). Culturally specific programs for foster care youth: The sample case of an African American rites of passage program. *Family Relations, 45*(2), 166–174.

Gordon, D. B. (1998). Humor in African American discourse: Speaking of oppression. *Journal of Black Studies, 29*(2), 254–276.

Grace, C. A. (1992). Practical considerations for program professionals and evaluators working with African-American communities. In M. A. Orlandi, R. Weston, & L. G. Epstein (Eds.) *Cultural Competence for Evaluators: A Guide for Alcohol and other Drug Abuse Prevention Practitioners Working with Ethnic/Racial Communities.* Rockville, MD: Office of Substance Abuse Prevention, U.S. Department of Health and Human Services, 55–74.

Green, J. W. (1999). *Cultural awareness in the human services: A Multi-Ethnic Approach.* Englewood Cliffs, NJ: Prentice-Hall.

Greene, B. (1997). Psychotherapy with African American women: Integrating feminist and psychodynamic models. *Smith College Studies in Social Work, 67*(3), 299–322.

Greene, B. (2000). African American lesbian and bisexual women. *Journal of Social Issues, 56*(2), 239–249.

Haight, W. L. (1998). "Gathering the Spirit" at First Baptist Church: Spirituality as a protective factor in the lives of African American children. *Social Work, 43*(3), 213–221.

Harvey, A. R., & Coleman, A. A. (1997). An Afrocentric program for

African American males in the juvenile justice system. *Child Welfare, 76*(1), 197–211.

Harvey, A. R., & Rauch, J. B. (1997). A comprehensive Afrocentric rites of passage program for Black male adolescents. *Health and Social Work, 22*(1), 30–37.

Hoopes, J. L., Alexander, L. B., Silver, P., Ober, G., & Kirby, N. (1997). Formal adoption of the developmentally vulnerable African American child: Ten year outcomes. *Marriage and Family Review, 25*(3/4), 131–144.

Johnson, P. D., & Kliewer, W. (1999). Family and contextual predictors of depressive symptoms in inner-city African American youth. *Journal of Child and Family Studies, 8*(2), 181–192.

Jordan, L. C., Bogat, G. A., & Smith, G. (2001). Collaborating for social change: The Black psychologist and the Black community. *American Journal of Community Psychology, 29*(4), 599–620.

Kamya, H. A. (1997). African immigrants in the United States: The challenge for research and practice. *Social Work, 42*(2), 154–165.

Kane, C. M. (2000). African American family dynamics as perceived by family members. *Journal of Black Studies, 30*(5), 691–702.

Lawrence-Webb, C. (1997). African American children in the modern child welfare system: A legacy of the Flemming Rule. *Child Welfare, 76*(1), 9–30.

Leslie, A. R. (1998). Using the moral vision of African American stories to empower low-income African American women. *Affilia: Journal of Women in Social Work, 13*(3), 326–351.

Lindsey, M. L. (1998). Culturally competent assessment of African American

clients. *Journal of Personality Assessment, 70*(1), 43–53.

Littrell, J., & Beck, E. (1999). Perceiving oppression: Relationships with resilience, self-esteem, depressive symptoms, and reliance on God in African-American homeless men. *Journal of Sociology and Social Welfare, 26*(4), 137–158.

McCabe, K., & Barnett, D. (2000). First comes work, then comes marriage: Future orientation among African American young adolescents. *Family Relations, 49*(1), 63–70.

McKinnon, J. (2001). The Black Population: 2000. U.S. Census Bureau.

McRoy, R. G., Oglesby, Z., & Grape, H. (1997). Achieving same-race adoptive placements for African American children: Culturally sensitive practice approaches. *Child Welfare, 76*(1), 85–104.

Miller, D. B., & MacIntosh, R. (1999). Promoting resilience in urban African American adolescents: Racial socialization and identity as protective factors. *Social Work Research, 23*(3), 159–169.

Mosley-Howard, G. S., & Evans, C. B. (2000). Relationships and contemporary experiences of the African American family: An ethnographic case study. *Journal of Black Studies, 30*(3), 428–452.

Phelps, R. E., Taylor, J. D., & Gerard, P. A. (2001). Cultural mistrust, ethnic identity, racial identity, and self-esteem among ethnically diverse Black university students. *Journal of Counseling and Development, 79*(2), 209–216.

Price, J. N. (1999). Schooling and racialized masculinities: The diploma, teachers, and peers in the lives of young, African American men. *Youth and Society, 31*(2), 224–263.

Resnicow, K., Soler, R. E., Braithwaite, R. L., Ben Selassie, M., & Smith, M.

(1999). Development of a racial and ethnic identity scale for African American adolescents: The survey of Black life. *Journal of Black Psychology, 25*(2), 171–188.

Robinson, L. (2000). Racial identity attitudes and self-esteem of Black adolescents in residential care: An exploratory study. *British Journal of Social Work, 30,* 3–24.

Robinson, T. L. (2000). Making the hurt go away: Psychological and spiritual healing for African American women survivors of childhood incest. *Journal of Multicultural Counseling and Development, 28*(3), 160–176.

Salem, D. A., Zimmerman, M. A., & Notaro, P. C. (1998). Effects of family structure, family process, and father involvement on psychosocial outcomes among African American adolescents. *Family Relations, 47*(4), 331–341.

Sanchez-Hucles, J. (2000). *The First Session with African Americans: A Step-by-Step Guide.* San Francisco: Jossey-Bass Publishers.

Schiele, J. H. (1996). Afrocentricity: An emerging paradigm in social work practice. *Social Work, 41*(3), 284–294.

Schiele, J. H. (1999). E. Franklin Frazier and the interfacing of Black sociology and Black social work. *Journal of Sociology and Social Welfare, 26*(2), 105–125.

Stevens, J. W. (1997). African American female adolescent identity development: A three-dimensional perspective. *Child Welfare, 76*(1), 145–172.

Stevens, J. W. (1998). A question of values in social work practice: working with the strengths of Black adolescent females. *Families in Society: The Contemporary Journal of Human Services, 79*(3), 288–296.

Stevenson, H. C., & Renard, G. (1993). Trusting ole' wise owls. *Professional Psychology, 24*(4), 433–442.

Thrasher, S., & Anderson, G. (1988). The West Indian family: Treatment challenges. *Social Casework, 69,* 171–176.

Tolleson, J. (1997). Death and transformation: The reparative power of violence in the lives of young Black inner-city gang members. *Smith College Studies in Social Work, 67*(3), 415–431.

U.S. Census Bureau. (2001). Current Population Survey. http://www.census.gov

Williams, J. H., Stiffman, A. R., & O'Neal, J. L. (1998). Violence among urban African American youths: An analysis of environmental and behavioral risk factors. *Social Work Research, 22*(1), 3–13.

Wilson, J. W., & Constantine, M. G. (1999). Racial identity attitudes, self-concept, and perceived family cohesion in Black college students. *Journal of Black Studies, 29*(3), 354–366.

Wright, O. L., Jr., & Anderson, J. P. (1998). Clinical social work practice with urban African American families. *Families in Society: The Journal of Contemporary Human Services, 79*(2), 197–205.

Latinos

Latinos (also known as Hispanics) are one of the fastest growing populations in the United States. This rapid growth is the result of a combination of high birth and high immigration rates. Although many Latinos are recent immigrants, some trace their roots in North America back to early Spanish explorers and indigenous (i.e., Native) people. In fact, some Latinos were living in what is now the Southwest before it became part of the United States.

The populations that we think of as Latinos today are a mixture of racial groups including Europeans, Africans, and indigenous people of North and South America. The common thread that binds Latinos together is a link to Spanish colonialism. Although a small country, Spain exerted a major influence throughout the Americas. Beginning with Columbus's Spanish-sponsored voyage in 1492, Spain sent numerous explorers to investigate and colonize the "new world." A strategy of forming alliances with prominent indigenous families was part of the colonizing process. As a result, Spaniards often had children by indigenous women. As Spaniards established plantations in the Caribbean, they imported African slaves, thus introducing another distinct population into the mix that would become Latinos. African, Spanish, and indigenous people mixed to greater or lesser degrees in different parts of North and South America, thus creating a multiracial Latino or Hispanic population. Although tremendous diversity exists among the various Latino groups, they are bound by the common thread of historical link to Spain and its legacy of language and values.

In 1990, 22.4 million Latinos in the United States constituted 9% of the population. By 2000, that number had risen to 35.3 million people or 12.5% of the U.S. population. An additional 3.8 million people were counted in Puerto Rico. Latinos trace their national origin to many different countries. Of the Latino population, 58.5% are Mexican, 9.6% are Puerto Rican, 3.5% are Cuban, and 28.4% are from other Latino groups (Guzman, 2001).

Latinos are a younger population than the U.S. population as a whole. The median age for Latinos is 25.9 compared with 35.3 in the general population. Indeed, 35% of all Latinos are under age 18. Latinos are geographically concentrated with 43.5% in the West, 32.8% in the South, 14.9% in the Northeast, and 8.9% in the Midwest. The states with the largest Latino populations are California (11 million) and Texas (6.7 million). Latinos are also an urban population with 46.4% living in cities. Although 27.9% of all Latinos over age 25 are high school graduates (compared with 33.1% of the U.S. population and 34.1% of whites), education status varies substantially by national origin. In 1999, 22.8% of Latinos lived in poverty compared with 7.7% of Whites (U.S. Census Bureau, 2001).

The terms *Spanish, Hispanic, Latino,* and *Chicano* have all been used as labels to represent people in the United States who trace their history and culture back to areas colonized by Spain. Some terms are more inclusive than others. These terms have somewhat different connotations, and people often have strong feelings about which terms they prefer. Issues of identity are situated within a historical and political context and are closely tied to the choice of ethnic labels such as *Latino, Hispanic, Chicano,* and *Rican.* Although there is no consensus about the preferred ethnic label, the ability of an individual to choose his or her preferred label or to have a label imposed by others reflects the struggle between self-determination and dominance. The right to choose a name is empowering (Comas-Dias, 2001).

The term *Hispanic* was introduced in the 1970s and used by the U.S. Census Bureau for those with cultural origins in Mexico, Puerto Rico, Cuba, Central America, and other Latin American countries. This term sometimes includes Spaniards and Brazilians. Although *Hispanic* is the term officially used and created by the U.S. Census Bureau, many people do not accept this label to represent themselves (de Leon Siantz, 1996; Padilla & Salgado de Snyder, 1992).

Before the creation of the label *Hispanic,* the term *Spanish* was frequently used. This label fits people from Spain but becomes problematic when used for people from North and South America. When used to represent people who do not see themselves as European, the term *Spanish* has troubling associations with Spanish colonizers. In addition, it cannot fairly represent people from a variety of national origins.

Some people prefer the label *Latino* as more representative of the amalgam of people linked by the Spanish colonial history (de Leon Siantz, 1996). However, given the extensive diversity among the people grouped under this label, when speaking of a specific group, it is preferable to use terms based on national origin (e.g., Ecuadoran, Dominican) rather than more encompassing terms such as *Hispanic* or *Latino* (Castex, 1994). In this chapter, when more-specific terms based on national origin are not practical, the term *Latino* will be used to represent this conglomeration of cultural groups. The word *Latino* can apply both to people in general and men specifically. When referring exclusively to women, the term *Latina* is used.

This chapter gives an overview of social work with Latino people. The significant diversity that exists within and among Latino groups sets the context for discussion. The chapter presents information on knowledge, skills, and values/attitudes necessary for cultural competence and presents issues for cultural competence on micro and macro levels.

KNOWLEDGE FOR CULTURAL COMPETENCE

The knowledge needed for culturally competent social work with Latinos can be divided into four broad areas: diversity, history, culture, and contemporary realities. Diversity serves as an overarching concept that informs the other areas. The history, culture, and contemporary realities of Latinos vary according to factors such as national origin, gender, class, and immigration status.

Diversity

The Latino population is heterogeneous in nationality, race, generational status in the United States, and socioeconomic status. Cultures are constantly undergoing change, thus creating diversity between those who follow older cultural traditions and those who follow newer cultural practices (Casas, 1992; Padilla & Salgado de Snyder, 1992).

Latinos can trace their origins to 26 different countries (Castex, 1994). Differences in national origin are likely to be associated with other differences, such as racial heritage and class. For example, many Latinos with roots in Mexico and South America have significant indigenous heritage, and Native cultures may have a major influence on their values and beliefs. Conversely, Latinos with roots in the Caribbean are likely to have African cultural influences. Cuban immigrants from the late 1950s and early 1960s who fled political turmoil associated with Fidel Castro's rise to power were typically well-educated professionals who spoke English. On the other hand, many Central Americans who came to the United States in the 1970s and 1980s fleeing political strife were generally unskilled, uneducated, and did not speak English. It is important to be knowledgeable about Latino subcultures and the affect of class, ethnicity, and biculturalism on Latinos (Applewhite, 1998).

When possible, it is important to look at data on Latinos separately based on national origin. When the many Latino groups are examined together as one group, diversity tends to be obscured. It is not possible to treat Puerto Ricans, Dominicans, and Colombians as one population and develop accurate assessments and treatment plans (Kail, Zayas, & Malgady, 2000). National origin has also been found to be a meaningful variable in understanding drinking behavior. Nielsen (2000) reports the results of the 1993 National Household Survey on Drug Abuse, a probability sample of people older than 18 in the United States. Her analysis compared 620 Cubans, 2467 Mexicans, 619 Puerto Ricans, and 756 Central and South Americans. She found that among male respondents, Mexican Americans reported the most frequent and heaviest drinking and greatest prevalence of drunkenness and alcohol related problems. Cubans rated the lowest on these measures with Puerto Ricans and other Latinos in between. Fewer differences were found across groups of Latinas. Differences in drinking persist among Latino groups after controlling for predictors of adult alcohol use. There are also differences in antecedents of alcohol use and drinking problems among various Latino groups. For example, depression is a major cause of drinking for Dominican men whereas acculturation seems to directly contribute to drinking problems for Columbian men.

Latinos differ considerably in the length of time they have been in the United States. Some are new arrivals whereas others are descended from people who arrived here centuries ago. There are also distinctions between voluntary and involuntary immigrants. People who chose to relocate here are often substantially different from those who fled to the United States after being forced from their homelands because of civil war, political strife, or harsh economic realities. Those who have entered the United States without permission find themselves in a particularly hostile environment and are unlikely to seek services even when in dire need. Migration itself is a source of stress compounded by an unfamiliar environment and culture shock (Padilla & Salgado de Snyder, 1992).

Although the Spanish language is often perceived to be a common denominator across Latino groups, Latinos from different regions speak different dialects of Spanish. Indeed, some Latinos do not speak Spanish at all and instead speak only English or indigenous languages (Castex, 1994). Service providers need to be knowledgeable about Latino clients' language preference and dialects, as well as speech and communication patterns (Applewhite, 1998).

Level of ability/disability is also something that varies among Latino people. The Latino population with disabilities is growing faster than their non-Latino peers. Persons with disabilities currently account for 15.3% of the Latino population in the United States. Information on Latinos with disabilities is limited because they are classified as White on many health surveys. In general, however, Latinos with disabilities are likely to wait longer as applicants for services. Once they have received a referral, they are more likely to be ineligible and are significantly less likely to receive academic training than non-Latinos. Structural discrimination results in Latinos with disabilities being more frequently unemployed, earning less money or in part time jobs (Zea, Belgrave, Garcia, & Quezada, 1997).

Cultural factors play a significant role in how a disability is perceived and experienced. The strong value placed on family may result in supportive attitudes and behaviors toward individuals with disabilities. The value of interdependence may support those adapting to a disabled status, especially when professional rehabilitation services are not readily available. The value of machismo, however, may foster denial of a disability or encourage returning to work too soon. Latino men may feel threatened by a loss of authority, yet they are not as likely as Whites to feel threatened by becoming financially dependent. The female role that includes tolerating adversity is compatible with the onset of disability, but passive resignation may inhibit women from benefiting from rehabilitation programs. Values of respect and deference to authority may affect the relationship with service providers and may disempower the client. The cause of a disability may be assumed to be supernatural, natural, or medical. Beliefs about whether a disability is changeable are also influenced by culture. This can lead to acceptance but inhibit rehabilitation. Immigrants and refugees who escape political violence may lack key family supports for coping with a disability (Zea et al., 1997).

Despite vast diversity, some common concerns are shared among many Latino people, particularly their social and health status. The Latino population can be described as growing, young, and poor. Latinos typically have large families and are likely to have limited health insurance and inadequate access to medical care (de Leon Siantz, 1996).

History

Understanding Latinos requires knowledge of the sociohistorical context of each particular group (Padilla & Salgado de Snyder, 1992). A brief overview of key points in the history of the largest Latino groups in the United States will assist helping professionals to understand the context of Latino clients.

Mexican Americans   Although most of the Mexican American population is a product of 20th-century immigration, the first Mexicans in the United States were not immigrants but, rather, were incorporated into the United States through military conquest and the annexation of an area that included parts of present day California, Arizona, New Mexico, Colorado, and Texas (Melendez, Rodriquez, & Figueroa, 1991). In 1848, the Treaty of Guadalupe Hidalgo led to Mexico ceding approximately half its territory to the United States. This area was populated by 75,000 Mexicans, as well as by many indigenous people (Gomez, 1992). Subsequently, most Mexicans that came to the United States were attracted by U.S. economic expansion compounded by Mexican political instability. Many Mexican immigrants have historically supplied cheap labor for agricultural production. Mexican immigration is characterized by fluctuating population flows that peak during periods of high labor demand in the United States and ebb when social policies have called for Mexicans to be forcibly returned to Mexico (Morales & Bonilla, 1993). Mexican Americans have responded to unjust policies and difficult living conditions in the United States by creating numerous advocacy and civil rights organizations (Marquez & Jennings, 2000).

Puerto Ricans   Puerto Ricans, the second largest Latino group in the United States, reside primarily in the Northeast. Puerto Rico has a long history of involvement with the United States. In 1898, Puerto Rico became a U.S. possession. In 1917, Puerto Ricans became U.S. citizens. By 1952, Puerto Rico had become a semiautonomous commonwealth. Although the dependent relationship between the United States and Puerto Rico led to citizenship for Puerto Ricans, those residing on the island of Puerto Rico cannot vote for the president and have no representation in the U.S. Congress because Puerto Rico is not a state (Morales & Bonilla, 1993). The political connections between the United States and Puerto Rico have made migration between the island and the mainland United States simple. Movements back and forth are common. Puerto Ricans have been active in transforming urban structures through their involvement in various social movements (Marquez & Jennings, 2000).

Cubans   The relationship between Cuba and the United States is highly political. Before the Cuban revolution of 1959, Cuba and the United States had close ties and Cuba was a common vacation spot for the American elite. In the wake of Fidel Castro's rise to power, many Cuban, middle-class, English-speaking professionals were welcomed to the United States as refugees. They adjusted easily to life in the United States, and today these Cuban-Americans have more socioeconomic characteristics in common with White Americans than with other Latino groups (Melendez et al., 1991). A subsequent wave of poorer, less-skilled refugees began arriving in the early 1980s. There was a significant public outcry and fear that this second wave of Cuban refugees consisted primarily of undesirable mental patients and prisoners expelled from Cuba by Castro (Morales & Bonilla, 1993). This second wave consisted primarily of men with African heritage. The United States opened its doors to both waves of Cuban refugees because of significant political differences with Castro's regime; yet the first wave of refugees received a warmer welcome because they were perceived to be similar to middle-class Americans in race, class, education, and values. The second wave of refugees was perceived as more threatening and difficult to assimilate.

Central Americans   During the 1970s, political instability in many Central American countries led many people to flee their homelands and seek safety in the United States (Morales & Bonilla, 1993). By definition, a refugee is someone fleeing persecution. Many Americans, however, perceived these migrants to be seeking entry to the United States for economic reasons. Thus, they are often viewed as undeserving of refugee status with its protections and benefits. Because of the substantial difficulty many Central Americans had proving their refugee claims, some entered the United States clandestinely and continue to live in the United States without the benefits of legal status. Today, some continue to be assisted by clergy, helping professionals, and a committed network of volunteers in the underground sanctuary movement. Others are exploited by unscrupulous smugglers, known as coyotes, who assist them in entering the United States illegally.

Culture

Latino cultures developed as a blend of indigenous, African, and Spanish cultures. These foundations can be seen to a greater or lesser extent in the various Latino populations. For example, strong elements of indigenous Nahuatl values continue to form the core of Chicano or Mexican American culture. A study of Chicanos and Whites found cohesiveness among Chicanos regarding fundamental values and beliefs regardless of age, gender, generation, or level of acculturation. This finding contrasts with widely held assumptions about acculturation and loss of culture as a primary identity after generations in the United States (Ordaz & De Anda, 1996). Key facets of Latino cultures include the value of interconnectedness, highly differentiated gender roles, and an emphasis on spirituality.

Interconnectedness Interconnectedness and interdependence, especially within the family, are highly valued by Latinos. Close, personal contact among people (*personalismo*) is highly valued. Interdependence is manifested in the value of familism or *familismo*. An individual's needs are generally subordinate to the collective. Family can provide lifelong intergenerational support and can be an important buffer against stress when adjusting to a new community that may be hostile and rejecting (Low & Organista, 2000).

The value of interdependence is highlighted by the emphasis placed on close family ties and a strong allegiance to the family. For example, honoring parents is an important value that takes precedence over other considerations (Galan, 1985). In American culture, a young adult displays maturity and responsibility by living independently, but in Latino communities, such behavior would be viewed as a selfish disregard of familial responsibility. Among Latinos, maturity and responsibility is often demonstrated by the young adult remaining in the parents' household and contributing to the support of the family (De Anda, 1984). Each member has responsibility for the well-being of the family.

The value of interdependence and strong connections to others can be used as motivating factors to encourage people to seek help. For example, Latinos' entry into substance-abuse treatment is largely motivated by a desire to improve relationships with or regain custody of children (Amaro, Nieves, Johannes, & Cabeza, 1999).

Although most social relationships have positive outcomes, excessive interdependence or lack of boundaries can be problematic. Some Latinos believe that people have the power to affect others in excessive or negative ways. For example, jealousy or over-admiration can result in a malady known as the evil eye. Envy, anger, and distrust can lead to accusations of witchcraft. Extreme interdependence makes an individual vulnerable to external, negative influences (Koss-Chioino, 1999).

Gender Roles Latino families often have highly structured gender roles. There are clear and distinct expectations for men and women. Men are expected to be strong, and women are expected to be submissive to male authority. Although distinct gender roles exist, it is important to recognize that not all Latinos fit these roles to the same extent. For example, Latinas are often stereotyped as passive and submissive, but many changes have taken place in marriages and families in the last decade. Many Latinas now work outside the home and may wield decision-making power about family finances. It is important to understand evolving gender roles within Latino families (Padilla & Salgado de Snyder, 1992).

Machismo is a culturally grounded expression of masculinity found in Latino cultures. Machismo includes an emphasis on self-respect and responsibility to provide and protect the family. Non-Latinos, however, have often focused on the negative, stereotypical aspects of machismo, such as dominance, aggression, and oppressive behavior toward women and children (Torres, 1998). Indeed, the stereotypical hypermasculine behavior, often associated with machismo, may be a backlash because of, or exacerbated by, oppression associated with racism and poverty in the United States (Mayo, 1997). A true understanding of the value of machismo can only be achieved when it is examined within a contemporary social, political, and economic context. For example,

> Puerto Rican men are often told that their culture, attitudes, and behavior are irredeemably sexist. . . . In truth, this perspective is secondary to the fact that the dominant culture does not permit them to explore adaptive options. They are not, for example, given access to economic opportunities equal to those of women in their culture; the result is a reversal of traditional gender roles in which Puerto Rican women become the primary source of income and achieve greater levels of economic self-sufficiency than the men. It is hardly surprising that, challenged at the very core of their traditional masculinity, many Puerto Rican men feel vulnerable and off balance, expressing dissatisfaction, discontent, and confusion, while struggling for emotional survival. (Torres, 1998, p. 17)

Latinas typically play a central role in the family that involves nurturing, caring, mediating conflicts, and preventing confrontations. This role varies depending on the larger context of acculturation and acceptance of modern gender roles. A Latina's sense of self is realized through connection to family, community, and the universe (Low & Organista, 2000). Non-Latinos often misinterpret this sense of self: "White feminists and mental health workers looking through the lens of the dominant culture may pathologize Latinas' subjugation of their needs to those of the family, thereby missing the ways that their role within the family contributes to both their survival and sense of security (e.g., self-esteem enhancing, central role in ministering to health and emotional problems of family members)" (Low & Organista, 2000, p. 140).

The Latina gender role is often referred to as Marianismo, the desire to emulate the self-sacrificing role played by the Virgin Mary in Catholic tradition. Marianismo is connected to a view of motherhood as sacred. In this role, women gain respect and power. There is a strong division between the concepts of a lady deserving protection and support and a prostitute to be outcast. These divisions are critical for victims of sexual assault. Hembrismo refers to a woman who can display strength, perseverance, and survival and can be a positive alternative to Marianismo. Sometimes hembrismo is used pejoratively for women who are too independent, but Latina feminists are reclaiming this term as relevant for contemporary gender roles in a bicultural context (Low & Organista, 2000).

Sometimes rigid gender roles in Latino families lead to dissatisfaction being expressed in culturally specific ways. The complaint pattern of depressed women in Puerto Rico differs in symptom frequency and intensity from standard psychiatric formulations (Koss-Chioino, 1999). *Ataques de Nervios* is a physical manifestation of strong emotions in Puerto Rican women and some other Latinas that occurs under particularly stressful psychological and social conditions. An *ataque* can sometimes appear similar to a fainting spell or seizure. Cultural and religious values discourage expressions of anger, assertiveness, and aggression, so *ataques* are a culturally acceptable way for women to vent strong feelings. A critical factor in distinguishing between those who suffer *ataques* and those who don't may be an ability to control anger (Rivera-Arzola & Ramos-Grenier, 1997).

Spirituality Spirituality has a fundamental shaping influence on the lives of many Latinos. Catholicism is a defining force of family and gender roles for Latino people (Acevedo, 2000; Ortiz-Torres, Serrano-Garcia, & Torres-Burgos, 2000). Latino Catholicism revolves around the concepts of life and death. This fatalistic belief system emphasizes that God will provide. There is a pervading sense that much of what happens is beyond an individual's personal control.

Most Latinos are Roman Catholic, but many espouse beliefs and practices influenced by indigenous and African belief systems such as Santeria among Cubans and Espiritismo among Puerto Ricans (Castex, 1994). Catholic saints often take on aspects of African or indigenous deities in syncretized or blended belief systems that are common in Latino communities across the country. Many people who espouse these belief systems continue to regard themselves as Catholics (Gann & Duignan, 1986).

Folk healers grounded in these syncretic belief systems play valuable roles in many Latino communities (Colon, 1996). Syncretic religions often function as mental health systems to help Latinos in the United States cope with alien environments. Active participation in these belief systems can be an important strength and should not be taken as a sign of psychological disturbance (Comas-Diaz, 1981; Queralt, 1984). Spirituality serves as a coping mechanism and support for many Latino people (Galvan, 1999; Paulino, 1998).

Contemporary Realities

It is important for helping professionals to have a clear understanding of the contemporary realities of Latino people, including extended family networks, social problems, strengths, issues based on immigration status, and issues of migrant workers.

Extended Family Networks   Latino families are typically large, intergenerational, and interdependent, and offer an important source of support to their members (Applewhite, 1998; Colon, 1996; Cox & Monk, 1993; Lopez, 1999). Extended family ties are highly valued and serve as a source of pride and security. Family networks may include grandparents, aunts, uncles, distant relatives, and fictive kin, that is, people tied to a family by custom through a mutual support network called *compadrazgo* (Lopez, 1999). The *compadrazgo* system can be a critical source of social and concrete support for Latinos who have limited access to formal support channels because of undocumented status, language, or cultural barriers. This kinship network serves as a resource for economic assistance, encouragement, and support. The *compadrazgo* system continues to be an important resource even among acculturated Latinos who do not follow common Latino religious practices or speak Spanish (Lopez, 1999).

The emphasis on respect and responsibility to family members often leads to elderly adults both being cared for and taking on caregiving responsibilities within the family. The elderly are often cared for within the family rather than through formal social services. When nursing homes are used, family members often continue to fulfill supportive caregiving responsibilities (Kolb, 1999). Likewise, Latino grandparents often take on roles in raising children (Burnette, 1999). Caregiving responsibilities generally fall to women in Latino families. Many Latinas experience increasingly complex roles as they age because of multigenerational family structures and the *compadrazgo* system (Lopez, 1999).

Social Problems   How problems are expressed is influenced by cultural factors. Latino culture encourages positive emotional expressions and discourages expression of anger and conflict, particularly for women. Complaining (including somatic complaints) can be a way to express repressed feelings of anger and frustration.

Latinas experience a high comorbidity of childhood abuse, substance abuse, mental health issues, and health problems (Amaro et al., 1999). Clearly, childhood abuse has serious implications for future well-being. For Latinas, sexual assault is also related to class issues. Poverty makes it difficult to escape dangerous neighborhoods, jobs, and individuals. The availability of services is related to an individual's class and influences whether needed assistance is likely to be available (Low & Organista, 2000).

Most Latinas live within a bicultural reality and view sexual assault as occurring within traditional Latino and modern American gender role systems. Traditional Latino gender roles facilitate self-blame for victims of sexual assault. The result of rigid application of traditional gender roles is shame and blame that prevent women from talking about assault with family and community members (Low & Organista, 2000).

Socioeconomic issues are often pressing concerns for Latinos. Most Latinos live in urban areas and hold unskilled or semiskilled jobs. Latinos in general, and youth in particular, are at high risk for physical and psychological problems

(Padilla & Salgado de Snyder, 1992) but they often encounter difficulty accessing adequate services. Barriers to care for Latino clients include language, discrimination, poverty, unemployment, and lack of knowledge of systems. Some Latinos do not have documentation that permits them to live or work in the United States, thus hindering their efforts to seek services in times of need. These barriers to services may in turn influence self-esteem and contribute to family dysfunction and abusive situations (Holland & Courtney, 1998).

Strengths Professional literature on Latinos usually focuses on socioeconomic challenges and ignores community strengths. Several key strengths have already been mentioned including strong supportive extended family and community networks, strong spiritual belief systems that serve as supports in everyday life as well as in times of crisis, and the value placed on human beings and personal interactions (*personalismo*).

Another important strength is cultural and community pride as expressed through the arts. For example, murals can serve important functions for youth. Communities can "claim" buildings as their own and transform space by painting murals. Messages in graffiti art reflect struggles of urban living and oppression. These messages are symbols of cultural pride. Religious and spiritual symbols in murals depict a community's past and hopes for the future. Murals also serve as memorials to dead community members and unrecognized heroes. Youth learn many skills through mural projects, including teamwork, communication, good work habits, and community participation (Delgado & Barton, 1998). This type of artistic expression can be an important way to reclaim blighted neighborhoods and reassert cultural pride.

Latino communities have also demonstrated considerable strength in the development of social movements in response to adversity (Marquez & Jennings, 2000). The Chicano movement in the 1960s and 1970s grew on a rising tide of activism generated by the larger civil rights movement. Likewise, Puerto Ricans became involved in struggles for social justice. Through these movements, Latinos demanded better working conditions, more access to education, and more equitable immigration policies.

Immigration Status Latinos, like other populations in the United States, possess a variety of legal statuses. Some are citizens whose families have been in the United States for generations, some are resident aliens who possess green cards and virtually all the rights of citizens, others are here on student visas, some arrive as refugees, some have special status through farmworker programs, and some do not have legal status in the United States.

Regardless of actual legal status, many Latinos face regular encounters in which they are presumed to be foreigners and sometimes presumed to be in the United States illegally. Such presumptions of status are based on racism and xenophobia (fear of foreigners). In 1986, the United States passed the Immigration Reform and Control Act (IRCA), which was designed to, among other things, sanction employers who hired workers without legal status to work in the United States. One widespread, unintended consequence of the

Act was to increase discrimination against people who looked or sounded foreign. For example, numerous employers were found guilty of refusing to hire Puerto Rican applicants who were unable to produce green cards during interviews. As citizens, Puerto Ricans could not possibly have green cards (identification that documents resident alien status).

Migrant Farm Workers   Some Latinos work as migrant farm workers. This population often consists of high numbers of immigrants recruited to the United States under programs that give them unique legal status so they can meet the needs of large agricultural producers.

Social workers need to be aware that Latino migrant workers may have special needs. Migrant farm workers are by necessity a highly mobile population that must relocate constantly to follow the seasonal harvesting of crops (Hibbeln, 1996). Although adequate data is scarce, Latino farmworkers tend to be poor, young men with limited education, limited English skills, and families to support. They face chronic seasonal unemployment, and because of their unique legal status, they are usually excluded totally or partially from federal laws that protect other workers including laws that restrict child labor. Children as young as 10 can legally work in the fields. Migrant workers face poor housing, limited access to medical care and a nomadic lifestyle that poses health problems. Malnutrition is a big problem. Most migrant farm workers qualify for food stamps but accessibility is too complex. Migrant farm workers experience hazardous working conditions, including exposure to pesticides. Lack of insurance and limited English proficiency serve as barriers to care (Hibbeln, 1996).

SKILLS FOR CULTURAL COMPETENCE

Helping professionals who work with Latinos need to possess a variety of basic skills. For example, cognitive behavioral approaches are relatively culture free or more open to cultural adaptation than most theoretical frameworks are; thus, cognitive approaches are likely to be appropriate with Latino clients (Low & Organista, 2000). A few skills are particularly important when working with Latino clients: language skills, the ability to recognize and confront bias, and the ability to conduct a culturally meaningful assessment.

Engaging

Latino clients may be reluctant to disclose intimate information to a helping professional who is perceived to represent an impersonal government affiliated office or agency. Historical interactions between Latinos and representatives of the dominant society such as helping professionals, as well as the precarious living circumstances of many Latinos, lead to fear and mistrust (Casas, 1992). Helping professionals can counteract these fears and generate trust using the Latino value of *personalismo*. Often establishing a connection on a human level will facilitate establishing a professional connection. A Latino client who asks a helping professional about his or her family is often trying to connect with the professional as a person rather than trying to be intrusive. Although the professional relationship must remain distinct from a personal relationship, when working with Latino clients, helping professionals may have more success engaging clients if they use some self-disclosure.

Awareness of clients' help-seeking behavior can also be an important element in engaging. An ethnographic study of battered Mexican immigrant women revealed that participants' attitudes about help seeking were more influenced by cultural factors such as gender roles and familism than by psychosocial stressors such as immigrant status and financial dependency (Acevedo, 2000).

Concern for the welfare of children can be a primary motivation for women seeking to leave abusive relationships. Study participants often held misconceptions about services that prevented them from seeking help. Some feared that seeking help would result in the loss of their children, or they did not know that help was available for violent relationships. Agency services were perceived as punishing or ineffective (Acevedo, 2000). Addressing misconceptions about the helping process is a key to effective outreach and engaging Latino clients.

Assessing

It is important to avoid stereotypes when conducting assessments. For example, although much has been written about rigid gender roles in Latino cultures, practitioners must be open to examining the reality of their clients' lives, even when this does not conform to the helping professional's preconceived ideas. For example, Latino men may function in caregiving roles. Puerto Rican men as caring fathers, husbands, support providers, and caregivers for the elderly contradicts stereotypes of distant men obsessed with machismo (Delgado & Tennstedt, 1997).

Helping professionals must be skilled in incorporating cultural factors into the assessment process (Applewhite, 1998). The cultural context influences how emotional distress is expressed and can be interpreted. Culturally based behaviors based on gender roles and expectations must also be considered (Koss-Chioino, 1999). If culture is not considered, culturally appropriate behavior may be labeled pathological. For example, helping professionals who are unfamiliar with Latino spiritual beliefs may mistakenly label a client's report of a conversation held with a deceased family member as a sign of psychiatric disturbance.

Using standardized assessment tools not normed for Latinos creates problems of reliability and validity. It is unclear whether such tools are capable of generating consistent, accurate results. Incorporating cultural variables is widely recommended as part of a meaningful assessment (Cuellar, 1998). Numerous instruments have been developed to assess cultural identity in Latino populations. These instruments typically examine issues such as language, food, and friendship preferences as ways of measuring cultural identity.

Latino-specific assessment tools include the Children's Ethnic Identity Questionnaire. This instrument assesses acculturation in children of Mexican descent, ages 3½ to 10, but its creators caution that it may be inappropriate for other Latino children (Bernal & Knight, 1997). Other Latino-specific instruments that assess cultural identity include the Measure of Acculturation for Chicano Adolescents, the Bilingualism/Multiculturalism Experience Inventory, the Acculturation Rating Scale for Mexican Americans, and the Behavioral Acculturation Scale (Baron & Constantine, 1997).

Helping professionals must closely examine the theoretical assumptions inherent in instruments that measure cultural identity or acculturation before incorporating these instruments in their work. Most cultural assessment tools are based on assumptions of a linear model of cultural identity, yet contemporary theories have begun to shift away from linear models.

Intervening

Most theories and models do not incorporate Latino-specific considerations. The Western values embedded in many counseling models may conflict with the values of Latino clients. For example, the emphasis on individuality and independence rather than interdependence with family and community is likely to lead practitioners to view Latino clients from a deficit perspective and attempt to change some of their culturally based values and strengths. Likewise, emphasizing self-determination when many Latino clients value deference to authority is likely to cause conflicts or lead to ineffective work. Different communication styles may also inhibit a productive social work relationship. A helping professional who emphasizes open, direct communication and emotional expressiveness may have difficulty interacting with Latino clients who value indirect, tactful communication, discretion, and emotional restraint, especially with anger (Low & Organista, 2000).

When working with Latino clients, listening in a holistic, nonjudgmental way is crucial. "The patients I see yearn to tell their story, historia, and they are hurting to be heard, aching to be listened to. They are often frustrated by being treated, or should I say mistreated, as parts" (Rojas, 1996, p. 224). After listening to a client's story for 20 minutes, it is easy to ask "what would you like to get out of this visit today?" and have the client prioritize areas for work. This, however, is likely to rush the Latino client. The willingness to listen in a thoughtful and patient way is crucial. Truly listening to a Latino client cannot be rushed and often takes significantly longer than 20 minutes before you summarize and set priority areas for work.

It is important to work with the client's agenda rather than have the helping professional impose his or her own ideas about what would be helpful. Latinas in abusive relationships often want to help their partners stop battering and preserve the family. Before you can honor these priorities, however, services must be available for batterers (Acevedo, 2000). To be responsive to Latina clients, helping professionals must be willing to accept the clients' priorities and goals as valid.

Some Latino clients have limited ability to speak English, thus skills in speaking Spanish or an indigenous language may be necessary (Applewhite, 1998). The ability to speak to a Latino client in the language that he or she is most comfortable in can be a key element in both outreach and engaging activities. Speaking in the client's language demonstrates the helping professional's willingness to take needed steps to effectively help the client.

There is significant pressure for Latinos to speak English, however, learning English may be an issue charged with sociopolitical overtones rather than simply mastering a skill. Ambivalent feelings about language may be closely associated with cultural identity and sense of self. What initially appears as resistance to learning English may instead be a symptom of a deeper conflict or fear of losing cultural identity or becoming associated with the dominant society (Paulino, 1998).

Helping professionals who do not speak Spanish may need to use interpreters during interactions with clients but using an additional person in interactions often distorts communication. It is an ethical imperative and often a legal mandate that clients have access to services in a language they can understand. Communication is more efficient and effective if the helping professional possesses the ability to speak the client's language to avoid the necessity of working through an interpreter.

Latinos face many forms of discrimination including that based on immigration status (or presumed status), accent, and race. Indeed, since 1992 the court system has recognized the legitimacy of discrimination based on accent (Sethi, 1994). Helping professionals must be able to recognize the affect of discrimination on their Latino clients and use their advocacy skills to further both micro- and macro-level change.

Helping professionals must also recognize racial and ethnic biases in their own organizations and practice settings. They must be skilled in confronting racism and discrimination experienced by many Latinos. Recognizing bias includes the ability to understand the ways that professional values, knowledge, and skills may clash with those of Latinos in a helping relationship (Applewhite, 1998). For example, empowering a client to become more independent from his or her family may conflict with a Latino client's values of interdependence.

VALUES/ATTITUDES FOR CULTURAL COMPETENCE

The values and attitudes that helping professionals bring to their work are an integral part of culturally competent practice. Key values that have particular relevance for working with Latino clients include valuing diversity, respecting extended family and natural support networks, respecting traditional beliefs and spirituality, and being open-minded and nonjudgmental.

It is important that helping professionals value cultural diversity and cultural integrity with a genuine and open appreciation of inter- and intragroup differences among Latinos (Applewhite, 1998). Latino cultures are grounded in a rich heritage and are not in any way inferior to the dominant society. Helping professionals cannot automatically assume that Latino clients need assistance assimilating into the dominant society. When Latino clients present problems of cultural fit, the helping professional can help them examine a variety of options rather than assume that clients must conform to dominant society standards to achieve a comfortable niche. Social workers need to recognize the significant sociopolitical dimensions associated with trying to eliminate an accent, learn English, or other aspects of fitting into American society. There is a strong push by society to conform to certain standards of language and behavior. A social worker who values diversity needs to ensure that he or she is not pushing the client toward assimilation and conformity but, rather, recognizes the legitimacy and value inherent in the client and his or her culture.

Helping professionals must demonstrate respect for the cultural resources and natural support systems Latinos use in problem solving. Respect includes valuing the strength of the nuclear and extended family and fictive kin, and the role Latino clients assume in this family constellation (Applewhite, 1998). A helping professional who does not respect Latino support networks might view Latino families as too large or having diffuse boundaries, thus the professional may miss the significant resources provided through these networks.

It is important that helping professionals respect the traditional beliefs, folk methods, and spiritual roles of Latinos in the folk healing process (Applewhite, 1998). A holistic approach that includes the spiritual as well as the physical and mental is important in working with Latino clients. A belief in the importance of harmony of body, mind, and spirit is found at the heart of folk healing practices such as Mexican Curanderismo (Rojas, 1996).

Respecting Latino spirituality may be challenging for helping professionals who misunderstand or feel threatened by belief systems that vary from their own. Helping professionals need to examine their feelings about different spiritual belief systems. Often Latino belief systems are stereotyped and distorted by the media in ways that are frightening to people unfamiliar with these spiritualities. A helping professional who values and respects diverse belief systems can begin to recognize and put aside stereotypical perspectives while educating himself or herself about these belief systems.

Being open-minded and nonjudgmental are key values associated with culturally competent helping; however, it is often difficult for helping professionals to espouse these values when clients display beliefs, values, and lifestyles that appear vastly different from those of the helper. For instance, a feminist social worker may have difficulty being nonjudgmental about rigid gender roles found in many Latino families. As part of remaining open-minded, helping professionals must strive to avoid stereotyping and actively seek to learn from clients about their values and priorities.

Helping professionals need to be open-minded about clients' choices and priorities, especially when they differ from those held by helping professionals. For example, "the Spiritist approach to treating depression distances angry feelings, displacing them onto spirit causes and images, thus avoiding their direct expression. This goes against the direction of the type of treatments advocated by feminist therapists because it encompasses an acceptance of the status quo" (Koss-Chioino, 1999, p. 347). Treatment that involves a spiritual aspect may be difficult for helping professionals to accept with an open mind if spirituality is not something they are comfortable including in their work or if the way they include spirituality is significantly different from indigenous Latino practices.

CASE EXAMPLE

Consuelo Ramirez is a Dominican immigrant who came to the United States five years ago with her husband and three children. Her children have been attending an after-school program at the multiservice, community-based agency where Annie Banks is employed as a family counselor. Recently, Consuelo disclosed to one of the staff in the after-school program that she is concerned about her daughter becoming too Americanized and wanting to act like her peers rather than behaving in a way Consuelo and her husband think is appropriate for a 14-year-old girl. The case has been referred to Annie to try to engage the family in counseling, but she is unsure how to proceed. Annie wonders, (1) What is the best way to connect with this family? (2) How might gender roles and expectations (in both the United States and the Dominican Republic) be meaningful issues in work with this family? (3) Are the issues in this case likely to be culture specific? Are they, perhaps, related to differential acculturation in this immigrant family? Or, are they just standard familial struggles around adolescent development?

As Annie proceeds with the case, she could consider the following:

- Engaging Latinos is often most effective when helping professionals recognize and use the value of *personalismo*. Self-disclosure can be a good way to establish the foundation for a meaningful helping relationship.
- Clients may have misconceptions about the helping process. Annie should be clear with the family about what family counseling is all about and allow the family to have maximum input into the goals of the work.
- Annie can seek out information on Dominican culture and how gender roles may function within this context. Asking family members about what they see as appropriate roles and expectations is a good source of information that is not skewed by stereotypes.
- Annie may want to seek consultation from a culturally competent supervisor or consultant to help her sort out whether issues are cultural, based on differential acculturation, or developmental.

CULTURAL COMPETENCE IN SOCIAL POLICIES

Policies often have a differential affect on various cultural populations. The result of the Immigration Reform and Control Act of 1986 was increased discrimination against many people, but the unintended consequences of this Act had a disproportionate impact on Latino people. Likewise, the refugee and asylum determination policies of the 1970s and 1980s were applied differently to Latinos than to other applicants. In a suit brought by the American Baptist Churches, it was determined that Central Americans applying for asylum status were virtually always denied. Denial of Central Americans was the norm, even when they presented more supporting evidence than did refugees from other parts of the world, particularly those from Southeast Asia. The U.S. District Court for Northern California mandated reexamination of all claims for asylum brought by Central American applicants in the mid-1980s (*American Baptist Churches, et al., plaintiffs, v. Richard Thornburgh, et al., defendants*, 760 F. Supp. 796; N. Dist. CA, 1991).

Many of the policies that are particularly meaningful for Latinos are related to immigration status or the presumption of foreignness. In 1994, Californians voted on Proposition 187, a measure designed to restrict Latinos and other immigrants without legal status in the United States from many benefits and services, such as the right to a public school education, that had previously been guaranteed by the U.S. Supreme Court (Torres-Gil & Kuo, 1998). This conservative measure passed and was seen as a harbinger of things to come for the rest of the nation. Ultimately, many of the provisions of Proposition 187 were deemed unconstitutional, but the sentiments that led California voters to support such a measure are still present and influence all interactions with Latinos (Mailman, 1995).

A similar reactionary philosophy permeates the English-only movement (Kiang, 1994). Some states have debated making English their official language. This movement is contrary to notions of cultural pluralism and respect for diversity and would force assimilation on Latinos and other people who seek to maintain their languages.

CULTURAL COMPETENCE IN SOCIAL AGENCIES

Simply offering services in Spanish or having bilingual interpreters available does not make a program culturally competent. Programs should be designed from a Latino cultural base (Ordaz & De Anda, 1996). For example, Amaro, Nieves, Johannes, and Cabeza (1999) describe the creation of a 12-month, culture/gender-specific residential substance abuse treatment program for Latinas and their children

Program planners must be knowledgeable about general cultural dynamics and the local community before they can develop relevant programs. Planners must be involved with community leaders and actively cultivate and promote partnerships. Using Latino lay people in roles such as health educators can be an effective outreach mechanism (Castro, Coe, Gutierres, & Saenz, 1996).

In evaluating agency services for cultural competence, evaluators can explore: (1) What is the racial/ethnic/national makeup of the Latino community being served? (2) How do people from different Latino subgroups differ from one another? How are they the same? (3) What is the history of the targeted Latino subgroup? (4) If the subgroup is composed of immigrants, did they leave their homelands voluntarily or involuntarily? (5) If recent immigrants constitute a large proportion of the targeted Latino community, what is the likelihood that they are in the United States without legal authorization? (6) How grounded is the targeted population in its cultural traditions? (Casas, 1992).

COMMUNITY INTERVENTIONS

Macro practice requires understanding the dynamics of community life, the contributions of mainstream and ethnic agencies, and the roles that Latinos play in their communities. Macro practice should engage the practitioner and community members in a mutual process at all levels, including problem identification, assessment, planning, goal setting, and implementation. Latino community members can serve as cultural guides and mentors. This will help empower them and foster self-determination. Macro work should consider strengths and weaknesses in the community, community leadership, and readiness for change (Applewhite, 1998).

In particular, helping professionals can use community-organizing skills to address discrimination and xenophobia. They can play a role in assisting grassroots organizations such as farmworkers' collectives and other advocacy organizations as they strive for just working and living conditions. Community interventions can also provide important support to bilingual and bicultural education and services when such programs and policies are threatened in an increasingly conservative political climate.

CONCLUSION

Latinos are a diverse population comprising people with roots in 26 different countries. Latinos trace their heritage, in varying degrees, to Spanish colonizers, indigenous people of the Americas, and enslaved Africans. Although immigration continues to fuel the growth of the Latino population, many Latinos, particularly Puerto Ricans and some Mexican Americans, come from families who have been citizens for generations. The presumption of foreignness, accompanying xenophobia, and negative stereotypes reinforce many social problems faced by this population. Social workers can recognize the strengths and resources of this diverse population and can use advocacy skills to confront the oppression faced by many Latinos.

Exercises

Exercise #1: Examining contemporary social policies

Examine the decision in the American Baptist Churches case (*American Baptist Churches, et al., plaintiffs, v. Richard Thornburgh, et al., defendants,* 760 F. Supp. 796; N. Dist. CA, 1991). Why were Central American asylum seekers treated differently than Southeast Asian refugee claimants were? Discuss how the attitudes about Latinos identified in this case may influence contemporary social policies.

Exercise #2: Reflecting on spiritual beliefs

Read at least three articles on syncretic Latino religious beliefs and practices such as Espiritismo, Curanderismo, and Santeria. Write a brief overview of one of these belief systems. Reflect on your own spiritual beliefs and answer the following questions: (1) In what ways is this belief system similar to my own? (2) In what ways is this belief system different from my own? (3) How might working with a client who had this type of belief system be difficult for me? (4) How might working with a client who had this type of belief system be easy for me?

Exercise #3 : Respecting different cultural contexts and value systems

Latina feminists have attempted to reshape traditional gender roles in ways that are supportive and nurturing for Latinas who experience domestic violence or sexual assault. If you had a Latina client who was in an abusive relationship but did not want to leave her partner, how could you go about helping her while showing respect for her cultural context and value system?

Additional Resources

Guzman, B. (2001). *The Hispanic Population: 2000*. U.S. Census Bureau. This report summarizes current census data on the Latino population. Information includes geographic locations, educational achievement, occupational distributions, and other basic demographic information. National origin of the largest Latino populations is presented.

Katz, S.R. (1997). Presumed guilty: How schools criminalize Latino youth. *Social Justice, 24*(4), 77–95. This article reports the results of a qualitative study of Latino youth in an urban school setting. The article poignantly recounts how stereotypes held by teachers ultimately shape their students and lead to self-fulfilling prophecies of involvement with drugs and crime. Helping professionals can clearly see the impact of culturally biased programs and institutions in this moving article.

Rodriguez, L.T. (1993). *Always Running, La Vida Loca: Gang Days in L.A.* New York: Simon & Schuster. This biography tells the story of a Mexican boy who arrives in the United States with his family. The narrative depicts how the boy's experiences with racism, xenophobia, and urban poverty lead him to become involved in a gang. The author recorded his experiences in this book when he saw his son being pulled in a similar direction. This first-person account can assist helping professionals understand the experiences of young Latino men and the process of disengaging from positive influences.

Torres, S. (1996). *Hispanic Voices: Hispanic Health Educators Speak Out*. New York: National League for Nursing Press. In this edited volume, Latino helping professionals share their perspectives on current issues among Latino people. A variety of topics are addressed including children, migrant workers, and women's spiritual well-being.

References

Acevedo, M. J. (2000). Battered immigrant Mexican women's perspectives regarding abuse and help-seeking. *Journal of Multicultural Social Work, 8*(3/4), 243–282.

Amaro, H., Nieves, R., Johannes, S. W., & Cabeza, N. M. L. (1999). Substance abuse treatment: Critical issues and challenges in the treatment of Latina women. *Hispanic Journal of Behavioral Sciences, 21*(3), 266–282.

American Baptist Churches, et al., plaintiffs, v. Richard Thornburgh, et al., defendants, 760 F. Supp. 796; N. Dist. CA, 1991.

Applewhite, S. L. (1998). Culturally competent practice with elderly Latinos. *Journal of Gerontological Social Work, 30*(1/2), 1–15.

Baron, A., & Constantine, M. G. (1997). A conceptual framework for conducting psychotherapy with Mexican American college students. In J. G. Garcia & M. C. Zea (Eds.), Psychological Interventions and Research with Latino Populations. Boston: Allyn & Bacon, 108–124.

Bernal, M. E., & Knight, G. P. (1997). Ethnic identity of Latino children. In J. G. Garcia & M. C. Zea (Eds.), Psychological Interventions and Research with Latino Populations. Boston: Allyn & Bacon, 15–38.

Burnette, D. (1999). Custodial grandparents in Latino families: Patterns of service use and predictors of unmet needs. *Social Work, 44*(1), 22–34.

Casas, J. M. (1992). A culturally sensitive model for evaluating alcohol and other drug abuse prevention programs: A Hispanic perspective. In M. A. Orlandi, R. Weston, & L. G. Epstein (Eds.) *Cultural Competence for Evaluators: A Guide for Alcohol and Other Drug Abuse Prevention Practitioners Working with Ethnic/Racial Communities.* Rockville, MD: Office of Substance Abuse Prevention, U. S. Department of Health and Human Services, 75–116.

Castex, G. M. (1994). Providing services to Hispanic/Latino populations: Profiles in diversity. *Social Work, 39*(3), 288–296.

Castro, F. G., Coe, K., Gutierres, S., & Saenz, D. (1996). Designing health promotion programs for Latinos. In P. M. Kato & T. Mann (Eds.) *Handbook of Diversity Issues in Health Psychology,* New York: Plenum Press, 319–345.

Colon, E. (1996). Program design and planning strategies in the delivery of culturally competent health and mental health prevention and treatment services to Latino communities. *Journal of Multicultural Social Work, 4*(4), 85–96.

Comas-Diaz, L. (1981). Puerto Rican Espiritismo and psychotherapy. *American Journal of Orthopsychiatry, 51*(4), 636–645.

Comas-Dias, L. (2001). Hispanics, Latinos, or Americanos: The evolution of identity. *Cultural Diversity and Ethnic Minority Psychology, 7*(2), 115–120.

Cox, C., & Monk, A. (1993). Hispanic culture and family care of Alzheimer's patients. *Health and Social Work, 18*(2), 92–100.

Cuellar, I. (1998). Cross-cultural clinical psychological assessment of Hispanic Americans. *Journal of Personality Assessment, 70*(1), 71–86.

De Anda, D. (1984). Bicultural socialization: Factors affecting the minority experience. *Social Work, 29,* 101–107.

de Leon Siantz, M. L. (1996). Profile of the Hispanic child. In S. Torres (Ed.), *Hispanic Voices: Hispanic Health Educators Speak Out.* New York: National League for Nursing Press, 13–25.

Delgado, M., & Barton, K. (1998). Murals in Latino communities: Social indicators of community strengths. *Social Work, 43*(4), 346–356.

Delgado, M., & Tennstedt, S. (1997). Puerto Rican sons as primary caregivers of elderly parents. *Social Work, 42*(2), 125–134.

Galan, J. (1985). Traditional values about family behavior: The case of the Chicano client. *Social Thought, summer*, 14–22.

Galvan, F. H. (1999). Sources of personal meaning among Mexican and Mexican American men with HIV/AIDS. *Journal of Multicultural Social Work, 7*(3/4), 45–67.

Gann, L. H., & Duignan, P. G. (1986). *The Hispanics in the United States: A History*. Boulder, CO: Westview.

Gomez, L. E. (1992). The birth of the "Hispanic" generation: Attitudes of Mexican-American political elites toward the Hispanic label. *Latin American Perspectives, 19*(4), 45–58.

Guzman, B. (2001). *The Hispanic Population: 2000*. U.S. Census Bureau.

Hibbeln, J. A. (1996). Special populations: Hispanic migrant workers. In S. Torres (Ed.), *Hispanic Voices: Hispanic Health Educators Speak Out*. New York: National League for Nursing Press, 162–192.

Holland, L., & Courtney, R. (1998). Increasing cultural competence with the Latino community. *Journal of Mental Health Nursing, 15*(1), 45–53.

Kail, B., Zayas, L. H., & Malgady, R. G. (2000). Depression, acculturation, and motivations for alcohol use among young Columbian, Dominican, and Puerto Rican men. *Hispanic Journal of Behavioral Sciences, 22*(1), 64–77.

Kiang, P. N. (1994). When Know-Nothings speak English only: Analyzing Irish and Cambodian struggles for community development and educational equity. In K. Aguilar-San Juan, *The State of Asian America: Activism and Resistance in the 1990s*. Boston: South End Press, 125–145.

Kolb, P. J. (1999). A stage of migration approach to understanding nursing home placement in Latino families.

Journal of Multicultural Social Work, 7(3/4), 95–112.

Koss-Chioino, J. D. (1999). Depression among Puerto Rican women: Culture, etiology and diagnosis. *Hispanic Journal of Behavioral Sciences, 21*(3), 330–350.

Low, G., & Organista, K. C. (2000). Latinas and sexual assault: Towards culturally sensitive assessment and intervention. *Journal of Multicultural Social Work, 8*(1/2), 131–157.

Lopez, R. A. (1999). Las comadres as a social support system. *Affilia, 14*(1), 24–41.

Mailman, S. (1995). California's Proposition 187 and its lessons. *New York Law Journal*. http://ssbb.com/article1.html, 3.

Marquez, B., & Jennings, J. (2000). Representation of other means: Mexican American and Puerto Rican social movement organization. *Political Science and Politics, 33*(3), 541–546.

Mayo, Y. (1997). Machismo, fatherhood and the Latino family: Understanding the concept. *Journal of Multicultural Social Work, 5*(1/2), 49–61.

Melendez, E., Rodriguez, C., & Figueroa, J. B. (Eds.). (1991). *Hispanics in the Labor Force: Issues and Policies*. New York: Plenum Press.

Morales, R., & Bonilla, F. (Eds.). (1993). *Latinos in a Changing U. S. Economy: Comparative Perspectives on Growing Inequality*. Newbury Park: Sage.

Nielsen, A. L. (2000). Examining drinking patterns and problems among Hispanic groups: Results from a national survey. *Journal of Studies on Alcohol, 61*(2), 301–328.

Ordaz, M., & De Anda D. (1996). Cultural legacies: Operationalizing

Chicano cultural values. *Journal of Multicultural Social Work,* 4(3), 57–67.

Ortiz-Torres, B., Serrano-Garcia, I., & Torres-Burgos, N. (2000). Subverting culture: Promoting HIV/AIDS prevention among Puerto Rican and Dominican women. *American Journal of Community Psychology,* 28(6), 859–887.

Padilla, A. M., & Salgado de Snyder, V. N. (1992). Hispanics: What the culturally informed evaluator needs to know. In M. A. Orlandi, R. Weston, & L. G. Epstein (Eds.) *Cultural Competence for Evaluators: A Guide for Alcohol and Other Drug Abuse Prevention Practitioners Working with Ethnic/Racial Communities.* Rockville, MD: Office of Substance Abuse Prevention, U. S. Department of Health and Human Services. 117–146.

Paulino, A. (1998). Dominican immigrant elders: Social service needs, utilization patterns, and challenges. *Journal of Gerontological Social Work,* 30(1/2), p. 61–74.

Queralt, M. (1984). Understanding Cuban immigrants. *Social Work,* 29(2), 115–121.

Rivera-Arzola, M., & Ramos-Grenier, J. (1997). Anger, Ataques de Nervios, and la Mujer Puertorriquena: Sociocultural Considerations and Treatment Implications. In J. G. Garcia & M. C. Zea (Eds.) *Psychological Interventions and Research with Latino Populations,* Boston: Allyn & Bacon, 125–141.

Rojas, D. Z. (1996). Spiritual well-being and its influence on the holistic health of Hispanic women. In S. Torres (Ed.), *Hispanic Voices: Hispanic Health Educators Speak Out.* New York: National League for Nursing Press, 213–229.

Sethi, R. C. (1994). Smells like racism: A plan for mobilizing against anti-Asian bias. In K. Aguilar-San Juan, *The State of Asian America: Activism and Resistance in the 1990s.* Boston: South End Press, 235–250.

Torres, J. B. (1998). Masculinity and gender roles among Puerto Rican men: Machismo on the U. S. mainland. *American Journal of Orthopsychiatry,* 68(1), 16–26.

Torres-Gil, F. M., & Kuo, T. (1998). Social policy and the politics of Hispanic aging. *Journal of Gerontological Social Work,* 30(1/2), 143–158.

U.S. Census Bureau. (2001). Current Population Survey. http://www.census.gov

Zea, M. C., Belgrave, F. Z., Garcia, J. G., & Quezada, T. (1997). Socioeconomic and cultural factors in rehabilitation of Latinos with disabilities. In J. G. Garcia & M. C. Zea (Eds.) *Psychological Interventions and Research with Latino Populations,* Boston: Allyn & Bacon, 217–234.

Asian Americans

Asian Americans are a rapidly growing population with a large proportion of foreign-born members. The size of the Asian American population has doubled every 10 years in recent decades. This enormous growth is largely because of immigration from Taiwan, China, Korea, the Philippines, and Southeast Asia (Okazaki, 1998). In 2000, there were 6,706,000 foreign-born Asian Americans in the United States, with 3,068,000 of these being naturalized citizens. Many of the foreign-born are relatively new arrivals: 40.9% arrived between 1990 and 2000 and 36.5% between 1980 and 1989 (U.S. Census Bureau, 2001).

In 1990, there were 6.9 million Asian Americans (2.8% of the U.S. population). For the 2000 census, 10.2 million people (3.6% of the U.S. population) identified themselves as Asian American. This is a 48% increase from the 1990 figure. In all, 11.9 million (4.2% of the U.S. population) identified themselves as either Asian American or part Asian American. This is a 72% increase from the 1990 figure.[1] Subsequent statistics include all those who identified as Asian American or part Asian American unless otherwise noted. The largest Asian American groups are Chinese (2.7 million), Filipino (2.4 million), and Asian Indian (1.9 million) (Barnes & Bennett, 2002).

---

[1]In 1990, the census did not allow people to designate more than one racial or ethnic group. Therefore, precise comparisons between 1990 and 2000 census figures are not possible, making it difficult to determine how much the Asian American population has grown.

Asian Americans are a young population with 38.9% being age 24 or younger compared with 32.5% of the White population. Asian Americans are well educated, with 28.7% having a bachelor's degree and 15.3% having an advanced degree, compared with 17% and 8.6% of the general population. Some Asian Americans face economic hardship with 10.7% living below the poverty line compared with 11.8% of the general population and 7.7% of White Americans. Asian American elders are hardest hit as 10.6% live in poverty compared with 9.7% of the general population and 7.6% of White elders. Elderly Asian American men fare worse than their female counterparts with 11.4% being impoverished compared with 9.9% of elderly Asian American women.

Geographically, 49% of Asian Americans live in the Western United States compared with 22.8% of the general population and 19.8% of White Americans. An additional 20% live in the Northeast, 19% in the South, and 12% in the Midwest. California has the largest Asian American population (4.2 million) followed by New York (1.2 million) and Hawaii (.7 million) (Barnes & Bennett, 2002). The Asian American population is divided between urban and suburban dwellers with 48.2% living in metropolitan areas outside central cities and 47.5% living inside central cities. This compares with 51.6% of the general population living in the suburbs and 29.3% in cities (U.S. Census Bureau, 2001).

Asian Americans are a heterogeneous population in ethnic composition, immigration history, language, religion, and other sociodemographic characteristics. Chinese and Japanese are the longest established Asian American groups and began arriving in the United States in the mid-1800s. Many other Asian American populations have arrived more recently as either immigrants or refugees (Choi, 2001).

It is not always clear which groups are considered Asian or Asian American. The continent of Asia extends from eastern Turkey to Siberia and includes the countries of Iran, Iraq, Israel, Jordan, Lebanon, Saudi Arabia, and Syria. The five former Soviet Republics of Kazakhstan, Kyrgyzstan, Tajikistan, Turkmenistan, and Uzbekistan are now classified by the International Olympic Committee as Asian nations. The U.S. Immigration and Naturalization Service, on the other hand, classifies people from the continent of Asia as Asians including those from the Middle East but excludes those from Turkey, Russia, and former Soviet Republics. The U.S. Census Bureau has still different criteria and doesn't consider people from the Middle and Near East (nations west of Pakistan) to be Asians; instead, Pacific Islanders are classified in the same category with Asians (Cho, 1997).

Although Pacific Islanders are often categorized with Asians, their histories and cultures are significantly different, and they are discussed in a separate chapter. Likewise, individuals from the Middle East are culturally distinct from other Asian groups and are discussed in other chapters. Most Asian Americans trace their origin to East Asia (e.g., China, Japan), South Asia (e.g., India, Pakistan), or Southeast Asia (e.g., Vietnam, Laos); Asian Americans who trace their ancestry to those major regions are the primary focus of this chapter.

In recent decades, the term *Asian American* has almost completely replaced the older term *Oriental* as the label used for the many groups with their roots in Asia. Although this term is generally considered acceptable, applying one label to many distinct cultural groups obscures diversity. It is generally preferable to use a more specific term based on national origin (e.g., Korean) or tribal/ethnic origin (e.g., Hmong) when speaking of members of a specific group.

This chapter gives an overview of social work with Asian Americans. The significant diversity that exists within and among Asian American groups sets the context for discussion. The chapter presents information on the knowledge, skills, and values/attitudes necessary for cultural competence, and presents issues for cultural competence on micro and macro levels.

KNOWLEDGE FOR CULTURAL COMPETENCE

The knowledge needed for culturally competent social work with Asian Americans can be divided into four broad areas: diversity, history, culture, and contemporary realities. Diversity serves as an overarching concept that informs all other areas. The history, culture, and contemporary realities of Asian Americans vary according to factors such as national origin, gender, generation in the United States, and immigration status.

Diversity

Various sources list Asian/Pacific Islanders as coming from more than 20 countries (Kuramoto, 1995), more than 20 ethnic groups speaking more than 30 languages (Harada & Kim, 1995), 26 different groups (Choi, 2001), tracing their roots to 28 countries of origin (Okazaki, 1998), or constituting more than 60 separate ethnic/racial groups and subgroups (Kim, McLeod, & Shantzis, 1992). Clearly, extensive diversity exists among these populations, including vast differences in acculturation, generation of immigration, history in the United States, culture, religion, dialect, educational achievement, and socioeconomic status (Kim et al., 1992; Okazaki, 1998). This extensive diversity continues to exist even when Pacific Islanders are not considered with Asian Americans. Only approximately 5% of the people grouped under the heading Asian/Pacific Islander are Pacific Islanders (Kuramoto, 1995). The diversity found among Asian American groups complicates attempts to understand their social and health needs and service usage. The heterogeneity of this population requires helping professionals to use subgroup-specific approaches (Harada & Kim, 1995; Yen, 1992).

National origin and ethnic differences within national groups account for significant diversity among the Asian American population. For instance, a Chinese American is likely to be quite different from an Indonesian American in education, economic status, culture, and a variety of other factors. Indeed, significant diversity exists among Chinese Americans. Chinese, the largest Asian American group, are heterogeneous in acculturation, foreign-born status, and country of origin. The Chinese community is made up of people from many different regions, socioeconomic backgrounds, and dialects. Chinese people come from Cambodia, Hong Kong, Malaysia, Mainland China, Laos, Singapore, Taiwan, Vietnam, and other Southeast Asian countries (Lee, 2000; Liu, 2001).

Koreans also constitute a large and growing segment of the Asian American population. Most Koreans are foreign-born and have arrived since the 1970s. The Korean American population has experienced significant expansion because of recent immigration. Many Korean immigrants have tended to settle in cities with Korean communities such as Los Angeles, New York City, Chicago, Honolulu, Seattle, and Washington, D.C. Koreans have come to the United States searching for better employment opportunities and a better education for their children. Most had some college before coming to the United States, but feel their English skills are inadequate. Indeed, many first-generation Korean immigrants are monolingual in Korean. Language difficulties and inadequate job opportunities lead to downward mobility for most Korean men. Many with higher education work in unskilled positions or start family-owned small businesses, often in high-risk inner city neighborhoods where families work together 12 hours a day, 7 days a week under stressful, self-sacrificing conditions (Rhee, 1997).

Assumptions that Filipino Americans share many cultural characteristics with other Asian American groups, such as Chinese and Japanese, are rarely based on empirical research. In fact, Spanish and American colonial influences have had a significant impact on shaping Filipino family structures, gender roles, and spiritual beliefs (Agbayani-Siewert, 1997). Indeed, the extensive diversity found within the Philippine Islands makes it difficult for Filipinos to conceive of themselves as belonging to a single national group (San Juan, 1994). Early Filipino immigrants were primarily farmworkers, but since the mid-1960s, most new arrivals have been professionals. In the Philippines, 80% of the people are poor and 30% of the children are malnourished, yet the Philippines continues to send its most highly educated professionals abroad, often to the United States, as doctors, nurses, scientists, and engineers. This phenomenon, known as "brain drain," is fueled by U.S. recruitment efforts to fill shortages of professionals such as nurses. Despite the high concentration of Filipino professionals in the United States, they have one of the lowest average incomes of all Asians (San Juan, 1994).

Asian Indians, on the other hand, have done especially well educationally and economically compared with other Asian groups (Cho, 1997). Despite their apparent success, many U.S.-born Asian Indians feel like second-class citizens stigmatized by their skin color, family background, and other ethnic characteristics. Racism prevents them from completely fitting into American society, thus leading them to have an ethnic life at home and an American public life with very little connection between the two (Radhakrishnan, 1994).

Considerable diversity exists among Southeast Asians in religion, urbanization, country of origin, cultural practices, language, and political views (Silka & Tip, 1994). The influx of Southeast Asians in the late 1970s and throughout the 1980s highlighted how different many of these populations were from the Asian groups that had previously arrived in the United States. Many did not experience the economic success that had come to be expected of Asian Americans. The best predictors of economic status for Southeast Asians in the United States are education, citizenship, and ethnicity. Most Southeast Asians have less than a high school degree, making them economically vulnerable. Citizenship is associated with bicultural competence and thus the ability to function adequately in the United States. Those who have not become citizens often experience economic difficulties. Southeast Asians who were ethnically Chinese and Chinese-Vietnamese fared better than did Laotians, Hmong, and Cambodians, probably because they came from more Westernized, urbanized societies and thus experienced less difficulty in making a transition to life in the United States. Speaking English is also linked with economic adjustment—English speakers are more employable. Length of residence in the United States has limited affect on economic well-being. Thus, time alone has not helped Southeast Asians become economically successful (Potocky & McDonald, 1995).

Asian Americans born in the United States tend to be significantly different from their foreign-born counterparts. Those born in the United States have few language or adjustment problems (Choi, 2001). Those who are foreign-born are more likely to have mental health problems (Okazaki, 1998). Tension often exists between second- and third-generation youth; many of both generations have negative views of newcomers and therefore do not want to be identified as Asian. Immigrant youth may loose respect for their parents and associate primarily with peer clusters. An extreme example of this is found in Asian gangs whose delinquent behaviors are increasing in some areas (Kim et al., 1992).

Asian Americans differ from each other in economic and cultural issues. For example, the stereotype of economically successful families that revere elders obscures important differences related to generation of immigration and educational level (American Psychiatric Association, 1994). Although class differences may not be readily apparent to outsiders, strictly enforced distinctions are often made between professionals, paraprofessionals, and blue-collar workers. Deep animosity also exists between some Asian groups (Silka & Tip, 1994; Yen, 1992). For example, in Sri Lanka, considerable strife and violence exists between the Sinhalese and Tamil populations, based partly on religious differences and Tamil struggles for independence.

Asian American elders have a bimodal pattern in education and income. Many have completed high school, but many others have no formal education at all. These differences are reflected in income as well. On average, those who immigrated more recently are likely to be poorer because they don't qualify for social security or pension benefits (Choi, 2001).

History

Given the recent immigration histories of many Asian Americans, it is helpful to know something about the history of their countries of origin, the history of United States involvement with that country, and the history of specific Asian

American groups in the United States. In particular, the history of the largest Asian American groups—the Chinese, Filipino, and Asian Indians—are presented. A discussion of historical perspectives on gender issues is also included.

Chinese Americans   Chinese began to arrive in the United States in large numbers in the 1840s in response to a demand for cheap labor (Liu, 2001). Because they came as laborers, early Chinese immigrants were predominantly men. Exclusionary practices and laws, along with Chinese values of interdependence, led these men to settle in close-knit communities known as Chinatowns (Cho, 1994).

In 1878, Chinese made up 2% of the total U.S. population but public attitudes and fears led to passage of the 1882 Chinese Exclusion Act, which severely restricted immigration. By 1900, Chinese immigration was at an all time low (Iglehart & Becerra, 1995; Liu, 2001). Small numbers of Chinese continued to come to the United States under restrictive immigration laws until the 1965 Immigration Act gave China (as well as other non-Western countries) a 20,000 per year immigration quota. Before 1978, when the United States established relations with Mainland China, most of these new arrivals came from Taiwan, and many were students. Most Chinese that came under this Act arrived as families.

The 1970s and 1980s led to the establishment of separate immigration quotas for the People's Republic of China, Hong Kong, and Taiwan. These quotas led to growing numbers of Chinese immigrants, many of whom were students or scholars. In the wake of the 1989 Tiananmen Square student protests and government crackdown, the U.S. government granted permanent residency to a large number of Chinese students and visiting scholars living in the United States (Liu, 2001). At this time, the Chinese government imprisoned many student leaders who advocated for greater freedom and were perceived by the government to be dissidents. Chinese student leaders who were pursing their education in the United States could not safely return to China without fear of imprisonment.

Filipino Americans   The Philippine Islands have experienced external domination and control for centuries. They were colonized by Spain for more than 300 years, followed by another 50 years of Japanese and American occupation. Exposure to these various cultural influences has led Filipino culture to develop quite differently than other Asian cultures have. For example, Filipinos typically espouse egalitarian family and gender roles (Agbayani-Siewert, 1997).

The colonial relationship between the United States and the Philippines has resulted in many Filipinos coming to the United States, and citizens of the Philippines serving in the U.S. military. In the early 20th century, Filipinos were prohibited from marrying Caucasians, and during the Depression, they could not own land or receive public assistance. In the 1930s, more than 175,000 Filipinos residing in the United States were officially designated "nationals," or wards under American tutelage that did not possess the rights of citizens. In

1934, the Tydings-McDuffie Act designated other Filipinos residing in the United States as aliens. These confusing and inconsistent policies continued a pattern of negative treatment of Filipinos. In 1940, all Filipinos were required to register and be fingerprinted like criminals (San Juan, 1994).

In their own country, under external domination, Filipinos came to occupy the lower strata in society. This status was later replicated in the United States. Under American occupation, Filipinos were exposed to democratic ideals while being subjected to colonized rule. In the United States, Filipinos continue to aspire to American ideals while experiencing both overt and covert racism that relegates them to second-class status. These experiences lead to a fatalism that is a realistic response to outside forces (Agbayani-Siewert, 1997).

Asian Indians   India was a colonial possession of Great Britain until it achieved independence in 1947–1948. The colonial system led to imposition of British forms of education and government that have shaped the character of modern India. Beginning in 1830, Asian Indians, primarily Sikhs, began arriving on the West coast of the United States as laborers. Their numbers reached 30,000 by 1910. Many of these migrants strongly supported over-throwing British rule in India, and thousands returned to Punjab to participate in a nationalist uprising in 1914. Most contemporary Asian Indian immigrants come to the United States as professionals or to seek a professional education and have not mobilized into large-scale social movements (Kumar, 2000).

The history of India is filled with divisions between Hindus, Muslims, and secular nationalists (Radhakrishnan, 1994). After independence from Britain, the countries of Pakistan and Bangladesh split off from India, largely based on religious and political divisions. These tensions continue to plague South Asia today.

Historical Perspectives on Gender Issues   Although early Asian immigration to the United States was heavily male, between 1950 and 1975, 51 to 60% of all immigrants from Japan, China, the Philippines, and Korea were women. A primary reason for women's immigration in this era was family reunification. Some of these women had married earlier Asian immigrants through long distance ceremonies and were coming to join their husbands. Others married U.S. military personnel who had been involved in the wars in Korea and Southeast Asia. Some women also came to the United States for jobs or as refugees (Fong, 1997).

The role of women in China changed dramatically following the founding of the People's Republic in 1949 when Mao legally equalized the sexes. Many women were well educated and worked in large numbers, although usually not in top leadership positions (Liu, 2001). These political changes in China began to challenge the strict hierarchical nature of families.

The U.S. military presence in Asia has often led to exploitive relationships between American men and Asian women, sometimes resulting in marital or child abandonment. This was most visible in the plight of Amerasian children who, along with their mothers and other family members, faced extensive persecution and ostracism in Vietnam when abandoned or not acknowledged by their American fathers (Fong, 1997).

Culture

Despite significant diversity, Asian Americans share many common values (Choi, 2001; Liu, 2001; Lorenzo, Pakiz, Reinherz, & Frost, 1995). Important cultural issues that social workers and other helping professionals need to understand include the value of collectivism, family structures, spirituality, harmony, and balance.

Collectivism   Asian socialization leads individuals to develop deep emotional interdependence and strong allegiance to roles and responsibilities—thus, a collective sense of self. Interdependence and affiliation are stressed over independence and individualism. Group needs are emphasized over individual needs; therefore, conflicts and confrontations that disrupt group harmony are to be avoided. This collectivism is grounded in hierarchical relationships, valuing of elders, and the importance of the extended family (Ino & Glicken, 1999; Silka & Tip, 1994). This worldview has its roots in Confucian, Buddhist, and Taoist philosophies that have been incorporated into many Asian cultures, particularly those from Japan, China, Korea, Taiwan, Vietnam, Cambodia, Thailand, and other areas of East Asia (Ino & Glicken, 1999). Asian Americans may experience some conflicts when exposed to bicultural socialization and contradictions between Asian collectivist values and American individualistic values (Ino & Glicken, 1999; Lorenzo et al., 1995).

Chinese culture emphasizes social relations and supports caregiving. Caregiving can be both an obligation and a stress for Asian American families of the mentally ill or elderly (Choi, 2001; Kung, 2001). Support of a kinship network can moderate the stress of caregivers but natural support systems may be reduced through immigration processes that divide families (Kung, 2001). Given the value placed on interdependence, social isolation of people who are mentally ill or disabled is unlikely in Chinese culture (Kung, 2001).

Family Structures   Family structures have a profound effect on values and belief systems (Yen, 1992). Family structures are also a reflection of values and beliefs. The Asian family is typically hierarchical, based on gender, generation, and age, with young women at the lowest level. Age and life experience are associated with wisdom and competency (Fong, 1997; Ino & Glicken, 1999; Lorenzo et al., 1995).

In Asian societies, family goes beyond living members and includes ancestors in the male family line and future descendants. The father is the leader of the household and carries responsibility for the family's economic and physical well-being, yet he still shows deference and loyalty to his parents and older siblings, whether they be living or dead. The wife is incorporated into the extended family of her husband. She becomes the emotional center of her family and is responsible for nurturing her husband and children. She has little public power and defers to her husband, mother-in-law, and the elders in her husband's extended family, yet exercises extensive emotional power and often acts as the relational and communication link between her husband and children (Ino & Glicken, 1999).

Duty to parents (filial piety) is a value found in many Asian cultures. For example, in Chinese families, parents have the highest authority and sacrifice for the good of the family is common. Even Americanized Chinese may hold these traditional values (Liu, 2001). Filial piety is also a strong value for Koreans, and adult children are expected to care for, respect, obey, and interact with parents in a polite and respectful manner. Sons are expected to care for elderly parents physically, emotionally, and financially. Daughters-in-law traditionally have the lowest status in the Korean household. This inferior status and rigid gender role places them in the position of caregiver and performer of household tasks for in-laws (Chang & Moon, 1997).

Filial piety leads to support and protection for parents as they age. Elders rely on their extended families, particularly children, for support. Living arrangements, and quality of interactions with support systems, are often the strongest predictors of Asian American elders' psychological well-being. However, elderly parents' sole reliance on children to meet instrumental and emotional needs can be draining for caregivers (Choi, 2001; Kung, 2001).

Rigid gender roles in which women have secondary status are common in most Asian cultures influenced by Confucianism. For example, long-standing patriarchal aspects of Korean culture give sons the right of inheritance whereas married daughters are no longer considered family members. This custom persists despite the 1989 Korean family law that, in principle, grants all children equal inheritance rights (Chang & Moon, 1997).

Asian American women's roles are often stereotyped and reinforced by stereotypes. The media promotes images of Asian American women as shy, docile, quiet, submissive, demure, exotic, and erotic. They are also portrayed as good housekeepers and dutiful wives who know their places (Fong, 1997). These stereotypes negate the development of a positive self-identity and contribute to feelings of inferiority and self-hatred for Asian American women. Even the more complimentary stereotypes are dehumanizing and promote Asian women as marriageable for White men.

Among Filipinos, sex roles are egalitarian rather than patriarchal. Filipinos place a high value on family, but they are also encouraged to be independent and competitive. This type of behavior may ultimately help raise the economic standard of living for both family and community. An individual's success or failure is viewed as a reflection on the family (Agbayani-Siewert, 1997).

It is important to view issues such as domestic violence within a cultural context. Chinese people tend to define themselves in relation to others (e.g., son, daughter, spouse) rather than as individuals. Chinese women internalize values of endurance, perseverance, and submissiveness to men as ultimate virtues. Most traditional Chinese women do not view leaving the abuser as a positive demonstration of self-assertiveness. Instead, such an act is viewed as exposing family problems to outsiders, bringing shame on the family, violating the values of perseverance and endurance, and undermining the family through divorce or separation. Rather than perceiving herself as an empowered survivor (as is commonly encouraged from a feminist perspective), a Chinese American woman who leaves an abusive situation may instead see herself as a bad person who brings shame to the family or causes family breakdown (Lee, 2000). Domestic violence is not always simply men against women. The husband's parents may be instigators of violence based on complex family dynamics. This sort of family violence is often viewed as acceptable (Lee, 2000).

Spirituality Spirituality is the foundation for many Asian American cultural beliefs and practices. In particular, Confucian, Taoist, and Buddhist spiritual traditions are major influences. These influences are prominent even among Christian Asian Americans.

Confucian philosophy emphasizes the needs of the group over those of the individual. The sense of being part of something greater than the self provides a sense of belonging and security (Liu, 2001). In Confucianism, virtue is exemplified by participation in appropriate social relationships and maintenance of social harmony at all levels of society. There are five essential relationships: sovereign and subject (also known as superior and subordinate), parent and child, older and younger brothers, husband and wife, and friends (Ino & Glicken, 1999). Filial piety is a central concept in Confucian thought. Confucianism is a pragmatic philosophy that guides behavior.

Taoism is more concerned with metaphysical and mystical matters. Tao is the cosmic process of the Way. Taoism teaches individuals to always act in accordance with nature, not against it. People can completely control neither nature nor destiny (Ino & Glicken, 1999).

Buddhism is guided by four noble truths: (1) life is suffering, (2) suffering originates from undue desires, (3) desire comes from ignorance and illusion, and (4) the road to salvation is enlightenment. Enlightenment, in turn, is achieved through eight noble paths. Concentration and meditation facilitate the ability to strive for enlightenment. The actions of this life have implications for the next life (Ino & Glicken, 1999); thus, actions should be taken with this in mind. Good deeds are reflected in advancing toward enlightenment in a future life. Bad behavior results in problems in future incarnations.

Indigenous belief systems predated Confucianism, Taoism, and Buddhism and still have influence in some areas of Asia. For example, before the Spanish occupation, Islamic and indigenous animistic beliefs were major spiritual influences in the Philippines. Many Filipinos espouse a polytheistic belief system blending indigenous beliefs and practices with Christian ideologies. There is a connection between a belief in powerful others and the importance of the family and group over the individual. The Tagalog phrase *Bahal na* expresses the power of God's will and an individual's limited control. Leaving things to fate cushions and explains defeats and barriers such as discrimination and oppression. These belief systems persist, although today more than 80% of Filipinos are Catholic (Agbayani-Siewert, 1997).

Harmony and Balance   Principles of social harmony and balance govern all interpersonal relationships (Ino & Glicken, 1999; Lorenzo et al., 1995). Conflicts must be minimized to maintain harmony. A violation of duty or social obligation can damage harmony within a family, group, or larger community. When harmony is disrupted, other family members use the mechanism of shaming to punish the offending individual (Ino & Glicken, 1999). Asian values support traits of passivity, deference, reserve, and emotional restraint (Shin & Abell, 1999).

Asian Americans often espouse a holistic view of health and illness. Traditional Asian medical systems are comprehensive and address aspects of the body, mind, and spirit (Dhooper & Tran, 1998; Kung, 2001). Physical and mental illness may be attributed to causes such as weakening of nerves, an imbalance of hot and cold, failure to be in harmony with nature, being cursed by evil spirits, or punishment for immoral behavior. In many Asian cultures, suffering is considered a natural and inevitable part of life; therefore, expressing emotions in response to suffering is discouraged and pointless. This perspective may result in the physical expression of emotional problems or delays in seeking help for problems (Dhooper & Tran, 1998).

In China, mental or physical impairments are often viewed as a punishment for parental or past life sins. Particularly in rural areas, religious consultation is sought to determine the causes and solutions for disabilities. Mental health is achieved through self-discipline, exercise of power, and avoidance of morbid thoughts. Emotional problems are associated with a weak character. Lack of a balanced diet and emotional disturbance during pregnancy are also seen as causes of disabilities. Mental illness may be caused by evil spirits or be a punishment from the gods. Disability is often viewed as shameful and is kept secret by families. Families (especially the family head) may feel shame and guilt. Chinese people may be more accepting of physical impairment caused by injury than of a congenital or mental problem (Liu, 2001).

Contemporary Realities

Effective work with Asian American clients requires understanding their contemporary realities. Areas that social workers need to be knowledgeable about include cultural transitions, social and health problems, concerns of the elderly, violence and oppression, and strengths.

Cultural Transitions   Cultures are constantly changing. Different members of the same Asian American family often take on varying degrees of American culture. These changes often cause significant stress as family roles shift. Differential rates of acculturation between parents and children can be destabilizing to families (Fong, 1997). Youth become Americanized more quickly than parents do, thus sometimes leading to a generation gap that contributes to an identity crisis and family instability (Kim et al., 1992). Intergenerational conflicts are heightened when children speak English and parents must rely on them for translation (Silka & Tip, 1994).

Changing gender roles are a source of conflict in many Asian American families (Silka & Tip, 1994). Asian American women espouse a blend of Asian and American values but the acculturation process is complex and nonlinear. The image of the accommodating Asian woman is being changed by American culture. Asian American women experience changes in their status as they become more employable outside the home (Fong, 1997; Kim et al., 1992; Rhee, 1997). Despite these changes in women's status, men are still more likely to fare better economically than women do. Even when Asian American women are employed full-time in professional or technical fields, they do not earn incomes commensurate with their education (Fong, 1997). Husbands' ideas about wives being subservient have also been slow to change (Rhee, 1997).

Age and length of time in the United States are associated with acculturation for Vietnamese Americans. Acculturation can be a functional ability in a host culture that does not necessarily require individuals to discard traditional values and a sense of a cultural self. Some theories say that ethnic enclaves hinder acculturation, but culturally familiar surroundings can support immigrants' adjustment and acculturation. Functional acculturation and cultural identification may be independent processes (Changming & Vu, 2000).

Several studies have sought to examine the relationship between acculturation and depression, but they frequently fail to look at moderating factors. Inconsistent findings are often the result. A study of 983 employed Chinese immigrants found that acculturation and socioeconomic status were strongly correlated, but it was not clear if acculturation led to higher socioeconomic status or vice versa. Socioeconomic status may be more predictive of depressive symptomology for women than men. This study found that acculturation had only an indirect influence on mental health. Indeed, the researchers identified a paradoxical effect: more acculturated people expressed more stress and depressive symptoms but more acculturation was also associated with higher socioeconomic status, which was associated with better mental health. A complicated relationship exists between acculturation and mental health (Shen & Takeuchi, 2001).

A study of 143 Chinese Americans in San Francisco examined cultural orientation and psychological well-being. Bicultural activity predicted psychological well-being but those who were grounded primarily in Chinese culture experienced less negative affect than either assimilated or bicultural individuals. It is important to assess cultural orientation in different life domains as this may vary (e.g., embracing some aspects of American culture such as foods may be distinct from other aspects like friendships) (Ying, 1995).

In contrast, a study of inner-city Asian American adolescents found those who had a high orientation toward their Asian culture experienced more depression than do those who were assimilated. Positive parent and peer relationships were associated with lower depression. No differences were found by gender, ethnic group, or socioeconomic status (Wong, 2001).

◊Social and Health Problems   When Asian Americans are seen as a problem-free, so-called model minority, they are touted as proof that racism is no longer a major social problem and impediment to educational and economic success. This has perpetuated neglect of social problems among Asian Americans (Miah & Kahler, 1997). One of the most pervasive problems of Asian Americans is underemployment. Those born in the United States typically fare well both educationally and economically, but many of the foreign-born have language difficulties that inhibit their employability or have credentials that are not readily transferable. This leads to many highly educated Koreans being underemployed (Shin, Berkson, & Crittenden, 2000).

Despite the model minority stereotype, Asian Americans rate as high or higher than White Americans on depression, somatization, and post-traumatic stress disorder measures. Rates and distribution of mental disorders are hindered by methodological and conceptual problems in the research, including making cross-cultural comparisons using assessment tools not normed for Asian Americans, and not taking into account population size, heterogeneity, and rapid demographic changes (Lee, Lei, & Sue, 2001). Data that points to ethnic differences in mental health raises important questions about how these ethnic differences should be interpreted. Asian Americans' responses might indicate more severe psychopathology or these apparent differences could be caused by cultural factors that are nonpathological (Okazaki, 1998).

Clinicians who see troubled clients and high suicide rates question the model minority view of Asian Americans based on academic achievement and upward mobility. For example, the suicide rate for 15- to 24-year-old Chinese Americans is 36% higher than the national average (Lorenzo et al., 1995). A study of 9th-grade Asian Americans found they were less delinquent and stronger academically than their White peers but they were significantly more isolated, more depressed, more anxious, less involved in school activities, less likely to seek help for problems, and more likely to internalize social problems. They had fewer role models and less social support. The psychosocial and emotional plight of Asian Americans highlights the need for proactive outreach programs (Lorenzo et al., 1995). Even though many Asian American adolescents demonstrate academic achievement, many also show significant distress. Only 42.5% of 153 who wrote essays on growing up Asian American expressed a positive attitude toward academic achievement although their academic behaviors were not problematic (Lee & Ying, 2001).

Concerns of the Elderly   Little research has been conducted on Asian American elderly (Miah & Kahler, 1997). This may be partly because of their invisibility as a minority group, yet the fastest growing segment of the rapidly growing Asian American population is women older than 75. Many Asians come to the United States with a goal of economic advancement, but after retirement they do not have the quality of life they expected. Ninety percent live in urban areas where they face overcrowding and poverty. Asian American elderly put in more work hours and retire later than other groups do. Most are foreign-born, so they have minimal or no social security benefits. The loss of traditional values, including loss of authority and respect, is seen as particularly disturbing to elderly Asian Americans (Miah & Kahler, 1997).

Elderly Asian Americans are vulnerable to depression. For elderly Chinese immigrants, predictors of depression include higher education, living alone, poor perceived health, dissatisfaction with family support, and total number of stressful life events (Mui, 1998). A study of 67 urban elderly Koreans reported depression much higher than that found in a Chinese sample. Elderly Korean women are more likely to be depressed than Korean men are. Depression may be related to stresses associated with immigration, language barriers, acculturation, financial hardship, poor health, social isolation, and splitting of the household. Changes in family composition and financial hardship were the most commonly reported life events. Perceptions of help from family and friends are strong predictors of mental health (Mui, 2001).

Violence and Oppression   Violence against women and elders is beginning to receive some attention from helping professionals, but this is still a largely hidden problem in many Asian American families. Identifying prevalence is difficult. There are problems with record keeping on specific ethnic groups, underreporting, and lack of service utilization because of cultural and language barriers (Lee, 2000). Research shows that wife abuse may be much more common among Korean immigrant families than among other ethnic or Asian groups. Factors that contribute to rates of violence include unusually high male domination, environmental factors such as immigration stress and adjustment difficulties for Korean men, heavy drinking, and permissive attitudes toward men's drinking in Korean culture (Rhee, 1997).

Attitudinal studies have documented a relatively high tolerance for domestic violence among Asian Americans. A study of 211 randomly selected Japanese American women in Los Angeles county revealed that 80% had experienced some type of partner violence during their lifetimes (52% physical violence, 76% emotional violence, 30% sexual violence). Some also experienced nonpartner violence (13% were abused by parents, and 18% knew of father's abuse toward mother). First-generation respondents reported more fathers' violence toward mothers. In addition, one-third reported experiencing sexual violence, three-fourths experienced no-contact sexual violence (e.g., obscene phone calls, voyeurism, flashing), 80% experienced property crime, and 19% were assaulted by someone other than their partner. First-generation Japanese Americans were most likely to experience sexual violence. The severity of victimization was higher for first generation women (Yoshihama, 2001).

Despite values that revere the elderly, studies are beginning to document elder abuse among Asian Americans. Many Asian American elders report having heard or seen abuse but do not disclose that they themselves have been abused. Lack of self-disclosure is probably related to strong cultural norms of shame and keeping concerns within the family (Chang & Moon, 1997). The most common forms of abuse identified among Korean American elders are (1) financial, (2) psychological (e.g., lack of respect for and inappropriate treatment by family members, especially cases where a daughter-in-law did not respect her mother-in-law properly, including expression of disagreement, using an inappropriate tone, and having inadequate interaction), (3) culturally specific abuse (e.g., adult children who have minimal contact with their parents, placing an elderly parent in a nursing home), (4) neglect (e.g., lack of attention and care, abandonment and pressuring parents to move out of adult children's homes), and (5) physical abuse (Chang & Moon, 1997).

Korean American elders typically define elder abuse only within the context of family relations. This may be because Korean society is strongly influenced by Confucianism and filial piety or perhaps their daily activities are restricted to their children's families because of cultural and language barriers. The nature of psychological and culturally specific abuse indicates that Korean elders apply their traditional norms and expectations in identifying abuse and maltreatment. Sons were typically identified as the culprits in financial abuse, and daughter-in-laws were identified as the primary perpetrators of psychological and culturally specific abuse (Chang & Moon, 1997).

Acts of racism and oppression against Asian Americans are rarely reported in the news, yet violence against Asians may be rising, especially violence perpetrated against Asian American shopkeepers in African American communities. Discussion of discrimination is often taboo (Yen, 1992), yet racism, discrimination, and subsequent alienation are common experiences for many Asian Americans (Kim et al., 1992; Lorenzo et al., 1995; Radhakrishnan, 1994). Stereotypes, discrimination, and exclusion are still common. Hate crimes against Asian Americans are rising, double standards in Affirmative Action continue to be applied, and glass ceilings are firmly in place (Cho, 1997).

Strengths   In trying to debunk the myth of the model minority, attention has shifted to a variety of social problems. Critiques of the model minority thesis emphasize how this obscures diversity and how some groups fare poorly. Conversely, some groups are doing well economically and educationally. Compelling educational success stories depict high SAT scores, significant college enrollments, and scientific achievements. Academic success often translates to economic accomplishments. Asian Americans experience lower unemployment rates, occupy more managerial and professional occupations, and have a higher percentage of households earning $100,000 or more than do White Americans. Among Asian Americans, Asian Indians fare particularly well (Cho, 1997).

Academic success may be connected to cultural values of interdependence, strong family connections, and orientation toward achievement (Kim et al., 1992; Lorenzo et al., 1995). The economic success of Asian Americans can often be explained by higher rates of labor force participation and more workers in the family (Fong, 1997).

A bicultural orientation can be a source of strength for Asian Americans. Valuing independence can promote a good fit in American society. Despite the American emphasis on independence, Korean Americans who value interdependence also fare well in psychological well-being (Hyun, 2001).

Asian American women have taken positive strides in establishing bicultural identities. There is a relationship between class and feelings of control. Those with educational and economic resources have a greater sense of control over their lives and may be more likely to accept American values

(Agbayani-Siewert, 1997; Fong, 1997). For example, Asian Indian American women are working to claim a new identity for themselves that combines U.S. and Indian features. Despite experiencing discord over two sets of expectations for women and men, they have internalized both egalitarian American attitudes and the gendered attitudes of their families regarding marriage, dating, and appropriate behavior. In a recent study, most Asian Indian women felt they were bicultural and their cultures could be successfully combined. "This way of thinking, or being culturally pluralistic, is not unlike an Indian philosophical way of thinking, which does not accept an 'either/or' (analytical) way of looking at reality, but believes in a 'both/and' (synthetic way of perceiving reality" (Srinivasan, 2001, p. 150).

SKILLS FOR CULTURAL COMPETENCE

The literature on Asian Americans frequently documents low service utilization and cultural and language barriers that inhibit seeking professional help. Social workers and other helping professionals need to be aware of these barriers and use their skills to minimize or eliminate impediments to service use.

Engaging

Social workers need to be skillful in conducting outreach and developing trust with Asian American clients. Skills in engaging are necessary in both identifying and bridging different expectations of the helping process. Engaging Asian American clients involves explicitly recognizing clients' dilemmas in seeking help and recognizing the emotions of shame and guilt. Social workers can reaffirm and strengthen the motivating factors that led to seeking help as part of the engaging process (Lee, 2000).

Asian Americans are often reluctant to acknowledge and seek help for personal problems; however, once problems are identified, they prefer professional to paraprofessional helpers. Professionals have recognized stature and command respect (Yen, 1992), thus fitting with the hierarchical relationships defined in Confucianism. On the other hand, Southeast Asians may place less emphasis on helpers with credentials than on those with culturally derived and sanctioned authority such as folk healers. Western helping professionals and Asian folk healers often operate with different concepts of health and disease. In traditional Asian healing, problems are not interpreted in psychological ways; therefore, talking about problems is not seen as meaningful (Silka & Tip, 1994).

Asking the client to provide information about his or her cultural background can be an important part of engaging. This shows that the helping professional is not willing to make assumptions about the client's culture based on a name or phenotypical features. Even if the helping professional has already determined the client comes from China, asking which part of China someone comes from can be helpful given the heterogeneity of the Chinese population (Liu, 2001).

Confidentiality is often seen as an important aspect of engaging clients from many cultural groups. For example, Koreans usually don't discuss family problems with strangers, or even close friends, because expression might result in social stigma. This poses a challenge for practitioners and agencies. Confidentiality is key to establishing a productive relationship (Rhee, 1997). Concerns over breaching confidentiality may limit work with families of the mentally ill, although involving the family can be critical in establishing a successful therapeutic bond (Kung, 2001).

On the other hand, Western ideas about confidentiality may differ from the needs and desires of some Asian American clients. In one particular example, an older man from Burma specifically requested that others know about his experiences as a refugee. In my experience, many Tamil clients who fled civil war in Sri Lanka requested that their family members be present during interviews, even though they knew they would be asked difficult questions about experiences with torture and other trauma. Although the presence of family members may have influenced the amount and type of information disclosed, the presence of family and friends was seen as facilitating, rather than hindering the process.

Educating the Asian American community about social problems and the role of helping professionals can establish an important foundation for conducting outreach and engaging clients. For example, publishing nonthreatening educational articles about the extent of problems such as domestic violence in Korean American newspapers may be a helpful strategy for outreach to prospective clients (Rhee, 1997). Social workers must reach out to Asian Americans and educate them on the roles played by helping professionals so they are seen as more than pill-givers (Kung, 2001).

Korean culture emphasizes collectivism; thus, those who are more traditional rely on more social support. Although many Korean immigrants have negative attitudes about professional help, *counselor* and *counseling* have become familiar terms in Korean, and using these terms could be more effective than other professional terms. Also, *counseling* is positively associated with children's education. This could be used for initial engaging before addressing a variety of issues (Shin et al., 2000).

Assessing

Social workers must be skillful in assessing Asian American clients within the clients' cultural contexts. Assessments will need to consider clients' cultures of origin and how clients fit or do not fit within those cultural values and norms. A culturally competent assessment is the first step to providing culturally competent services for Asian Americans (Okazaki, 1998), yet little empirical evidence indicates what constitutes culturally competent assessment with these populations. Little has been done to adapt standardized assessment tools for use with Asian Americans. There are currently no data to guide researchers and clinicians on distinguishing between culture and pathology in Asian Americans. Indeed, development of culturally appropriate assessment tools or modification of existing assessment instruments for use with Asian Americans is quite limited compared with the work that has been done on culturally appropriate assessment of other cultural groups (Okazaki, 1998). Of the assessment tools that do exist, most have been developed for Southeast Asian refugees (Okazaki, 1998). One exception is the Homesickness and Contentment scale developed to measure emotional and psychological adjustment of Asian Americans in a new culture. This culturally sensitive tool considers the private nature of Asians (Shin & Abell, 1999).

In conducting assessments with Asian American clients, it is important to consider that self-report measures may be influenced by the cultural norm of moderation in expressing feelings and emotions (Mui, 1998). In fact, Asian American values may influence responses to any assessment tool, thus challenging the validity and reliability of tools not specifically normed for a particular Asian American population. Helping professionals who conduct assessments without using standardized instruments will need to consider how an Asian American client's values, norms, and communication patterns influence the material presented.

An assessment that focuses primarily on clinical issues is likely to be limited and miss major societal issues such as experiences with xenophobia and racism. The Person-in-Environment perspective may be an appropriate assessment framework to examine political and social realities as well as the cultural context of clients such as Filipino Americans (Agbayani-Siewert, 1997).

Intervening

Several steps can be taken to maximize cultural competence in social work interventions, including involving the Asian American community in decision making; using bilingual/bicultural staff; using resources within the Asian American community such as churches, clubs, and associations; using culturally tailored interventions such as supportive, directive, and personal relationships that include the family; having flexible scheduling and informality to encourage free communication; striving for differential assessment of cultural issues and pathology; and recognizing the importance of cultural familiarity for those who feel alienated. Combining indigenous helping and Western methods may be particularly meaningful for elderly Asians. English as a Second Language programs may be an important service to offer at agencies because there is a strong connection between an inability to communicate and many social and psychological problems (Miah & Kahler, 1997).

Language and other communication problems often prevent Asian Americans from seeking or receiving adequate professional help. Whenever possible, bilingual professionals can be used to minimize language difficulties (Kuramoto, 1995). Given the many different Asian languages, however, this presents a challenge.

Even when conducting sessions in English, social workers may need to modify how they communicate with Asian clients. For example, for Asian American clients to save face and reduce embarrassment, a social worker may need to use indirect communication and euphemisms in telling a client's family about a mental health diagnosis. Psychiatric labels are likely to be experienced as blunt and stigmatizing. A helping professional who is skillful in communicating within a client's cultural context is likely to be most effective.

Interventions need to be compatible with Asian American clients' value systems. For example, independent living as a treatment goal for clients who are mentally ill may conflict with core Chinese values. More appropriate goals might include helping families to find balance in providing assistance without being overindulgent, and encouraging clients to take on self-care responsibilities rather than striving for separation from the family (Kung, 2001).

Given Asian American clients' concerns about losing face, empathy assumes a particularly significant role in establishing a trusting working alliance. For example, when working with adolescents, family can be involved but because of the emphasis on harmony, balance, and family hierarchy, Western modes of family therapy must be modified. Instead of confronting the family together, a social worker can function as a mediator or broker between the family and adolescent (Lorenzo et al., 1995).

Helping professionals must become skillful in interpreting their Asian American clients' communication patterns. Indirect communication is common among Chinese Americans, including nonverbal messages that must be understood within context (Liu, 2001). Communication, as an aspect of social interaction, is highly contextual and tends to flow downward from superior to subordinate, often in the form of directives. Both verbal and written communications are indirect, in the passive tense, and at times may appear convoluted. Furthermore, much of the communication is nonverbal, especially where the conduct and not the content is the most meaningful. These principles of Asian communication styles maintain vital social harmony in any interpersonal interaction (Ino & Glicken, 1999, p. 528).

Asian Americans who are newly arrived in the United States are often unfamiliar with Western psychiatric concepts and may express intense concern for loss of face (Lorenzo et al., 1995). The individualism deeply rooted in American counseling is often problematic for Chinese clients (Liu, 2001). Individualistic crisis therapies negate the importance of family and thus are not meaningful. Helping professionals must consider how changes in the client would affect the family (Ino & Glicken, 1999).

Literature on working with Southeast Asian clients rarely uses an empowerment perspective. Southeast Asians group have little political voice despite their significant numbers in some areas (Silka & Tip, 1994). Work with Asian American clients needs to move beyond clinical work and include a focus on strengths and empowerment on both micro and macro levels.

Chinese medicine often prescribes herbs so use of medicine is seen as acceptable and familiar to address a range of problems. Clients, however, often expect quick symptom relief and are reluctant to continue a long course of medication that might upset the balance in the body. This has implications for treatment of mental illness (Kung, 2001) and other chronic conditions that may require long-term use of medication.

When Asian refugees come in contact with the American health-care system, their unfamiliarity is often replaced with confusion and distrust. Because of their experiences with traditional healers in Asia, many expect the physician to identify their illness by feeling their pulse. American diagnostic procedures such as X-rays are often interpreted as part of treatment. When these procedures do not cure an ailment, trust in both the doctor and the helping process are undermined (Dhooper & Tran, 1998).

Modifying professional skills and models to fit within the cultural context of an Asian American client is likely to be necessary for maximum effectiveness. Western helping practices and Asian medicine can coexist to the benefit of clients. Many Asian Americans use both. The broad bio-psycho-social perspective emphasized in social work can easily accommodate the cultural belief systems of Asian clients (Dhooper & Tran, 1998).

There should be cultural compatibility between intervention models and client groups. When psychoeducational family group treatment was evaluated with Chinese and Malay families in Singapore, incompatibilities were identified between the models and clients in beliefs, worldviews, and treatment expectations. These incompatibilities resulted in difficulties in clients complying with their expected roles. In particular, different explanations for mental illness and different levels of acceptance of community mental health services were sources of problems. There were several areas of incompatible treatment expectations: (1) Under the psychoeducational model, all family members were expected to attend the program, yet in East Asian belief systems the client is the problem and family is not in need of treatment. (2) The psychoeducational model encourages disclosure of personal and family issues, yet Asian clients valued inhibition in self-disclosure and minimization of problems. (3) The model encourages families to practice coping skills and strategies to handle client behaviors, but the families value deference to authority and expect to be told what to do. (4) The psychoeducational model does not lend itself to quick and easy solutions, yet this is precisely what many Chinese and Malay families expect. Cognitive behavioral interventions, on the other hand, were particularly successful in facilitating participation in activities and goal achievement (Bentelspacher, DeSilva, Goh, & LaRowe, 1996).

An emphasis on psychodynamic counseling obscures issues such as discrimination and acculturation and, therefore, limits social workers' understanding of clients' life situations (Agbayani-Siewert, 1997). A client-centered focus may be problematic for Chinese Americans who expect a more authoritative approach. The cultural emphasis placed on controlling emotions may inhibit disclosure (Liu, 2001). Chinese families of people with a mental illness expect practical help; thus, informative programs are often helpful. Structured vocational programs may be both practical and culturally congruent with the high value placed on work in Chinese culture (Kung, 2001). Stress, vulnerability, and social support may be an appropriate framework for helping Chinese families understand mental illness. This framework may fit with ideas about balance and harmony (Kung, 2001).

VALUES/ATTITUDES FOR CULTURAL COMPETENCE

Self-reflection and examination are key values for culturally competent social workers. When working with Asian American clients, it is important for helping professionals to assess their own locus of control. For example, do they feel individuals have control over their lives and destiny (a value prominent in American culture) or do they feel many things are beyond human control and are guided by fate or destiny (a value prominent in many Asian cultures)? Lack of self-awareness is likely to result in imposing values on the client (Agbayani-Siewert, 1997).

Helping professionals must be able to recognize their own culturally based assumptions and biases. Many Western assumptions may be problematic with Southeast Asians. For example, "coining," the process of lightly running a hot coin over a child to reduce fever, is common among some Asian people, yet this practice is often misunderstood and reported as child abuse (Silka & Tip, 1994; Sinclair, 2000). Talking to unseen others and believing in the power of spirits may be interpreted as signs of psychological disturbance by Western service providers. Likewise, the Western belief that disclosing emotional concerns and inner secrets is helpful stands in sharp contrast to Asian beliefs that this is shameful. Assumptions can lead to cultural misunderstandings (Silka & Tip, 1994).

Having an understanding attitude toward traditional Asian medicine is important in working toward compliance with Western regimes. Chinese Americans may not reveal to Western practitioners their use of traditional medicine for fear of disapproval. Thus, clinicians have limited knowledge of clients' use of dual systems. It is important to respect clients' views of problems, even when the helping professional does not comprehend or believe in Chinese interpretations of symptoms (e.g., lack of balance) (Kung, 2001).

CASE EXAMPLE

May Choi is an elderly Korean American woman preparing to leave the hospital after a short stay for a fractured hip. Mike Ortiz, the hospital social worker, is responsible for discharge planning. He is in the process of arranging for May to return to the home of her son and daughter-in-law where she has lived for 10 years following the death of her husband. May complains that her daughter-in-law is abusive and has ignored her. She stated that if Mike wants to ensure her adequate care, he should get the daughter-in-law to act appropriately. Mike wonders if he should explore the possibility of discharging May to a nursing home rather than a potentially abusive family situation. In consultation with his supervisor, Mike reflects on the following questions: How can he determine what living environment is in the client's best interest? How do Mike's and May's differing views of independence, interdependence, and family roles and responsibilities influence the case? How do culturally influenced views of elder abuse affect this case and the actions that Mike needs to take?

The following issues are salient in reflecting on this case:

- Mike needs to do a more thorough assessment to determine whether May's home environment is safe. Although May's complaints may not rise to legal standards of abuse or neglect, he needs to be careful not to minimize May's concerns and perceptions of her home situation.
- May's preliminary disclosure of her concerns indicates that she and Mike have developed a level of trust that will facilitate their work together. They can build on this important foundation.
- Mike needs to examine his own values and how these may influence what he views as appropriate steps to take.
- Good supervision will be a key element in helping Mike reflect on value differences that he and May have about independence, interdependence, family roles, and responsibilities and how these influence what is deemed an appropriate living situation.
- Asking May her views and opinions will be central to determining how to handle the case. Mike knows it is important to take time to explore these issues with May rather than to put together a discharge plan with minimal client input.

CULTURAL COMPETENCE IN SOCIAL POLICIES

Policies that target Asian Americans have often had a negative and disruptive impact, beginning with early restrictive, racially based immigration laws. Xenophobic and racist fears, fueled by a wartime climate led to a policy of forcing Japanese and Japanese Americans in the Western United States to be relocated to internment camps during World War II. The Japanese and Japanese Americans were forced to leave behind homes, businesses, and the lives they had built and spend years confined in camps in remote areas. This deprivation of liberty occurred despite no specific charges being lodged against any of the people sent to the camps.

In the 1970s, resettlement policies for Southeast Asians continued to be culturally disruptive. In the wake of United States military withdrawal from Southeast Asia at the culmination of the Vietnam War, the United States developed policies to relocate many now-vulnerable Southeast Asian allies to the United States. Federal resettlement policies focused on placing these refugees in nuclear family units in communities across the United States. In fact, most of these refugees came from cultures that valued large extended kinship networks that served as important social supports. The effect of the resettlement policy was to disrupt one of the few supports still functioning for this vulnerable population (Silka & Tip, 1994).

Other policies originate as reactions to growing Asian American communities and their attempts to have a voice in their new homeland. For example, Lowell, Massachusetts, underwent rapid demographic changes during the 1980s, which led it to become the second largest Khmer (Cambodian) community in the United States (Kiang, 1994). As the Khmer began to develop a number of positive community-based initiatives, some other residents of the area felt threatened by the growing assertiveness of the Southeast Asian community. As a result, in this and similar communities, English-only referendums were passed (Silka & Tip, 1994). Such policies exclude those who do not have a strong command of English from full participation in community activities, political processes, and social services. English-only movements are the antithesis of programs that promote bilingualism and biculturalism, and they break down cultural strengths by denying people the use of their native language.

Social policies may affect Asian American populations even when they were not specifically targeted to these groups. For example, the growing movement to criminalize spousal abuse has helped Chinese women who experience domestic violence to avoid some stigma and self-blame (Lee, 2000). This and similar policies may help empower those who experience violence to step forward and make positive changes in their lives despite cultural barriers that inhibit this type of disclosure.

CULTURAL COMPETENCE IN SOCIAL AGENCIES

Cultural and language barriers inhibit service utilization of Asian Americans in general and elders in particular. Providers and policy makers create barriers by failing to recognize the needs of Asian Americans (Choi, 2001). Agency administrators and Boards of Directors need to review their policies and procedures to determine how they may inadvertently be creating barriers to serving Asian Americans.

Several factors have been associated with successfully engaging Asian youth in alcohol and drug prevention. These factors may have broad applicability to enhancing services for Asian Americans. Agencies that successfully served Asian American youth were well known, had community credibility, and were part of the community infrastructure. Most staff and management were bilingual, bicultural Asians. The Asian American community recognized and supported these agencies as contributing to Asian Americans and to the community at large. Agency services emphasized cultural pride, ethnicity, language, traditions, holidays, ceremonies, and enhancing self-esteem for Asian Americans. Programs emphasized group activities and community service. Cultural norms, philosophy, religion, and values were supported and reinforced. Specific services were presented in a larger context of issues important to Asian American youth (Kuramoto, 1995).

Ethnic agencies need to expand and diversify their services. Mainstream agencies need to include Asian content in sensitivity training, increase bilingual/bicultural staff, conduct needs assessments, disseminate information on services targeting Asians, and engage in outreach to clients (Choi, 2001). The Asian American community is likely to benefit from a combination of culturally specific services and culturally competent services offered through mainstream agencies.

COMMUNITY INTERVENTIONS

Little quality research is available to inform the development of community-based interventions. Research has been limited by the existence of few large-scale, empirical studies. Asian Americans need to be over-sampled in large-scale research to identify interracial differences. Large samples will allow for inclusion of multiple subgroups of Asian Americans, thus providing more information on this heterogeneous population (Choi, 2001). Qualitative research in which the distinct voices of various Asian Americans are presented is also critical in yielding information that will help social workers develop and implement appropriate interventions.

Much of the literature on interventions with Asian Americans focuses on the micro level and neglects important issues like empowerment, advocacy, and community development. Community-based empowerment activities may occur through grassroots organizations. A number of examples are available from the Southeast Asian (primarily Khmer) community in Lowell, Massachusetts. Grassroots groups tackled problems of basic living among Southeast Asians such as housing, jobs, and basic survival skills. Mutual aid groups used empowerment strategies and developed community resource centers. Indigenous leaders were central in mobilizing resources. With leadership provided through the Buddhist temple, the Khmer community developed a program to teach youth to read and write Khmer to slow cultural erosion and alleviate generational stress. The community was able to set up newspapers and television programs in Khmer. Community efforts focused on improving educational access. These community-based efforts illustrate how outreach programs initiated with government funding or through universities can support basic survival skills (Silka & Tip, 1994).

Community activism has been important in pushing for educational reform, compliance with bilingual education mandates, and desegregation. Many newer Asian immigrants, particularly Southeast Asians, experience political disenfranchisement, anti-immigrant sentiment, and racial intolerance (Kiang, 1994). Social workers can use macro-level skills and knowledge gained from similar struggles in other communities of color to assist in building a community where tolerance and respect allow different cultural groups to peacefully coexist.

Development of multi-ethnic coalitions can be instrumental in bringing about community change (Kiang, 1994). Social workers can draw on their skills in mediation, advocacy, and coalition building to help community residents develop positive solutions to their problems.

The development of spiritual centers can strengthen communities and help to enhance the quality of life for community members. The 1984 founding of a Buddhist temple in Lowell, Massachusetts, became the first significant symbol of the Khmer community's presence in the area. The temple attracted a large number of Khmer from other parts of the United States who now saw Lowell as a desirable place to live (Kiang, 1994). Social workers and other community activists can lend support to members of the Asian American community as they seek to establish religious, cultural, and social institutions that support and serve the community.

A macro-level perspective is helpful in understanding and addressing issues of Asian American gangs. Increases in school dropouts and gang membership is associated with economic downturns, limited job opportunities, lack of family support systems, and academic and social problems that accompany cultural and linguistic alienation. Some gangs have formed specifically to defend their members against racial harassment in schools or neighborhoods (Kiang, 1994). These are all issues that can be addressed through policies and macro-level change.

Anti–Asian American violence and bigotry continues to exist despite and sometimes because of the economic and educational success of some Asian Americans. This bigotry is often obscured when racism is seen as Black and White. Indeed, racial insults against Asian Americans are often trivialized or dismissed as hypersensitivity (Sethi, 1994). Social workers and other helping professionals who are not Asian American can take a particularly important step in acknowledging the presence and destructive nature of anti-Asian bigotry. Non-Asians can serve as allies and bring this issue to the public's attention as an important area in need of change.

Although anti-Asian violence receives little attention, it is carried out with the same viciousness and heinous disregard for human life as any hate crime. In 1986 in New Jersey, a group called the Dotbusters was responsible for vandalism of houses and businesses as well as harassment and assaults of Asian Indians on the street. One 28-year-old man was beaten into a coma. The *Jersey Journal* published a letter from the Dotbusters threatening all Asian Indians and promising to drive them out of Jersey City. A 30-year-old executive was bludgeoned to death with bricks, yet the public was reluctant to see the crime as racially motivated despite the fact that his White companion was left unharmed (Sethi, 1994). Social workers need to be concerned about racism against Asian Americans just as they are about racism against other communities of color. The social work commitment to social justice must be a core component of culturally competent work with Asian Americans.

CONCLUSION

Asian Americans are a heterogeneous population in national origin, religion, class, educational background, and generation of immigration. Given the significant proportion of Asian Americans who are foreign-born, social workers must also have an understanding of how the immigration process may interact with cultural issues. Much of the attention that Asian Americans receive from helping professionals focuses on clinical issues or individual change, so it is important for social workers to recognize that societal issues such as racism and xenophobia significantly affect the lives of many Asian Americans. Macro-level as well as micro-level interventions are needed to address the root causes of many concerns of Asian American clients.

Exercises

Exercise #1: Reflecting on Confucianism
Review the *Sayings of Confucius*. Various versions are available from a number of different publishers. Identify the sections that discuss filial piety. Reflect on how these teachings may influence the lives of contemporary Asian Americans.

Exercise #2: Media perspectives on Asian Americans
Monitor local and national media for one week including newspapers, television, and the popular press. What content is presented on Asian Americans? How does this content challenge or reinforce images of Asian Americans as a model minority?

Exercise #3: Reviewing internment and reparations policies
Research the development and implementation of the Japanese internment and subsequent reparations policies. Identify the driving and opposing forces behind each. Reflect on each of these policies in light of social work values as articulated in the *Code of Ethics* of the National Association of Social Workers.

Additional Resources

Aguilar-San Juan, K. (1994). The State of Asian America: Activism and Resistance in the 1990s. Boston: South End Press. This edited book provides information on activism in various Asian American populations. Content includes advocacy around stereotyping and grassroots empowerment efforts. Asian Americans as activists is a subject often neglected in the social science literature.

Barnes, J. S., & Bennett, C. E. (2002). *The Asian Population: 2000*. U.S. Bureau of the Census. This report gives a concise overview of the contemporary Asian American population. Information includes geographical dispersement, age, education, immigration status, and other demographic information. National origin of major Asian groups in the United States is included.

Choi, N. G. (2001). *Psychosocial Aspects of the Asian-American Experience: Diversity within Diversity*. New York: Haworth Press. This edited book provides information on social work and other helping interventions with Asian Americans. The book presents empirical work as well as reviews of the state of the knowledge base. Some content on Pacific Islanders is also included.

Rabbit in the Moon. (1999). Wabi-Sabi Productions. This video uses interviews and historical accounts to depict the internment of Japanese and Japanese Americans in the United States during World War II. The video provides a foundation for discussing racism and the impact of social policies on populations in the United States.

References

Agbayani-Siewert, P. (1997). The dual world of Filipino Americans. *Journal of Multicultural Social Work*, 6(1/2), 59–76.

American Psychiatric Association. (1994). *Ethnic Minority Elderly: A Task Force Report of the American*

Psychiatric Association. Washington DC: American Psychiatric Association.

Barnes, J. S., & Bennett, C. E. (2002). *The Asian Population: 2000.* U.S. Bureau of the Census. http://www.census.gov/population/www/cen2000/briefs.html.

Bentelspacher, C. E., DeSilva, E., Goh, T. L. C., & LaRowe, K. D. (1996). A process evaluation of the cultural compatibility of psychoeducational family group treatment with ethnic Asian clients. *Social Work with Groups,* 19(3/4), 41–55.

Chang, J., & Moon, A. (1997). Korean American elderly's knowledge and perceptions of elder abuse: A qualitative analysis of cultural factors. *Journal of Multicultural Social Work,* 6(1/2), 139–154.

Changming, D., & Vu, P. (2000). Acculturation of Vietnamese students living in or away from Vietnamese communities. *Journal of Multicultural Counseling and Development,* 28(4), 225–242.

Cho, M. (1994). Overcoming our legacy as cheap labor, scabs, and model minorities: Asian activists fight for community empowerment. In K. Aguilar-San Juan, *The State of Asian America: Activism and Resistance in the 1990s.* Boston: South End Press, 253–273.

Cho, P. J. (1997). Asian American experiences: A view from the other side. *Journal of Sociology and Social Welfare,* 24(1), 129–154.

Choi, N. G. (2001). Diversity within diversity: Research and social work practice issues with Asian American elders. In N. G. Choi (Ed.) *Psychosocial Aspects of the Asian-American Experience: Diversity within Diversity.* New York: Haworth Press, 301–319.

Collmeyer, P. M. (1995). From "Operation Brown Baby" to "Opportunity": The placement of children of color at the Boys and Girls Aid Society of Oregon. *Child Welfare,* 74(1), 242–263.

Dhooper, S. S., & Tran, T. V. (1998). Understanding and responding to the health and mental health needs of Asian refugees. *Social Work in Health Care,* 27(4), 65–82.

Fong, L. (1997). Asian-American women: An understudied minority. *Journal of Sociology and Social Welfare,* 24(1), 91–111.

Harada, N. D., & Kim, L. S. (1995). Use of mental health services by older Asian and Pacific Islander Americans. In D. K. Padgett (Ed.), *Handbook on Ethnicity, Aging, and Mental Health,* Westport, CT: Greenwood Press, 185–202.

Hyun, K. J. (2001). Is an independent self a requisite for Asian immigrants' psychological well-being in the U.S.? The case of Korean Americans. In N. G. Choi (Ed.) *Psychosocial Aspects of the Asian-American Experience: Diversity within Diversity.* New York: Haworth Press, 179–200.

Iglehart, A., & Becerra, R. M. (1995). *Social Services and the Ethnic Community.* Boston: Allyn & Bacon.

Ino, S. M., & Glicken, M. D. (1999). Treating Asian American clients in crisis: A collectivist approach. *Smith College Studies in Social Work,* 69(3), 525–540.

Kiang, P. N. (1994). When Know-Nothings speak English only: Analyzing Irish and Cambodian struggles for community development and educational equity. In K. Aguilar-San Juan, *The State of Asian America: Activism and Resistance in the 1990s.* Boston: South End Press, 125–145.

Kim, S., McLeod, J. H., & Shantzis, C. (1992). Cultural competence for evaluators working with Asian-American communities: Some practical considerations. In M. A. Orlandi, R. Weston,

& L. G. Epstein (Eds.) *Cultural Competence for Evaluators: A Guide for Alcohol and other Drug Abuse Prevention Practitioners Working with Ethnic/Racial Communities.* Rockville, MD: Office of Substance Abuse Prevention, U.S. Department of Health and Human Services, 203–260.

Kumar, A. (2000). *Passport Photos.* Berkeley: University of California Press.

Kung, W. W. (2001). Consideration of cultural factors in working with Chinese American families with a mentally ill patient. *Families in Society: The Journal of Contemporary Human Services, 82*(1), 97–107.

Kuramoto, F. H. (1995). Asian Americans. In J. Philleo & F. L. Brisbane (Eds.) *Cultural Competence for Social Workers: A Guide for Alcohol and other Drug Abuse Prevention Professionals Working with Ethnic/Racial Communities.* Rockville, MD: Center for Substance Abuse Prevention, 105–155.

Lee, J., Lei, A., & Sue, S. (2001). The current state of mental health research on Asian Americans. In N. G. Choi (Ed.) *Psychosocial Aspects of the Asian-American Experience: Diversity within Diversity.* New York: Haworth Press, 159–178.

Lee, M. (2000). Understanding Chinese battered women in North America: A review of the literature and practice implications. *Journal of Multicultural Social Work, 8*(3/4), 215–241.

Lee, P. A., & Ying, Y. (2001). Asian American adolescents' academic achievement: A look behind the model minority image. In N. G. Choi (Ed.) *Psychosocial Aspects of the Asian-American Experience: Diversity within Diversity.* New York: Haworth Press, 35–48.

Liu, G. Z. (2001). *Chinese Culture and Disability: Information for U.S. Service Providers.* Center for International Rehabilitation Research Information and Exchange. Buffalo: University at Buffalo, State University of New York.

Lorenzo, M. K., Pakiz, B., Reinherz, H. Z., & Frost, A. (1995). Emotional and behavioral problems of Asian American adolescents: A comparative study. *Child and Adolescent Social Work Journal, 12*(3), 197–212.

Miah, M. R., & Kahler, D. R. (1997). Asian-American elderly: A review of the quality of life and social service needs. *Journal of Sociology and Social Welfare, 24*(1), 79–89.

Mui, A. C. (1998). Living alone and depression among older Chinese immigrants. *Journal of Gerontological Social Work, 30*(3/4), 147–166.

Mui, A. C. (2001). Stress, coping, and depression among elderly Korean immigrants. In N. G. Choi (ed.) *Psychosocial Aspects of the Asian-American Experience: Diversity within Diversity.* New York: Haworth Press, 281–299.

Okazaki, S. (1998). Psychological assessment of Asian Americans: Research agenda for cultural competency. *Journal of Personality Assessment, 70*(1), 54–70.

Potocky, M., & McDonald, T. P. (1995). Predictors of economic status of Southeast Asian refugees: Implications for service improvement. *Social Work Research, 19*(4), 219–227.

Radhakrishnan, R. (1994). Is the "ethnic" authentic in the diaspora? In K. Aguilar-San Juan, *The State of Asian America: Activism and Resistance in the 1990s.* Boston: South End Press, 219–233.

Rhee, S. (1997). Domestic violence in the Korean immigrant family. *Journal of Sociology and Social Welfare, 24*(1), 63–77.

San Juan, E. (1994). The predicament of Filipinos in the United States:

"Where Are You From? When Are You Going Back?" In K. Aguilar-San Juan, *The State of Asian America: Activism and Resistance in the 1990s.* Boston: South End Press, 205–218.

Sethi, R. C. (1994). Smells like racism: A plan for mobilizing against anti-Asian bias. In K. Aguilar-San Juan, *The State of Asian America: Activism and Resistance in the 1990s.* Boston: South End Press, 235–250.

Shen, B., & Takeuchi, D. T. (2001). A structural model of acculturation and mental health status among Chinese Americans. *American Journal of Community Psychology, 29*(3), 387–418.

Shin, H., & Abell, N. (1999). The Homesickness and Contentment scale: Developing a culturally sensitive measure of adjustment for Asians. *Research on Social Work Practice, 9*(1), 45–60.

Shin, J. Y., Berkson, G., & Crittenden, K. (2000). Informal and professional support for solving psychological problems among Korean-speaking immigrants. *Journal of Multicultural Counseling and Development, 28*(3), 144–159.

Silka, L., & Tip, J. (1994). Empowering the silent ranks: The Southeast Asian experience. *American Journal of Community Psychology, 22*(4), 497–530.

Sinclair, B. P. (2000). Putting cultural competence into practice. *AWHONN Lifelines, 4*(2), 7–8.

Srinivasan, S. (2001). "Being Indian," "Being American": A balancing act or a creative blend? In N. G. Choi (Ed.) *Psychosocial Aspects of the Asian-American Experience: Diversity within Diversity.* New York: Haworth Press, 135–158.

U.S. Census Bureau. (2001). Current Population Survey. http://www.census .gov

Wong, S. L. (2001). Depression level in inner-city Asian American adolescents: The contributions of cultural orientation and interpersonal relationships. In N. G. Choi (Ed.), *Psychosocial Aspects of the Asian-American Experience: Diversity within Diversity.* New York: Haworth Press, 48–64.

Yen, S. (1992). Cultural competence for evaluators working with Asian/Pacific Island-American communities: Some common themes and important implications. In M. A. Orlandi, R. Weston, & L. G. Epstein (Eds.) *Cultural Competence for Evaluators: A Guide for Alcohol and Other Drug Abuse Prevention Practitioners Working with Ethnic/Racial Communities.* Rockville, MD: Office of Substance Abuse Prevention, U.S. Department of Health and Human Services, 261–291.

Ying, Y. (1995). Cultural orientation and psychological well-being in Chinese Americans. *American Journal of Community Psychology, 23*(6), 893–912.

Yoshihama, M. (2001). Model minority demystified: Emotional costs of multiple victimizations in the lives of women of Japanese descent. In N. G. Choi (Ed.) *Psychosocial Aspects of the Asian-American Experience: Diversity within Diversity.* New York: Haworth Press, 201–224.

Pacific Islanders CHAPTER

Pacific Islanders are indigenous people descended from the original peoples of Hawaii, Guam, Samoa, and other Pacific Islands. Twenty-five different Pacific Island cultures are included within the designation Asian/Pacific Islander (Okazaki, 1998). Pacific Islanders come from diverse backgrounds in Polynesian, Micronesian, and Melanesian cultures (Grieco, 2002). Polynesian island groups include Native Hawaiian, Samoan, Tongan, Tahitian, and Tokeleuan. Micronesian island groups include Chamorro (also known as Guamanian), Mariana Islanders, Saipanese, Palauan, Carolinian, Kosraean, Pohnpeian, Chuukese, Yapese, and I-Kiribati. Melanesian island groups include Fijian, Papua New Guinean, Solomon Islanders, and Ni-Vanuatu (Grieco, 2002). The largest Polynesian groups are Hawaiians, Samoans, and Tongans. The largest Micronesian group is Chamorros/Guamanians. The largest Melanesian group is Fijians (Mokuau, 1995).

The 2000 U.S. census documented 874,000 Pacific Islanders; 399,000 of these identified solely as Pacific Islanders (.1% of the U.S. population), and an additional 476,000 (.2% of the U.S. population) identified as part Pacific Islander.[1] Information on Pacific Islanders living in the U.S. areas of Guam, American Samoa, the Commonwealth

---

[1]These figures are taken directly from the U.S. Census Bureau report edited by Grieco. The fact that they do not add up precisely may be because of rounding errors, but this is not detailed in the census documents.

of the Northern Mariana Islands, and the U.S. Virgin Islands is not included in census figures (Grieco, 2002).

Pacific Islanders were the only population identified by the U.S. census in which reporting two or more races was more common than was reporting one. Pacific Islander and Asian was the most common combination (138,802 people or 29% of Pacific Islanders), followed by a combination of Pacific Islander and White (112,964 people or 24% of Pacific Islanders), a combination of Pacific Islander, Asian, and White (89,611 people or 19% of Pacific Islanders), and some other combination (35,108 people or 7% of Pacific Islanders) (Grieco, 2002).

The 1990 census documented 365,000 Pacific Islanders. The 2000 figure for Pacific Islanders only represents a 9.3% increase in population. The 2000 figure that includes Pacific Islanders of mixed heritage represents a 140% growth in the Pacific Islander population.[2] Subsequent percentages are based on all Pacific Islanders. These vary only minimally from figures for those who identify solely as Pacific Islanders. Most Pacific Islanders live in the Western United States (73%), 14% live in the South, 7% in the Northeast, and 6% in the Midwest. Fifty-eight percent live in either Hawaii or California. The cities with the largest Pacific Islander populations are Honolulu (58,130), New York City (19,203), Los Angeles (13,144), and San Diego (10,613) (Grieco, 2002).

Native Hawaiians are the largest Pacific Islander group, accounting for almost half of this population. In 2000, there were 401,000 Native Hawaiians, 133,000 Samoans, 93,000 Chamorros/Guamanians, and smaller populations of other Pacific Islanders. Native Hawaiians were the Pacific Islander population most likely to be mixed with other groups (65%). Tongans and Fijians were the least likely to be mixed with other groups (25% and 28% respectively) (Grieco, 2002).

The categories Melanesian, Micronesian, and Polynesian were developed by Europeans based on geography, cultural variations, linguistic distinctions, and perceived racial categories among Pacific Islanders. Melanesia means black islands, and in the 19th century, Melanesians were typically described as savages. Lighter-skinned Polynesians, on the other hand, were viewed as sensual and hospitable. Using these categories today may perpetuate racist assumptions and may be more misleading than illuminating (Linnekin, 1997). Because of the problems associated with the categories Polynesian, Micronesian, and Melanesian, the broader term *Pacific Islander* is used throughout this chapter to refer to the indigenous people of the Pacific Islands except when content is taken directly from another source that relies on these distinctions. When possible, specific Pacific Islander groups are identified and these more specific terms used (e.g., *Native Hawaiian, Samoan*).

This chapter gives an overview of social work with Pacific Islanders. The social science literature on Pacific Islanders is quite limited and focuses prima-

[2]In 1990, the census did not allow people to designate more than one racial or ethnic group. Therefore, precise comparisons between 1990 and 2000 census figures are not possible, making it difficult to determine how much the Pacific Islander population has grown.

rily on Native Hawaiians. A relatively comprehensive knowledge base exists on the closely related Polynesian group, the Maori of Aotearoa/New Zealand. Although Maori are not typically considered Pacific Islanders, content on this group is included in this chapter because it informs practice with Pacific Islanders and because some Maori do reside in the United States, particularly in Hawaii. The significant diversity that exists within and among Pacific Islander groups sets the context for discussion. The chapter presents information on knowledge, skills, and values/attitudes necessary for cultural competence and includes issues for cultural competence on micro and macro levels.

KNOWLEDGE FOR CULTURAL COMPETENCE

The knowledge needed for culturally competent social work with Pacific Islanders can be divided into four broad areas: diversity, history, culture, and contemporary realities. Diversity serves as an overarching concept that informs the other areas. The history, culture, and contemporary realities of Pacific Islanders vary according to factors such as national origin, colonial relationship to the United States, and immigration status.

Diversity

There is limited information available on many Pacific Islander groups. Because of their small numbers, few Pacific Islander groups have received attention from social scientists and helping professionals. Indeed, when Pacific Islanders are categorized with Asian Americans, almost all the attention focuses on various Asian American groups. Pacific Islanders are a virtually invisible population, although some reside in significant numbers in Hawaii and California and in lesser numbers throughout the United States. This limited information may contribute to erroneous generalizations about Pacific Islander populations. In fact, the extent of diversity among and within Pacific Islander populations is unclear.

Pacific Islanders are a heterogeneous population. Some are indigenous to islands that have become part of the United States (like Hawaiians); some have immigrated as nationals (like some Samoans) or migrated as citizens (like some Chamorros/Guamanians). Others reside in Pacific homelands affiliated with the United States through territories (such as some Samoans and Chamorros/Guamanians), commonwealths (like Northern Mariana Islanders), or free association (such as Palauans) (Mokuau, 1995).

A compelling similarity among Pacific Islanders is the common experience of colonization (Linnekin, 1997). In many ways, their contact with various European and American forces has been one of the primary shaping forces of contemporary Pacific Islander existence. The colonial relationship between each of the Pacific Islands and the United States is somewhat different. These historical and contemporary legal relationships influence the conditions under which Pacific Islanders came or can come to the United States and the legal status they enjoy once here.

There is broad variation in the level of traditionalism among these populations (Mokuau, 1995). Pacific Islander populations that have had extensive contact and mixing with other populations may experience and practice their traditions differently than do more isolated populations. Also, Pacific Islanders who reside on the mainland United States may have fewer cultural resources and supports than do those remaining in their traditional territories. *connection to land*

History

The history of Pacific Islanders can be viewed in three stages: (1) pre-European contact, (2) initial contact, and (3) colonization, displacement, and relocation. Understanding this history helps us understand the variations and similarities among Pacific Islander populations and puts contemporary realities within context.

Pre-European Contact Western Pacific volcanic activity created many islands and atolls that served as stepping-stones for migrations throughout the Pacific. For example, Eastern Polynesian ancestors of the Maori probably sailed from the Marquesas or Society islands, possibly from Pitcairn Island and the southern Cook Islands (Denoon, Mein-Smith & Wyndham, 2000). The first canoes of the Maori arrived in Aotearoa/New Zealand about 1,000 years ago (Gregory, 2001). The Maori view themselves as close relatives of Native Hawaiians and Tahitians. Before European contact, Pacific Islanders maintained long-distance exchange and marriage relationships. These cultures did not exist in isolation from each other despite significant distances. Rather, interactions between islands were once common, but declined with Western contact (Linnekin, 1997).

Settlement in some parts of the Pacific Islands is documented well before 10,000 B.C. These populations then spread throughout the islands of the Pacific. Between 1000 B.C. and A.D. 500, Polynesia had rapid population growth, and agricultural expansion and intensification. Extensive trade took place between islands, and social stratification began to develop. Large-scale movements of island people were common by the 16th century. Despite great distances from large landmasses, Pacific Islanders had some limited contact with outside populations, including Asian merchant ships early in the first millennium. Pacific Islanders also experienced contact with, and settlement of, some islands by South American indigenous people in the middle of the first millennium. Some castaways from Spanish galleons also made their way to Pacific Islands and were incorporated into these populations (Denoon, 1997).

Native Hawaiians originally migrated to the Hawaiian Islands from Tahiti about A.D. 750 (Hurdle, 2002). They share a common ancestry with people across the Pacific from New Zealand to Easter Island (Braun & Browne, 1998).

Initial Contact Spanish explorers landed in the Solomon Islands in 1568 while looking for gold. Like many subsequent encounters, this contact was initially positive, but soured as Spaniards' demands for food, combined with scarce island resources, led to confrontations and mutual massacres. During the 17th century, Spain's dominance of the Pacific receded and English and Dutch encroachments grew. Dutch Captain Abel Tasman arrived in New Zealand in 1642 then later sailed to Tonga. The British landed in Tahiti in 1767 and arrived in Hawaii in 1778 (Meleisea & Schoeffel, 1997).

Although there had been some earlier contact, Captain James Cook of England is touted as the discoverer of Australia and New Zealand and, indeed, the primary colonial explorer throughout the Pacific. Cook's attitude was that any resistance by indigenous people would not be tolerated. Seafaring agents of European powers became colonizers of the Pacific Islands. These Europeans considered societies like Tahiti to be Paradise and the nakedness (interpreted as sexual availability) of Polynesian women spawned many legends. Indigenous people were depicted as childlike.

European contact led to extreme depopulation of all the Pacific Islands. The Europeans brought many diseases with them, especially in 18th century. Pacific Islanders were particularly vulnerable to European-carried diseases because the remoteness of their islands left them with no immunities. Exact depopulation numbers are unclear but severe (Denoon et al., 2000). Hawaii provides just one example of the devastation brought by colonial contact. In 1778, European contact began to drastically reduce the Native Hawaiian population through measles, tuberculosis, venereal diseases, leprosy, influenza, and other infectious diseases. In response to this decimation, Asians were imported to Hawaii as laborers. The former monarchy of Hawaii was colonized by the United States in the mid-1800s. Native Hawaiians have experienced generations of intermarriage with other Pacific Islanders, Asians, Europeans, and Americans (Hurdle, 2002). Asians outnumbered Native Hawaiians in Hawaii by the 19th century (Braun & Browne, 1998).

Colonization, Displacement, and Relocation   Many Pacific Islander territories have been colonized by the United States and thus exposed to Western cultures (e.g., Hawaii as a state, American Samoa and Guam under U.S. jurisdiction) (Mokuau, 1995). The largest Pacific Islander groups, Hawaiians and Samoans, both became American by virtue of colonization. The kingdom of Hawaii was overthrown by the U.S. military in 1893 and was administered by the U.S. Department of the Interior until it became a state in 1959. American Samoa became a U.S. territory in 1900 and was initially administered by the Navy as a coaling station until it came under supervision of the Department of the Interior (Braun & Browne, 1998).

The United States is the second most important destination for contemporary Pacific Islanders (after New Zealand where they constitute 11% of the population). Nearly half of the Pacific Islander population in the United States is born here. American Samoa is both a destination for migrating Pacific Islanders and a stepping-stone to the United States for Western Samoans and Tongans.

Migration patterns shift based on the economies of the United States and New Zealand. American Samoans and Chamorros from Guam have had free access to the United States since 1951 and 1950 respectively. Many have served in the U.S. military since World War II. In 1960, Micronesian citizens of trust territories became eligible for financial assistance for education in the United States but experienced limited entry for employment until termination of their trusteeship in 1986 (or 1994 for Palauans). Entry for education was easier, so Micronesians tend to have educations above the national average, but because many are still in school, they often live below the poverty line (Nero, 1997).

Stereotypical images of Pacific Islanders developed during initial colonization and persist today. Europeans and Americans both perpetuated the colonial assumption that Pacific Islanders were politically incompetent and foreign intervention was needed to end chronic instability and warfare (Linnekin, 1997). Historians portrayed Pacific Islanders as helpless to withstand European advancement. Judgmental attitudes depicted Pacific Islanders as lazy. As part of standard colonial assimilationist practices, early formal education in the islands was conducted almost exclusively by missionaries (Linnekin, 1997).

Extensive movement and relocation of Pacific Islanders occurred with colonization. Many whole communities were relocated. For example, the U.S. government removed some Pacific Islander communities when their homelands were used for testing nuclear weapons during World War II. Some relocated peoples such as Bikinians continue connections with the United States. Through this arrangement, they retain a separate status within the independent Marshall Islands. Bikinians and former residents of the other "Atomic Atolls" Utrik, Enewetak, and Rongelap, also receive food and income from trust funds in compensation for their removal from their homelands (Nero, 1997).

Some relocated communities have fared better than others. Many Marshallese have come to the United States. Their government opened a consulate in Newport Beach to serve their Southern California community. They also have a large population in Hawaii (Nero, 1997). On the other hand, relocation and financial payments have proved to be inadequate substitutes for land for Bikinians and Banabans. The Bikini community has been moved to Rongerik then to Kwajalein then to Kili and unsuccessfully tried to use part of its financial settlement to buy land in Hawaii. Today, most Bikinians live on islands of the Majuro Atoll. Substantial payments have been unable to secure adequate living places, and payments have led to factions and divisions within the community. Indeed, financial payments have often exacerbated tensions between individual rights and collective needs of Pacific Islanders (Nero, 1997).

No community better exemplifies the damaging effects of essentialising notions of identity, mixed heritage, and international mobility than the Chamorros of Guam, . . . The first colonised in the Pacific, the indigenous people of the Mariana Islands were reduced to 5 percent of their precontact numbers by diseases and warfare with Spain. Finally vanquished by 1700, a mere 3000 survivors were resettled on Guam, where they began reconstructing their lives. They became Catholic, married members of the Spanish, Philippine, and Mexican ruling class, and incorporated many elements from those cultures. From their own heritage they maintained their language, the strength of the extended family with its matrilineal bias, and a preference for hierarchies in which status is demonstrated by generosity. (Nero, 1997, p. 449)

Chamorros have lived in many places and have experienced many cultural influences. Elite Chamorros emphasized their Spanish heritage, and some people have questioned their authenticity as a Pacific Island people. In the 19th century, some Chamorros settled in Saipan with Spanish encouragement, whereas others traveled to Hawaii and the United States as whalers. In 1899, when the United States claimed Guam after the Spanish American war, Chamorros on Guam were separated from those of Saipan. Other Mariana Islands and Carolines became territories of Germany then Japan. Many Chamorros relocated throughout the Carolines and Marshalls, and many on Guam joined the U.S. military. In 1978, the Federation of Guamanian Associations of America estimated that 55,000 Chamorros lived in California, and 47,000 continue to reside in Guam. The history of these people raises questions of identity: Who is a Chamorro or Guamanian? Is Guamanian a hybrid successor to Chamorro culture? Although the specific situation of the Chamorros is distinct, it also illustrates the many changes that Pacific Islanders have faced during the last two centuries.

Culture

Pacific Islander cultures share many similarities because of extensive contact between, and interrelationships among, island groups. Some common themes across Pacific Island groups include (1) the value of the collective manifested in relationship to family, community, and the spiritual world, including an emphasis on genealogy; (2) strong relationships between humans, animals, and plants; (3) protocols and procedures guided by spiritual beliefs; and (4) self-empowerment, renewal, independence, and pride as articulated through the sovereignty movement that emphasizes self-determination (Mokuau, 1995). Several key areas of culture are important for social workers to understand, including spirituality, family networks, values, gender roles, balance, and harmony.

Spirituality   Spirituality is a key element of Pacific Islander cultures. For example, prayer is the foundation of Hawaiian healing practices. Communication on a spiritual level creates trust. When two spirits or souls meet, healing takes place (Morelli, Fong, & Oliveira, 2001). In another illustration, as part of their spiritual belief system, some Pacific Islanders, like the Maori, bury the placenta of a newborn child to link that person to the land (Gregory, 2001). Spiritual health is considered more important than physical health, thus many Pacific Islanders are very accepting of people with an illness or disability (Braun & Browne, 1998).

Family Networks   'Ohana (family) is the center of life in Hawaiian culture (Morelli et al., 2001; Rezentes, 1996). Interdependence "is exemplified by

Hawaiian values of *'ohana* or family, which designates an entire community rather than being restricted to blood relationships, and *kokua*, which refers to help given without needing to be requested and without expectation of payment" (Gotay et al., 2000, p. 530). The Hawaiian value placed on extended families emphasizes a need for harmonious relationships and maintenance of good will (Hurdle, 2002).

Oral histories and genealogical traditions are a meaningful component of contemporary Pacific Islander life (Linnekin, 1997). Oral exchange of genealogies, history, traditions, and legends is passed from one generation to the next to perpetuate culture (Morelli et al., 2001). *Waka* (canoe) is a powerful metaphor for unity in Aotearoa/New Zealand. People trace ancestry to a particular canoe that arrived in Aotearoa/New Zealand, and this is the basis for their family networks. The canoe their original ancestor traveled in is used in introductions and self-identification (Bishop & Glynn, 1999).

For the Maori, like many Pacific Islander cultures, community is based on a collective strength including sharing, nurturing, supporting, and empowering interdependent groups. Community networks are anchored in the nested systems of *whanau, hapu,* and *iwi. Whanau,* the extended family, is the primary building block of community. Family membership gives a sense of identity and culture. *Hapu,* typically translated as subtribe, is comparable to a Native American clan system. This network of extended families is connected by a common ancestor and governed by a hereditary chief. An *iwi* or tribe is an economically and socially self-sufficient grouping through which political decisions are made and land is vested. Each *iwi* maintains one or more *marae* (a meeting house that serves as a spiritual center) where social and political decisions are made. *Iwi* and *hapu* are associated with certain *waka* or canoes that ancestors arrived in. A clear sense of identity, role, place, and responsibility are grounded in *whanau, hapu,* and *iwi.* Relatedness to, and responsibility for all parts of the environment are integral concepts in Maori culture (Gregory, 2001).

In many Pacific Islander cultures, family connections extend beyond human beings and incorporate other members of the living world. Hawaiian tradition holds that the taro plant is the older brother of humankind, thus establishing roles and responsibilities among junior and senior siblings (Linnekin, 1997).

Values   In recent years there has been a resurgence of cultural identity including language revitalization, reclaiming traditional land, developing traditional music and dance, traditional healing, and culturally based social and health services among Native Hawaiians (Hurdle, 2002). Hawaiian values that influence family relations and help-seeking behavior include *mana* (energy that permeates and links all things), *lokahi* (harmony and unity), *pono* (rightness or proper order), *'ohana* (extended family and social supports), *kokua* (mutual help and cooperation), and *kuleana* (role). Explicit roles are based on age, gender, class, and ability. Respect is accorded to elders for their roles as teachers and keepers of culture (Braun & Browne, 1998).

Kawa/tikanga or protocol is very important in how things are conducted among Maori people (Bishop & Glynn, 1999). For Maori, knowledge is powerful and to be protected for the benefit of the group, not the individual. Prohibitions and benefits are ascribed to knowledge transmission. Not all knowledge is for everyone. Indeed, some cultural knowledge is considered *tapu* (sacred or forbidden) (Bishop & Glynn, 1999; Gregory, 2001).

Gender Roles   Women in island societies rarely acted according to the European male explorers' expectations of passivity, devaluation, and dependency but because men interacted primarily with men, this is what is recorded (Linnekin, 1997). Preconceptions of Europeans shaped their interactions with islanders. According to Edward Said, "Distancing, stereotypic visions of the exotic not only informed European colonialism but continue to pervade Western representations of colonised peoples. Representing the culture or the past of an indigenous people is implicitly a matter of political power" (Linnekin, 1997, p. 12).

Balance and Harmony   Balance and harmony are central concepts in many Pacific Islander cultures. Soothing or preventing conflict, shame, and interpersonal disruption is very important for Hawaiians (Morelli et al., 2001). Traditional Hawaiian values require a balance between humility and pride (Rezentes, 1996). In Hawaiian culture, illness and misfortune are often caused by an imbalance of *mana* or loss of *pono*. Restoring *pono (ho'oponopono)* involves prayer and self-scrutiny for those who are out of balance, problem definition, restitution, and forgiveness (Braun & Browne, 1998). Likewise, for the Maori, good health is a combination of physical, mental, familial, and spiritual health. Poor health or mental illness may refer to disruptions in any of these areas (Gregory, 2001).

Contemporary Realities

Data on Pacific Islanders is often aggregated with Asians and thus obscures their health and social status (Braun & Browne, 1998). Many of the contemporary realities of Pacific Islanders are the direct result of colonization and efforts to counteract its effects. For example, in Aotearoa, Maori are 12 to 15% of the population but constitute almost 50% of those in prison. They are three to four times more likely to experience social problems, their unemployment rate is three times higher, they have a higher school dropout rate and a lower life expectancy than do the descendants of the Europeans that colonized their land (Gregory, 2001). Social workers need to be aware of contemporary realities of Pacific Islanders, including alcohol and drug use, social and health issues, homelands, and strengths.

Alcohol and Drug Use   There are few studies of alcohol and drug use among Pacific Islanders but a growing body of descriptive and preliminary data exists (Mokuau, 1995). When statistics on Pacific Islanders and Asians are combined, it makes accurate assessment of alcohol and other drug prevalence impossible. Even when Pacific Islanders are listed separately from Asians, they aren't typically separated by Islander group (Mokuau, 1995).

Social problems such as substance abuse may result from a breakdown of cultural values associated with colonization or immigration (Mokuau, 1995). Conversely, using tradition can be helpful in preventing alcohol or drug use. In the traditional worldview, alcohol and drugs block the path to spirituality. Reconnecting spiritually can be an important form of prevention. Use of indigenous peer educators also helps in prevention (Mokuau, 1995).

Among Asian Pacific Islander groups, only Hawaiians drink at rates similar to those of Whites (Kim, McLeod, & Shantzis, 1992). A survey in Hawaii found that Native Hawaiians experience more serious problems with alcohol, tobacco, and illicit drugs than do other populations in the state (Mokuau, 1995).

Relaxation and camaraderie are the hallmarks of Native Hawaiian drinking behavior. This type of social drinking is not necessarily linked to problem behavior. Drinking gatherings emphasize the cultural values of affiliation, rest, and celebration. Hawaiian male youth in rural areas spend weekends drinking with friends at beaches or parks. To drink beer and "talk story" is a cultural form of communication that is personal and nonconfrontative. The storytelling context preserves relationships (Mokuau, 1995). Considerably less information is available on other Pacific Islander populations, but the limited data suggests that Samoans experience alcohol and other drug problems. Alcohol is also becoming an increasing problem in various island homelands, particularly for men (Mokuau, 1995).

Social and Health Issues   Hawaiians often live far from Western medical care and are less likely to have comprehensive insurance. In the 1980s, federal legislation established the Native Hawaiian Health Care System on each major island and scholarships for training Native Hawaiian health care providers. This resulted in more community-based care designed to increase health status (Braun & Browne, 1998).

Hawaiians have a 34% higher death rate than do other U.S. groups, which reflects high rates of cancer, heart disease, and cerebrovascular disease. Native Hawaiians have a shorter life expectancy, and higher rates of suicide, child abuse and neglect, substance abuse, and criminal conviction than other groups do. Their low income, limited use of health care, and infrequent prenatal care results in a high incidence of low birth weight and premature infants (Hurdle, 2002). Native Hawaiian women also have the lowest screening rates and the highest breast and cervical cancer mortality rates in Hawaii (Gotay et al., 2000).

In general, Pacific Islanders are a relatively young population with low income and education (Mokuau, 1995). Among Pacific Islanders, Samoans are at particular risk of poverty (Braun & Browne, 1998).

Extensive economic interdependence exists among Tahiti, American Samoa, and the former U.S. Trust Territory of Micronesia. Countries that maintain a close relationship with their former colonizer enjoy a better standard of living (e.g., American Samoa is much better off than Western Samoa).

Economic interdependence spans long distances as Pacific Islanders in the United States and other countries send substantial amounts of money to relatives in the islands (Nero, 1997).

Hawaiian Homelands   Hawaiian homelands are public lands held in trust by the state of Hawaii for the benefit of Native Hawaiians. There are currently 62 Hawaiian homeland areas. The Hawaiian Homes Commission Act of 1920 created a program where these lands are leased to Native Hawaiians. Twenty-three percent of the people in the state of Hawaii live on Hawaiian homelands. Eighty-three percent of these are people who are Native Hawaiian or Native Hawaiian in combination with one or more other Pacific Islander groups. Fourteen percent of people who are exclusively Native Hawaiian live on Hawaiian homelands, making them the people most likely to live on the homelands. Eight percent of the population who are Native Hawaiian combined with something else live on the homelands (Grieco, 2002).

Strengths   Some aspects of Pacific Islander culture enhance the ability of Pacific Islanders to cope with stressful situations. For example, among Native Hawaiians, there is often a fatalistic acceptance of dementia symptoms. A common saying, "more makule, more pupule" translates roughly as "the older you get, the more mixed up you get." Among Native Hawaiians, there is an expectation that someone in the family will accept the honorable role of caring for an elder with dementia. Participation in Western medical care for dementia is more likely if the doctor is known to a friend or family member (Braun & Browne, 1998).

Many Pacific Islanders, particularly Native Hawaiians, have retained a strong sense of themselves as independent cultures despite colonization, resulting in a strong sense of self-determination. Indeed, decolonization and empowerment are strong themes among many Pacific Islanders as well as the Maori of Aotearoa/New Zealand. This emphasis on the inherent strengths of being indigenous, or the people of the land, can be an important foundation for community empowerment.

SKILLS FOR CULTURAL COMPETENCE

Culturally competent helping professionals need to be able to demonstrate a variety of helping skills such as listening, communicating, and networking within a cultural context. Without a cultural dimension, general skills cannot lead to culturally appropriate helping. The competent professional brings culture-specific skills in Pacific Islander protocols to the helping relationship.

Engaging

Skills in outreach are important in accessing and serving this often-invisible population. Outreach begins with recognizing where Pacific Islander populations are located and identifying their social service needs. For example, staff at a social service agency and health clinic located in Oakland, California,

Conflicts of/what we are right [handwritten marginal note]

began to recognize that their neighborhood had a significant Tongan population. Once this was identified, outreach workers developed culturally appropriate strategies to engage the Tongan population and bring them to the agency for services and medical care.

Helping professionals can do several specific things to facilitate engaging Pacific Islander clients. These culturally specific elements need to be used in combination with more generalized social work techniques for engaging. Awareness and following of cultural protocols can be very important in engaging Pacific Islander clients (Rezentes, 1996). In particular, the protocols of removing shoes during a home visit, accepting or offering food and drink, and self-disclosure of genealogy can be meaningful in engaging.

When making a home visit with Pacific Islanders, removing shoes is an important gesture. For many Pacific Islanders, wearing shoes in the home is considered trampling on the ancestors and is a highly offensive act. Upon entering a home, the helping professional can look to see if shoes appear to be kept by the door and the client is either barefoot or in slippers. This can be an indication that the client follows this protocol. A helping professional who does not follow this practice will be viewed as extraordinarily disrespectful and insensitive.

Food and drink are frequently offered as signs of hospitality to helping professionals making a home visit. Despite the professional teaching that this may blur roles and boundaries in the professional relationship, following these protocols can be very important in engaging Pacific Islander clients. Even partaking of a minimal amount of food and drink is considered acceptable. Likewise, helping professionals may want to consider having some food and drink available for Pacific Islander clients during office visits. This could be as simple as offering a cup of coffee or cookies. This basic gesture can be significant in beginning the engaging process.

For many Pacific Islander people, family genealogy is a key component of identity. Traditional greetings may include recitations of the names of ancestors and how they are related to a particular individual. This type of disclosure sets the stage for interactions between people. In a similar vein, some initial self-disclosure by the social worker can set the context for a productive discussion (Rezentes, 1996). As part of an early discussion of roles and expectations, the social worker may disclose facts such as how long he or she has been at the agency and how long he or she has lived in the community.

Assessing

Many Pacific Islanders have been exposed to a variety of cultural influences and many are of mixed cultural heritage themselves. Assessment of cultural identity along a linear continuum is frequently oversimplified and is not meaningful for most Native Hawaiians (Rezentes, 1996). Individualized assessments must be used to determine whether a culturally based intervention would be a good fit for clients (Morelli et al., 2001). Assessing clients' connection to traditional Pacific Islander cultures is an important part of explor-

[handwritten margin note:] lots of talk about cultural assessments. Will we see any?

ing who they are, what issues are important to them, and what type of assistance is likely to be most effective. It is important for helping professionals to avoid having stereotypical preconceptions guide their work; therefore, a thorough assessment is crucial to culturally competent practice.

Assessments of Pacific Islander clients, as in assessments of other populations, need to include an examination of the social environment. Exploring the context for work includes examining stressors and supports such as the relationship of the particular Pacific Islander group to the United States and the client's connection to existing culturally based social structures in the community.

The literature of the helping professions has begun to stress the importance of using culturally appropriate assessment tools rather than instruments normed for use with other cultural groups, but little work has been done in this area with Pacific Islanders. Few standardized instruments have been normed for Pacific Islander populations. A taskforce that undertook an extensive search of assessment tools used to measure substance abuse and related concepts with Pacific Islanders found that most measures do not have established reliability and validity with this population (Center for Substance Abuse Prevention, 2000). Helping professionals need to avoid using standardized instruments with this population, or use such instruments with extreme caution, noting their inadequacies and how these may translate into misleading scores.

Intervening

A number of culturally based social work interventions have been developed for Pacific Islanders, particularly in Hawaii. The development of culturally based interventions has proceeded even though culturally based assessments have received limited attention. Many of these interventions incorporate traditional forms of healing. For example, *ho'oponopono* is a family-based conflict resolution strategy performed by a *kahuna* (traditional healer) in ancient times to maintain community harmony. The practice was adopted in the 1970s by a therapeutic children's center when it became apparent that Native Hawaiian children were not making adequate progress. Mental health workers initiated meetings with Hawaiian elders and *kahuna* that resulted in revitalizing the use of *ho'oponopono*. These methods have since been adapted and used in schools, residential youth treatment centers, and Hawaiian churches (Hurdle, 2002).

The traditional process of *ho'oponopono* bears some similarities to family therapy (Rezentes, 1996). It takes place within the extended family network and involves identifying the problem with all involved parties, discussing the effect on the family system, identifying possible solutions to the problem, and implementing the chosen solution. *Ho'oponopono* is a solemn ritual of traditional healing based on a shared cultural tradition with clear roles for participants. The ritual has a spiritual focus and is based on cultural values that call for a resolution to restore harmony (Hurdle, 2002).

[handwritten margin note: Holistic approach - spirituality]

[handwritten margin note: FAMILY Centered Interventions]

Family systems components are important in substance abuse treatment for Pacific Islander women (Morelli et al., 2001). Incorporation of family was a primary consideration in the development of a culturally based, woman-centered, residential program for pregnant and postpartum substance-abusing Asian/Pacific Islanders in rural Hawaii. This program used Hawaiian healing practices or deep cultural therapy and community-based supports such as elder-guided, infant-mother bonding (Morelli et al., 2001).

In the past, most programs have not recognized women's treatment needs such as child care. In the United States, there is significant stigmatization of women who abuse alcohol or drugs, especially if they are pregnant. This stigma and the associated fear of losing their children are barriers to treatment. The Hawaiian deep cultural therapy used in the program consisted of *ho'oponopono* (conflict resolution), deep culture (storytelling), *lo'i* (taro patch), and *lomilomi* (massage therapy). The underlying principles of these traditional healing practices are in harmony with women's relational needs and provide a foundation for healing (Morelli et al., 2001). The Hawaiian deep cultural therapy was instrumental in the recovery process of 68% of the women in the program. These practices helped the women reconnect with their spirituality, face their emotional pain, confront the effects of their substance abuse, and begin the healing process. Sixty-six percent said Hawaiian parenting classes were helpful in developing parenting skills, positive attitudes, and knowledge (Morelli et al., 2001).

Interventions can be examined and modified to appropriately fit Pacific Islander populations. For example, the Gandhian approach to family social work that examines nonviolent ways to resolve problems has been found to be compatible with Pacific Islander values such as prioritizing the needs of the family before the individual (Fong, Boyd, & Browne, 1999). Likewise, cognitive behavioral, systems, and existential therapies have proven useful with Native Hawaiians (Rezentes, 1996).

Advocacy is an important skill when working with Pacific Islander populations. As many of these populations struggle to correct past and ongoing social injustice, they often seek reparation for displacement and seek a stronger voice for self-determination. Social workers and other helping professionals can serve as advocates for Pacific Islanders as they struggle with issues of self-determination and access to quality, culturally appropriate services.

Empowerment is a crucial skill that goes with advocacy. Social workers can help Pacific Islanders strengthen their own abilities to bring about positive change in the lives of individuals, families, and communities. Family empowerment has been identified as an important component of culturally competent work with Pacific Islanders (Fong et al., 1999). One particular way Pacific Islander clients can be empowered is to help them challenge the stereotypes that caricature them and negatively influence their self-images. For example, many Maori in New Zealand, much like the indigenous people of the United States, have internalized the perspective that depicts them as suffering widespread devastation when Europeans introduced alcohol. Maori were portrayed as helpless victims without the strength to resist this overwhelming temptation. In reality, historical records do not support the stereotype of instantaneous widespread cultural destabilization with the introduction of alcohol. Reframing the stereotype with historical information can be empowering and encourage community self-determination (Mancall, Robertson, & Huriwai, 2000). In working with Maori people, cultural affirmation is critical. Helping professionals need to be willing to affirm Maori cultural identity and empower Maori clients to explore and develop culturally meaningful aspects of their lives (Weaver, Nikora, & Moeke-Pickering, 1998).

A study that examined the specific elements of cultural competence with Maori people revealed that several key skills are important when working with this population. Most importantly, listening and communication skills are necessary for culturally competent helping. A helping professional needs to listen, be patient, give people time to express themselves, and seek feedback. Communication skills include an ability to interpret nonverbal behavior and the ability to interpret communication within specific cultural contexts. For example, Maori often express various feelings through their eye movements. Interpersonal skills are also critical for culturally appropriate helping. These include skills in group work, facilitation, interviewing, networking, conflict resolution, and the ability to work within culturally based family structures, social structures, and various components of the community. Helping professionals must also be able to work within cultural protocols. Helping professionals need to understand Maori culture and norms and be able to use Maori social structures (Weaver et al., 1998).

Culturally appropriate approaches to research design, program implementation, educational materials, and evaluation were used in a health promotion program for Native Hawaiian women. This project was community driven, with Native Hawaiian representation in all phases from grant proposal development to data interpretation. The intervention was grounded in the significance of social support in Hawaiian culture. Hawaiian women functioning as lay health educators provided support and education. Information was delivered in groups in traditional talk story fashion. It was theorized that information would spread throughout the community, not just to those in educational and support groups. Ultimately, the intervention was successful in increasing cancer-screening behaviors (Gotay et al., 2000).

Stereotypes have often influenced the way research has been conducted and the way programs have been implemented with Pacific Islander populations. For example, the deficit perspective often held by researchers has led them to examine the inability of Maori culture to cope with problems rather than framing research questions in a different way. The assumption that Maori culture is inferior to that of the colonizer has permeated research. As Maori have pushed for self-determination, they have challenged researchers to alter their ways of conducting research. Research on Maori must be based on Maori epistemologies and conducted in culturally appropriate ways. Researchers must share power and control to promote Maori self-determination (Bishop & Glynn, 1999).

VALUES/ATTITUDES FOR CULTURAL COMPETENCE

Culturally competent helping professionals need to bring certain attitudes and values to their work. They need to be humble, open to learning, and respectful. They need to go beyond tolerating cultural differences to truly valuing and affirming Pacific Islander culture, values, and identities, and advocating for cultural and social justice. Without these attitudes and values, cultural knowledge and skills cannot lead to competent helping.

In working with Pacific Islanders, helping professionals must value decolonization and self-determination. Decolonization means the ability and willingness of members of the dominant society to recognize how their group has systematically devalued the culture of the colonized group and imposed their own values, beliefs, and ways of doing things. Valuing self-determination of colonized groups involves letting go of oppression and cultural imposition and supporting colonized groups in their right to assert their own values, beliefs, and ways of doing things. These values were identified as key elements in working with Maori clients as well (Weaver et al., 1998). Helping professionals need to recognize and work through the impact of colonization on themselves as well as on their clients.

Social justice is a primary component of culturally competent helping. It is important to be aware of cultural differences and perspectives. Helping professionals need to be nonracist and place a priority on equality and equity issues. They need to avoid using generalizations or holding negative stereotypes about Maori people (Weaver et al., 1998). Using a strengths perspective, helping professionals must question stereotypes about Pacific Islanders including the beliefs that they are incompetent, promiscuous, and lazy. These stereotypes undermine Pacific Islanders' sense of self and their abilities to bring about positive changes in their communities.

A study of culturally competent helping practices with Maori people revealed that it is crucial for helping professionals to display humility and openness. Helping professionals must not make assumptions. They need to be nonjudgmental, nondomineering, and unbiased, as well as flexible, humble, relaxed, and patient. Helping professionals need to emphasize the importance of the client's values and welfare. They must be considerate, understanding, and supportive, while expressing caring in a genuine and responsible fashion (Weaver et al., 1998).

Demonstrating respect for Maori values is also an important component of cultural competence. Helping professionals need to understand and respect Maori values, concepts, beliefs, attitudes, and family decision making. This includes understanding and embracing sacredness (*tapu*). Helping professionals need to show respect for clients, including their cultures, voices and skills, beliefs and attitudes, and cultural practices. Helping professionals must recognize the importance of being indigenous and *tangata whenua* (literally "the people of the land"). Helping professionals need to emphasize and focus on links such as *whakapapa* (genealogy). It is important to value a person's place as a member of a *whanau* (family), *hapu* (subtribe/clan), and *iwi* (tribe) (Weaver et al., 1998).

CASE EXAMPLE

Leann Curtis, a social worker at Bennett School for the Deaf, received a referral from a colleague at an elementary school on the north side of Oahu. Warren Perry, an 8-year-old with a hearing impairment, is in need of specialized services and his current elementary school is not equipped to meet his educational needs. Recently, he has been acting out in school. His family walked out on a conference with Warren's teacher and is seen as uncooperative by school personnel. In preparation for her initial contact with Warren and his family, Leann reviewed Warren's records and learned that his family is a blend of Native Hawaiian and Maori. She consulted a local Native Hawaiian elder who recommended she engage the family through a home visit. Upon her arrival, Leann saw the family had left their shoes at the door, so she did the same. As part of her role introduction, she told the family a bit about herself and her family of origin. Toward the end of her visit, Leann brought up the unsuccessful contacts the family had with their previous school and asked how she could be more helpful. They disclosed that during the most recent meeting, the teacher sat on her desk as she listed the behavioral problems Warren was exhibiting in the classroom. In Maori culture, sitting on a table or desk is considered highly offensive, disrespectful, and a significant violation of cultural protocol. This behavior, along with the teacher's abrupt manner led the family to believe that the school and its personnel had no interest in understanding or helping Warren; thus, there was no point in wasting time in an unproductive meeting.

The following considerations were relevant in approaching the case in a culturally competent manner:

- Leann took time before initiating contact with the family to learn something about common protocols in Pacific Islander families. When she arrived at the home, she saw indications that these protocols are observed in this particular family so she began to follow them. As she introduced herself, she mentioned the contact she had with the Native Hawaiian elder and her hopes that with the family's guidance she will be able to assist them in the ways they deem most appropriate.
- Leann knows that this family has been labeled as resistant and uncooperative, so she was careful not to push her own agenda of placement in Bennett School and put the family in a defensive posture.
- As part of her engaging work with this family, she spent the bulk of her time listening to the concerns expressed by the family. She has set a comfortable climate and has demonstrated her interest in the family. This

encouraged them to begin to disclose some vital information about what
went wrong in earlier contacts with school personnel.

- Leann's efforts have facilitated the early stages of engaging. The family has begun to trust her based on her demonstrated interest and
respect for their culture and her contact with the elder before her visit.
She has done a good job of laying the foundation for a productive
working relationship.

CULTURAL COMPETENCE IN SOCIAL POLICIES

Although most helping professionals will not be familiar with many of the
laws and social policies that specifically target various Pacific Islander populations, culturally competent professionals should understand some general
policy themes. Policies have, and continue to, define the relationship between
the United States and various Pacific Islander groups. Policies define the
nature of the various colonial relationships including efforts for the United
States to decolonize or withdraw from involvement with various Pacific
Island nations. These policies define who can come to the United States,
under what circumstances, and what their legal status is likely to be once
within the United States.

Indeed, members of the largest Pacific Islander population in the United
States, Native Hawaiians, have become defined as U.S. citizens. In many
ways, their situation is comparable with that of American Indians, and
indeed, sometimes Native Hawaiians are defined as Native Americans. In
fact, however, there is considerably less federal law defining a unique indigenous status for Native Hawaiians and a government-to-government relationship with the United States. Native Hawaiians have far fewer legal
protections and social programs designed to meet their needs than other
indigenous Americans do. No treaties exist between Native Hawaiians and
the federal government, Native Hawaiians are not organized into separate
tribes or nations, and they have no reservations. This lack of protection
through laws and social policies makes Native Hawaiians a particularly vulnerable population. Social policies need to be understood within a context of
colonization and the need for social justice. Helping professionals must take
an activist stance in confronting unjust policies and shaping new policies in
culturally competent and just ways.

Largely because of their colonial histories, Pacific Islanders experience significant social problems that deserve attention from policy makers. For social
policies to be culturally appropriate, they must support biculturalization of
Pacific Islander and Western treatment interventions (Morelli et al., 2001).
One example of a social policy that specifically targets the needs of Pacific
Islanders is the Native Hawaiian Health Care Improvement Act of 1988 (P.L.
100–579). This act funded programs on most of the Hawaiian Islands to provide culturally based health care, health education, and health promotion
(Hurdle, 2002).

CULTURAL COMPETENCE IN SOCIAL AGENCIES

Some social agencies have made significant efforts to incorporate cultural dimensions in their programs. Traditional Hawaiian healing practices are now used in some prisons, schools, residential treatment facilities, and family services (Hurdle, 2002).

Very little has been written about incorporation of traditional protocols in management and administration. As agencies begin to move toward cultural competence, it is important to ask whether the foundation of agency services include Pacific Islander epistemologies or whether they are based exclusively on Western ways of knowing and doing. The attitude of superiority inherent in colonization makes it difficult to acknowledge alternative ways of doing things as valid. The split between "professional" and "grassroots" is likely to continue, but a blending of traditions in social service agencies could significantly benefit Pacific Islander clients.

COMMUNITY INTERVENTIONS

Macro-level interventions and community development have an important role to play in decreasing the social and health problems of Pacific Islanders. In the mid-1990s, the Queen Emma Foundation in Hawaii targeted rural communities on the island of Oahu that had high concentrations of Native Hawaiians with health and social problems. The foundation employed a culturally competent community development strategy that allowed the community members to identify their own problems and help create needed programs and services.

The Ahupua'a Access and Support Model used by the Queen Emma Foundation was based on ancient Hawaiian values. This model outlines a framework for support of communities based on levels of access; all levels are interdependent and holistic and rest on the foundation of *lokahi* (unity). The primary support system is the family, both nuclear and extended, with the community (*malama'ohana*) being of secondary support. The community level is envisioned to support a *pu'uhonua* (place of refuge); historically, this was a particular location that provided refuge and protection to people in need. The *pu'uhonua* is now being reframed as a community center that provides services such as outpatient medical care, counseling services, or respite care (Hurdle, 2002, p. 190).

This development project was a result of a community visioning process. Ultimately, the project resulted in the creation of a child-care center, farmer's market, health promotion program, and healthy lifestyle program that included nutritional instruction based on a traditional Hawaiian diet. Traditional healers play an integral role in the clinics (Hurdle, 2002).

Research agendas and concerns are usually determined by the dominant/colonizing culture. Typically, researchers are the primary beneficiaries of research. Research does not usually benefit indigenous people; however, this need not be the case. Examples from the Maori of Aotearoa/New Zealand illustrate how non-indigenous researchers and service providers can work respectfully within an indigenous cultural context. Research can be done consciously within *Kaupapa Maori* (Maori philosophy) and address concerns about initiation, benefits, representation, legitimation, and accountability in research. Researchers can consciously step out of the Western paradigm that defines distinct roles for those who do research and those who are researched. These roles can be reframed according to the research participant's domain (Bishop & Glynn, 1999). Cultural competence requires that researchers work with Pacific Islander populations in supportive, rather than in exploitive, ways.

Culturally inappropriate research is not only exploitive but tends to generate inappropriate and stereotypical information. Such information serves as a faulty foundation for practice and, thus, perpetuates cultural incompetence. Often research has simplified Maori knowledge so that it could be understood by outsiders, thus leading to distortions believed by non-Maori and Maori alike. Researchers are seen as experts and Maori voices are silenced (Bishop & Glynn, 1999).

Bishop and Glynn (1999) identified the keys to culturally appropriate research within a Maori context: (1) *Whakawhanaungatanga* (establishing relationships in a Maori manner). The relationship is fundamental and involves participatory research that addresses power and control concerns. Researchers must be involved as participants in the research, not simply outsiders. (2) *Tino rangatiratanga* (self-determination) is an emphasis on indigenous autonomy and control. (3) Knowledge as *taonga tuku iho* (treasures passed down from ancestors) consists of cultural messages that guide life today (Bishop & Glynn, 1999).

CONCLUSION

The limited information available on culturally competent social work practice with Pacific Islanders is often confounded with the information on Asian American populations. In striving for cultural competence, helping professionals can draw on the broader social science knowledge base that documents the significant impact that colonization has had on Pacific Islander populations. In their work with these populations, social workers must reflect on their own roles, which may inadvertently contribute to perpetuating colonization or can consciously support decolonization, self-determination, and empowerment.

Exercises

Exercise #1: Reflecting on the Hawaiian sovereignty movement and client self-determination

Review the recent literature on the Hawaiian sovereignty movement. Compare and contrast how the values reflected in this movement fit with the value of client self-determination in a one-on-one relationship with a social work client.

Exercise #2: Practicing an introductory protocol

Genealogy is an important part of introductions in Pacific Islander protocols. Write a one-page description of how you might introduce yourself and your background when you first meet a Pacific Islander family. Reflect on your level of comfort or discomfort with self-disclosure and how you could reach a comfortable level of disclosure that is engaging without being too revealing or focused on yourself.

Exercise #3: The development of social policies for Native Hawaiians

Even though Native Hawaiians and American Indians are both populations indigenous to what is now the United States, very different social policies have been developed for these groups. Review the literature and begin to examine why American Indians have substantially more legal protections than Native Hawaiians do. What implications does this have for the development of future social policies that address the needs of Native Hawaiians and other Pacific Islanders?

Additional Resources

Denoon, D., Firth, S., Linnekin, J., Meleisea, M., & Nero, K. (1997). *The Cambridge History of the Pacific Islands*. Cambridge: Cambridge University Press. This book provides an overview of the history and contemporary realities of Pacific Islanders. It is a useful tool for familiarizing helping professionals with the different Pacific Islander populations and their struggles with colonization and decolonization.

Grieco, E. (2002). *The Native Hawaiian and Other Pacific Islander Population: 2000.* U.S. Bureau of the Census. This census report presents current information on the Pacific Islander population in a concise form. Information includes geographical distribution, age, poverty status, and other demographic information as well as a brief description of Hawaiian homelands. This is a useful resource for becoming familiar with the different Pacific Islander groups.

Hurdle, D. E. (2002). Native Hawaiian traditional healing: Culturally based interventions for social work practice. *Social Work, 47*(2), 183–192. This article describes traditional indigenous Hawaiian healing methods and how they can be used with social work clients in a contemporary context. This content is useful for assisting helping professionals in integrating culture in their work with Pacific Islanders.

Rezentes, W. C. III (1996). *Ka Lama Kukui Hawaiian Psychology: An Introduction.* Honolulu: A'ali'i Books. This book, written by a Native Hawaiian helping professional, describes traditional Hawaiian beliefs and helping practices. The author presents how these traditional concepts can be integrated in the helping relationship.

References

Bishop, R. L., & Glynn, T. (1999). Researching in Maori contexts: An interpretation of participatory consciousness. *Journal of Intercultural Studies, 20*(2), 167–186.

Braun, K. L., & Browne, C. V. (1998). Perceptions of dementia, caregiving, and help seeking among Asian and Pacific Islander Americans. *Health and Social Work, 23*(4), 262–274.

Center for Substance Abuse Prevention. (2000). *Core Measures: Phase II.* Rockville, MD. Center for Substance Abuse Prevention.

Denoon, D. (1997). Human settlement. In Denoon, D., Firth, S., Linnekin, J., Meleisea, M., & Nero, K. (Eds.), *The Cambridge History of the Pacific Islands.* Cambridge: Cambridge University Press, 37–79.

Denoon, D., Mein-Smith, P., & Wyndham, M. (2000). *A History of Australia, New Zealand, and the Pacific.* Malden, MA: Blackwell.

Fong, R., Boyd, C., & Browne, C. (1999). The Gandhi technique: A biculturalization approach to empowering Asian and Pacific Islander families. *Journal of Multicultural Social Work, 7*(1/2), 95–110.

Gotay, C. C., Banner, R. O., Matsunaga, D. S., Hedlund, N., Enos, R., Issell, B. F., & DeCambra, H. (2000). Impact of a culturally appropriate intervention on breast and cervical screening among Native Hawaiian women. *Preventive Medicine, 31,* 529–537.

Gregory, R. J. (2001). Parallel themes: Community psychology and Maori culture in Aotearoa. *Journal of Community Psychology, 29*(1), 19–27.

Grieco, E. (2002). *The Native Hawaiian and Other Pacific Islander Population: 2000.* U.S. Bureau of the Census. http://www.census.gov /population/www/cen2000/briefs.html, accessed 6/3/02.

Hurdle, D. E. (2002). Native Hawaiian traditional healing: Culturally based interventions for social work practice. *Social Work, 47*(2), 183–192.

Kim, S., McLeod, J. H., & Shantzis, C. (1992). Cultural competence for evaluators working with Asian-American communities: Some practical considerations. In M. A. Orlandi, R. Weston, & L. G. Epstein (Eds.), *Cultural*

Competence for Evaluators: A Guide for Alcohol and other Drug Abuse Prevention Practitioners Working with Ethnic/Racial Communities. Rockville, MD: Office of Substance Abuse Prevention, U.S. Department of Health and Human Services, 203–260.

Linnekin, J. (1997). Contending approaches. In Denoon, D., Firth, S., Linnekin, J., Meleisea, M., & Nero, K. (Eds.), *The Cambridge History of the Pacific Islands.* Cambridge: Cambridge University Press, 3–36.

Mancall, P. C., Robertson, P., & Huriwai, T. (2000). Maori and alcohol: A reconsidered history. *Australian and New Zealand Journal of Psychiatry, 34*(1), 129–134.

Meleisea, M., & Schoeffel, P. (1997). Discovering outsiders. In Denoon, D., Firth, S., Linnekin, J., Meleisea, M., & Nero, K. (Eds.), *The Cambridge History of the Pacific Islands.* Cambridge: Cambridge University Press, 119–151.

Mokuau, N. (1995). Pacific Islanders. In J. Philleo & F. L. Brisbane (Eds.), *Cultural Competence for Social Workers: A Guide for Alcohol and Other Drug Abuse Prevention Professionals Working with Ethnic/ Racial Communities.* Rockville, MD: Center for Substance Abuse Prevention, 159–188.

Morelli, P. T., Fong, R., & Oliveira, J. (2001). Culturally competent substance abuse treatment for Asian/ Pacific Islander women. In N. G. Choi (Ed.), *Psychosocial Aspects of the Asian-American Experience.* New York: Haworth Press, 263–280.

Nero, K. (1997). The end of insularity. In Denoon, D., Firth, S., Linnekin, J., Meleisea, M., & Nero, K. (Eds.), *The Cambridge History of the Pacific Islands.* Cambridge: Cambridge University Press, 439–467.

Okazaki, S. (1998). Psychological assessment of Asian Americans: Research agenda for cultural competency. *Journal of Personality Assessment, 70*(1), 54–70.

Rezentes, W. C. III (1996). *Ka Lama Kukui Hawaiian Psychology: An Introduction.* Honolulu: A'ali'i Books.

U.S. Census Bureau. (2001). Current Population Survey. http://www.census .gov

Weaver, H. N., Nikora, L. W., & Moeke-Pickering, T. M. (1998). *The cultural edge: Helping professionals and Maori clients.* Unpublished manuscript.

CHAPTER | # Jewish Americans

There are two major Jewish cultural groups in the United States, the Ashkenazim, Jews of central and eastern European descent, and the Sephardim, Jews of Spanish descent. Before the peak of the Spanish Inquisition in 1492, Sephardism was the primary form of Jewry in the world but with that dispersion their numbers decreased. Now Sephardim represent only a small minority of the U.S. and world Jewish populations. Jewish Americans are divided among three primary levels of religiosity—Orthodox, Conservative, and Reform.

The National Jewish Population Survey of 1990 identified 4,210,000 Americans who were born Jewish and whose religion was Judaism, and an additional 185,000 who converted to Judaism, for a total U.S. Jewish population of 4,395,000. In addition, 1,120,000 were born Jews but stated they did not practice any religion (Falk, 1995). Of the core Jewish American population, which excludes people born Jewish but following another religion, 18.9% are under age 15 and 16.9% are age 65 and over. This relatively old population contains proportionately one-third more elderly people than does the U.S. population as a whole (Council of Jewish Federations, 1990). The declining birth rate will not replace the Jewish population from generation to generation (Falk, 1995).

Almost all (90.6%) of the core Jewish American population were born in the United States. Jewish Americans struggle with the reoccurring concern of whether changes in third- and fourth-generation Jews will lead to the vanishing of American Judaism. There is a clear intergenerational pattern of assimilation and an increasing remoteness from Judaism with each generation a family is in the United States. Most converts to Judaism are women age 30 to 50 who marry a Jew. Overall, the number of converts is low, and 30% who reported they had become Jewish had not gone through a formal conversion process. The population that reported either being born or raised Jewish but currently practicing another religion is primarily offspring of intermarriages. This group is also predominantly female (Council of Jewish Federations, 1990). Including secular Jews, in 1992, 2% of the U.S. population was Jewish. This continues a decline from 2.9% in 1968, and 3.7% in 1937 (Falk, 1995).

Examining Jewish identity raises questions of whether Jews are an ethnic, cultural, or religious group. Although there is no simple answer, the definitions used in the Jewish Population Survey (Council of Jewish Federations, 1990) suggest that the common tie among Jews is religion, whether or not they are active practitioners. There are some ethnic commonalities among some groups of Jews as reflected in the Ashkenazim and Sephardim distinctions, but there is significant ethnic and cultural diversity among Jews as well. A small minority of Jews is of non-European descent. Of the core Jewish population in the United States, 2.4% are African American and 1.9% are Latino. The largest group of American Jews (47.6%) report they are of Ashkenazic origin. An additional 8.1% are Sephardic, and 44.3% do not know their ethnic heritage, or provided a variety of answers (Council of Jewish Federations, 1990).

The U.S. Jewish population has a high proportion of college graduates and a declining gender gap in education. The stronger the attachment to Judaism, the smaller the gender gap (Council of Jewish Federations, 1990). In 1990, more than 20% of Jewish men had completed an undergraduate degree (without postgraduate education), and an additional 30% had gone beyond this to achieve some postgraduate education. This compares with 13.2% and 11.3% of non-Jewish White men. Nearly 25% of Jewish women are college graduates and an additional 25% have graduate degrees compared with 11% and 6% of non-Jewish White women. Although Judaism has emphasized study as a key virtue, higher education with its scientific bent may be considered anti-religious and may ultimately contribute to increasing secularization (Falk, 1995).

Choice of marriage partners has changed significantly during the last few decades. More than half the people who were born Jews are married to non-Jews. Less than 5% of interfaith marriages involve a non-Jew converting to Judaism. This is likely to be an underestimate of interfaith relationships because it does not include marriages resulting in divorce or relationships outside marriage (Council of Jewish Federations, 1990). Traditionally, Jews are matrilineal; thus, only those born of a Jewish mother are considered Jewish. Tracing descent through the female line has persisted despite other aspects of Jewish culture being patriarchal. In recent times, matrilineal descent, combined with the high rate of intermarriage, has raised the divisive issue of who can be considered Jewish. The Reform denomination now recognizes anyone who has either a Jewish mother or a Jewish father to be Jewish (Falk, 1995).

The term *Jew* covers a broad range of people and reveals little about cultural identification or how someone practices his or her faith. The specific categories, Orthodox, Conservative, and Reform, and even more specific designations within those categories (e.g., Hasidic as a form of Orthodox) are likely to be more meaningful. In this chapter, specific terms are used when possible.

This chapter gives an overview of social work with Jewish Americans. The social work literature on this population is limited, so this chapter also draws on the broader social science literature as well as on literature on social work with Jews in Israel. The significant diversity that exists within and among Jewish Americans sets the context for discussion. The chapter presents information on knowledge, skills, and values/attitudes necessary for cultural competence and presents issues for cultural competence on micro and macro levels.

KNOWLEDGE FOR CULTURAL COMPETENCE

The knowledge needed for culturally competent social work with Jewish Americans can be divided into four broad areas: diversity, history, culture, and contemporary realities. Diversity serves as an overarching concept that informs the other areas. The history, culture, and contemporary realities of Jewish Americans vary according to factors such as ethnicity and degree of religiosity.

Diversity

There are significant distinctions among Jewish Americans along ethnic and cultural lines. Differences exist between Ashkenazim and Sephardim; within Ashkenazim between Germans and Eastern Europeans; and within Sephardim based on geographical distribution (Schwartz, 1999). These national and ethnic distinctions have implications for how culture has developed and continues to be expressed.

Sephardim are associated with Jewish Spanish high culture and retained a Castilian Spanish identity for centuries in exile. Spanish-Portuguese Sephardim dominated the religious, social, and economic life of American Jewry and Jewry throughout the Western hemisphere during the U.S. colonial and early federal periods. By the 1830s, Sephardim were overwhelmed by German-speaking Ashkenazim from central Europe, and these newer immigrants served as the foundation for the future American Jewish community (Cohen, 1993).

Sephardim translates as Iberian and refers to this population's historic association with Spain and to a lesser extent Portugal. Sephardim spoke Judeo-Spanish, Greek, or Arabic. They developed distinct religious practices, songs, and poetry. In modern times, the term *Sephardic* is also applied to Jews of non-Iberian backgrounds who have become part of Sephardic communities and in Israel to those who identify as Sephardim on cultural grounds. Of the nearly 15 million Jews world wide, only 10% are Sephardim (Cohen, 1993).

Both Sephardim and Ashkenazim observe the basic tenets of Judaism and abide by the authority of the Babylonian Talmud, but their different cultural

and historical backgrounds have shaped their rituals, liturgy, and general attitude toward Jewish law. Sephardim emphasize the joyful and sustaining
aspects of following the commandments rather than their absolute observance.
Sephardic music reflects Iberian and Arabic influences. "As for the *piyutim*
(hymns), it has been said that the Ashkenazic ones are 'mediators between the
Nation and its God,' while those of the Sephardim are 'mediators between the
Soul and its Creator'" (Papo, 1993, p. 280).

Jewish Americans also exhibit significant diversity in their religiosity.
Indeed, many are secular and do not practice Judaism, whereas others interpret traditional teachings more or less flexibly. Religiosity is often divided into
the three categories of Orthodox, Conservative, and Reform, with the latter
being the most liberal.

There is a significant split between Orthodox and non-Orthodox Jews.
Orthodox may see non-Orthodox as non-Jews and non-Orthodox may see
Orthodox as outdated relics (Falk, 1995). Study of the Torah is the most fundamental principle of Orthodox Judaism, and this branch is more structured
than Reform or Conservative traditions are (Falk, 1995). There are many differences between Reform, Conservative, and Orthodox branches of Judaism,
yet all share similarities. Of the three branches, Orthodox Judaism is the most
strongly grounded in tradition and has its roots in both Sephardic and
Ashkenazic heritage. Reform Judaism has its roots in German Ashkenazic traditions and was a prominent movement when many Jews were emigrating from
Germany to the United States, before and after the Civil War. Reform Judaism
emphasized a restructuring of the liturgy to make it more accessible, eliminated
many rules governing daily life so Jews were less visibly distinct from other populations, and essentially focused on modernizing the ancient faith to make it
more attractive. The American Conservative movement in Judaism was created
to fill the gulf between what was seen as the extremes of Orthodoxy and the
overliberalization of Reform Judaism (Cowan & Cowan, 1996).

There are also clear distinctions within the three major branches. For
example, among the Orthodox, the Hasidim have come to stand out as ultra-
Orthodox and there are distinct types of Hasidim. All Hasidim trace their origin to the movement started by Israel ben Eliezer (1700–1760), but the
different sects vary based on which rebbe or charismatic leader they follow
and the customs of that group. Hasidic communities are frequently insular and
actively opposed to what they see as the corrupting forces of contemporary
secular society. Hasidim tend to be suspicious of outsiders. Boundaries are an
important part of self-maintenance. Insulating members from a secular host
community operates as protection against assimilation (Heilman, 1995;
Shaffir, 1995).

History

Jews have a long history that continues to influence contemporary cultural
expression in the United States. That history includes centuries in Europe,
Asia, and other parts of the world before coming to the United States, early
immigration to and life in the United States, and the Nazi Holocaust and its

aftermath. Understanding this history gives helping professionals a context for understanding Jewish American clients.

Development and Dispersement of European Jewish Cultures   Under Muslim rule (beginning in the 8th century and dwindling between the 12th and 15th centuries), Iberian Jews were the premier Jewish community in Europe and developed many of the traits that shaped Sephardim. Iberian Jews were *dhimmi* or protected people. They were seen as inferior and subject to heavier taxes but lived in greater physical and emotional comfort than in any other Christian or Muslim country of the time. They participated in many occupations and had regular professional contact with Muslims. Significant interaction led to Muslim influences on Jewish life, dress, institutions, architecture, philosophy, governance, and culture. During this Jewish golden age, poetry, writing, and philosophy flourished (Cohen, 1993).

The Sephardim were also influenced by the Christian reconquest of Iberia (between the 12th and 15th centuries). The Sephardim continued to enjoy quasi-autonomous status under Talmudic law during Christian rule as they had with Muslims. At this time, Jewish intellectual mysticism flourished. Jews took on a prominent role in administration and diplomacy as the Christian reconquest continued. Jews were charged with organizing royal finances and collecting taxes. Their knowledge of both Christian and Muslim cultures made them ideal diplomats. Unlike in other Christian areas, the Jews of Iberia had substantial professional, social, and cultural contact with non-Jews. In spite of and in some ways because of these key roles, Jews were easy scapegoats and were seen as an impediment to non-establishment leaders seeking political change. Thus, Jews experienced growing prejudice and propaganda, including charges of host desecration, well poisoning, and ritual murder. These myths were exploited to raise popular discontent against the Jews (Cohen, 1993).

As Christians reconquered more of the Iberian Peninsula, conversion became the official policy of Spanish kingdoms like Castile and Aragon. This lasted until the Edict of Expulsion that forced all Jews out of Spain in 1492 and a comparable order that banned Jews from Portugal shortly thereafter. Expulsion was deemed necessary because it was felt that Jews who had forcefully been converted to Christianity could not be trusted and might secretly be practicing Judaism. The Inquisition sought to apprehend and punish heretics.

Many Jews who left Spain settled in the Muslim world, particularly in parts of the Ottoman Empire. These refugees encountered Jewish populations in their new homes who often felt threatened by the newcomers' skills and culture. The Ottoman Jewish community was socially isolated and politically fragmented. Sephardic heritage was consolidated through a movement for political unification of Jewish life that included systematization of the Kabbalah (mystical teachings related to God, the universe, and the Torah), focus on education to transmit sacred traditions of Judaism, channeling Jewish faith and practice through structures of traditional thought and law, and preservation of 15th century Castilian as the primary Sephardic language (also known as Espanyol, Judezmo, or Ladino) (Cohen, 1993).

In the 19th century, there was a gradual recession from centrality of Sephardic life through increased acculturation and secularization. Sephardism was also weakened by Nazi decimation of Sephardic Jews in lands once under the Ottoman Empire (Cohen, 1993). Sephardim have immigrated throughout the world for three reasons: religious zeal, economic opportunity, and fear of persecution. They have mixed with people from various continents, resulting in a very diverse population (Cohen, 1993).

Hasidism developed in Eastern Europe in the mid 18th century as an alternative to traditional rabbinical Judaism. This reform movement saw Judaism as rigid and overly scholastic and sought to change it into a faith grounded in "egalitarianism, charismatic leadership, and ecstatic devotion to God. Hasidism arose from the ashes of 18th-century Poland, where Jewish culture and society had deteriorated into political anarchy, financial impoverishment, and spiritual malaise. As such, it can best be understood as a revitalization movement" (Belcove-Shalin, 1995a, p. 4).

The founder of Hasidism, Israel ben Eliezer, taught that God was everywhere and could be praised through music, dance, and stories as well as through study and prayer. Legitimizing nonscholarly forms of communion and placing them on the same level as formal Torah study radically democratized Jewish worship (Belcove-Shalin, 1995a). Hasidic teachings later became systematized and rebbes' authority grew. As Hasidism spread in Eastern Europe, other Jews resisted and condemned the Hasidim's "insular lifestyle, contempt for the Torah, unseemly shouting, singing, and dancing during prayer, excessive feasting and merrymaking, and the 'cult of the rebbe'—as well as of the frivolous innovations in the liturgy, prayer sequence, and the method of ritual slaughter" (Belcove-Shalin, 1995a, p. 6).

Early Immigration and Life in the United States   In 1654, 23 Jewish refugees arrived in New Amsterdam fleeing the Portuguese reconquest of Recife, Brazil. Governor Peter Stuyvesant attempted to deport them but desisted after being reminded of the number of Jewish stockholders in the Dutch West Indian Company. Jews came to New Amsterdam (later New York) in increasing numbers and eventually New York became the city with the largest Jewish population in the history of the Jewish people. Eventually, the Jews of the United States became the largest Jewish community in the world (Karp, 1998).

The first significant Jewish immigration to the United States was Sephardic. In this first wave of immigration, small numbers came from the Netherlands and England in the 17th century. Between 1899 and 1913, several thousand came from the Mediterranean region bringing the total Sephardic population to approximately 15,000 (Schwartz, 1999).

After 1908, large numbers of Sephardic immigrants settled on the lower east side of New York City. Social agencies were concerned about the already overburdened area and encouraged resettlement elsewhere, but most stayed. Sephardim were often rejected by Ashkenazim. Sephardim were gradually absorbed into American economic life, although many had arrived speaking no English or Yiddish (a language common among European Jews) and worked in sweatshops (Papo, 1993).

Sephardic immigration to the United States, predominantly from the former Ottoman Empire, peaked between 1908 and 1924 when the United States severely limited Jewish immigration. By then, the United States had approximately 70,000 Sephardic immigrants with half of these living in the greater New York area. Substantial Sephardic communities also existed in Atlanta, Chicago, Cincinnati, and Los Angeles (Cohen, 1993).

The first wave of Ashkenazic immigration to the United States was 1820 to 1880. Approximately 200,000 German Jews came to the United States fleeing nationalistic and anti-Semitic laws. A second wave of immigration occurred between 1880 and 1924 and contained 2.5 million Eastern European Jews (Schwartz, 1999).

The different Jewish populations did not have contact with each other before their arrival in the United States; thus, tension and discord developed here, particularly between German and Eastern European Jews. Americanized German Jews feared their social status would decrease if they were associated with the new Eastern European arrivals. There were significant differences in practices and values of these groups. German Jews had a long history of assimilation, unlike the Orthodox, separatist Eastern Europeans. Germans were less observant and did not speak a distinct language like Yiddish. On the other hand, Sephardim tended to live a culturally separate life in their host countries centered around religion. Despite regional distinctions, Sephardim shared a common culture and language based on their history in Spain. Sephardic practices were foreign to U.S. Ashkenazim and were not well tolerated. The two groups kept separate educational, social, and religious institutions. Racism was also a factor, and Ashkenazim disparaged Sephardim for their darker skin. Likewise, Sephardim disparaged Ashkenazim, calling them Protestants or hatless Jews because of their reform practices (Schwartz, 1999).

Small Hasidic congregations began appearing in the United States in 1875. Some minor rebbes and emissaries came to the United States in the early 20th century. Another wave of leaders settled along the eastern seaboard and in the Midwest after World War I. Large masses of rebbes and their followers did not arrive until after World War II. By the 1960s, the Hasidic population of New York City was believed to be between 40,000 and 50,000. Because of a high birth rate (families typically have 5–6 children), and a growing number of new adherents, the Hasidic population has doubled in 20 years. There are an estimated 250,000 Hasidim in the world, with 200,000 of these in the United States, and 100,000 of these in New York State. The Hasidim have established particularly strong communities in the neighborhoods of Crown Heights, Williamsburg, and Boro Park, Brooklyn. The largest Hasidic communities outside metropolitan New York are in Montreal, Chicago, and Los Angeles (Belcove-Shalin, 1995a).

Although they enjoyed a certain amount of material and social success, German Jews were often barred from civic, fraternal, and social organizations;

thus, they formed their own. Other European Jews and Sephardim were more likely to form cultural organizations upon their arrival in the United States because they were more concerned with cultural maintenance (Schwartz, 1999). Sephardim established mutual aid societies that became the center of social and community life. Later, large federations were established that were open to all Jews. These federations coordinated fundraising activities and social and educational services (Papo, 1993).

In 1924, federal restrictions slowed Jewish immigration to a trickle, thus raising the issue of a potential loss of culture. Likewise, high rates of Sephardic intermarriage led to significant cultural loss and a diminishing perception of them as a distinct group (Schwartz, 1999).

The Holocaust and Its Aftermath   Jews have experienced pogroms and exiles throughout their history. The most significant one in recent times is the persecution and mass killings of millions of Jews in Europe under Nazi rule during World War II. This recent memory continues to affect the lives of American Jews. Broadly defined, Holocaust survivors are European-born Jews who experienced the Holocaust either in hiding, in the underground resistance, as refugees, or in concentration or forced labor camps (Sorscher & Cohen, 1997).

Afraid of what they saw as overpowering acculturative and secularizing forces in America and the nationalistic heresy of Israel, many Hasidic leaders warned their followers not to leave their homes in Europe as Nazism gained power. Thus, many Hasidic communities were wiped out, leaving few survivors. A few surviving Hasidic leaders did establish communities in the United States. One of the primary cultural survival strategies that they employed was to emphasize customs of the past (Heilman, 1995).

The Nazi Holocaust has significantly affected the children of survivors. This transgenerational impact includes the following: (1) detrimental effects such as traumatic after-effects, phobias, depression, recurrent imagery, pessimism, and other mental health problems; and (2) adaptive effects such as creativity, altruism, group affiliation, and ethnic identification. Significant variation exists in individuals' responses to Holocaust trauma. Parents' communication patterns (i.e., what is stated about the Holocaust) influence children's responses. Despite the significant and lasting effects, few controlled, empirical studies have been conducted on the psychological effects of Holocaust trauma on the children of survivors (Sorscher & Cohen, 1997).

The limited response of Americans, including American Jews, to Nazi atrocities is an issue that divides the Jewish community. This has become a controversy as "historians have shown that the American Jewish community was at best complacent about the mass murders of Jews in Europe between 1933 and 1945. Even after the war was over, Jewish organizations sought to return the survivors to Poland and other hotbeds of anti-Jewish hatred" (Falk, 1995, p. 364). American Jews and Jewish organizations felt ill prepared to cope with Holocaust survivors in the United States and, thus, were reluctant to extend their assistance.

Culture

Understanding several key elements of Jewish culture will help facilitate the work of helping professionals with their Jewish clients. First among these areas are ongoing struggles associated with identity and assimilation. It is also important for helping professionals to have a basic understanding of key Jewish rites and values.

Identity and Assimilation   Fear of cultural loss through assimilation has been a prominent theme among Jewish Americans for more than 100 years. "American Jews, like other Jews before them, have lived within a paradox of faith and fear—the faith that they are an eternal people, and the fear that their generation may be the last. The survival of every Jewish community has been conditional" (Karp, 1998, p. ix). In every generation, survival of the next generation is the priority.

Some Jews view the tradition of matrilineal descent as antiquated, dysfunctional, and contributing to the decline of the Jewish American population. They point out that Judaism was established by Abraham, a man who was born a Chaldean and, thus, is not based in biology (Falk, 1995). Even if socialization rather than biological heritage were the primary criteria for Jewish identity, it is likely that the population would continue to decline. Indeed, the contemporary Jewish community is faced with a paradox: overall their numbers are decreasing and each succeeding generation is becoming more assimilated into the American mainstream, yet the small, ultra-Orthodox Hasidic sect is actually growing in numbers and influence.

Hasidic communities are an example of resistance to assimilation. Hasidim survive from the past but are not identical with it. They are part of the modern world struggling against powerful social forces that would either sweep them away or transform them. The process of cultural and social survival itself has led to change. As more Jews become acculturated and secularized, Hasidim stand out as anti-acculturation.

> In the process, these erstwhile radical mystics and religious revolutionaries who challenged the rabbinic status quo when they first emerged in the late eighteenth century have become redefined as among the most conservative elements in Jewish life, the ultra-Orthodox or—in the increasingly popular Hebrew term *Haredim*—those whose attachment to ritual and religious tradition is anxiously maximal. As Haredim, they are a minority of a minority, approximately 25 percent of the nearly 10 percent of Jews who call themselves "Orthodox." But they are a minority that has been, at least on the surface, able to maintain their alternative lifestyle and values in the face of the secularizing and acculturative trends. Long after they were expected to disappear, they have continued to exist. (Heilman, 1995, p. xii)

Rites   Ceremonial rites of passage aid in the negotiation of life stage transitions. Traditionally, the bar or bat mitzvah marks the transition from childhood to adulthood—bar mitzvah for males and bat mitzvah for females. Participation in this important rite of passage may be associated with lower delinquency among Jewish adolescents. This pivotal ritual helps them understand and accept their responsibilities as adults (Falk, 1995).

These rites are based on 1,500 years of traditions. At age 13, a boy goes through a ceremony in which he recites a blessing, reads from the Torah, and delivers a speech in Hebrew. After his bar mitzvah, the boy is considered to be a man and can give witness in a Jewish court, is held responsible for his wrongdoing, and can be counted as one of a group of 10 adults, or *minyan*, needed for a prayer service (Kahn, 1995).

Bat mitzvah is the more recently developed female counterpart to bar mitzvah and is increasingly acceptable in more liberal congregations. This ritual reinforces generational values and customs of traditional Jewish practices. This transition offers a sense of connectedness to the community. This can be a part of psychosocial growth and development for an individual.

During the last 20 years, adult bar and bat mitzvahs have begun to happen for those who chose not to, or were unable to, complete the ritual at the typical time. A study of adult bat mitzvahs found that often women who study for their bat mitzvahs are making important statements about their commitments as Jews. This is a mechanism for women who grew up in assimilated Jewish families to claim the Jewish identities their families had denied. For assimilated Jews in search of their cultural identity, bat mitzvah may help them to connect with past, present, and future generations of Jews (Kahn, 1995).

Values   Major values important to Jewish Americans include justice, self-reliance, education, and families. Justice is a key value in Jewish cultural traditions. "Admonitions to do that which is just have been the core of Jewish existence. The whole concept of *halacha,* the law, rests on the concept of justice so that, as we have seen, Jews ranging in observance from Reform to Orthodox consult *halacha.* To be a Jew depends therefore first, and foremost, on absorbing into one's personality a concern with social justice *in this world*" (Falk, 1995, p. 367, emphasis in original). An outgrowth of this concern with justice is social action, and many Jews have been actively involved with a variety of social agendas.

Self-reliance is emphasized in Jewish culture (Falk, 1995). It is important to be able to rely on yourself because others may prove unreliable. This value may be an outgrowth of the centuries of persecution experienced by Jewish people throughout the world and a sense of recurrent victimization.

The strong value placed on education is evidenced by the large numbers of Jewish Americans completing college and graduate school and their subsequent occupational distribution. The Jewish community is better off economically than most Christian denominations are. This may make poverty particularly painful for the Jews who experience it. Educational and professional achievements are expectations in the Jewish community. In particular, young adults are expected to have secured an education and economic stability before marriage (Falk, 1995). Religious education can also be an important way to preserve culture (Papo, 1993).

In general, Judaism comes from a patriarchal tradition although Reform branches are much more accepting of gender equality than their Orthodox counterparts are. The clear gender roles and guidelines for married life found in Orthodox Judaism can be appealing to young Jewish adults struggling with the contested nature of these roles in contemporary society (Davidman & Stocks, 1995).

Among the Hasidim, there is no place for singles, who are considered half a person. Hasidim have institutionalized mechanisms, such as matchmakers and arranged marriages, for ensuring their members marry. Highly regulated dating is allowed only when young adults are ready for marriage. After a few dates, the suitability of a potential marriage partner is determined. Hasidim are opposed to divorce. Selflessness, devotion, and unconditional acceptance of the partner are encouraged in marriage. Romantic love is de-emphasized because feelings are fleeting. An emphasis is placed on the roles they will play, such as spouse and parent. Strict gender roles emphasize the importance of marriage and childbearing for women. Biological differences are thought to be the root source for the distinct natures of men and women. Women are seen as naturally selfless and devotional. Sexuality is related to Godliness and should only exist within marriage. Jewish laws also establish boundaries for when sexuality can be expressed within marriage. There is an emphasis on modesty, and touching is strictly regulated in public and in the home. Birth control is generally forbidden (Davidman & Stocks, 1995).

A study of the Lubavitcher Hasidim revealed that family is central in religious life. Breakdown of the family is attributed to loss of boundaries in contemporary life. Loyalty, respect, and trust are key family values. There is a strong belief that if the family were to return to a traditional form, other societal ills would disappear (Davidman & Stocks, 1995).

Contemporary Realities

It is important for social workers to move beyond a historical foundation of knowledge and have a basic understanding of the contemporary realities of Jewish Americans. Key contemporary realities include anti-Semitism, loss of culture and population, gender roles, home and exile, and strengths and continuity.

Anti-Semitism and Oppression   Anti-Semitism and oppression have been a shaping force among Jews historically and continue to be so in contemporary times. In reflecting on their lives, oppression was a theme identified by members of a group of Russian Jewish immigrants.

> The entire group concurred that it was ultimately due to anti-Semitism that they sought to immigrate to America. Discrimination against Jews for promotions in factories and for entrance to universities was a frequent topic of conversation . . . In light of this oppression, it is interesting to note that virtually all group members stated that they had chosen immigration not so much for themselves but for their children and grandchildren and their futures. All members

conveyed that living with anti-Semitism and oppression in Russia was a way of life, onerous as it was, towards which they had adapted. The conclusion from their point of view is that immigration to America held the possibility of hope for a better life for future generations but that their generation's suffering was too profound to permit them to envision or enjoy any future of their own. (Feinberg, 1996, p. 47)

Anti-Semitism and oppression are fueled by stereotypes and myths. One such myth is that Jews possess specific traits such as a talent for commerce and finance, aversion to soldiering, obsession for religion, clannishness, and xenophobia. "Derived from the myth is the implicit notion of a demonic power possessed by Jews. As a result of this power, Jews, the paucity of their numbers notwithstanding, can control powerful institutions and even entire kingdoms. Connected to the myth is the conception of a 'Jewish problem' nettling every government and requiring special attention" (Cohen, 1993, p. 6). These stereotypes, which have existed for centuries, provide a historical precedent for Hitler's belief that the "final solution" was eradication of Jewish people from all countries.

Accusations of connections with the occult and demonic powers fuel the contemporary anti-Semitism of American right-wing extremist and neo-Nazi groups. Such groups often believe that Jews have infiltrated and are secretly running the United States government (referred to as Zionist Occupied Government or ZOG). These extremist groups believe Jews must be destroyed as Aryan Whites, the true Americans, assert their rightful place in the United States.

Loss of Culture and Population   Jewish Americans face the challenge of maintaining the integrity of their faith and culture while coexisting with non-Jewish culture and society. Maintaining both is difficult, especially when they are not living within the physical boundaries of a Jewish community (Karp, 1998). Opportunities for social mobility and the American emphasis on assimilation undermined maintenance of a Jewish cultural identity. Those who wanted to retain their culture had to take deliberate steps to do so (Karp, 1998).

Increasing secularization has been identified as a threat to Jewish cultural continuity. Evidence of this trend includes the following facts: More than half of Jewish Americans marry non-Jews; 3,186,000 American households contain Jews, yet only 56.8% of these households are entirely Jewish; 700,000 children with at least one Jewish parent are being raised in another religion; the Jewish American population is dispersed across the United States, thus weakening major centers of Jewish life; divorce is relatively common; non-Jewish religious practices are widespread among American Jews (e.g., 28% of Jewish households have a Christmas tree some times or every year, yet only 22% of Jews light Sabbath candles every week); and 72% of Jewish Americans do not belong to any Jewish organization (Falk, 1995).

Participation in Jewish rites and rituals, a key element of Jewish identity, has been dwindling. Only 61% of Jewish Americans fast on Yom Kippur, 59%

attend synagogue on high holy days, 11% attend synagogue weekly, and 17% eat only kosher foods (Falk, 1995). The most widely observed ritual in the Jewish community is the bar or bat mitzvah, although this has often been secularized. Most Jewish Americans (85%) have a bar mitzvah, including 36% who say they have no religion. This rite plays a major role in maintaining contemporary Jewish identity, even in a secularized form (Falk, 1995).

Ultra-Orthodox Jews like the Hasidim are also shaped by their fears of secularization and assimilation. They once faced hostile societies that kept Jews at bay. Now they are confronted with enticing, attractive societies where Orthodox Jews can enter a mainstream contemporary existence. In response, they have adopted a defensive posture and have developed their own schools and insular communities to protect their children from what they view as the inferior but tempting outside world. Another survival strategy is to entice more Jews to become Hasidim. They maintain separate customs and language, and they protect themselves by amassing money and political power. All these efforts are to ensure cultural survival (Heilman, 1995).

Gender Roles   Gender roles for Jewish Americans vary significantly with the degree of assimilation and level of religiosity. For example, even though overall Jewish women are likely to be highly educated like their male counterparts, among Orthodox Jews women are still often expected to focus their energies on creating a home for their husband and children. Jewish women in Israel, especially those from Asian or African backgrounds, still live in a traditional society of male authority and female submissiveness. The role of the woman is homemaking and child care. Almost half (45%) of women work outside the home but often part-time, in occupations dominated by women, and they earn less money. Traditional Judaism is patriarchal and women occupy passive roles. In marriage, the man blesses his wife, gives her a Religious Marriage Certificate, and retains the right to divorce her (Rabin, Markus, & Voghera, 1999). Despite these patriarchal realities, in Israel, Jewish women are more likely than Arab women to file for divorce in domestic violence situations, thus indicating they feel some power (Rabin et al., 1999).

Home and Exile   Exile and the search for a home is a significant theme in Jewish identity. Throughout history, Jewish populations have been repeatedly uprooted. This history is reflected in a longing for home and the promised homeland. The concepts of home and exile are intertwined in both sacred texts and contemporary existence. In rebuilding communities in exile, the Hasidim participate in a divine cosmic drama in which man assists God. This intense community building has proved a successful buffer against acculturation that has characterized much of Jewish existence in the United States (Belcove-Shalin, 1995b). The strong presence of the Hasidic community in Brooklyn has resulted in transforming and traditionalizing the style of dress and worldview of other Orthodox Jews, including a more stringent separation of the sexes. Building schools is a key part of this community transformation.

Strengths and Continuity   Despite ongoing fears of cultural loss, Jewish Americans are finding a variety of ways, from Reform to Orthodox, to express new visions of Jewish identity. As the new millennium opens, Reform Judaism has embraced a new traditionalism including a network of day schools that are transforming Jewish education. There is wide evidence of a cultural and spiritual renaissance, including Jewish studies at many universities, continually expanding student bodies at seminaries, and many highly educated and religiously committed Jews. Still, many fears remain. The high rates of intermarriage and degree of assimilation continue to raise a challenge to survival (Karp, 1998).

Judaism remains despite secularization. The social aspects of being Jewish continue even with a decreased emphasis on religion. The Reform movement, which blends tradition and innovation, may lead secular Jews to return to Judaism and their ancestral roots. For example, the new practices of accepting the child of a Jewish father and a non-Jewish mother as Jewish and allowing gay membership may encourage secular Jews to join reform congregations (Falk, 1995).

On the more traditional side, Hasidim have a high birth rate and high profile beyond their actual numbers. Many Hasidic groups are headquartered in Brooklyn where they have amassed political clout. Their high number of voters enables them to have a significant influence on the surrounding community (Belcove-Shalin, 1995a).

SKILLS FOR CULTURAL COMPETENCE

Given the integration of Jewish Americans into the American mainstream, many skills used by helping professionals are likely to be useful with this population. For Jewish Americans from more insular communities, social workers may need to hone skills in engaging, trust building, and outreach.

Engaging

Ultra-Orthodox communities have taken steps to separate themselves from mainstream America and thus are not likely to participate in social services in large numbers. The strong emphasis on self-reliance is likely to produce self-help resources within the Jewish family and community that are sought out in times of need. Social workers who seek to offer services to this community will need to assess the level of need and work closely with trusted members of the community if they expect to gain access to this population. Rather than seeing this population in large numbers, it is more likely that social workers may occasionally encounter ultra-Orthodox clients in venues such as hospitals where their contact with helping professionals is less than voluntary. Social workers need to listen carefully to clients' stated needs and be conscious of any recommendations that may be perceived as contrary to clients' beliefs and values.

Given the high value placed on education by many Jewish Americans, it may be helpful for a social worker to identify his or her credentials as part of the engaging process. It may also be reassuring to Jewish American clients to see the helping professional's degrees, certifications, and license displayed in his or her office or interviewing room. In some cases, it may also be engaging to discuss the empirical foundation for the helping techniques being used and how success will be measured in this particular case.

Engaging and gaining trust can be a process that takes time. As the work continues, clients may watch for signs of anti-Semitism or bias in the helping professional's language and actions. The absence of such bias and ongoing expressions of willingness to truly listen to the client's concerns are likely to strengthen the engaging process. One well-known Jewish helping professional of German descent described the suspicion that was always present in the back of his mind when he interacted with non-Jews. He vigilantly listened for any hint that might indicate prejudice and confirm his suspicions that virtually all non-Jews were anti-Semitic (Hammerschlag, 1988). It is likely that some Jewish American clients have similar suspicions. If a helping professional finds indications that this is the case, explicitly discussing these fears can be helpful in engaging and moving forward into a productive helping relationship.

Some Orthodox Jews, the Hasidim in particular, have strong beliefs about cross-gender touching. For example, it would be considered highly inappropriate for a male social worker to greet a female client with a handshake. Social workers need to be aware of such proscriptions and alter their greetings accordingly. Although it is not possible to be aware of all such beliefs, social workers must always be alert for cues that clients are comfortable or uncomfortable. Maximizing clients' comfort will help set the stage for ongoing, productive work.

Assessing

Many of the standardized assessment tools currently in use by helping professionals have been normed for European American populations. Thus, it is likely these tools may be reliable and valid with clients from the assimilated Jewish American population. These tools may have more questionable applicability to Jewish American clients from more insular, less assimilated communities.

A few assessment instruments have been developed particularly for Jewish American clients. Notably, the Brenner Scale of Jewish Identification has been developed to measure multidimensional aspects of Jewish identity. Subsequent versions of this tool contain some modifications (Sorscher & Cohen, 1997).

As with other clients, comprehensive assessments that include examining the social environment as well as strengths and weaknesses within the client are needed. Interactions between the client and various aspects of the environment also need to be examined as part of the assessment process. Many researchers and helping professionals emphasize examining the Holocaust and its impact on survivors and future generations of Jewish Americans; thus, including a historical dimension by using tools such as multigenerational genograms can be an important facet of an assessment.

Intervening

Jewish Americans may seek help for a wide variety of social and health problems. Thus, a variety of interventions may be useful. Social workers may be called to do interventions for culturally specific issues such as trauma related to the Holocaust and culturally related struggles with loss, oppression, and identity.

Research is beginning to explore the transgenerational effect of parental Holocaust trauma. Indeed, some authors suggest that parental wartime experiences be explored with all Jewish clients born after World War II (Sorscher & Cohen, 1997). There appear to be distinct gender differences in how Holocaust survivors cope with trauma. Women openly acknowledge psychological effects of trauma, but men are more stoic. Exploring what parents said about Holocaust experiences can be an important aspect of helping interventions (Sorscher & Cohen, 1997).

Groups can be used to enhance the memory and capacity for reminiscence among elderly Jewish Russian immigrants. Groups offer an important context for elders to synthesize their stories and find meaning in their present lives (Feinberg, 1996). A group of elderly, Russian Jewish immigrants identified the following themes that organized how they convey their stories: loss, oppression, struggle with identity, and reminiscence. Losses that they experienced included loosing their homeland, family, and friends. These losses were tied in with their experiences with oppression and sense of identity.

> Each member addressed the issue of the loss of family and friends who either remained in Russia by choice or were unable to immigrate. In addition, there were painful recollections of family and friends who died in Russia as a result of the political oppression of Jews. Isaac informed the group that he had been imprisoned for six years in a Russian labor camp because it was discovered that he gave a small amount of money to support a Jewish political dissident whom he revered. He tearfully recounted being devastated by the news that his mentor died in prison. Especially poignant losses presented in the group were those involving children and the emotional reactions of affected members were still fresh after many years. Rebecca, an 82-year-old former teacher, informed the group at the third meeting about her son's sudden death six years ago in Russia. She suspected that it was a suicide after he took a controversial political position against the hierarchy at the factory. (Feinberg, 1996, p. 46)

VALUES/ATTITUDES FOR CULTURAL COMPETENCE

Along with basic social work values, it is important for helping professionals to demonstrate respect, empathy, and a belief in social justice when working with Jewish Americans. As with all populations, it is important that social workers display respect for their Jewish American clients. Given the extraordinary diversity in this population, some Jewish American clients are likely to value and be knowledgeable about their cultural heritage but others will not. Social workers must acknowledge that either stance is acceptable. Jewish

Americans who do not hold culture to be a primary part of their lives should not be condemned or exalted for this perspective just as those who make Jewish cultural traditions a central focus must not be judged, either positively or negatively, for this position.

Assimilated Jewish Americans are likely to share many of the values of their helping professionals. More Orthodox Jews, however, may have values, life choices, and gender roles that are significantly different from those of many helping professionals. Social workers need to demonstrate respect for the values of their Jewish clients, regardless of whether social workers share these same values.

It is important for social workers to be able to empathize with Jewish Americans who experience persecution, oppression, and anti-Semitism. Social workers need to be able to understand the various ways these experiences may be internalized. Helping professionals must be willing to recognize oppression as a contemporary phenomenon despite the educational, professional, and economic success of many Jewish Americans. Because most Jewish Americans are White, their experiences with oppression may be trivialized, minimized, or viewed as historical artifacts rather than contemporary realities. Helping professionals must be willing to examine their own feelings and beliefs about the oppression experienced by Jewish Americans. It is important for helping professionals to be willing to take an activist stance against continuing injustice.

CASE EXAMPLE

Harvey Lowenberg, an assistant principal at a large urban high school, recently sought counseling through his Employee Assistance Program. Patrice Miller, a second-year MSW intern has been assigned to work with Harvey.

He complained of sleep disturbances and difficulty concentrating. In the second session, he revealed that he has a strained relationship with his widowed father, a Holocaust survivor in poor health. Harvey's father lives 30 miles away but is becoming increasingly unable to live alone. They have never had a good relationship and their communication has been particularly sparse since the death of Harvey's mother, three years ago. As an only child, Harvey feels he must accept the burden of caring for his father, but the stress of considering this has begun to affect his work performance and relationship with his wife.

The following considerations are relevant in approaching the case in a culturally competent manner:

- Patrice has done some reading about the intergenerational effects of the Holocaust, but she struggles with how to bring up this subject. In particular, she wonders about the ethics of raising this issue. She is afraid this might be her own agenda because this was not what Harvey identified as the presenting problem.
- As an African American, Patrice is particularly sensitive to stereotyping. She wonders if she is making stereotypical assumptions that the roadblock in the father-son relationship is somehow related to the Holocaust.

- Patrice raises her concerns with her supervisor who validates her concerns and gives her suggestions on raising these issues in a sensitive and productive way. Her supervisor recommends that she pursue discussions of the meaning of family and beliefs about caretaking responsibilities in future sessions with Harvey. By exploring these larger areas related to Harvey's presenting problem, Patrice can begin to examine any culturally specific issues related to intergenerational Holocaust trauma that may be relevant in this case.

CULTURAL COMPETENCE IN SOCIAL POLICIES

Historically in various parts of the world, Jews have been the targets of policies that have sought to convert, displace, and annihilate them. In the United States, the Jewish population has not typically been singled out as the target of particular social policies. However, more generalized social policies have sometimes had a differential impact on the Jewish American population. Indeed, the effect of social policies is often hidden unless explicit efforts are made to examine both their positive and negative consequences for different populations.

The federal programs that solidified distinctions between African Americans and Whites inadvertently opened the doors of opportunity to many Jewish Americans. For example, the GI Bill of Rights, also known as the 1944 Servicemen's Readjustment Act, extended educational and occupational benefits to veterans. These benefits were not extended equally to women and African American veterans and served primarily as a large-scale affirmative action program for White males. This policy helped open the doors to higher education for Jewish American men in many universities that had previously restricted Jews. Federal programs targeting veterans also facilitated homeownership in the growing suburbs for many Jewish Americans (Brodkin, 2001).

One Jewish American author reflects on the experiences of her family and other Jewish Americans,

> The myth that Jews pulled themselves up by their own bootstraps ignores the fact that it took federal programs to create the conditions whereby the abilities of Jews and other European immigrants could be recognized and rewarded rather than denigrated and denied. The GI Bill and FHA and VA mortgages were forms of affirmative action that allowed male Jews and other Euro-American men to become suburban homeowners and to get the training that allowed them—but not women vets or war workers—to become professionals, technicians, salesmen, and managers in a growing economy. Jews' and other white ethnics' upward mobility was the result of programs that allowed us to float on a rising economic tide. (Brodkin, 2001, p. 42)

Hasidim were designated a disadvantaged minority under President Johnson's Great Society programs and thus benefited greatly from government initiatives. Federal aid has continued with the ongoing recognition of the Hasidim as an underprivileged community. This has enabled extensive community-building efforts in Boro Park, Brooklyn. Today, Boro Park is 85%

Hasidic rather than the heterogeneous community it was a few years earlier. Federal policies have been instrumental in helping this Jewish American community develop a strong infrastructure (Belcove-Shalin, 1995b). The strong community that has been supported by federal initiatives has, however, come into conflict with other communities. For example, African Americans once resided in larger numbers in Boro Park before being supplanted by the growing Hasidic population. Continuing tension exists between these groups.

CULTURAL COMPETENCE IN SOCIAL AGENCIES

As with other cultural groups, social agencies serving Jewish Americans have often either ignored culture or have sought to modify it. Sometimes this has been true even of Jewish organizations.

One early example of this phenomenon is Seattle's Settlement House, founded in 1906 by elite, Americanized Jews to serve poor immigrant Ashkenazic and Sephardic Jews. Although Christian-influenced Americanism dominated the early settlement house movement, this example presents a distinctly Jewish adaptation. Settlement house workers demonstrated a preference for preserving Ashkenazic over Sephardic culture. They also promoted the use of English and a secular Judaism that led to the Americanization of the Jewish population they served (Schwartz, 1999). Seattle's settlement house had a dual mission: socialize Jewish immigrants to American culture and secularize Orthodox, Eastern European Jews. "The ideal American Jew was both an ideal American and an ideal Jew, practicing an Ashkenazic Judaism stripped of its ethnic and orthodox overtones" (Schwartz, 1999, p. 35).

Jewish communities have established an extensive network of agencies that focus on social, cultural, and recreational needs. Unlike other agencies under ethnic auspices, agencies under Jewish sponsorship typically serve a wide variety of clientele including many non-Jews. Jewish agencies may or may not include a particular focus on meeting the cultural needs of Jewish American clients.

COMMUNITY INTERVENTIONS

Many Jewish Americans do not live in specific geographical communities any more with the exception of some Orthodox Jews, particularly the ultra-Orthodox Hasidim. This lack of a geographical community hinders opportunities for community-based interventions. Indeed, the blending of Jewish Americans into mainstream American society has limited macro-level interventions with this population.

Community interventions that do exist in Jewish American communities tend to be grassroots efforts. These efforts may include activities such as building schools and community centers. Although social workers may not always play significant roles in initiating grassroots efforts, policy makers and community activists can help ensure that funding resources are available for these types of projects.

Social workers indigenous to Jewish communities may have significant roles to play in community development and other macro-level interventions. Indeed, the values emphasized among many Jewish Americans may lead them to enter the helping professions. The Judeo-Christian ethic of compassion and caring is the foundation for many people who choose to become social workers or other helping professionals. The Jewish value of justice may also lead Jewish Americans to become social activists or community organizers. These professional skills, combined with membership in a Jewish community, can lead to positive change and community building.

CONCLUSION

In reflecting on the Jewish American experience, the intertwined themes of loss and continuity are particularly prominent. Assimilation has been a major force among Jewish Americans, yet despite dwindling numbers and cultural attachment, there are some signs of renewal in both Reform and Orthodox traditions. Oppression and anti-Semitism are shaping influences, both historically and in contemporary times. Social workers and other helping professionals can serve their Jewish American clients with an understanding of these phenomena and integrating this understanding and skills with the values of respect, empathy, and social justice. This combination will maximize cultural competence with the Jewish American population.

Exercises

Exercise #1: Visiting a synagogue
Contact a local synagogue and inquire about visiting a service that is open to the public. Ask if there are particular protocols that you need to be aware of to participate in the service respectfully (e.g., for women, wearing a skirt of a certain length). After your visit, write a brief reflection paper that discusses how you felt during your experience, similarities and differences between this experience and other religious services you have experienced, and how what you observed may inform your work with Jewish American clients.

Exercise #2: Increasing knowledge and empathy through literature
Read the Pulitzer Prize winning book *The Complete Maus* (Spiegelman, 1997). This short work, written in the form of a comic book, details the lives of European Jews (depicted as mice) under Nazi rule (with Nazis depicted as cats). In particular, the story reflects the experiences of a father who experienced the Holocaust discussing this with his adult son. What does this book have to say about intergenerational issues related to Holocaust trauma? What issues are identified for children of survivors?

Exercise #3: Interview a Jewish refugee
Contact a local refugee resettlement agency for assistance in identifying a Jewish refugee who might be willing to talk about his or her experiences. During an interview, inquire about what life was like being a Jew in his or her former country. What is life like as a Jewish refugee in the United States? What would be the most important things for social workers to know and do so they can help Jewish refugees? Report your findings to the class.

Additional Resources

Eisenberg, R. (1995). *Boychiks in the Hood: Travels in the Hasidic Underground.* New York: HarperCollins. Eisneberg describes his travels to Hasidic communities throughout the world. In part, this is a journey of self-discovery for an author with Hasidic roots yet little knowledge of this culture. This insightful and humorous book is a good tool for helping professionals to learn both about Hasidic cultures and the changing nature of cultural identity.

Brodkin, K. (2001). How Jews Became White. In P. S. Rothenberg (Ed.), *Race, Class, and Gender in the United States.* New York: Worth, 30–45. This article describes how social policies have helped shape the lives of Jewish Americans and subsequently how others perceive them. In addition to reviewing social policies, Brodkin provides a personal perspective on how her family benefited from these policies.

Council of Jewish Federations. (1990). *1990 National Jewish Population Survey.* Although this resource is becoming somewhat dated, it presents key demographic information on the Jewish population not available through other sources such as the U.S. census. The report also presents information on the changing nature of the Jewish American population.

Cowan, N. M., & Cowan, R. S. (1996). *Our Parents' Lives: Jewish Assimilation and Everyday Life.* Tuscaloosa: University of Alabama Press. This book presents an overview of issues in the daily lives of Jewish Americans and describes how this population has adapted to life in the United States. The book is based on interviews of Eastern European Jews born between 1895 and 1915. The voices of these people provide important insights for helping professionals working with this population.

References

Belcove-Shalin, J. S. (1995a). Introduction: New World Hasidism. In J. S. Belcove-Shalin (Ed.), *The New World Hasidim: Ethnographic Studies of Hasidic Jews in America.* Albany: State University of New York Press, 1–30.

Belcove-Shalin, J. S. (1995b). Home in exile: Hasidim in the new world. In J. S. Belcove-Shalin (Ed.), *The New World Hasidim: Ethnographic Studies* of Hasidic Jews in America. Albany: State University of New York Press, 205–236.

Brodkin, K. (2001). How Jews became White. In P. S. Rothenberg (Ed.), *Race, Class, and Gender in the United States.* New York: Worth, 30–45.

Cohen, M. A. (1993). The Sephardic phenomenon: A reappraisal. In M. A. Cohen & A. J. Peck (Eds.), *Sephardim in the Americas: Studies in Culture and*

History. Tuscaloosa: American Jewish Archives and the University of Alabama Press, 1–79.

Council of Jewish Federations. (1990). *1990 National Jewish Population Survey.*

Cowan, N. M., & Cowan, R. S. (1996). *Our Parents' Lives: Jewish Assimilation and Everyday Life.* Tuscaloosa: University of Alabama Press.

Davidman, L., & Stocks, J. (1995). Varieties of fundamentalist experience: Lubavitch Hasidic and fundamentalist Christian approaches to contemporary family life. In J. S. Belcove-Shalin (Ed.), *The New World Hasidim: Ethnographic Studies of Hasidic Jews in America.* Albany: State University of New York Press, 107–133.

Falk, G. (1995). *American Judaism in Transition: The Secularization of a Religious Community.* Lanham, MD: University Press of America.

Feinberg, R. I. (1996). Use of reminiscence groups to facilitate the telling of life stories by elderly Russian Jewish immigrants. *Smith College Studies in Social Work, 67*(1), 39–51.

Hammerschlag, C. (1988). *The Dancing Healers: A Doctor's Journey of Healing with Native Americans.* San Francisco: HarperCollins.

Heilman, S. C. (1995). Foreword. In J. S. Belcove-Shalin (Ed.), *The New World Hasidim: Ethnographic Studies of Hasidic Jews in America.* Albany: State University of New York Press, xi–xv.

Kahn, N. E. (1995). The adult bat mitzvah: Its use in the articulation of women's identity. *Affilia, 10*(3), 299–314.

Karp, A. J. (1998). *Jewish Continuity in America: Creative Survival in a Free Society.* Tuscaloosa: University of Alabama Press.

Papo, J. M. (1993). The Sephardim in North America in the Twentieth Century. In M. A. Cohen & A. J. Peck (Eds.), *Sephardim in the Americas: Studies in Culture and History.* Tuscaloosa: American Jewish Archives and the University of Alabama Press, 267–308.

Rabin, B., Markus, E., & Voghera, N. (1999). A comparative study of Jewish and Arab battered women presenting in the emergency room of a general hospital. *Social Work in Health Care, 29*(2), 69–84.

Schwartz, A. (1999). Americanization and cultural preservation in Seattle's Settlement House: A Jewish adaptation of the Anglo-American model of settlement work. *Journal of Sociology and Social Welfare, 26*(3), 25–47.

Shaffir, W. (1995). Boundaries and self-presentation among the Hasidim: A study in identity maintenance. In J. S. Belcove-Shalin (Ed.), *The New World Hasidim: Ethnographic Studies of Hasidic Jews in America.* Albany: State University of New York Press, 31–68.

Sorscher, N., & Cohen, L. J. (1997). Trauma in children of holocaust survivors: Transgenerational effects. *American Journal of Orthopsychiatry. 67*(3), 493–500.

Spiegelman, A. (1997). *The Complete Maus.* New York: Pantheon Books.

Arab Americans

Arabs are one of the fastest growing populations in the world as well as in Western countries. The 2000 census identified 1.2 million Arab Americans—an increase of 38% from 1990 (de la Cruz & Brittingham, 2003). Their median age is 30.2. More than half (59.3%) were born in the United States. Almost half of the foreign-born Arab population (49%) are naturalized citizens. Generally, Arab Americans are an educated population with 82.4% having attained at least a high school degree, 36.3% having at least a bachelor's degree, and 15.2% having a graduate degree. Despite their high education levels, 14.5% of Arab Americans live in poverty (U.S. Bureau of the Census, 1998).

In December 2003, the U.S. Census Bureau issued its first report ever on people of Arab ancestry. The U. S. Census Bureau notes that there is still a lack of consensus about who falls under the definition of Arab. For purposes of the report, most people from Arabic-speaking countries are categorized as Arab. The largest Arab American populations were Lebanese (37%), Syrian (12%), and Egyptian (12%). Arab Americans are spread evenly across all regions of the United States (de la Cruz & Brittingham, 2003).

The census is likely to undercount Arab Americans because many are suspicious of government authorities and conceal their ethnic affiliation. Instability in the Arab world contributes to their growing numbers in the United States, and current unofficial estimates place the number of Arabs in the United States at about 2½ to 3 million

(Hassoun, 1999; Nobles & Sciarra, 2000). Wayne County, in Southeastern Michigan, has one of the largest concentrations of Arabs in the United States, with more than 100,000. There are many Arab groups in Wayne County including Egyptians, Iranians, Iraqis, Jordanians, Kaldeans, Lebanese, Moroccans, Palestinians, Saudis, Syrians, and Yemeni (U.S. Commission on Civil Rights, 2001).

Early Arab immigrants like those from Lebanon and Syria in the 1870s, as well as those from Yemen in the 1960–1980s, typically came looking for work. Later populations arrived fleeing political instability. In particular, refugees came from Syrian territory occupied by Turkey in 1939, from Iraq following the Ottoman massacres, from Palestine when they were expelled by Israelis in 1948 and 1967, and from Lebanon during the civil war beginning in 1975 and after the Israeli invasion of 1982. Early Arab immigrants were 90% Christian. By the middle of the century, proportions began to shift and eventually Arab immigrants became 90% Muslim. In the last decade, the percentage of Christians has begun to rise again (Haddad, 1997).

Political events in the 20th century led to a sense of unity among some Arab nations and among Arab Americans (Haddad, 1997; Nobles & Sciarra, 2000; Shain, 1996). Arab nations such as Syria, Egypt, and Jordan that arose after the creation of Israel as a Jewish state are committed to nationalism and the union of Arab nations. Rather than seeing themselves as separate political entities, they see the boundaries dividing Arabs as temporary (Nobles & Sciarra, 2000). Arabic, the official language of all Arab countries, is the fourth most widely spoken language in the world. This is another unifying factor among Arab peoples (Nobles & Sciarra, 2000).

Bedouin is the term applied to all Arabic-speaking, nomadic tribes in the Middle East. These tribes predate the establishment of either Christianity or Islam. Today most Bedouin are Muslim, although a few are Christian. Traditionally, they are nomadic, but Bedouin society is undergoing rapid change. Of 100,000 Bedouin in the Negev (Southern Israel), 40% are now in villages and 60% are semi-nomadic, living in rural areas (Al-Krenawi & Graham, 1999).

The term *Syrian* was initially a catchall label for all people from the eastern end of the Mediterranean (Shakir, 1997). Historically, early Arab immigrants were referred to as Syrians, Syrian-Lebanese, Arabs, or Arabians. Use of terms was inconsistent. More recently, they have become identified and identify themselves as Arab Americans (Suleiman, 1997). The term *Arab American* is used throughout this chapter to refer to people in the United States who trace their heritage to one or more of the 21 Arab countries in North Africa or the Middle East. More specific national or tribal terms are used when possible so the diversity of this group is not obscured.

This chapter gives an overview of social work with Arab Americans. The social work literature on this population is fairly limited, so this chapter draws on the broader social science literature as well as the literature on social work with Arabs in the Middle East. The chapter presents information about knowledge, skills, and values/attitudes necessary for cultural competence, and reviews issues for cultural competence on micro and macro levels.

KNOWLEDGE FOR CULTURAL COMPETENCE

The knowledge needed for culturally competent social work with Arab Americans can be divided into four broad areas: diversity, history, culture, and contemporary realities. Although some of the social work knowledge base is universally applicable, the distinct cultural, economic, religious, and political characteristics that distinguish Arab societies from Western, postindustrial societies require the development of specific knowledge pertaining to social work with Arab Americans (Haj-Yahia, 1997). Diversity serves as an overarching concept that informs other key areas of knowledge. The history, culture, and contemporary realities of Arab Americans vary according to factors such as religion, national origin, and generation in the United States.

Diversity

Different groups of Arabs (e.g., Palestinians, Lebanese, Yemeni) have different traditions and religious beliefs. There is also significant diversity among Arab Americans based on their generational status in the United States. Failure to understand the differences among Arab groups promotes stereotyping. For instance, today many Americans assume that Arabs are all Muslim. Muslims are also assumed to be terrorists. More understanding of the diversity of Arab Americans would help reduce this type of stereotyping (U.S. Commission on Civil Rights, 2001).

There are many differences among Arab people, including those based on ethnic, linguistic, tribal, regional, religious, socioeconomic, and national identities. In some ways, Arab peoples have deep social and class distinctions and are politically fragmented, transnationally and within national boundaries. Likewise, the Arab world has been exposed to Western cultural norms and these influences have been experienced differently in various Arab communities and societies (Al-Krenawi & Graham, 2000; Haj-Yahia, 1997).

Many Arabs are Muslim (followers of the Islamic faith), but the terms *Arab* and *Muslim* are not synonymous and cannot be used interchangeably. In fact, some Arabs are Muslim and some are Christian (Faragallah, Schumm, & Webb, 1997; Katz & Lowenstein, 2002). Indeed, less than half the Arabs in the United States are Muslim (Faragallah et al., 1997; Shain, 1996). There are an estimated six million Muslims in United States, with only 15% of these being Arab (Al-Krenawi & Graham, 2000).

Differences between Muslims and Christians may cause significant divisions among Arab immigrants. Arab Christians have more reasons than their Muslim counterparts to leave Islamic cultures where they may be unwelcome or experience persecution. Christian Arabs are likely to experience less cultural conflict once in the United States. This may accelerate acculturation. Educational attainment may also moderate traditional values (Faragallah et al., 1997).

It is often assumed that Muslim Arabs have more difficulty acculturating to life in the United States than other immigrants do (Faragallah et al., 1997). Extreme religious affiliation, particularly with Islam, may be a force for maintaining traditions. Muslim Arabs may be more traditional and less accepting of Western culture than are their Christian counterparts, thereby hindering their acculturation. One small study, however, refuted the hypothesis that Muslim Arab Americans are more traditional than their Christian Arab counterparts (Faragallah et al., 1997).

Sometimes, even within one country, different groups of Arabs have vastly different experiences and backgrounds. For example, Israeli Bedouin have somewhat different experiences than do other Arabs in Israel. These traditionally nomadic, predominantly Muslim, Arabic speakers historically lived in self-sufficient tribal groups in the desert. They interacted with other Bedouin tribes and with settled agrarian and urban populations. When Israel was established in 1948, Israeli Bedouin were increasingly pushed by the Israeli government onto allotted land and into an agrarian lifestyle, similar to reservations for Native Americans in the United States. In this process, they became separated from other Arabs by the Israeli border. They were considered loyal citizens of Israel and some served in the military. The 1967 war and invasion of the West Bank and Gaza Strip created an influx of Arab workers into Israel and renewed contact between the Bedouin and other Arabs. Subsequently, Israelis began to view Bedouin in a negative light similar to other Arabs. Extreme and rapid social change in recent decades has led to the deterioration of strong family-based tribes. The young often become socially isolated from elders and their culture (Elbedour, Bastien, & Center, 1997).

Arab Americans differ considerably based on their generational status in the United States. Some identify with symbols of their old countries without taking an interest in domestic or foreign affairs, but others may not identify at all as members of an Arab community. The notion of pan-Arab solidarity and Arab Americans as a group developed only after the 1967 Arab-Israeli war. Those who arrived in the United States during the last 30 years are more likely to identify as Arab American or with a specific Arab nationality than are earlier immigrants and their descendants (Nobles & Sciarra, 2000; Shain, 1996).

History

Understanding the history of a group is important to understanding the group's contemporary circumstances and providing culturally appropriate services. A brief review of history prior to emigration to the United States as well as a review of historical experiences in this country is helpful in shedding light on the background of the Arab American population.

History before Arrival in the United States   In ancient times, Arabs were nomads inhabiting the Arabian peninsula. Islam rose in the 7th century and spread over parts of Asia, Africa, and Europe, thus carrying with it Arabic culture and language. The term *Arab* is used today for all the countries that were conquered by Muslim Arabs, although some of the inhabitants of these regions are Arabs by speech, rather than by ethnicity or religion (Nobles & Sciarra, 2000).

The 7th and 8th centuries were the peak of the Arab empire. By the 13th century, Europe prospered and Arab societies were in decline (Nobles & Sciarra, 2000). Under the Ottoman Empire, Lebanon, Syria, Palestine, and Israel were all part of greater Syria (Shakir, 1997). The Arab world was divided after World War I, including a 1917 agreement to make Palestine a Jewish homeland. The decline of Arab dominance and subsequent European ascendancy has had a significant impact on Arab ideas and feelings. Imposition of foreign languages and cultures and the U.S. involvement in Israel have led to feelings of betrayal and open psychological wounds. Thus, some Arabs blame European colonialism for problems such as poverty, psychological conflicts, and most of all, the loss of Palestine (Nobles & Sciarra, 2000). Some Arabs believe that the West takes away moral values and family ties as well as freedom. Since the mid-1970s, some Arabs have viewed the spread of Islamic fundamentalism as an antidote to Western domination.

History in the United States   Arab immigrants have been coming to the United States since at least 1854. Between 1971 and 1992, nearly 600,000 immigrants came from Iran, Iraq, Jordan, Lebanon, Egypt, Syria, and Turkey (Faragallah et al., 1997). Like many other immigrants, Arab Americans come to the United States for political, economic, and social reasons. Although Arab Americans have settled across the country, a significant secondary migration has led many to relocate to Michigan where they are attracted by the size and diversity of the Arab American population (U.S. Commission on Civil Rights, 2001).

Details of early Arab immigration are unclear because statistics are inconsistent and fragmented. Accuracy is obscured because Arab immigrants came from various parts of the multinational Ottoman Empire. By 1899, immigration officials noted the large numbers of people coming from the Ottoman province of Greater Syria and added "Syrian" as a classification. By World War I, approximately 100,000 Syrian immigrants had arrived in the United States. By World War II, Syrian immigrants and their descendants numbered 206,000 (Naff, 1997; Nobles & Sciarra, 2000).

Virtually all the pre–World War II Syrians were Christians from Mount Lebanon (Naff, 1997; Nobles & Sciarra, 2000). A few thousand of these were Palestinians who were referred to as Syrians until Syria and Lebanon attained independence after World War II. Early Syrian immigrants were primarily uneducated farmers and artisans who were poor, but not destitute. They were attracted by U.S. industrialization and urbanization and came to earn money with the hope of returning home in a few years. Many Syrians became travel-ing peddlers, and by the late 1890s, distinctly Syrian communities had been formed throughout the United States. The anti-alien movement after World War I led to the Johnson-Reed Act of 1924, which restricted Syrian immigra-tion to a quota of 100. This Act was not repealed until 1965 (Naff, 1997).

By the mid-20th century, most Arab immigrants were Muslims. Many of them were Palestinians displaced after the 1948 establishment of Israel. Some Iraqis and Syrians also came to the United States to escape political conflict. From the mid-1960s to the present, most Arab immigrants have been profes-sionals and entrepreneurs fleeing war and political unrest. Many were edu-cated, young, affluent, and sought U.S. citizenship (Nobles & Sciarra, 2000). These Arabs came to the United States more consciously as immigrants rather than as sojourners. They came as either students or members of the educated elite (Suleiman, 1997). These immigrants came from many Arab nations that had recently gained independence and were more politicized and nationalistic than their earlier counterparts.

U.S. foreign policy led to a major shift in how Arab Americans viewed themselves. In particular, the favoritism shown Israel in the 1967 Arab-Israeli war shocked Arabs in the United States and gave birth to a politicized Arab-American identity (Haddad, 1997). These political events became the rallying point or common cause that joined Arab Americans together (Shain, 1996). The ethnopolitical awakening of Arab Americans rose with the civil rights movement and was fueled by anti-Arab sentiments connected to world events. Anti-Arab feelings in the United States were exacerbated by the 1973 oil embargo and subsequent price hikes, the U.S. boycott of the PLO in 1975, and the increasing power of the pro-Israeli lobby. The 1978 Abscam operation, in which FBI agents disguised as Arabs sought to corrupt members of Congress, politically galvanized Arab Americans (Shain, 1996).

In response to frustration with caricatures of Arab culture and Muslim religion in the 1970s and 1980s, there was a rise of activism and establishment of Arab American institutions such as the National Association of Arab Americans (1972), the Arab-American Anti-Discrimination Committee (1980), and the Arab American Institute (1985). Palestinian refugees and immigrants who had recently lost their homeland were a driving force in this activism. In 1982, Israel's invasion of Lebanon raised significant Arab American protest, but internal divisions within organizations failed to trans-late community mobilization and American public support into political gains (e.g., no congressional condemnation of Israel's role in the massacres, no halt in arms flow to Israel, and no cut in aid). These setbacks led to Arab American disillusionment and retreat (Shain, 1996).

Arab American community opinion was openly divided during the Gulf war. According to a poll in February 1991, Muslims were 1.5 times more likely to oppose the war than were non-Muslims. Jordanians and Palestinians were more than twice as likely to oppose the war as were other Arab Americans. The general public challenged the loyalty and patriotism of Arab

Americans. Diaspora organizations previously united under the Palestinian cause were no longer able to stifle intra-Arab conflicts, and Arab American coalitions splintered (Shain, 1996).

Anti-Arab rhetoric, government policies, and public sentiment continued to grow following the 1993 World Trade Center and the 1995 Oklahoma City bombings. Arab Americans were blamed and held collectively accountable regardless of the source of violence. Arab American communities became targets of discrimination and political persecution (Shain, 1996). This trend continued with the 2001 destruction of the World Trade Center and attack on the Pentagon.

Culture

Despite the extensive national, political, religious, and tribal diversity, Arab societies have common attributes, based on a shared geographic environment and place in history. Thus, cultural commonalities unite the diverse transnational Arab population (Al-Krenawi & Graham, 2000; Haj-Yahia, 1997).

Family Structures   Arab society is based on the patrilineal extended family that is a source of both financial and emotional support (Al-Krenawi & Graham, 2000; Haj-Yahia, 1997; Nobles & Sciarra, 2000). For the Bedouin, as with other Arabs, blood bonds are stronger than any other and require deep commitment and responsibility. Bedouin have a hierarchical family order where males dominate females and old dominate young (Al-Krenawi & Graham, 1999). Families have complimentary roles that emphasize patriarchy, primary group relations, spontaneity, and expressiveness. The extended family is based on a patriarchal line (*hamula*), and this is the most important kinship structure. In some Arab cultures like the Bedouin, several *hamula* constitute a tribe (Al-Krenawi & Graham, 2000). Eldest sons play a significant role within Arab families. Children grow up with numerous nurturing caregivers (Nobles & Sciarra, 2000).

Arab society has a collectivist rather than individualistic orientation. Arab society espouses some individualist values such as personal achievement, influence, power, and prestige, but the collectivist values such as group affiliation prevail. Family members are expected to share responsibilities, achievement and influence, joy and grief, success and failure, reputation, aspirations, and convictions. There is a strong focus on relationship status such as motherhood, fatherhood, brotherhood, and family solidarity. Relationships beyond the family, such as those with neighbors and small local groups, are the foundation for local solidarity. People introduce themselves by identifying their relatives and where they live. Subsequently they may describe their ethnic or sectarian ties. Relationships based on more than one type of connection are the strongest (Haj-Yahia, 1997).

Gender Roles   Traditionally, there are strong gender differences in Arab societies. Men constitute the authority in the household, economy, and political structure. Women may be perceived as weak, powerless, subservient, and sub-missive. They are often unable to leave the family setting without an escort. Women's social status is typically contingent on marriage and children, espe-cially producing sons (Al-Krenawi & Graham, 1999). Female economic, social, and physical dependence in a male-dominated society seems to play a major role in domestic violence (Rabin, Markus, & Voghera, 1999). Arranged marriages are common and women often do not work outside the home. Women may endure years of marital problems to avoid the stigma of divorce. In Islamic tradition, fathers have custody of boys after age 7 and girls after age 9 (Al-Krenawi & Graham, 2000; Rabin et al., 1999).

In Arab families, men and women have specific rights and duties. Actions of the individual reflect on the family. In Arab culture, girls' activities are restricted to protect family honor. In a patrilineal society, responsibility and group membership derive from the paternity of a child; thus, sexual chastity and honor become imperative qualities for females. In this way, women are a fundamental, valued, and crucial element in the creation and maintenance of an Arab identity (Ajrouch, 1999). In the United States, adolescent girls feel tension between honoring their parents' wishes and the perceived freedom of American girls. There is much more permissiveness for males. Boys feel a responsibility to uphold family honor and often scold sisters about their behavior. In the extreme, male family members may kill a female member thought to have shamed the family. Restrictions on females become exagger-ated in an atmosphere of perceived threats (i.e., the independence of American society). Some parents believe that teaching Islam is a way to teach children who they are as Arabs in the United States. The fear of God is used to instill expected behaviors (Ajrouch, 1999).

The status of women in the Arab world fluctuates because of conflicts between traditionalists and reformers. Women's status in any particular coun-try is likely to reflect the group that currently holds sway (Nobles & Sciarra, 2000). The status of Arab women in the United States is both complex and changing. The challenge of negotiating different sets of cultural ideals and val-ues is particularly conflictual for Arab American women. Additional conflicts exist because their attachment to the United States (land of their birth or immigration) is at odds with this country's hostile policies in Middle East (Shakir, 1997).

A study of the Lebanese community in Dearborn, Michigan, examined interpretations of ethnic identity among adolescents and their parents. Both gender and religion were identified as primary aspects of Arab American identity. The adolescents viewed gender as particularly salient. Female behavior is the defining characteristic of both Arab and American identity. Parents, on the other hand, saw religion as the defining characteristic of Arab identity. Religion is the justification for parents' behavioral expecta-tions (including gender roles) for their children. Although there is a clear relationship between gender and religion as key characteristics of Arab American identity, which aspect is stressed reflects a distinct generational difference (Ajrouch, 1999).

Despite some adaptations, the behavior of Palestinian American women in public remains distinctly different from dominant society norms. There are also variations among Palestinian American women. Differences are rooted in class distinctions. Middle-class Palestinian American women often wear American clothes, whereas lower class women wear more-traditional clothes and cover their hair. Palestinian American women are generally not allowed to date. Occasional exceptions are made among middle-class families if she is of marriageable age and the date is a prospective marriage partner who is also an Arab Muslim. Palestinian society has a tradition of arranged marriages between cousins. Although most women now choose their own partners, usually they only get to know a man after a formal engagement or under close supervision. Virginity is expected at marriage. Being in public with an unrelated man is scandalous and makes marriage difficult. Men, on the other hand, are allowed to date and live with women outside marriage. Marriage to a Palestinian Muslim is preferred for men as well, but other marriage partners are acceptable (Cainkar, 1997).

Values   Not all Muslims are Arab, nor are all Arabs Muslim, yet Islam has a significant influence on the Arab world where religion regulates daily behavior. Arab values include an emphasis on fatalism, predetermination, and God's will. Belief in God and piety are important, regardless of religious affiliation. There is a general belief among Arabs that religion should be taught in schools and promoted by governments. Established beliefs or practices should not be subjected to interpretation or modification (Nobles & Sciarra, 2000).

Belief in predestation is not interpreted as belief that an individual must yield to reality but, rather, he or she is experiencing a temporary sense of powerlessness until circumstances change. Although there is often a belief that events are dictated by divine will rather than personal choice, there is also a value that emphasizes self-determination, free will, and the need to control and change reality (Haj-Yahia, 1997).

Arab cultural values and perspectives are often alien to Western society, and to some principles and values of the social work profession as well (Haj-Yahia, 1997). For example, Arab school systems emphasize rote learning and memorization rather than interpretation and analysis. Conformity is emphasized over independent thought and creativity. The teacher is a strong authority figure who emphasizes society's authoritarian, hierarchical nature and respect for elders. Adults are seen as source of wisdom, knowledge, and authority (Al-Krenawi & Graham, 2000). These values differ from how most social workers look at the learning process and interactions between those who guide and those who learn. These different perceptions may lead to conflicting expectations in the social work relationship.

The Arab emphasis on hierarchical structures conflicts with Western value orientations, thus causing tension, ambiguity, and anxiety for some Arab Americans (Haj-Yahia, 1997). The value of conformity and obedience also conflicts with American value systems. Arab values that discourage independence and initiative may contribute to Arab Americans' reluctance to express disagreement or to challenge instructions (Haj-Yahia, 1997).

Cultural values are shaped by environmental forces. Living within a context of constant conflict or war influences self-perception and values. Arab children in the Gaza Strip and West Bank have been living under Israeli occupation since 1967. For 80% in the West Bank, this is their traditional homeland, and the other 20% are refugees from other parts of Israel. The Gaza Strip population is extremely poor and made up almost entirely of refugees. A study of drawings made by children of the West Bank and Gaza Strip revealed that they see themselves primarily as martyrs for the Intifada (the struggle to return to the 1948 borders established for Israel and Palestine). In contrast, Bedouin Arab children, who have not lived with the same level of conflict and displacement as Arab children from the West Bank and Gaza Strip, see themselves as having a variety of life options rather than necessarily being martyrs (Elbedour et al., 1997).

There is a tension between compliance and rebellion in Arab societies. Sometimes the values of self-control, patience, submission, and security lead to helplessness, passive endurance of humiliation, and avoiding confrontation. On the other hand, Arabs also have a tradition of revolutions, uprisings, and struggles for freedom. Such rebellions produce heroes, who are immortalized and glorified for their resistance to oppression (Haj-Yahia, 1997). Living under oppressive conditions may lead to the rise of leaders who use violent means to achieve what they see as a struggle for liberation.

The cultural emphasis on the group has both advantages and disadvantages. Collectivist values engender cooperation, commitment, mutual trust, harmony, and psychological peace of mind. People support each other and there is a strong sense of belonging. This sense of connection is reflected in the proverb, "Paradise without people is not worth living in" (Haj-Yahia, 1997). Collectivist values, however, may also lead to social pressure to conform at the expense of freedom, individuality, independence, and self-reliance. An individual with ambitions that do not fit with goals of the collective may face ostracism (Al-Krenawi & Graham, 2000; Haj-Yahia, 1997). Strong themes of honor and shame permeate everyday life (Al-Krenawi & Graham, 2000; Nobles & Sciarra, 2000).

Hospitality and generosity are highly valued. People are judged by how they treat guests (Nobles & Sciarra, 2000). Lack of hospitality can be an expression of hostility or other negative feelings. For example, anger at guests may be expressed by refusing to offer them coffee. Likewise, a family saddened by a member's deteriorating health may not serve dinner to guests as a reflection of their sorrow (Katz & Lowenstein, 2002). Examining the context can help social workers assess and understand clients' actions.

Many Arabs have fluid notions of time that are less structured than Western ideas. For example, families may have difficulty limiting visiting hours at a hospital. Hours should be flexible, when possible. Social workers can advocate on behalf of Arab clients in the case of inflexible visiting hours.

Making and keeping appointments at fixed times or ending sessions promptly may be a source of difficulty (Al-Krenawi & Graham, 2000).

Shifting Identities   Many Arab Americans, especially early immigrants, blended easily into U.S. society. The assimilationist tendencies of early Arab immigrants became strengthened as World War I cut them off from their homelands and the United States fought against the Ottoman Empire, their former colonizer (Suleiman, 1997).

Many American-born Arabs, both Christians and Muslims, have integrated into American society. However, there is a growing shift among the younger generation of Muslims to move away from an Arab identity to a Muslim identity. Recently arrived immigrants and exiles, who tend to observe the faith more strictly when abroad as a way of asserting their identity, have led to a revival of Muslim identity in the United States. Arab Americans who favor coalitions are anxious about the shift to Islamic identification that excludes Christian Arabs, the majority of Arab Americans (Shain, 1996).

A study of Arab Americans found that longer residence in United States, younger age at immigration, not recently visiting the homeland, and Christianity are associated with higher acculturation. Discrimination experiences are associated with less life satisfaction in the United States but not acculturation in general (Faragallah et al., 1997).

Contemporary Realities

The contemporary concerns of Arab Americans can be broadly grouped into areas related to the status of Arab Americans in U.S. society and politics and to relations between the United States and the Arab world; especially the U.S. position regarding the Israeli-Palestinian conflict (Shain, 1996). International political relationships are influential in shaping the experiences and perceptions of Arabs in the United States. Social workers need to be knowledgeable about several key contemporary realities of Arab Americans, including cultural transitions, economic status, health, stereotypes, discrimination, community social structures, and the world situation.

Cultural Transitions   Arabs are experiencing transitions in their home societies as well as in the United States. Conflicts arise between following tradition, heritage, and fundamentalism and future-oriented modernism. Some call for defying the past, but others espouse a static fundamentalism, adhering to the well known and rejecting the unknown. These tensions have existed for centuries. In classical Arab thought, innovation and creation can only come from God; thus, anything other than strict preservation of tradition is sacrilegious. On the other hand, Arab societies have experienced periods of great creativity and innovation, placing them on the cutting edge of scientific knowledge (Haj-Yahia, 1997).

Israeli Arab village elders report a decline in community closeness and support. Elders, once respected community leaders, owners of land, and sources of wisdom, are now relegated to being advisors, with no real leader-ship roles. Leadership now happens through village institutions. These changes, however, have not displaced the norm of respect and family care for the elderly. Societal changes have led to more women pursuing educational and employment opportunities, thus affecting the ability of the elderly to mobilize family and community support. Changes in family and community necessitate development of formal social services such as homecare. When homecare is necessary, some families request that care be provided by a member of the extended family employed by an agency. This is an ideal way of providing social services in a culturally acceptable way. Families are typically satisfied with this service (Katz & Lowenstein, 2002).

Although Arab culture is characterized by a hierarchy of power, influence, prestige, and seniority, this is counteracted by an emerging ideology that strives for equality and that combats discrimination and a system of privileges. Fundamentalism is tied into debates between religion and scientific, secular culture. The growing divide between Islamic fundamentalism and modern secularism may lead to a split within the Arab American community and between fundamentalist Arabs and non-Arabs. Some Arab Americans make conscious attempts to reconcile the sacred and secular and blend future-oriented elements into classic Arab heritage, thus, avoiding isolation and confinement to the past (Haj-Yahia, 1997).

Economic Status   Despite stereotypes that Arabs have vast wealth from oil, many Arabs experience economic vulnerability, both in their original homelands and in the United States. For example, there is considerable economic hardship for Arabs in Jaffa, a part of Tel Aviv, Israel. They live in dilapidated and overcrowded dwellings and have a high rate of unskilled labor accompanied by low income. Most families live in serious economic distress along with extreme psychological stress. They experience high rates of school dropouts, juvenile delinquency, alcohol and drug abuse, and increasing rates of divorce (Savaya, 1998)

The economic status of Arab Americans varies considerably. Despite often feeling that they are unwelcome and their status is unequal, many Arab immigrants have done well financially (Faragallah et al., 1997). In the United States, Arabs are disproportionately involved in retail trades. In part, this is because of industrial downsizing and loss of a manufacturing base in urban areas like Chicago, leaving few options. Historically, retail trades have led to upward mobility but this niche is not capable of absorbing growing numbers of immigrants. Thus, Arab Americans are experiencing growing unemployment (Cainkar, 1999). Arab Americans are often victims of employment discrimination. Those with high levels of education may not have an opportunity to work in their field. For many professionals, retail is the only avenue for economic survival (U.S. Commission on Civil Rights, 2001).

Health   Arab immigrants in the United States often work long hours under stressful conditions, which places them at risk for health problems. The combination of lifestyle changes, dietary changes, and stress associated with adaptation to a new cultural environment needs to be examined for health consequences. Many Arab Americans work in the auto industry in Detroit and are exposed to pollutants and unhealthy factory conditions. A community-based health study of 300 Arab Americans in Detroit revealed problems with hypertension, high cholesterol, and diabetes. Differences were found between populations from Yemen, Syria/Lebanon, Jordan/Palestine, and Iraq, as well as between men and women. Large numbers of unemployed and those without adequate health insurance and language skills may be associated with undiagnosed or untreated disease. In the United States, dietary practices of Arab Americans have become less nutritious over time (Hassoun, 1999).

Affective disorders are often viewed as having a somatic origin so mental health treatment is expected to be similar to medical treatment in its timeliness and lack of client involvement. Expression of physical symptoms is more acceptable and common. Mental illness is often perceived as linked to the supernatural, that is, not quite human, not quite angelic. Mental illness is regarded with respect and fear of God. It may be helpful to explicitly include religious concepts in the helping process (Al-Krenawi & Graham, 2000).

Perceptions that problems may have a supernatural origin are consistent regardless of educational level (Al-Krenawi & Graham, 2000), although they may be more prominent among older Arabs (Katz & Lowenstein, 2002). Traditional healing may be used as well as Western ways of helping. Traditional healers treat spiritual and mental issues, and Western methods are sought for medical or somatic disorders. Helping professionals can integrate activities with traditional healers and validate their use by clients (Al-Krenawi & Graham, 2000).

Stereotypes   The U.S. media strongly reinforces stereotypes of Arabs as being wealthy, terrorists, unfriendly nomads, or belly dancers (Nobles & Sciarra, 2000). Some Arabs Americans tend to deny or minimize their heritage because of stereotyping. Some continue to successfully engage with mainstream society and are likely to be successful, to advocate secularism, and to emphasize commonalities across cultures and religions. Others, particularly more recent immigrants, tend to remain withdrawn from American culture (Nobles & Sciarra, 2000). The considerable impact of negative media attention related to world events makes Arabs feel unwelcome in the United States and makes acculturation more difficult and less desired (Faragallah et al., 1997).

Arab Americans are one of the few groups that can still be stereotyped with impunity (Faragallah et al., 1997; Shakir, 1997; Stockton, 1997). Negative portrayals abound in textbooks and the media. The key symbol of the alien world of Arab Americans is Islam. Islam is seen to represent danger, aggressiveness, terror, and devastation (Shakir, 1997; Stockton, 1997). The linking of Arabs and Islam obscures diversity and promotes stereotypes.

Discrimination   Although all immigrants risk encountering discrimination, the experience may be somewhat different for Arab Americans. Some Arabs master English, do not have distinctive features, and do well economically, thus blending into mainstream America relatively easily without being recognized as minorities. If they are recognized as Arabs, however, they may encounter intense discrimination based on stereotypes. Discrimination against Arab Americans may be more tolerated in the United States than is discrimination against other minorities (Faragallah et al., 1997).

An investigation into civil rights violations perpetrated against Arab Americans identified three major areas of concern: (1) racial profiling and detention at airports and ports of entry, (2) denial of due process in deportation hearings, and (3) discrimination. Extensive mistrust exists between Arab Americans and law enforcement entities; thus, discrimination may not be documented because of fear of police authorities (U.S. Commission on Civil Rights, 2001).

It is important to understand the shaping forces of identity for those who live with intergroup conflict. Strong, long-term, emotional responses develop with relation to the conflict itself, one's own group, and members of other groups. Free-form drawings provide insight into how people see themselves within a social context. A study of Arab children in Israel found that those exposed to the most conflict organize their identities in a way that includes their enemies as well as themselves; thus, conflict becomes self-perpetuating (Elbedour et al., 1997). These children learn to see themselves only as avengers and are not able to picture a world where they are not reacting to and interacting with their enemies. The discrimination and stereotyping experienced by Arab Americans may have similar outcomes.

Issues of discrimination often arise in educational settings, particularly related to lack of bilingual education and lack of cultural accommodation. Many Arab American school children are refugees fleeing wars in their homelands. They often dress and follow social customs that are different from mainstream America. Arab American children are often harassed and ridiculed by other students. Many incidents have been reported where school personnel have been insensitive and unwilling to support Arab American students. English is often not their primary language, and the lack of bilingual programs hinders students from getting a quality education. Allegations have also been made that schools are reluctant to hire Arab American faculty (U.S. Commission on Civil Rights, 2001).

Anti-Arab racism is frequently tolerated in the United States. This is not a fringe phenomenon but, rather, is common in mainstream society (Abraham, 1997). Terrorist incidents and subsequent media portrayals trigger threats and violence against Arab Americans throughout the United States. Anti-Arab racism and hate crimes rose during the Gulf War. The war raised latent anti-Arab American feelings and derogatory references that were openly expressed on talk shows, bumper stickers, t-shirts, pins, and posters (Abraham, 1997). Stereotypes and discrimination have been compounded by reactions to the terrorist attack on the Pentagon and destruction of the World Trade Center on September 11, 2001. Revelations that the attacks were carried out by Arab Islamic fundamentalists further solidified the belief of many Americans that being Arab, being Muslim, and being a terrorist were virtually synonymous.

Likewise, the increasing violence in Israel early in the 21st century presented the news media with almost nightly images of Palestinians as suicide bombers. Fear of differences and of the unknown fuel the fires that lead many people to believe that the actions of a highly publicized few accurately characterize the sentiments and behaviors of millions.

Community Social Structures   Communities vary, but examination of the social structures within one particular Arab American community can be enlightening. Chicago has a population of approximately 150,000 Arabs, 57% of whom are Palestinians. Communitywide Palestinian organizations declined after the Gulf War. The community in general displayed less pride, strength, and resilience. A needs assessment conducted in 1996–1997 found that 30% of the Arab American community were unemployed and 30% were in low-paid employment. Overall, 66% were receiving some kind of public assistance. Half of Chicago's Arab population is children under age 14; thus, most Arabs living in poverty in Chicago are American-born children. Most Arab Americans in Chicago (70%) do not speak English well. This is a major barrier to successful life in the United States, yet there are no Arab-oriented English language programs to address this need. The majority (70%) reported disliking their neighborhoods because of crime, drugs, gangs, and shootings, but said they could not move for economic reasons.

Lack of community infrastructure exacerbates high service need. Residents reported needing assistance with a wide range of problems, including alcoholism, drug abuse, and domestic violence. Divorce and delinquency are no longer unusual. Arab street gangs and theft rings victimize and instill fear and distrust among Arab American community members. Many parents feel their children are out of control. The lack of a strong, insular Arab community hinders self-help, but few external programs are available to address the growing need (Cainkar, 1999).

The Chicago needs assessment identified a lack of informal community networks and institutional support. Middle-class Arabs began departing for the suburbs in the late 1980s. This vacuum was partly filled by a rise in religious adherence to Islam, particularly among the poor, that provided a new source of strength and pride among Muslim Arabs in Chicago. Islamic institutions arose to address some of the educational needs of the community. This rise in Islam, however, did not counteract the declining involvement of external social service providers and led to a backlash of rising discrimination against Arab Americans (Cainkar, 1999). The snapshot provided by this needs assessment, that of one particular imperiled community, is not a picture commonly seen by the American public or most service providers.

The World Situation   The ecological context, including the world situation, significantly affects the lives of Arab Americans. Issues that have contributed to upheaval in Arab American communities include the Gulf War, Middle East peace process, and the resurgence and expansion of radical Islam. External factors have created a crisis of identity and political purpose among

Arab Americans (Shain, 1996). For some Arab Americans as well as Arabs around the world, U.S. military involvements in Arab contexts such as Afghanistan and Iraq may fuel resentment and images of the United States as an imperialist society.

Stereotyping and discrimination now provide a negative bond that unites Arab Americans. Racism and discrimination have an insidious effect on the psychological development and self-concept of people. The prevalence of these factors in the daily lives of Arab Americans raises frightening questions such as, "At what point will this create a hatred that raises stereotypes of terrorism to the level of a self-fulfilling prophecy?" "Are we already at that point?" and "How can a mutually reinforcing cycle of oppression and violence be stopped?"

SKILLS FOR CULTURAL COMPETENCE

Some general skills are likely to be appropriate and helpful in working with Arab American clients. Other skills, particularly those related to interactions and relationship building, will need to be modified to accommodate the values of hierarchical authority commonly found in Arab societies.

Engaging

Engaging, the process of establishing an effective relationship with a client, is influenced by who the social worker is as well as by factors within the client. Although it is sometimes helpful for professionals and clients to come from a shared cultural background; this can also have limitations. For example, an Arab American battered woman may be reluctant to see an Arab American helping professional because extended families have such far-reaching powers. The Arab American helping professional is likely to be associated with a specific family clan. In this situation, a woman may feel that confidentiality and unbiased assistance are not realistic (Rabin et al., 1999).

Mental health services can be stigmatizing, particularly for Arab American women. Participating in such services could damage marital prospects or increase the likelihood of separation or divorce. In Arab countries, a husband could use this information as leverage to obtain a second wife. To facilitate service usage, it is helpful to integrate services into a nonstigmatizing framework or physical setting such as a medical clinic (Al-Krenawi & Graham, 2000). Providing economic assistance can be another way of overcoming barriers to service usage. Offering concrete services can be a first step to engaging clients in therapeutic work (Al-Krenawi & Graham, 1999; Savaya, 1998).

Overcoming mistrust and negative views of helping professionals are crucial aspects of engaging Arab American clients. There may be an expectation that helping professionals are likely to disregard religious values. In such a context, it can be difficult to establish trust. To overcome mistrust, social workers can educate themselves about the religious, cultural, and national background of the client. It is important to develop an understanding of how Arabs view health, medicine, Western society, how they are viewed in the West, and their use of traditional healing systems (Al-Krenawi & Graham, 2000).

An awareness of Arab American cultural norms is important in engaging. How helping professionals present themselves is also important. For many Arab Americans, dressing well is associated with self-respect. Therefore, a social worker's casual appearance may be perceived as disrespectful. Social workers should be careful about self-disclosure. Information that is perceived to be negative may adversely affect their status in an Arab American client's eyes whereas positive information (e.g., connection to a famous person) can lead to admiration (Nobles & Sciarra, 2000).

Displaying hospitality is important in engaging. For example, if eating or drinking, a helping professional can invite the client to eat or drink as well. A helping professional drinking coffee during an interview who does not extend an offer of a beverage to a client may offend that person (Nobles & Sciarra, 2000).

It is helpful to be aware of Arab American norms of physical distance and touching. A shorter physical distance between people is common among Arab Americans. People of the same gender often repeatedly touch each other or hold hands during conversation as a sign of friendship (Nobles & Sciarra, 2000).

Following culturally specific etiquette can be important in engaging. Shaking hands when a client arrives or departs is important. Social workers need to be particularly aware of how Arab American clients may interpret their nonverbal behavior. For example, sitting so that the soles of one's shoes face the other person is considered an insult. Leaning against a wall or keeping hands in pockets may be interpreted as a lack of respect (Nobles & Sciarra, 2000).

Gender can be a crucial dynamic when working with Arab American clients. Indeed, a cross-gender social work relationship may be difficult or impractical. For example, an Arab American male client may have difficulty accepting a female social worker's directions, partly because other senior men in his family may not approve. When working with families, acknowledging the patriarchal family structure by addressing the father first as head of family is important. Social workers need to avoid challenging traditional power hierarchies or roles because this is likely to alienate the family (Al-Krenawi & Graham, 2000). If cross-gender social work relationships are attempted, it is important to socialize the client about the professional nature of the relationship and the boundaries that are protected by professional standards. When a male social worker is working with a female Arab American, referring to the client as "my sister," maintaining minimal eye contact, keeping physical distance between the client and worker, and integrating the family in the work are likely to increase comfort and productivity (Al-Krenawi & Graham, 2000). These techniques clearly establish the social work relationship as being within a nonsexual context.

Personal and informal interventions are typically used before bringing problems to formal institutions. Formal relationships are made as informal and personal as possible (Haj-Yahia, 1997). For Arab clients, it may be difficult to accept the formal distance between the social worker and client emphasized in Western helping (Al-Krenawi & Graham, 2000; Haj-Yahia, 1997). For Arabs, it is more important to build a relationship than solve a problem. Relationships are built on trust. The helping professional can relax formality with a client of the same gender but it is important to maintain even greater distance in cross-gender relationships (e.g., minimal eye contact) to avoid the appearance of impropriety (Al-Krenawi & Graham, 2000).

Many social workers have developed an egalitarian approach to their work. This may need to be modified when working with Arab American clients who value traditional hierarchical structures. An egalitarian approach may be viewed as personal and may contradict Arab American expectations of professional distance and objectivity. Social workers may need to modify their approach so displays of openness, support, empathy, sharing, and respect are viewed as professional, and not personal (Haj-Yahia, 1997).

In a related area, helping professionals may need to hone skills in clearly establishing boundaries with their Arab American clients. Boundaries must be clearly delineated early in the social work relationship. The value many Arab Americans place on personal relationships may lead them to interpret the social worker's attempts at engaging behavior in a personal rather than pro-fessional light. Likewise, Arab Americans may question the honesty and sin-cerity of helping professionals when they set boundaries after having developed a relationship and established confidence (Haj-Yahia, 1997).

Assessing

In conducting an assessment, it is important to consider acculturation and its differential effect on families. This can be done by taking a detailed history, including length of time outside the country of origin, and exploring the rea-sons for and conditions under which immigration occurred. It is also impor-tant to assess social and familial support and the degree of religious affiliation (Krenawi & Graham, 2000). Few assessment tools have been developed espe-cially for this population, but at least one measure has been established to assess acculturation of Arab American immigrants (Faragallah et al., 1997).

It is important to do a through assessment of the environmental context including social stress related to stereotyping, discrimination, and limited com-munity support. Examining community resources and stressors gives a fuller picture of the context within which the client lives. Along with this, an assess-ment needs to examine the family, group, tribal, and cultural context of the client (Al-Krenawi & Graham, 1999).

Intervening

Arabs are more likely to seek concrete assistance rather than psychological services; however, provision of basic necessities such as financial assistance may open the door to requests for other types of services (Savaya, 1998). Interventions with Arab American clients need to consider various factors including gender roles, individuals' places within families and communities, patterns of service use, and level of acculturation. Short-term, directive treatment is likely to be most effective. Work with Arab Americans needs to consider factors such as passive and informal communication patterns, belief in predetermination and external control, and culturally specific idioms of distress. When appropriate, modern and traditional helping systems may be integrated to assist Arab American clients (Al-Krenawi & Graham, 2000).

Interventions with Arabs should include the family, community, and tribal context. The Arab emphasis on extensive family involvement can be a resource but often makes the social worker's job more complicated. Social workers may view families as over-involved, codependent, enmeshed and overprotective but the family may consider their level of involvement appropriate and anything less to be neglect (Al-Kenawi & Graham, 2000). When working with Arab American families, it is important to remember that speaking directly to other family members or confronting them is contrary to cultural norms and is likely to lead to frustration and resistance. Indirect communication is more culturally congruent (Nobles & Sciarra, 2000).

Individualistic interventions are usually not productive with Arab Americans. Behavioral and cognitive therapies tend to be more suitable than psychodynamic approaches (Al-Krenawi & Graham, 2000). Short, directive treatment may be effective, but rigid timeframes may be perceived by Arab American clients as cold or unreasonable. Social workers are expected to be like teachers, by explaining problems, supplying information, and providing solutions with little or no input from clients. Social workers are considered authority figures. Arab American clients are likely to conform to what is advised, at least on the surface, since disagreement or confrontation is considered rude. Arab American clients are likely to appear passive throughout the helping process (Al-Krenawi & Graham, 2000). Differences in communication patterns must be considered when non-Arab American social workers work with Arab American clients.

> In conversation, Arabs are accustomed to repetitions of the same idea or issue for purpose of emphasis. Repeated responses are therefore needed for reassurance; if a statement is made softly and not repeated, an Arab may wonder if the speaker really means what he or she is saying. This originates in the Arabic language, which uses many different phrases with the same meaning. Therapists should not be surprised if a client keeps asking for reassurance by asking "really?" (Nobles & Sciarra, 2000, p. 189).

Arab clients may view self-disclosure as revealing weakness or being disloyal to the family and community. Arab American clients' communications are typically restrained, formal and impersonal. They may describe their problems using a complex system of metaphors, proverbs, and culturally specific expressions of distress. For example, depression may be described as "a dark life," or fear described as "my heart fell down." Communication is indirect, circular, and non-specific. It may be difficult for Arab American clients to understand social workers' more direct communication styles. Miscommunication can be frequent in the helping relationship and may lead to early termination or nonuse of services (Al-Krenawi & Graham, 2000).

Helping professionals must appreciate both the ecological context of clients' lives and their personal perceptions of their circumstances, problems, and resources. Social work techniques must be culturally appropriate (i.e., home visits can be essential to establishing a professional relationship rather than meeting in a more formal setting). Joining children in their games can help social workers build on families' strengths and resources. This culturally appropriate way of developing trust can enable a social worker to assess the situation and give an opportunity for modeling and reinforcing positive behaviors. Provision of concrete services like clothing, food, and cash assistance is often interpreted as evidence of the social worker's sincerity, recognition of the family's urgent needs, and ability to help (Al-Krenawi & Graham, 1999).

When social workers encounter large cultural gaps with their Arab American clients, they may consider seeking a cultural consultant acceptable to the family who can act as a broker. This may be someone affiliated with an agency or a community member (Al-Krenawi & Graham, 2000).

Issues of termination can be raised early in the work. Termination can be stressful because a client may not expect the relationship to end. It can be helpful to indicate that the client can reestablish contact at any time should another difficult situation arise. If termination appears abrupt, the helping professional may be seen as untrustworthy, cold, and inconsiderate (Nobles & Sciarra, 2000).

Advocacy skills are necessary to help Arab American clients combat discrimination and oppression. Social workers can use advocacy skills to assist clients experiencing employment discrimination, harassment in schools or the workplace, or discrimination based on racial profiling. It is also important for helping professionals to confront bigotry outside the professional context. For example, confronting an acquaintance who makes a bigoted statement about Arab Americans demonstrates that racism and stereotyping will not be tolerated. As committed individuals take a stand, the societal context that allows bigotry against Arab Americans, will begin to change.

VALUES/ATTITUDES FOR CULTURAL COMPETENCE

Respect for clients' cultural and religious beliefs are key aspects of cultural competence. Social workers need to avoid actions that imply a particular culture or belief system is superior to others. Cross-cultural interaction can be valued by social workers as enriching for both them and their clients. Helping professionals need to avoid emphasizing clients' assimilation or acquisition of American cultural values (Nobles & Sciarra, 2000).

Social workers typically espouse values of self-determination and free will, but these may conflict with an Arab American emphasis on God's will and predestination (Haj-Yahia, 1997). To successfully negotiate value conflicts with Arab American clients, helping professionals must remain nonjudgmental. This can be particularly challenging when clients' value systems conflict with fundamental professional values. Social workers need to find a way to honor clients' value systems within the helping process.

It is important to develop a positive alliance based on acceptance, respect, trust, and validation of the client's current situation. Helping professionals must demonstrate an ability to balance their roles as professionals with knowledge, respect, and a willingness to work within cultural systems (Al-Krenawi & Graham, 1999).

Helping professionals need to be self-reflective and examine their beliefs and stereotypes about Arab Americans. As members of American society, helping professionals are constantly exposed to stereotypical images and negative messages about Arab Americans and in particular Muslim Arab Americans. It is important for helping professionals to critically examine their own feelings about this population and how these may influence their work. Recognizing the existence of bias is an important first step. Once recognized, these feelings can be examined in supervision and steps can be taken to minimize their impact on the helping relationship.

CASE EXAMPLE

Sophia Collins is the Supervisor of Prevention Programs at a mid-size community agency. She has noticed that some of her caseworkers have had cases of Arab Americans who have been harassed and attacked in the wake of the destruction of the World Trade Center. In particular, she has noted that many children have been harassed into leaving extracurricular activities, are afraid to walk back and forth to school, and are becoming increasingly isolated. Sophia and her staff of three decide to conduct a focus group of Arab Americans as the first step in developing a program to address the emerging needs of the community's children. Sophia remembers that Leila Aswad, a former client who has been instrumental in referring others, is involved with the local Arab Parent Coalition and invites her to meet with the staff about their ideas.

The following considerations are relevant in approaching the case in a culturally competent manner:

- Sophia has taken an important step in identifying a grassroots leader who is familiar with the agency and can serve as a broker between the agency and the Arab American community.
- The focus group needs to provide food and a clear statement of purpose to engage the community members. At this initial meeting, Sophia can begin to facilitate clarification of the problem and a definition of roles to be taken on by community members and agency staff.
- Community members are likely to have many thoughts about their needs, and this may be an important opportunity for them to vent. Sophia realizes, however, that she needs to have a clear set of goals for the meeting such as receiving guidance about prevention efforts the agency can develop to address the community's needs. She needs to keep in mind the agency's function, mission, and capabilities, and try to match these with the community's expressed needs.

- Sophia will want to consult with Leila about particular protocols to follow during the focus group and any subsequent programming that is developed. In particular, she is interested in knowing how she, as a woman in a leadership position, can best reach out to male members of the Arab American community for their guidance and support.

CULTURAL COMPETENCE IN SOCIAL POLICIES

A number of social policies specifically target Arab Americans (e.g., hearings based on secret evidence, profiling at airports). These policies are of great concern in Arab American communities and are seen to reinforce stereotypes, discrimination, and lack of Arabs' acceptance in U.S. society. Policies should be carefully evaluated for their intent, success, and unintended consequences. Arab Americans continue to express dismay and outrage that in a country that espouses freedom and tolerance, policies often infringe on their basic rights and liberties. These concerns include differential treatment by policy makers in general and specific policies that allow the use of secret evidence and racial profiling. Other policies may not specifically target Arab Americans but have a particular impact on this population.

Income maintenance policies such as public assistance have had some success in addressing the needs of changing Arab American families. Although historically, extended families provided assistance and there is a strong mandate in Arab cultures for husbands to support families, sometimes these systems break down in contemporary Arab American communities. Poor Arab American families may go without services because of barriers such as shame, language, and transportation problems. A 1993 study (conducted before welfare reform restrictions) revealed that by the early 1990s, there had been some success at overcoming these barriers. Attitudes in the Arab American community toward accepting welfare were becoming more positive. Women controlling money may lead to some shifts in gender-based power dynamics within families (Aswad, 1999). More investigation is needed of how these changes may or may not be continuing under Temporary Assistance to Needy Families.

During the Gulf War, the FBI issued a press release that made no distinction between their hate crime unit that examines victimization of Arab Americans and the units that are investigating potential terrorist activity. The Arab American community found it disconcerting that a law enforcement agency that should be protecting them could be targeting them as well. These practices led to increasing suspicion and unwillingness by Arab Americans to talk to the FBI for fear that the FBI was gathering secret evidence (U.S. Commission on Civil Rights, 2001).

Indeed, one of the policies most vehemently opposed in the Arab American community is the federal government's practice of using secret evidence. Under the Federal Antiterrorism and Effective Death Penalty Act of 1996, the federal government can present "secret evidence" in court against legal immigrants who are not citizens and are considered a threat to national security. The use of secret evidence in certain immigration proceedings was first authorized in 1955, but the 1996 law, passed in the wake of the World Trade Center and Oklahoma City bombings, has led to the increased use of secret evidence against immigrants. The evidence is only heard by a judge and therefore cannot be challenged by the accused. Suspects can be arrested and deported without ever seeing the evidence against them. Arab Americans are disproportionately affected by this law. Most of the immigrants being held in U.S. jails under this law are Muslim Arabs. Any past statements attributed to the accused individual, statements that should be protected by the First Amendment, can be used against individuals in deportation hearings (U.S. Commission on Civil Rights, 2001). The U.S. Commission on Civil Rights found that the secret evidence provision needs serious legal scrutiny because these proceedings appear to be politically motivated and target specific communities. The suspension of constitutional rights inherent in the use of secret evidence threatens the civil liberties of all Americans (U.S. Commission on Civil Rights, 2001).

In 1997, the White House Commission on Aviation Safety and Security was established and released a report with 53 recommendations to improve safety and security, including a proposal for passenger profiling. In 1998, the Computer Assisted Passenger Screening (CAPS) was instituted throughout the airline industry. The Federal Aviation Administration claims profiling is not discriminatory and does not target any group based on race, national origin, or religion. Customs officials have the power to detain people at airports and border crossing for lengthy periods, sometimes days, when there is reasonable suspicion of contraband. This has been upheld by the Supreme Court (U.S. Commission on Civil Rights, 2001). Arab Americans have significant concerns, not against profiling per se, but against the way it is done. Profiling, as it is currently practiced, is based on stereotypes such as those that abound in movies that portray Arabs Americans as criminals and Muslims as terrorists. Profiling is offensive and not effective (U.S. Commission on Civil Rights, 2001).

The U.S. Commission on Civil Rights found that Arab Americans and Muslims *are* being disproportionately selected by the airline-profiling program based on a belief that Arab Americans and Muslims fit a common physical or traveling description of terrorists. The system operates in a discriminatory manner and needs independent review. In particular, the secrecy surrounding profiling criteria is a serious problem. To date, CAPS has not identified a single traveling terrorist (U.S. Commission on Civil Rights, 2001).

The profiling policy has a far-reaching effect on U.S. society. Federal policies and programs that target Arabs and Muslims depict these people as foreign and separate from the American mainstream and therefore less deserving of civil rights and equal treatment in the eyes of the American public (U.S. Commission on Civil Rights, 2001).

CULTURAL COMPETENCE IN SOCIAL AGENCIES

Some Arab American communities have developed their own social service agencies to provide culturally appropriate help. For example, the Arab Community Center for Economics and Social Services, (ACCESS), founded in the early 1970s in Wayne County, Michigan, has a staff of Arabic-speaking social workers. Its location in the heart of the community has made services much more accessible (Aswad, 1999). This agency addresses issues of police profiling, physical abuse, and verbal threats. Clients are encouraged to seek legal assistance, but many feel when they sue a police officer they take their lives in their own hands, so reporting is limited. ACCESS reports some reduced discrimination in Dearborn where 22% of the population and 54% of young people are Arab American. The hiring of more Arab Americans in law enforcement will likely lead to additional improvements in relations between Arab Americans and the rest of the Dearborn community (U.S. Commission on Civil Rights, 2001).

Mainstream agencies can strive to improve services to Arab American clients. One common recommendation for enhancing services to diverse populations is to hire indigenous social workers. Beyond this, agencies must look at how Arab American social workers fit within the agency and how agency structures, policies, and ways of doing things can be modified to integrate these professionals (Haj-Yahia, 1997).

COMMUNITY INTERVENTIONS

The Chicago Arab American community presents examples of creative, effective community interventions. In the mid-1990s, a significant service vacuum existed in the Chicago Arab community. This community had few internal supports, overwhelming language and cultural barriers, as well as hostile encounters with external social service organizations. In 1995, a group of predominantly Arab American women activists began meeting to strategize how to meet their community's needs. They formed the Arab-American Action Network (AAAN), began developing social programs, and sought external funding for their plans. Initially, city government and local foundations were reluctant to work with AAAN, but after persistent efforts, funders became more responsive. The AAAN received a block grant from the mayor's office to establish an after-school program. Additional funding was obtained for youth vocational training. Foundation funding enabled AAAN to offer family counseling, parenting classes, crisis intervention, and liaison and mediation services. These beginnings opened the door to other funding in recognition of the community's efforts. This process of community transformation continued as members of the Arab American community sought funding for an assessment to document the size and needs of the community. The needs assessment was also instrumental in developing recognition and political leverage (Cainkar, 1999).

The experiences of the Chicago Arab American community demonstrate how a poor community with virtually no infrastructure was able to develop and sustain a grassroots movement for positive change. Social workers can seek out and partner with such grassroots movements. Social work skills such as advocacy, program development, and grant writing can be instrumental in assisting Arab American communities to develop a community infrastructure and self-sustaining institutions.

CONCLUSION

The status of Arab Americans is inseparable from the context of world events. This group is highly stigmatized and subject to stereotyping and discrimination. To provide culturally competent services to this population, social workers need to examine their own feelings and stereotypes and critically reflect on how these may negatively influence their work. Likewise, it is important to examine how value differences between social workers and their Arab American clients may have an impact on the relationship. Key social work skills like advocacy are important tools necessary in combating the oppression experienced by this group.

Exercises

Exercise #1: Reflecting on the status of Arab American women
Bint Arab: Arab and Arab American Women in the United States (1997) by Evelyn Shakir reports the stories of Arab American women in both historical and contemporary times. Chapter 15, "Collage," presents short reflections of Arab American women on their lives. Review the reflections of five different Arab American women. Write a 3- to 5-page paper reflecting on your own thoughts about how gender, culture, and immigrant status interact in the lives of these women.

Exercise #2: Challenging stereotypes
Identify some of the commonly held stereotypes about Arab Americans. Analyze where these stereotypes may have originated and what factors perpetuate them. Reflect on how stereotypes may influence the life of an Arab American child.

Exercise #3: Confronting anti-Arab bigotry
Role play with a classmate how you could respond to someone who states that the local Arab American mosque should be burned to the ground because it serves as a haven for terrorists. Discuss whether you would respond differently depending on whether the statement is made by one of your family members, a casual acquaintance, a client, or your supervisor.

Additional Resources

McCarus, E. (1997). *The Development of Arab-American Identity*. Ann Arbor: University of Michigan Press. This edited book presents background information that can assist helping professionals to better understand their Arab American clients. Chapters cover a variety of topics including early Arab immigration, racism and violence, religious identification, and Arab women in the United States

Nobles, A. Y., & Sciarra, D. T. (2000). Cultural determinants in the treatment of Arab Americans: A primer for mainstream therapists. *American Journal of Orthopsychiatry, 20*(2), 182–191. This article is tailored for helping professionals working with Arab American clients. Various cultural issues and their implications for the helping process are reviewed.

Suleiman, M. W. (1999). *Arabs in America: Building a New Future*. Philadelphia: Temple University Press. This edited book on the Arab American experience covers a number of areas of particular interest to helping professionals. Topics include family and ethnic identity, attitudes toward welfare, grassroots responses to the deteriorating safety net, health, and political processes.

U.S. Commission on Civil Rights. Michigan State Advisory Committee. (2001). *Civil Rights Issues Facing Arab Americans in Michigan*. Washington DC: The Commission. This report describes the results of an investigation into complaints of racism and discrimination in a large Arab American community in Detroit. The report contains powerful first person narratives of experiences with discrimination as well as government findings and recommendations. This is a good resource for assisting professionals to understand the impact of social policies on this population.

References

Abraham, N. (1997). Anti-Arab racism and violence in the United States. In E. McCarus (Ed.), *The Development of Arab-American Identity*. Ann Arbor: University of Michigan Press, 155–214.

Al-Krenawi, A., & Graham, J. R. (1999). Social work intervention with Bedouin-Arab children in the context of blood vengeance. *Child Welfare, 78*(2), 283–296.

Al-Krenawi, A., & Graham, J. R. (2000). Culturally sensitive social work practice with Arab clients in mental health settings. *Health and Social Work, 25*(1), 9–22.

Ajrouch, K. (1999). Family and ethnic identity in an Arab-American commu-nity. In M. W. Suleiman (Ed.), *Arabs in America: Building a New Future*. Philadelphia: Temple University Press, 129–139.

Aswad, B. C. (1999). Attitudes of Arab immigrants toward welfare. In M. W. Suleiman (Ed.), *Arabs in America: Building a New Future*. Philadelphia: Temple University Press, 177–191.

Cainkar, L. (1997). Palestinian women in American society: The interaction of social class, culture, and politics. In E. McCarus (Ed.), *The Development of Arab-American Identity*. Ann Arbor: University of Michigan Press, 85–105.

Cainkar, L. (1999). The deteriorat-ing ethnic safety net among Arab immigrants in Chicago. In M. W. Suleiman (Ed.), *Arabs in America: Building a New Future*. Philadelphia: Temple University Press, 192–206.

De la Cruz, G. P., & Brittingham, A. (2003). *The Arab population: 2000*. U. S. Bureau of the Census. http://www.census.gov/2003pubs/c2kbr-23.pdf. Accessed 2/12/04.

Elbedour, S. Bastien, D. T., & Center, B. A. (1997). Identity formation in the shadow of conflict: Projective drawings by Palestinian and Israeli Arab children from the West Bank and Gaza. *Journal of Peace Research, 34(2)*, 217–231.

Faragallah, M. H., Schumm, W. R., & Webb, F. J. (1997). Acculturation of Arab-American immigrants: An exploratory study. *Journal of Comparative Family Studies, 28(3)*, 182–203.

Haddad, Y. Y. (1997). Maintaining the faith of the fathers: Dilemmas of religious identity in the Christian and Muslim Arab-American communities. In E. McCarus (Ed.), *The Development of Arab-American Identity*. Ann Arbor: University of Michigan Press, 61–84.

Haj-Yahia, M. M. (1997). Culturally sensitive supervision of Arab social work students in Western universities. *Social Work, 42(2)*, 166–174.

Hassoun, R. (1999). Arab-American health and the process of coming to America: Lessons from the metropolitan Detroit area. In M. W. Suleiman (Ed.), *Arabs in America: Building a New Future*. Philadelphia: Temple University Press, 157–176.

Katz, R., & Lowenstein, A. (2002). Family adaptation to chronic illness in a society in transition: The rural Arab community in Israel. *Families in Society: The Journal of Contemporary Human Services, 83(1)*, 64–72.

Naff, A. (1997). The early Arab immigrant experience. In E. McCarus (Ed.), *The Development of Arab-American Identity*. Ann Arbor: University of Michigan Press, 23–35.

Nobles, A. Y., & Sciarra, D. T. (2000). Cultural determinants in the treatment of Arab Americans: A primer for mainstream therapists. *American Journal of Orthopsychiatry, 20(2)*, 182–191.

Rabin, B., Markus, E., & Voghera, N. (1999). A comparative study of Jewish and Arab battered women presenting in the emergency room of a general hospital. *Social Work in Health Care, 29(2)*, 69–84.

Savaya, R. (1998). Associations among economic need, self-esteem, and Israeli Arab women's attitudes toward and use of professional services. *Social Work, 43(5)*, 445–454.

Shain, Y. (1996). Arab-Americans at a crossroads. *Journal of Palestinian Studies, 25(3)*, 46–59.

Shakir, E. (1997). *Bint Arab: Arab and Arab American Women in the United States*. Westport, CT: Praeger.

Stockton, R. (1997). Ethnic archetypes and the Arab image. In E. McCarus (Ed.), *The Development of Arab-American Identity*. Ann Arbor: University of Michigan Press, 119–153.

Suleiman, M. W. (1997). Arab-Americans and the political process. In E. McCarus (Ed.), *The Development of Arab-American Identity*. Ann Arbor: University of Michigan Press, 37–60.

U.S. Bureau of the Census. (1998). CPH-L-149. Selected Characteristics for Persons of Arab Ancestry: 1990. http://www.census.gov. Accessed 7/11/02.

U.S. Commission on Civil Rights. Michigan State Advisory Committee. (2001). *Civil Rights Issues Facing Arab Americans in Michigan*. Washington DC: The Commission.

Immigrants
and Refugees

The vast majority of people in the United States are the descendants of those who came here from elsewhere. People relocate from one country to another for many different reasons. This has been true throughout human history and will continue to be true in the future.

we should be taught these!

People arrive in the United States with a variety of legal statuses; some come temporarily as students or short-term workers, others come as refugees who fear for their lives; still others come hoping to build a new life here and adjust their immigrant status periodically on the way to achieving permanent residency or citizenship. Migrants come to the United States under a multitude of legal conditions (and some illegal). The fine distinctions between these statuses are beyond the scope of this chapter; however, one key distinction for social workers to understand is that migration to the United States is more or less voluntary, depending on the situation in an individual's home country.

simplifying

Broadly speaking, immigrants are those who choose to relocate to a new country, often for economic reasons and hopes for more opportunities and a better life. Refugee status, on the other hand, is much more narrowly defined by international law. The 1951 United Nations Convention on the status of refugees states a refugee is a person who has left his or her country and cannot return because of a well-founded fear of persecution based on race, religion, nationality, membership in a particular social group, or political opinion (United Nations, 2002). For someone to attain the status of refugee, he or she must prove a reasonable fear of persecution on one of these five grounds if he or she had remained in, or were to return to, his or her homeland. To apply for refugee status, someone must already be outside his or her home country. Often, someone who is granted refugee status lives in a refugee camp in a country near his or her homeland, then is accepted for resettlement in another country such as the United States. Someone who flees his or her homeland and arrives in the United States without having applied for refugee status can apply for asylum. Asylum is similar to refugee status except that the applicant has already arrived in the United States before initiating a claim. In the strict sense, refugee is a term that connotes a particular legal status that has already been granted, but often this term is applied more casually to asylum-seekers as well.

Immigrants and refugees come from a wide variety of cultures in many parts of the world; thus, there is no distinct refugee or immigrant culture in and of itself. Indeed, some of the material in previous chapters will apply to refugees and immigrants, depending on their cultures of origin (e.g., Cuban refugees, Chinese immigrants). There are, however, common bonds among refugees and immigrants. Immigration status, both in its psychological and legal aspects, has a major influence on identity. This important layer of identity interacts with other layers such as culture and gender.

Immigration now accounts for 35% of U.S. population growth, and that figure is rising (Muller, 1994). The 2000 census identified 17,758,000 noncitizens and 10,622,00 naturalized citizens living in the United States (U.S. Census Bureau, 2001). Although some of these noncitizens may hold a temporary status (e.g., student visa) and plan to return to their homelands, most of the noncitizens and all of the naturalized citizens are immigrants. Of the foreign-born population, 4,355,000 are from Europe, 7,246,000 are from Asia, 14,477,000 are from Latin America (primarily Mexico), and 2,301,000 are from other areas. Asia, Africa, and Europe (in that order) are the major refugee-producing regions (United Nations High Commission on the Status of Refugees, 2002).

The term *immigrant* can include all people who come to the United States, including those who are more specifically termed refugees or asylum-seekers. At times, the term *immigrant* is used to distinguish a voluntary newcomer from a refugee who feels he or she has no choice but to flee his or her homeland to escape persecution. In reality, the legal designations of refugee and asylee are confounded with political ideas about which countries currently have social conditions that lead to persecution of their own citizens. Some immigrants experience compelling conditions in their homeland (e.g., famine, economic decline) that lead them to leave, although they feel their choice was not entirely voluntary. Even though there are differences between the terms *immigrant* and *refugee*, they do not accurately portray the differences in the lives of people who bear these labels.

Service providers who work with immigrants and refugees are increasingly using the term *newcomer* to represent those who have recently come to the United States and, thus, are facing a variety of adjustment issues, regardless of their legal status. *Newcomer* is an inclusive term that does not make distinctions based on reasons for leaving. This term will be used in this chapter when referring to the broad population of people who have come to the United States. The legal distinctions and policies associated with immigration and refugee status necessitate the use of the terms *immigrant* and *refugee* in certain contexts; thus, those terms will be used in this chapter as well.

This chapter gives an overview of social work with newcomers to the United States. The significant diversity that exists within and among newcomers sets the context for discussion. The chapter presents information about knowledge, skills, and values/attitudes necessary for cultural competence, and reviews issues for cultural competence on micro and macro levels.

KNOWLEDGE FOR CULTURAL COMPETENCE

The knowledge needed for culturally competent social work with newcomers can be divided into four broad areas: diversity, history, stages of migration, and contemporary realities. Diversity serves as an overarching concept that informs other areas of knowledge. The history, migration experiences, and contemporary realities of newcomers vary according to factors such as national origin, reasons for emigrating, gender, and age.

Diversity

Newcomers are a very diverse population. Their experiences in the United States are likely to vary significantly based on age at arrival, year of immigration, and degree of choice in immigration (Silka & Tip, 1994). There is also significant variation in English competence, even among particular groups of newcomers such as Asian refugees (Dhooper & Tran, 1998).

Newcomers arrive in the United States from all over the world. National origin is often linked to reasons for emigrating (Swingle, 2000). Economically depressed areas lead some people to emigrate, and oppressive, politically unstable areas produce refugee flows.

Most Asians come to the United States as immigrants seeking education or employment. Southeast Asians, on the other hand, have come to the United States primarily as refugees. The Vietnamese are the largest Southeast Asian refugee group in the United States (Ngo, Tran, Gibbons, & Oliver, 2001). Many Southeast Asian refugees have also arrived in the United States after fleeing genocide in Cambodia.

South and Central America are sources of many newcomers to the United States. Because the United States is on friendly terms with many South and Central American governments, most newcomers from these areas do not qualify as refugees, regardless of their reasons for leaving. Most arrive either as immigrants or without legal status.

Both immigrants and refugees come from the various African nations. Some experience persecution that qualifies them for refugee status (i.e., Somalis), and others come as immigrants (i.e., Kenyans).

The proportion of European newcomers has declined during the last century, but immigration has continued to a greater or lesser extent from certain regions. In particular, instability in Poland led many to emigrate to the United States in the early 1980s, and instability in the former Czechoslovakia and Yugoslavia led to emigration in the 1990s and early part of the 21st century.

Some of the most recent European migrations have been from the former Soviet Union. Since the early 1970s, more than 500,000 Soviet Jews have been resettled in the United States. They tend to be older and have smaller families than other refugee groups do. Typically, both men and women are highly educated and two-thirds have a college degree. Around 70% held professional, technical, or white-collar jobs in the Soviet Union (Vinokurov, Birman, & Trickett, 2000). In 1993, when the Soviet Parliament granted its citizens the right to travel, there were more refugee arrivals from the former Soviet Republics (49,559) than from any other country. Historically, Soviet arrivals have been predominantly Jewish, but this changed with the 1991 dissolution of the Soviet Union (Kropf, Nackerud, & Gorokhovski, 1999).

The experience of being a newcomer in the United States varies for men and women. A study of Soviet Russian Jews found, as in other refugee populations, women are more alienated than men. Unlike other newcomer populations, however, Soviet women did not differ from men in acculturation or work status. These findings need further exploration to determine how and why Soviets differ from other refugee populations (Vinokurov et al., 2000). The comparable education levels of Soviet men and women may be part of the reason why fewer gender differences are found in this population compared with some others.

Differential acculturation among family members is especially problematic for men. Shifting family roles and gender expectations are often a source of stress. Men may feel displaced when women earn the sole or primary income, and women may experience difficulty adjusting to this new role. As a result, inner-city Khmer women (refugees from Cambodia) have been found to use high levels of sleeping pills and alcohol. Frequent, intentional drug overdose has also become a problem for these women (Dhooper & Tran, 1998).

Immigration-related stress may exacerbate violent behaviors within families. Violence is sometimes triggered by role reversal when wives find jobs more easily than their husbands do. Women immigrants may also feel more vulnerable and less able to seek help if they are psychologically threatened by loosing their status or socially isolated because of cultural and language barriers (Lee, 2000).

Newcomers tend to have different experiences based on age. Age of arrival in the United States is associated with psychological adaptation among Soviet Jewish refugees (Vinokurov et al., 2000). Indeed, youth often adapt to life in the United States more easily than their parents do. Role reversal is common when parents don't speak English well (Kim, McLeod, & Shantzis, 1992).

Immigrant adolescents experience simultaneous developmental and cultural transitions. They are in the process of developing their own identities and desire to fit in but are confronted with choices of fitting into their home culture or U.S. culture. They are also confronted with being perceived differently, depending on their social context. For example, immigrant Russian Jewish adolescents are viewed as Russian in the United States but Jews in Russia. These adolescents typically deal with the double identity crisis of adolescence and cultural transitions through one of four patterns: clinging to their old cultural identity, attempting to eradicate it, vacillating between United States and Soviet identities, or integrating the two (Berger, 1997). On the other hand, Khmer refugees who came to the United States when they were very young experienced little of the trauma and subsequent mental health sequela associated with the genocide of Pol Pot, thus experiencing minimal trauma-related adjustment problems (Berthold, 2000). Age at the time of trauma and immigration both influence the experiences of refugees.

Adjustment stress may be particularly overwhelming for older adults (Kropf et al., 1999). Middle age and elderly refugees are at high risk for physical and emotional problems because of the incongruence between the roles of elders in their homelands and the United States and differential acculturation among family members (Dhooper & Tran, 1998). The developmental tasks of older adults include integration or being satisfied with the life they have lived. For example, older Soviet immigrants often experience despair over lost opportunities and roads not taken under the former rigid political regime. They may not have had resources, opportunities, or skills to pursue their goals. Often the Soviet government forced older adults to migrate with their families. This forced choice may be resented and result in a sense of depression and loss (Kropf et al., 1999).

History

Migration patterns vary over time. In the United States, policies governing immigration have vacillated between being liberal and restrictive. These policies have had a shaping influence on the experiences of newcomers.

Pre-1965 Immigration   Before 1924, the United States experienced high and relatively unrestricted immigration. In particular, the United States encouraged immigration from Western Europe because these people were considered likely to assimilate easily (Swingle, 2000).

Despite this relatively free access, there has always been some anti-immigrant sentiment, and immigrants have historically made convenient scapegoats for many of society's ills. As these anti-immigrant sentiments grew, isolationist practices, the post–World War I economic recession, and rising bigotry led to the restrictive Immigration Act of 1924 (Muller, 1994). Under this Act, most non-European countries were restricted to a quota of 100 immigrants per year.

Many Americans—who fantasize that historically the United States was an ethnically homogenous utopia that only recently become subject to the divisive influences of culturally different immigrants—manifest xenophobic sentiments. Speaking of the quota system based on national origin, one social worker stated, "Yearning for a fond and dimly remembered Protestant,

Anglo-Saxon, rural, un-neurotic, monolithic culture is nostalgic nonsense and is itself a psychotic baying at the moon" (Bernard, 1959, p. 67).

Post-1965 Immigration   In 1965, the immigration quota system was significantly relaxed, and many more individuals from non-European countries were allowed entry to the United States. In 1975, because of the war in Vietnam, Southeast Asian refugees began coming to the United States. The first wave of these refugees consisted of educated, affluent professionals. This well-connected, elite group adjusted quickly to life in the United States. Subsequent groups of Southeast Asian refugees have been farmers, fishermen, and laborers and have had significant difficulty becoming acclimated to their new lives in the United States, despite resettlement programs (Segal, 2000).

The new wave of Vietnamese escaped from their Communist-controlled country by boats between the late 1970s and early 1980s or spent time in "reeducation" camps. They experienced multiple traumas, including rape, being lost, starvation, witnessing the death of loved ones, and torture. These experiences make them particularly vulnerable to psychiatric disorders such as depression and posttraumatic stress disorder (PTSD) (Ngo et al., 2001).

Also, in the mid-1970s, after decades of political and economic destabilization, the Cambodian government began a campaign of genocide against its own people. In 1975, Khmer Rouge leader Pol Pot closed the country to outside contact, sent the urban population to workcamps in the countryside, and "reeducated" citizens considered dangerous or disloyal. Between 1975 and 1979, an estimated 1.5–3 million men, women, and children, or 20–40% of the entire Cambodian population, were killed by their own government. Survivors witnessed mass executions and suffered starvation, torture, destruction of their communities, slave labor, brainwashing, beatings, and loss of loved ones. Their suffering often continued in refugee camps before resettlement (Berthold, 2000; Uehara, Morelli, & Abe-Kim, 2001). Approximately 330,000 Khmer refugees have been resettled in the United States (Berthold, 2000).

The dramatic growth of the immigrant population in the 1980s and 1990s, particularly from Asia and Latin America, fueled many Americans' fears of economic dependency. Roughly 675,000 legal permanent residents enter the United States annually seeking employment or as part of the family reunification program. Another 120,000 are admitted annually as refugees. An estimated 275,000–300,000 immigrants enter the United States illegally each year, primarily from Mexico (Swingle, 2000).

Stages of Migration

Newcomers go through distinct stages during their migration. Although there is significant variation in the content of these stages, this framework is useful for helping social workers understand the experiences of newcomer clients (Drachman & Halberstadt, 1992).

Premigration   Many factors play a role in the decision to migrate, including social, economic, political, and kinship issues (Kamya, 1997). Some newcomers decide to emigrate based on the actions of family members that emigrated earlier. For many populations, particularly those in the Caribbean, it is common for one person to come to the United States first, then once economically established, send money for other family members to follow. With this type of immigration pattern, it often takes many years of planning and saving money for family members to be reunited in their new homeland.

Economic circumstances are one of the most common reasons for people to emigrate. For centuries, people have come to the United States searching for a better life. The standard of living in the United States is substantially better than in many parts of the world; thus, people find economic reasons for relocation compelling.

Political situations also compel individuals to choose to come to the United States. For those living under repressive governments with little political freedom, life in the United States can be an appealing alternative. There are, however, those who would prefer not to leave their homelands. They may feel that fleeing to the United States or another safe country is their only option because of persecution or imminent danger.

It is important for social workers to understand the social, political, and economic factors that clients experienced before departure from their homelands. Some experienced abrupt exile or flight, whereas others may have waited years for governmental permission to leave. The primary issues that arise during this contemplation or premigration stage include anxiety about separation from family and friends and leaving a familiar environment. Decisions must be made about who leaves and who is left behind. This stage may involve life-threatening circumstances, persecution, violence, and loss of significant others (Drachman & Halberstadt, 1992).

Transit Newcomers experience a wide variety of transit experiences. For some, their departure is orderly and quick. For others, the journey to a new homeland takes years and involves stops in multiple countries. Sometimes the journey is dangerous and earlier trauma is compounded. Many newcomers live in a refugee camp or detention center for either brief or long periods before coming to the United States. Once they achieve refugee status, they must await a foreign country's decision about whether they will be accepted for resettlement. For most newcomers, whether voluntary or forced migrants, loss of significant others is a compelling issue (Drachman & Halberstadt, 1992). Some are able to weather these stressors of migration more successfully than are others because of the interaction among an individual's internal resources, available support, and external stressors (Kamya, 1997).

The experience of Khmer refugees who escaped the genocide of Pol Pot, gives an example of the transit experiences of some refugees. Hundreds of thousands of Khmer fled to the Thai-Cambodian border. During their escape, they were subjected to rape, death, or injury from stepping on land mines. After crossing the border, they risked imprisonment and torture in Thailand. Once in Thai refugee camps, their safety was still not ensured, and shelling, grenade, and bandit attacks were common. Even after relocating to a new country, many continued to experience trauma related to separation from family, isolation, discrimination, adjusting to a new culture, and community violence (Berthold, 2000).

Resettlement   Building a life in a new country involves many challenges. Refugees have access to short-term services to help with their adjustment, but both refugees and immigrants face a similar set of challenges. Some of the critical variables typically encountered during the resettlement phase are the following: (1) cultural issues, (2) reception from host country, (3) opportunity structure of host country, (4) discrepancy between expectations and reality, and (5) degree of cumulative stress throughout the migration process (Drachman & Halberstadt, 1992). In particular, newcomers are likely to experience transitions in family structures, economic circumstances, and cultural dynamics. Changes resulting from relocation have psychological, spiritual, affective, and cognitive consequences. Newcomers often experience stress in their new homelands, including conflicts with their new society, interpersonal conflicts, and role conflicts (Kamya, 1997).

Immigration is often associated with major family disruption and loss of social supports. Immigrants may experience significant changes in traditional family roles (Segal, 2000). For instance, the ways that men and women interact in the United States may be significantly different from gender roles in newcomers' countries of origin. Parents and children are likely to experience significant role changes as children tend to adapt to United States cultural norms and learn English more quickly than their parents do.

Often newcomers attempt to replicate their traditional family structures in the United States. This is frequently difficult; however, when possible, the traditional family structure may prove to be an important support system. For example, most Southeast Asian refugees live in large extended family households where they are able to pool resources for better economic success (Potocky & McDonald, 1995).

Newcomers often experience economic stress and feelings of personal failure if they are unemployed or underemployed. They are required to spend much of their energy on basic survival needs and therefore have little room for other concerns like emotional support, disciplining children, and building social skills (Kim et al., 1992). After resettlement, most refugees live in overcrowded poverty situations. For most Southeast Asians, this means downward mobility (Dhooper & Tran, 1998). Refugees such as the Khmer may relocate to communities where they experience ongoing community violence. Exposure to violence is associated with violent behavior, psychological problems, and other risk behaviors in adolescents (Segal, 2000).

Resettlement programs usually offer employment well below the professional status of Soviet Jewish refugees. This downward mobility often leads to significant psychological stress. Although findings vary, studies suggest that only 40 to 50% of Soviet refugees are employed in their fields of specialization (Vinokurov et al., 2000).

Immigration involves adjusting to a new cultural environment (Kamya, 1997). Ultimately, newcomers must decide to what extent they wish to adopt

United States values and norms. These are major factors in deciding whether to pursue U.S. citizenship. Changing citizenship often represents a significant change in self-perception and sense of identity. For refugees, it may mean the death of a dream of one day being able to return to their homeland. These feelings frequently inhibit refugees from seeking U.S. citizenship (Potocky & McDonald, 1995).

Contemporary Realities

Newcomers are exposed to many stressors. Some newcomers are able to weather these stressors more successfully than others are. The foundations of resilience are likely to be a combination of internal resources and social supports. It is important for social workers to have an understanding of the resilience and vulnerability experienced by newcomers. In particular, social workers need to be aware of issues relating to cultural adaptations, health and mental health, and xenophobia.

Resilience   Immigrants with higher self-esteem and internal strengths have greater coping resources and are better at enduring stress (Kamya, 1997). Trauma can lead to a variety of psychological and behavioral problems including depression, anxiety, and alcoholism, but not all who experience trauma suffer equally. Some are able to muster internal strengths and social supports that successfully ameliorate the impact of potentially devastating experiences. Some of the factors that influence newcomers' resilience include their cultural beliefs, religious beliefs, socialization experiences, available coping strategies, and available social and psychological support (Ngo et al., 2001).

Work seems to be a protective factor that enhances other areas of functioning for newcomers. For example, Soviet Jewish refugees who gain employment in their earlier occupation tend to have higher income, higher acculturation, more comfort speaking English, more life satisfaction, and less alienation (Vinokurov et al., 2000). There is likely a bidirectional, reinforcing relationship between work and resiliency; work supports resilience and resilience enhances work opportunities.

A study of Vietnamese refugees found those who are more acculturated tend to have lower levels of depression. This raises the question, what motivates or enables a newcomer to acculturate or not acculturate? Some researchers have proposed that acculturation is a mechanism for coping with stress. Studies on the relationship between acculturation and mental health have mixed findings. A balance between cultures is probably the most helpful for successful adjustment. The impact of premigration trauma may vary depending on an individual's level of acculturation. A study of Vietnamese Americans found that premigration traumatic experiences had a stronger association with depression among those with lower acculturation (Ngo et al., 2001).

Newcomers also contribute to the resilience of society. For example, newcomer demands for new housing were a significant factor in the U.S. economic recovery of the 1990s. Newcomers also stimulate demand for public services such as education (Muller, 1994). Thus, newcomers' resilience enhances more than their own lives. Contrary to popular stereotypes, newcomers make a significant contribution to the well-being of U.S. society.

Vulnerability   The stresses of adjusting to life in a new country may cause newcomers to be vulnerable to social and health problems. It may also be that premigration and transit experiences such as exposure to trauma renders some newcomers, particularly refugees, vulnerable to a variety of problems. Refugees experience a sense of loss and grief. War and violence have destroyed old ways of life, and traditions are often devalued in their new land. The demands to learn a new language, customs, and skills can be overwhelming (Dhooper & Tran, 1998).

Refugees tend to be poor and live in unhealthy, unsafe environments characterized by a lack of health and mental health services. Culturally appropriate, high quality, comprehensive services are rare, and refugees often lack the resources to access and pay for services. Many do not have health insurance and those that have Medicaid often do not use services to the extent needed because of cultural and language barriers (Dhooper & Tran, 1998).

Most refugees have experienced extensive physical and psychological trauma (Dhooper & Tran, 1998). Multiple traumas compound each other and increase vulnerability.

> The experience of being a refugee is cumulative. The actual or threatened experiences of persecution or witnessing atrocities; separation from or loss of family members that has not been mourned because of uncertainty about their fate and preoccupation with survival or denial; mismatch of new alliances hastily formed in refugee camps for companionship; and numerous incongruities between a refugee's knowledge, skills, and expectations and the expectations of the new environment in the country of resettlement wound a battered psyche. (Dhooper & Tran, 1998, p. 71)

The high exposure to violence experienced by many refugees may make them vulnerable to mental health problems. A study of 144 Khmer adolescents found that one-third had symptoms of PTSD, and two-thirds had symptoms of clinical depression. The number of violent events they experienced predicted their level of PTSD, personal risk behaviors, and grade point average, but not their level of depression or problem behaviors at school (Berthold, 2000). Risk factors for serious psychiatric disorders include experiencing a high degree of family loss or separation, spending a long time in refugee camps, multiple traumas, unemployment, limited education, limited English proficiency, and few emotional and material resources. Premigration stressors are strong predictors of depression and anxiety even after five years in the United States, although this varies depending on refugee group (Dhooper & Tran, 1998).

Cultural Adaptations   Many newcomers experience conflicts between the expectations of their home culture and that of the United States. These include different expectations for gender roles and child-parent relationships (Segal,

2000). For example, youth in the United States may expect greater freedoms than those traditionally found in newcomers' cultures of origins.

For refugees from Vietnam, adjustment to life in the United States has been a long and difficult process. They must come to terms with the factors that forced them from their homes and resulted in separation from family, friends, and support systems. They often experience stress associated with loss and grief over loved ones, social isolation, and strained family relationships. Changes in social status and culture shock are common. The psychological stress experienced by refugees may reduce their capacity to adjust to a new cultural environment (Segal, 2000).

A study of American-born and foreign-born Hmong young adults revealed they interpret their cultural identities differently. For those born in the United States, being Hmong and being American are unrelated concepts, whereas those born in Asia see being Hmong and being American as negatively related. In other words, those born in the United States experience culture as fluid or orthogonal rather than as an either/or phenomenon (Tsai, 2001).

Issues of identity and sense of self emerge as newcomers go through the challenges of adjusting to life in a new country. Elderly Russian Jewish immigrants often migrate seeking a better life for their children but have paid little attention to their own developmental needs. The statement of one elderly Russian Jewish newcomer reflects a sense of being lost: "Isaac stated that, when he was finally leaving Russia by plane, he had no preference about where the plane might land. He indicated that his focus was on leaving Russia where his identity was bound and that he would land on foreign soil dominated by a foreign language and no heritage of his own" (Feinberg, 1996, p. 47). Although he was grateful for the opportunity to come to the United States, his "experience reflected difficulty establishing a sense of continuity of self in light of having immigrated late in life" (Feinberg, 1996, p. 48).

Health/Mental Health   Newcomers, particularly refugees, may experience a number of physical health problems. For Southeast Asian refugees, health problems are often related to premigration factors including physical trauma, lack of medical care, starvation, malnutrition, diseases, and high-risk health behaviors common in their native lands. They also experience the physical sequelae of acculturation-related stress, diseases common in the United States, and lack of fit between their health needs and the health-care system's services (Dhooper & Tran, 1998). Major mental health problems of this population include PTSD, depression, and anxiety.

Some newcomers express trauma symptoms in physical ways. This often conflicts with Western perceptions of trauma-related problems. For example, survivors from the Cambodian Killing Fields see their somatic complaints as authentic pain, but professionals tend to label it *psychopathology* (Uehara et al., 2001).

Some of the health and mental health problems of refugees have proven to be intractable. Refugees who fled the Khmer Rouge continue to experience disturbing and disabling symptoms even decades later. Clinical studies provide mixed evidence for effectiveness of treatment. Some have found treatment to be effective, but others have not (Uehara et al., 2001).

There is limited information about the health and mental health of elderly immigrants. Depression may be common because of limited resources, physical frailty, and stressful life events. Older Chinese immigrants are at higher risk for depression than are older Whites, probably because of risk factors such as poverty, low educational achievement, poor physical health, and high rates of family disruption. Depressed Chinese elders are less likely to be identified by professionals or receive services than depressed White elders (Mui, 1998).

Xenophobia   The current U.S. political climate is one of fear and suspicion of newcomers as evidenced by restrictive policy reforms (Kropf et al., 1999). Indeed, xenophobia, or fear of foreigners, is a key factor that inhibits integration of newcomers into U.S. society (Mayadas & Elliott, 1992). Xenophobia has both structural and interpersonal components, and its effects are found in social policies, institutionalized discrimination, lack of accommodation, and interpersonal prejudice. The influx of newcomers is perceived as straining cultural homogeneity and is therefore seen as threatening. This is particularly true during economic recessions, when Americans may perceive strangers who look, act, and speak differently as particularly threatening (Mayadas & Elliott, 1992). Anti-immigrant sentiment is currently the highest it has been since the Great Depression and has led to major changes, such as reversing the long-standing policy of accepting any refugee who fled Cuba. Now, those who seek entry into the United States as refugees from Cuba are confined in Panama or at the United States naval base in Guantánamo Bay while their cases are reviewed (Muller, 1994).

> Anti-immigrant feeling is a simple sentiment with complex roots, some of them social and racial, and some seeming more practical. Immigrants are blamed for overcrowded schools, rising hospital deficits, and high welfare costs—indeed, for virtually everything that ails American society. Nothing ails this country more than the poverty of a large segment (one-third) of the black population, and the stagnant or declining wages among Americans of all races and all but the highest income levels, and fingers are being pointed at the immigrants. Not too many years ago, the sight of a Korean shopkeeper or a Salvadoran construction worker would have been taken by many citizens as reassuring evidence of the American Dream's lasting power. Now such recent arrivals are likely to be seen as alien interlopers who are taking good jobs from hard-working Americans. (Muller, 1994, p. 66)

Xenophobia leads to negative feelings toward a variety of foreigners, but some are perceived in a more negative light than others are. For example, in the United States ambivalence toward newcomers from Africa is compounded with racism (Kamya, 1997). Previous overt hostility between the United States and Soviet Union may leave residual anti-Soviet feelings against newcomers from the former Soviet Union (Kropf et al., 1999).

SKILLS FOR CULTURAL COMPETENCE

Some general skills are likely to be appropriate and helpful with newcomer clients. Other skills, such as those associated with using interpreters, assessing trauma, and confronting xenophobia may be particularly relevant with this population.

Engaging

Language and cultural barriers often inhibit newcomers from seeking services. Mistrust of authority and fear of exposure are common among refugees because of their experiences. Helping professionals are considered authority figures associated with organizations. Thus, many refugees may limit disclosure because they have difficulty trusting social workers (Segal, 2000).

Helping professionals must establish rapport and trust before gathering information. Refugees may feel the less they disclose, the safer they are. To establish rapport, helping professionals can educate themselves about both general and specific refugee experiences and the newcomers' culture. This will help build understanding and trust (Segal, 2000).

Self-disclosure, when used cautiously, can increase credibility with newcomers. Likewise, displays of empathy and understanding promote relationship building (Segal, 2000). To get past newcomer clients' suspicions, social workers could present themselves as persons as well as professionals. Limited self-disclosure may facilitate this process. For example, a social worker might share that she relocated to this community two years ago and initially it was difficult learning to negotiate the city's transportation system.

It can be particularly challenging to successfully engage clients when language barriers exist. If the social worker and client do not speak the same language, it will be necessary to involve an interpreter in the work. Ideally, the interpreter is someone with training in interpreting within the social work context. It is important that the interpreter communicate fully with the social worker without adding to, deleting from, or modifying the client's statements. The interpreter should be able to help the social worker understand the subtle nuances of the client's communication. Using clients' children as interpreters is highly problematic and is likely to upset family roles. It is best to avoid this practice. Parents may be reluctant to disclose some information to children, and even though they may speak English, children may not have the adult vocabulary necessary to fully communicate information the social worker needs. Working through an interpreter increases the opportunity for miscommunication between helping professionals and clients, but sometimes it is the only option.

The way that an office or interview space is arranged can influence the engaging process. It is helpful to have images that depict different cultures in an accessible and respectful way. For example, messages and symbols that promote collegial relationships between United States and the former Soviet

Republics can help overcome barriers in engaging Soviet immigrants (Kropf et al., 1999).

Assessing   One of the most critical skills for social workers who work with newcomers is the ability to competently conduct a differential assessment. For instance, a helping professional needs to be able to distinguish between issues related to culture, mental health, trauma, and a variety of other factors. This is particularly complicated because many of these factors interact with each other. For example, when working with elderly Asian immigrants, assessment of depression is complicated by cultural issues, and it may be difficult to identify the root cause of the problem (Mui, 1998).

Two overarching questions guide helping professionals' decisions about the methods used to assess newcomers: Do Western psychological concepts, diagnostic categories, and assessment tools apply to non-Western populations? If so, which populations do they fit and how well? Use of standardized assessment tools is often problematic with newcomers because these tools tend to assume some cultural commonality among respondents and are rarely available in multiple languages and dialects. An additional dilemma is that translators are not always familiar with Western psychological concepts, thus making translated instruments less meaningful. Even standardized tools that have been modified for particular populations tend to use an individualistic psychological framework. They also rely on reporting feelings and experiences to strangers. Both individualistic frameworks and expectations of self-disclosure may be culturally incongruent for many newcomers (Silka & Tip, 1994).

Assessment tools may not be applicable across cultures. One study of child abuse among Vietnamese refugees produced such inconsistent and unexpected findings that the researcher was led to significantly question the use of standardized tools. These problems were encountered even after translation and back-translation methods had been employed in an attempt to make the assessment tool usable with this population (Segal, 2000).

Many assessment instruments have been adapted or developed specifically for use with various newcomer populations. Most notably, the Harvard Trauma Questionnaire (HTQ) was developed for assessing trauma in refugees from Vietnam, Cambodia, and Laos (Mollica et al., 1992). The various versions of the HTQ have been used extensively by different researchers (e.g., Berthold, 2000; Ngo et al., 2001). Other assessment tools for newcomers include the General Ethnicity Questionnaire and variations such as the General Ethnicity Questionnaire–Hmong Version that assess cultural orientation in various life domains (Tsai, 2001) and the Vietnamese version of the Center for Epidemiological Studies–Depression Scale (Ngo et al., 2001). Another scale was developed to assess Russian and American acculturation as separate domains (Vinokurov et al., 2000). There is some support for the cross-cultural validity of instruments that have been used with other refugee populations when working with African immigrants (Kamya, 1997).

Adapting assessment tools for use with different cultural populations can be a difficult process. Imprecise item translation raises challenges of reliability and validity with translated instruments. For example, a question may be interpreted too literally (Ngo et al., 2001). There have also been questions about whether the HTQ, one of the most widely used assessment tools for refugees, is biased against women. The HTQ items may more accurately reflect experiences of men because they tend to be the targets of war trauma and re-education camps, whereas women may not have experienced these directly (Ngo et al., 2001).

Whether or not standardized tools are used in conducting assessments, several domains need to be explored when working with newcomers. Assessments need to include experiences with trauma, including premigration experiences with war, torture, imprisonment, assaults, and loss of loved ones. Helping professionals can ask clients how they perceived these events and their own level of threat or safety. It is important to explore the reasons for flight, refugee camp experiences, and experiences with the immigration process (Ngo et al., 2001). Helping professionals also need to examine stressors and supports that newcomers experience after relocating. Exposure to community violence in the United States is particularly relevant for mental health problems of Khmer adolescents (Berthold, 2000). Helping professionals need to assess postmigration stressors such as economic, employment, sociocultural, language, family, and acculturation issues. It is important to examine whether earlier trauma has effected current functioning (Ngo et al., 2001).

Intervening

In selecting interventions, one critical theme that social workers need to remember is the tension associated with either overtly or covertly helping clients assimilate into U.S. society compared with preserving their cultural traditions. Social workers need to find a balance of assisting clients to function in the larger culture while valuing their own sociocultural context (Berger, 1997; Kamya, 1997; Ngo et al., 2001). As part of examining cultural identity issues, helping professionals can provide an opportunity to mourn losses and offer education about U.S. norms. Helping professionals can normalize and validate various patterns of adjustment. Services may need to be offered in other languages as well as in English (Berger, 1997).

Social support has a direct effect on mental health outcomes (Berthold, 2000). This is particularly meaningful for immigrants and refugees who may have left support systems behind. Mobilizing support systems is an important intervention.

Another skill that may be useful in working with newcomers is the ability to be directive. Directiveness is particularly helpful with Vietnamese refugees, given their cultural respect for authority. This is more helpful than the non-directiveness often emphasized in social work practice (Segal, 2000). Social workers may need to make a particular effort to alter their usual nondirective approach.

Social workers may be involved in intervening in family issues such as child rearing. Physical discipline acceptable in home countries like Vietnam may not be acceptable in the United States. At the same time, families may feel they are losing control of their children, experiencing internal conflicts caused by differential acculturation, and may be at a loss about what to do (Segal, 2000).

When working with newcomers, it is important to understand and work within their family structure. This is often an extended network like a clan system. Helping professionals can communicate with and mobilize the family leader. Meaningful interventions must be based on an understanding of clients' culturally conditioned responses to stress, incorporating new ideas into the assessment and intervention based on current research, and teaching life skills appropriate for survival in the United States. Concrete assistance such as facilitating the search for missing family members can be an important intervention because reunification is very therapeutic (Dhooper & Tran, 1998).

Many interventions for newcomers, particularly refugees, are likely to be related to coping with trauma (Silka & Tip, 1994). Helping professionals and researchers need to strive to develop and implement culturally congruent interventions that fit with refugees' beliefs about problems and their solutions. For example, the Buddhist belief in karma, that current life reflects past life, influences how refugees perceive and react to their traumatic experiences. This is an important consideration in working with Buddhist clients because clients may feel some personal responsibility for their trauma (Ngo et al., 2001).

Survivors of the Cambodian Killing Fields often view helping professionals and systems of care as causes of suffering rather than sources of help (Uehara et al., 2001). For example, a helping professional who is perceived as minimizing the importance of complaints of pain may be viewed as adding to the problem. Helping professionals need to understand survivors' perspectives, desires and explanatory models if they are to be effective in working with refugees. It is important to identify conflicts between survivor and professional explanatory models such as conflicts around the appropriateness and meaning of somatic pain (Uehara et al., 2001).

As part of their listening skills, helping professionals must become strong enough to listen to stories of atrocity, pain, and suffering without becoming numb or denying the reality of these experiences. Empathizing with experiences of torture is difficult, emotionally draining, and involves professionals imagining themselves in the unimaginable scenes described by survivors (Uehara et al., 2001). This personal and emotional involvement conflicts with what professionals are taught about professional distance but can be crucial in developing empathy.

Schools have an important role to play in addressing problems of traumatized youth. Youth who have experienced trauma and violence frequently have difficulty concentrating and develop various symptoms that interfere with their ability to learn. They may become withdrawn or disruptive. School-based services that promote early problem identification, referral, and counseling can enable newcomer youth to take better advantage of educational opportunities. These services must be culturally and linguistically relevant and welcoming to newcomer youth (Berthold, 2000).

Given the increasing xenophobia in U.S. society, advocacy skills will continue to be a crucial part of a social worker's repertoire. Newcomers, particularly those with limited English skills and those who have been exposed to trauma, are a very vulnerable population. It is important for social workers to be able to help them cut through bureaucratic practices and access the services to which they are entitled.

It is also important for social workers to use their advocacy skills to demand responsive programs that truly meet the needs of newcomers rather than simply providing short-term, concrete assistance with the unrealistic expectation of long-term economic self-sufficiency. Social workers must advocate for programs that go beyond English and vocational skills and include ongoing counseling and adjustment assistance.

Social workers need to use their skills to fight against the growing institutionalization of xenophobia in social policies. Many refugees and asylum seekers in the process of being resettled in the United States or having their claims heard have been stranded in a legal limbo after the terrorist attacks on New York City and Washington, D.C., on September 11th, 2001. Social workers can advocate for the timely handling of these applications and for keeping U.S. borders open instead of closing them as a reaction to the attacks. Likewise, social workers need to consider how new laws such as the Patriots Act give sweeping new powers to law enforcement with few checks and balances, thus reinforcing preexisting xenophobia.

Approaches to work with refugees must include a political and preventive approach. The trauma experienced by many refugees cannot be cured and sometimes is difficult to ameliorate at all. Clearly, prevention has the potential to be much more effective than any treatment approach. Social workers and other helping professionals must advocate for eradicating refugee-producing situations around the world (Uehara et al., 2001).

VALUES/ATTITUDES FOR CULTURAL COMPETENCE

Social workers must validate and support their clients. This is particularly important with survivors of torture who often feel discredited by those who hear their stories. It is important for social workers to believe in clients' credibility and offer ongoing support (Weaver & Burns, 2001).

Hearing the stories of trauma victims is stressful. To avoid becoming numb and uncaring, social workers must take care of themselves. Quality supervision is a key element of self-care and helper wellness. This can be a meaningful source of support for professionals at all stages of their careers, not just those new to the helping professions. Being able to express feelings in a safe, understanding, and confidential setting is critical in preventing burnout when working with populations such as refugees.

It is important for social workers to be aware of their own values and those embedded in the helping professions. Social workers must be wary of approaching newcomers from a foundation of ethnocentrism that may lead them to disparage trauma survivors' reports of pain, pathologize somatic complaints and complainants, and increase clients' experiences of distress and suffering. Helping professionals may presume that what they label as somatic complaints are less real than other maladies are. Such presumptions place social workers at odds with newcomer clients who continue to complain of intractable pain. Social workers need to examine their beliefs about what complaints are "real," and ensure they do not undermine or minimize newcomer clients' beliefs, perceptions, and concerns. This is a particularly important value when social workers find themselves in the role of gatekeepers for medical and welfare systems (Uehara et al., 2001).

Self-awareness and reflection on one's own values are critical for social workers assisting newcomers. Social workers need to critically examine their own beliefs and feelings about whether newcomers should be expected to assimilate into U.S. society and to what degree. For instance, should social work clients be encouraged or perhaps pushed into learning English? Should newcomers be expected to become citizens? What is the role of client self-determination in these decisions?

CASE EXAMPLE

Dung Tran, a homeless man in his 50s, arrived at the Fifth Street Men's Shelter where social worker Roberto Garcia met with him to discuss his needs. Dung's English was limited, but from what Roberto could determine, Dung came to the United States in 1980 and received brief assistance from a resettlement organization. His expressed need now is for food and shelter but Roberto's approach at the shelter is to work on long-term independence and self-sufficiency in addition to temporary provision of concrete services. Dung said little about his life circumstances or what led him to become homeless. Roberto knew little about Southeast Asian refugees and had a lot of difficulty understanding Dung. He located a Southeast Asian self-help organization in a nearby community and contacted them for consultation and interpretation services. The self-help organization informed Roberto that they have had sporadic contact with Dung during the past 10 years. Their group has limited funding and thus has not been able to provide the ongoing mental health counseling needed by so many refugees. By coordinating with the self-help organization, Roberto was able to identify and make a referral to a culturally appropriate supportive living arrangement.

The following considerations are relevant in approaching the case in a culturally competent manner:

- Roberto realized that he would not be able to do any long-range planning with Dung without the help of an interpreter. Both language barriers and concerns about safely disclosing to a stranger must be adequately addressed.

- Consultation with someone at the Southeast Asian self-help organization enabled Roberto to learn about pertinent cultural issues as well as issues related to refugees and trauma.
- This case reveals the problems that many refugees experience when short-term resettlement assistance is terminated. Addressing basic needs such as language and vocational skills does not begin to address the issues of trauma that often last a lifetime. The failure to address trauma often impedes the ability to learn vocational or language skills, thus reducing the effectiveness of such services. Advocacy efforts are necessary to bring about significant restructuring of resettlement efforts, however, in a xenophobic and conservative political climate, services for newcomers are likely to be reduced rather than enhanced.

CULTURAL COMPETENCE IN SOCIAL POLICIES

Three major types of policies significantly affect newcomers. Immigration policies govern who is allowed to come to the United States and under what circumstances. Resettlement policies target refugees and determine what assistance is available to help them adjust to life in the United States. In addition, social service policies that apply to a broad spectrum of people in the United States often have specific provisions or implications for newcomers.

Immigration policies can be divided into three major categories: (1) regulation of legal immigration related to employment or family reunification, (2) regulation of immigration for humanitarian reasons (e.g., refugees, asylees), and (3) control of illegal entries. Each type is governed by different rules, goals, and eligibility for benefits (Kropf et al., 1999).

Immigration policies have shifted with public sentiment and the political climate over the years, as noted in the earlier historical review. Initially open policies became more restrictive in the 1920s as more people from non–Western European countries sought entry to the United States. These restrictive policies did not experience significant change until 1965.

Policies were developed to define and assist refugees following World War II and the revelations of the atrocities committed under Nazi Germany. Since then, various groups have entered the United States under refugee admission policies. After Castro came to power in 1959, many refugees were admitted to the United States from Cuba. In the late 1970s and early 1980s, a major flow of refugees came from Southeast Asia. During the late 1980s, 94% of those admitted as refugees came from Communist countries. Because refugees flee persecution with few resources, they are entitled to special assistance designed to lead to economic self-sufficiency and the same public benefits as U.S. citizens (Kropf et al., 1999).

The U.S. Refugee Act of 1980 provides federal assistance through the Office of Refugee Resettlement. This assistance consists of teaching basic skills such as English, vocational skills, and providing medical care to help newly arriving refugees become self-sufficient as quickly as possible (Segal, 2000). Although some skilled, English-speaking refugees (i.e., the first wave of Cuban refugees) have become self-sufficient quickly, most Vietnamese refugees arrived with low literacy, education, and skills that were not transferable to the U.S. context, resulting in longer dependency than envisioned by policy makers. Resettlement assistance is always short term and is not available to non-refugee newcomers. Eligibility for refugee status and resettlement assistance changes depending on the circumstances in the country of origin. With changes in the former Soviet Union, Soviet immigrants are no longer automatically considered refugees, leading to significant changes in their eligibility for benefits (Kropf et al., 1999).

Health-care policies and approaches have often created barriers to service usage for newcomers, rather than facilitating access. The U.S. health-care system is money-driven, acute-care oriented, and based on episodic encounters between patients and care providers. It does not fit the needs of refugees. There is no sustained, comprehensive approach to the problems of this population. Refugees tend to have multiple physical and mental health problems that are intense and complex and must be considered within the context of their painful past and cultural perspectives. The ignorance of health care providers about the customs, cultures, and experiences of refugees is the primary barrier to meaningful care (Dhooper & Tran, 1998).

The welfare reform provisions of 1996, particularly the original version, had a harsh impact on newcomers. The Personal Responsibility and Work Opportunity Reconciliation Act of 1996 portrayed immigrants as an undeserving group and an economic drain on U.S. society. Elderly immigrants were especially hard hit when denied Supplemental Security Income (SSI) and food stamps. Fortunately, the Balanced Budget Act of 1997 restored some benefits because of a sympathetic media portrayal of the dire consequences for elderly immigrants such as loss of nursing home care (Swingle, 2000; Torres-Gil & Kuo, 1998).

Although access to some of these benefits has been restored, many newcomers fear they will be considered a public charge and be deported. This has led to significant service underutilization and subsequent social and health consequences. For example, fewer immigrant women are getting prenatal care, and children are not being immunized or participating in nutrition programs (Swingle, 2000).

Under welfare reforms instituted in 1996, hundreds of thousands of legal immigrants are threatened with the loss of federal funding unless they become naturalized citizens. Social workers are caught in a value dilemma of supporting the client's self-determination regarding citizenship status or urging citizenship. Pursuing U.S. citizenship may be perceived as a loss of cultural roots and connection to their homelands (Pinto, 2002).

Social workers need to advocate, organize, and mobilize if they are to serve newcomer communities effectively. Legal immigrants, particularly those who have not become citizens are vulnerable to conservative and harsh policy measures such as California's Proposition 187, which attempted to eliminate state services to immigrants, and Proposition 209, which banned the use of affirmative action programs based on race, as well as federal efforts to do the same. In the next few years, it is likely that federal efforts to reduce the budget deficit will result in additional policies that will negatively affect newcomers. Social workers must be vigilant advocates to prevent significant service cuts (Torres-Gil & Kuo, 1998).

CULTURAL COMPETENCE IN SOCIAL AGENCIES

Social, health, welfare, and educational institutions have largely failed to respond to newcomer groups, despite the fact that this population is often poor, unskilled, and in ill health. Newcomers use these services much less than the general population (Mayadas & Elliott, 1992).

Care systems vest power in professionals; thus, conflicting experiences of refugees are often discredited or ignored. We need a fundamental reorganization of systems of care and new models of healing that restore self-definition and control to newcomers, especially refugees who are trauma survivors. Survivors must be able to present their stories in their own terms. The moral and social injuries wrought by atrocities can only be resolved with moral and social solutions (Uehara et al., 2001).

Many newcomers do not have a good command of the English language. It is difficult for them to fully comprehend the services that are being offered to them; thus, they cannot adequately give informed consent or participate as partners in setting goals and working toward change. Agencies must offer interpreters as part of both their ethical and legal responsibilities. Many agencies concerned about costs do not provide access to interpreters, which makes them culturally incompetent and out of compliance with federal mandates.

COMMUNITY INTERVENTIONS

Refugee services are largely uncoordinated, and many refugees stop receiving services after only a few months. Social workers can play an important role in developing coalitions and coordinating services offered by different agencies. Social workers can also be influential in modifying the policies and programs of agencies by serving on boards and advisory committees (Dhooper & Tran, 1998).

Social workers can use community organization knowledge and skills to forge links between social agencies and newcomer communities, enhancing the fit between agency services and client needs. Connecting with refugees requires dedicated outreach efforts that include visiting communities and identifying and contacting key persons such as leaders and traditional healers. It is important for social workers to learn first hand about newcomer communities and their needs (Dhooper & Tran, 1998).

Community organizers can work to stimulate better relations among newcomers and existing residents. Community interventions can be used to prepare both newcomers and neighborhoods for mutual acceptance. Local institutions such as churches, schools, and community centers are ideal locations for building bridges to exchange cultural view points, foods, and life styles, thus fostering intercultural learning (Mayadas & Elliott, 1992).

The isolation of ethnic enclaves may lead to the perception that refugees are successfully resettled. This may also help some refugee populations like the Vietnamese save face or reduce feelings of embarrassment and humiliation (Segal, 2000). Outreach programs will need to recognize these factors and proceed with sensitivity.

Empowerment of refugee communities has received little attention (Silka & Tip, 1994). Refugee communities may serve as surrogates for lost extended family networks, providing both emotional and material support (Segal, 2000). Social workers can play a key role is supporting community leaders and helping newcomers access resources to enhance their natural strengths.

Many social ills disproportionately affect immigrants. Social workers must be involved in societal level change (Kamya, 1997). This includes involvement in the creation of policies and programs that are responsive to all people, including newcomers.

CONCLUSION

The issues of newcomers are directly related to policy considerations and the social climate that allows or restricts their entrance to the United States and access to social programs. Clearly, knowledge of policies and advocacy skills go hand-in-hand with clinical competence in serving these populations. It is important for social workers to recognize the premigration and transit experiences of newcomers and how these may influence their abilities to successfully adapt to life in the United States. Many newcomers, especially refugees, continue to experience the impact of trauma, and most, to some degree, must deal with issues of loss and cultural transition. In a society with increasing diversity caused by immigration, coexisting with a climate of increasing xenophobia, social workers must understand and be equipped to deal with the many challenges faced by their newcomer clients.

Exercises

Exercise #1: Volunteer work with refugees
Make a commitment to do some volunteer work at a refugee shelter or resettlement agency for a semester. At the beginning of your experience, identify three goals you would like to meet to enhance your own learning. The goals must be focused on enhancing your knowledge and experience, not the services you will provide during your time there. Keep a weekly journal of your time with the refugees and your reflections on your interactions. At the end of the semester, evaluate the progress you have made on your three goals.

Exercise #2: Policy review
Examine the Personal Responsibility and Work Opportunity Reconciliation Act of 1996 (welfare reform). Advocates for newcomers vehemently opposed

this policy, particularly its earlier version, because of the harsh impact it would have on noncitizens. Analyze the current policy and identify how it has a differential impact on this population. Or, if you choose, examine another major federal policy and identify how it affects the newcomer population.

Exercise #3: Interview a newcomer

Interview someone who is not a U.S. citizen. You can identify someone to interview through foreign student associations, word of mouth, or with the assistance of your instructor. Ask them questions about their feelings, perceptions, and experiences such as the following:

- What led you to come to the United States?
- What did you think the United States would be like before you came here?
- How does this compare to what you think of the United States now?
- What do you think is the hardest thing for newcomers to adjust to once they arrive here?
- What could Americans do to make things easier for newcomers?

Report the findings from your interview to the class.

Additional Readings

Bhabha, J. (1996). Embodied rights: Gender persecution, state sovereignty, and refugees. *Public Culture, 9,* 3–32. This article describes the tension between human rights and the sovereignty of nation states as it plays out in the arena of refugee policy. Women who apply for refugee status based on claims that they have been persecuted because they are women are the particular focus of the article. The author exposes the politics behind U.S. refugee policies and uses specific cases to illustrate her points.

Eastmond, M. (1996). Luchar y Sufrir—Stories of life and exile: Reflexions on the ethnographic process. *Ethnos 61*(3/4), 231–250. This article presents the stories of two very different refugees from El Salvador. This intimate portrait helps social workers understand and empathize with people who have become refugees.

Fadiman, A. (1997). *The Spirit Catches You and You Fall Down: A Hmong Child, Her American Doctors, and the Collision of Two Cultures.* New York: Farrar, Straus, & Giroux. This award-winning book depicts the story of a refugee family who experience ongoing cultural misunderstandings and conflicts with the medical establishment regarding the treatment of a young girl with a severe form of epilepsy. After years of professional contact, the family interacts with a social worker who begins to approach the case in a culturally competent way. The book provides insight into both positive and negative interactions between helping professionals and this refugee family. This is a moving story of the dire consequences of cultural incompetence.

Mayadas, N. S., & Elliott, D. (1992). Integration and xenophobia: An inherent conflict in international migration. *Journal of Multicultural Social Work, 2*(1), 47–62. This article examines the values and fears that are inherent in debates about immigration. In particular, the roles of economic variables and xenophobia are examined. This article is a useful complement to other literature that focuses on clinical issues of working with newcomers.

References

Berger, R. (1997). Adolescent immigrants in search of identity: Clingers, eradicators, vacillators, and integrators. *Child and Adolescent Social Work Journal, 14*(4), 263–275.

Bernard, W. S. (1959). American immigration policy in the era of the dispossessed. *Social Work, 4*(1), 66–73.

Berthold, S. M. (2000). War traumas and community violence: Psychological, behavioral, and academic outcomes among Khmer refugee adolescents. *Journal of Multicultural Social Work, 8*(1/2), 15–46.

Dhooper, S. S., & Tran, T. V. (1998). Understanding and responding to the health and mental health needs of Asian refugees. *Social Work in Health Care, 27*(4), 65–82.

Drachman, D., & Halberstadt, A. (1992). A stage of migration framework as applied to recent Soviet emigres. *Journal of Multicultural Social Work, 2*(1), 63–78.

Feinberg, R. I. (1996). Use of reminiscence groups to facilitate the telling of life stories by elderly Russian Jewish immigrants. *Smith College Studies in Social Work, 67*(1), 39–51.

Kamya, H. A. (1997). African immigrants in the United States: The challenge for research and practice. *Social Work, 42*(2), 154–165.

Kim, S., McLeod, J. H., & Shantzis, C. (1992). Cultural competence for evaluators working with Asian-American communities: Some practical considerations. In M. A. Orlandi, R. Weston, & L. G. Epstein (Eds.) *Cultural Competence for Evaluators: A Guide for Alcohol and Other Drug Abuse Prevention Practitioners Working with Ethnic/Racial Communities.* Rockville, MD: Office of Substance Abuse Prevention, U.S. Department of Health and Human Services, 203–260.

Kropf, N. P. Nackerud, L., & Gorokhovski, I. (1999). Social work practice with older Soviet immigrants. *Journal of Multicultural Social Work, 7*(1/2), 111–126.

Lee, M. (2000). Understanding Chinese battered women in North America: A review of the literature and practice implications. *Journal of Multicultural Social Work, 8*(3/4), 215–241.

Mayadas, N. S., & Elliott, D. (1992). Integration and xenophobia: An inherent conflict in international migration. *Journal of Multicultural Social Work, 2*(1), 47–62.

Mollica, R. F., Caspi-Yavin, Y., Bollini, P., Truorg, T., Tor, S. I., & Lavelle, J. (1992). The Harvard Trauma Questionnaire: Validating a cross-cultural instrument for measuring torture, trauma, and posttraumatic stress disorder in Indochinese refugees. *Journal of Nervous and Mental Disease, 180*(2), 110–115.

Mui, A. C. (1998). Living alone and depression among older Chinese immigrants. *Journal of Gerontological Social Work, 30*(3/4), 147–166.

Muller, T. (1994). The immigrant challenge. *Wilson Quarterly, 18*(4), 65–71.

Ngo, D., Tran, T. V., Gibbons, J. L., Oliver, J. M. (2001). Acculturation, premigration traumatic experiences, and depression among Vietnamese Americans. In N. G. Choi (Ed.), *Psychosocial Aspects of the Asian-American Experience: Diversity within Diversity.* New York: Haworth Press, 225–242.

Pinto, R. M. (2002). Social work values, welfare reform, and immigrant citizenship conflicts. *Families in Society: The Journal of Contemporary Human Services, 83*(1), 85–92.

Potocky, M., & McDonald, T. P. (1995). Predictors of economic status of Southeast Asian refugees: Implications for service improvement. *Social Work Research, 19*(4), 219–227.

Segal, U. A. (2000). Exploring child abuse among Vietnamese refugees. *Journal of Multicultural Social Work, 8*(3/4), 159–191.

Silka, L., & Tip, J. (1994). Empowering the silent ranks: The Southeast Asian experience. *American Journal of Community Psychology, 22*(4), 497–530.

Swingle, D. B. (2000). Immigrants and August 22, 1996: Will the public charge rule clarify program eligibility? *Families in Society: The Journal of Contemporary Human Services, 81*(6), 605–610.

Torres-Gil, F. M., & Kuo, T. (1998). Social policy and the politics of Hispanic aging. *Journal of Gerontological Social Work, 30*(1/2), 143–158.

Tsai, J. L. (2001). Cultural orientation of Hmong young adults. In N. G. Choi (Ed.), *Psychosocial Aspects of the Asian-American Experience: Diversity within Diversity.* New York: Haworth Press, 99–114.

Uehara, E. S., Morelli, P. T., & Abe-Kim, J. (2001). Somatic complaint and social suffering among survivors of the Cambodian Killing Fields. In N. G. Choi (Ed.), *Psychosocial Aspects of the Asian-American Experience: Diversity within Diversity.* New York: Haworth Press, 243–262.

United Nations High Commission on Refugees. (2002). http://www.unhcr.ch

U.S. Census Bureau. (2001). Current Population Survey. http://www.census.gov

Vinokurov, A. Birman, D., & Trickett, E. (2000). Psychological and acculturation correlates of work status among Soviet refugees in the United States. *International Migration Review, 34*(2), 538–559.

Weaver, H. N., & Burns, B. J. (2001). "I shout with fear at night": Understanding the traumatic experiences of refugees. *Journal of Social Work, 1*(2), 147–164.

CHAPTER | # Advocating for Change

In many ways, helping professionals are involved in journeys to the Four Directions. Contemporary helping professionals are likely to encounter clients from all over the world; some newcomers and others with strong roots in the Americas. Culturally competent service provision requires responding to these clients in ways that are both knowledgeable and respectful of their cultural background.

The history and contemporary realities of diverse groups in the United States contain a number of common themes. One common struggle is the tension between how much tradition will be retained versus how much modernity or U.S. culture will be adopted. This struggle is not always based on choice. People from many cultural backgrounds have been pressured to accommodate just to survive in the United States. For example, the newcomer who does not speak English is likely to have difficulty establishing economic stability. Some policies, such as requiring Native Americans to attend boarding schools, forced certain norms and values on this population. Questions of cultural retention and adaptation resonate at the community as well as the individual level. This raises the issue, at what point is culture lost to assimilation? Indeed, this issue has preoccupied Jewish American thought for decades. Some predict Jewish Americans will become so Americanized and secularized they will cease to exist as a distinct population.

The populations reviewed in this book have experienced societal oppression in one way or another. For some, like African Americans, oppression is highly visible and has roots firmly grounded in history. The oppression felt by other groups such as Asian Americans and Jewish Americans is no less damaging, although it may be veiled by factors such as economic success. Some populations experience oppression that is closely linked with xenophobia. For instance, many Latinos and Arab Americans are perceived as foreigners who do not, and cannot, fit into the U.S. mainstream, regardless of how long they or their families have resided in the United States. Newcomers are perceived as a threat, likely to overwhelm the American way of life; thus, their numbers must be quelled. For some populations, such as Pacific Islanders and Native Americans, their experiences with oppression are linked with marginality in a way that makes them virtually invisible. For all groups, experiences with oppression are also influenced by factors such as gender, religion, class, and sexual orientation.

The characteristics of the American population are constantly changing as shifting immigration trends bring new populations to the United States. Events in other parts of the world such as wars and famine lead to flows of immigrants and refugees. In addition to being knowledgeable about groups of people that are already in the United States, helping professionals are constantly being challenged to learn about newly arriving cultural groups. Likewise, U.S. foreign policy has significant implications, not only for who comes to the United States but also how Americans are perceived and even the well-being of people around the world who will never come to the United States. For example, U.S. involvement in Afghanistan has significant implications for who will receive aid and what types of aid they will receive. Helping professionals can raise their voices to help shape U.S. policy, thus changing the lives of people around the world.

CULTURAL COMPETENCE ON THE MICRO LEVEL

The principles of cultural competence are most commonly associated with direct practice or micro level interventions. Certain knowledge, skills, and values/attitudes are necessary for culturally competent work with various populations. It is important that helping professionals model and communicate the importance of culturally appropriate work so others learn by their example.

Interventions with Clients

Much of the social work knowledge base has erroneously presumed to be culturally neutral. Thus, theories and interventions have been applied to clients without consideration for whether they are culturally congruent, appropriate, or productive. Attempts to tailor some theories and interventions to different populations have often resulted in only minor alterations without questioning the guiding philosophies behind them. For example, questions on an assessment tool may be literally translated without regard for whether concepts are meaningful across cultures.

Often without being aware of it, social workers and other helping professionals have contributed to cultural erosion by applying, unquestioningly, Western-based methods. Social workers need to be conscious and self-reflective in considering implications of the work they do. In some instances, assisting a client to adapt and develop life skills for survival within the mainstream culture may be appropriate; however, this should always involve awareness by the helping professional and informed consent by the client.

Influencing Colleagues

Because the helping professions emphasize characteristics such as self-awareness, empathy, good communication skills, and the desire to help others, helping professionals are in an ideal position to model and teach multicultural skills (Sue et al., 1998). Social workers and other helping professionals have an opportunity to be in the vanguard that supports respect for people of all cultures and demands that oppressive conditions be changed.

This change must begin by influencing colleagues. Not all helping professionals see cultural competence as a priority in their work or in their lives. Those who do can model this important value for their colleagues. Those in supervisory, administrative, or educational capacities also need to help those with whom they work understand the importance and magnitude of cultural competence. Those who minimize and dismiss cultural competence as political correctness need to be taught otherwise. One of the most effective ways to influence others is through example. Beyond stating the importance of cultural competence, helping professionals must demonstrate its centrality in their daily actions.

CULTURAL COMPETENCE ON THE MACRO LEVEL

The principles of cultural competence are applicable at all levels of practice. Policy makers, administrators, and community organizers must be knowledgeable about different cultures and integrate this knowledge with skills and values that honor diversity. Only when cultural competence is implemented at all levels can it reach its maximum effectiveness at any level.

Influencing Social Policies

Social policies guide practice. They influence such factors as what services are available, who is entitled to services, and for how long. Social policies have long had a differential impact on the various populations in the United States. Indeed, some policies, such as resettlement assistance for refugees and the Indian Child Welfare Act, target specific populations. Policies influence the people that helping professionals work with and the types of services that helping professionals are able to provide. Even clinicians who focus their work on micro-level interventions with individual clients, families, or groups need to be aware of how policy shapes their work and their clients' lives.

Awareness of how social policies affect clients is the first step in taking an active role in influencing policies. Various constituencies constantly lobby to influence policies. Some social workers and other helping professionals have raised their voices in this arena. Many others have not. Helping professionals, particularly those who work directly with clients, are in an excellent position to ensure that policy makers hear the voices of these clients. These professionals can show how their clients will be affected by proposed policies or are affected by policies already in place. By building bridges between clients and policy makers, helping professionals can play an important role in shaping policy. Often ethnic communities feel disenfranchised, voiceless, or too overwhelmed by other concerns to speak out on policies that affect them. Social workers and other helping professionals can use empowerment and advocacy skills to assist ethnic community members to influence policies.

Influencing Social Agencies

Helping professionals have the power to influence agencies to be more responsive to the diverse clients they serve. It is a mistake to assume that an individual practitioner can be culturally competent within an environment that neglects culture. Agency leaders must reflect on how services, practices, and administrative procedures are or are not compatible with the cultural populations they serve.

In striving for cultural competence, agencies need to develop specific plans for reaching out to diverse populations. Outreach may include going into ethnic communities to foster communication and trust as a way of encouraging clients to seek needed services, or contacting community leaders for help in establishing connections. Outreach efforts need to involve recruiting culturally diverse people for various roles within the agency. Having community members serve on agency boards or advisory groups is an excellent way of building bridges and establishing resources to help the agency become culturally responsive.

All agency personnel need opportunities for regular training related to working with different kinds of clients. Agency administrators can ensure that quality educational opportunities are available and required. Administrators must communicate that such educational opportunities are a valuable part of staff's responsibilities and must provide adequate time and financial support for attendance. Employees who are expected to seek training on their own time or use their own money are given the message that cultural diversity training is not an important or integral part of the agency and its priorities.

Agency leaders, including those in administrative capacities and those who serve on boards, play an important role in setting agency priorities and communicating what is valued. Unless cultural competence is established as an integral part of the agency, it is likely to never be fully implemented into agency policies and practices. Without full integration, the hands of helping professionals are tied.

Even helping professionals who are not in leadership capacities play an important role in integrating cultural competence throughout their agencies. Indeed, the new helping professional who arrives at the agency with fresh eyes is often able to see how things can be done differently. New staff can serve as an important catalyst that initiates movement toward increased cultural competence.

Influencing Professional Education

Professional education is the vehicle for developing culturally competent professionals. Schools need to fully integrate the principles of cultural competence throughout the curriculum. Cultural competence is not an issue that should be addressed solely in practice or human behavior classes. Cultural competence must be addressed in policy and research classes as well as in field placements.

Cultural competence must become a reality in the structure of educational programs as well as throughout the curriculum. Administrators and faculty must look at how programs are structured to make them accessible and welcoming to a wide variety of students. A program with a culturally competent infrastructure will be likely to attract diverse faculty, staff, and students, thus reinforcing the program's responsiveness to diverse communities. Examining structural and educational policy issues requires a significant and sincere commitment to change. This may be a challenging process for many schools but it is necessary to develop a culturally competent educational process. In turn, this institutional change provides an excellent model for training helping professionals to change external policies and structures.

Students in both undergraduate and graduate programs play an important role in shaping how the profession responds to different types of people. Students often come to the profession with new perspectives. They raise questions about why things are the way they are and why they can't be done differently. Sometimes, helping professionals and educators who have been in the field for a long time get in routines and assume that things are being done in the most appropriate ways. Challenging assumptions and established ways of doing things can help move the helping professions along the journey to cultural competence. Students often bring strong backgrounds in grassroots organizations and indigenous knowledge from their own communities. This knowledge can be a critical factor in shaping the professional knowledge base in culturally competent ways.

Influencing Communities

Social workers and other helping professionals can begin to influence communities and societies to develop increased tolerance and respect for different kinds of people. Research and practice literature clearly indicate that clients are influenced by their social environments. Environments that are hostile and oppressive significantly affect the well-being of individuals who live there. Thus, it seems clear that helping professionals must concern themselves with societal change before they can begin to address the root causes of many clients' problems.

Helping professionals can use community organization skills to facilitate communication between diverse groups in the community. This may involve agency-sponsored community forums to facilitate a dialogue between long-term residents and new immigrants to the community. This may also involve building bridges between diverse communities. Assisting members of isolated ethnic communities to recognize their commonalities can be the first step in building a coalition that can work toward improving conditions for all. For instance, members of the Mexican American and Vietnamese community may come to realize they have similar concerns about bilingual, bicultural education and the responsiveness of the school system. Collectively, they have more power to influence school district decisions and demand that resources be put into programs that meet priorities defined by community residents.

Helping professionals can assist communities, including political leaders, to hear and be responsive to the voices of disenfranchised or new community members. Often communities perceive new arrivals as different and threatening. Community reactions to newcomers may inhibit communication and set up barriers between different groups within the same community. In these situations, helping professionals can facilitate communication and ease tensions. If problems have already arisen between different components of the community, helping professionals may need to draw on conflict resolution skills.

Influencing the Profession

Helping professions are made up of individuals, each of whom has a voice that can be used to influence their profession. Likewise, professions are typically represented by membership organizations with elected leadership who take their priorities and direction from the membership. Helping professionals have an opportunity to shape their profession through these organizational channels. Unfortunately, many fail to use this avenue.

Professional organizations have a key role in advancing cultural competence. As noted earlier, membership organizations in various helping professions have identified cultural competence as an imperative and have listed it as such in their codes of ethics. Some organizations have developed separate documents that describe and emphasize the importance of cultural competence. For example, the National Association of Social Workers has recently developed and adopted Standards for Cultural Competence that have also been endorsed by the Council on Social Work Education as the standard for the social work profession. It is important that professional organizations continue to take leadership in articulating the need for cultural competence and setting standards accordingly.

The various helping professions seem to follow parallel paths in recognizing the need for cultural competence. Social work, psychology, counseling, nursing, and related professions have all prioritized cultural competence and have begun to operationalize this concept and develop professional standards.

Unfortunately, there is minimal cross-pollination among the helping professions. Only a few high-profile scholars such as Derald Sue have become widely recognized across professions. Increased interprofessional dialogue would be an important step in moving cultural competence closer to reality.

Models for interdisciplinary dialogue exist on a smaller level. For example, some universities have initiated conferences that encourage "conversations in the disciplines." This is an opportunity for scholars from various fields to convene at workshops or conferences around an area of interest such as cultural competence. Likewise, interdisciplinary centers provide opportunities for professionals from different disciplines to meet, exchange ideas, develop collaborative projects, and advance the knowledge base of the helping professionals across disciplinary lines. Indeed, this model may be useful in professional training programs. Social work doctoral programs like those at Columbia University and the State University of New York at Buffalo require that students take classes in other disciplines and have scholars from other fields serve on their committees as full members (not just outside readers with minimal roles). It is in the best interest of the people we serve to stimulate interprofessional dialogue and collaboration in further developing the study of cultural competence.

CONCLUSION

Cultural competence requires integration of knowledge, skills, and values/attitudes related to work with diverse populations. This integration must happen at all levels of practice including clinical work, agency administration, policy development, and community organization. Although the majority of helping professionals may work directly with clients, they cannot be fully culturally competent if agency practices or national policies restrict their ability to implement services in a culturally meaningful way. Attention to the community and societal context of clients' lives must be included in culturally competent service provision. All these areas are integrally related.

Social workers and other helping professionals are change agents who must use their skills to influence a variety of individuals and systems. Before helping professionals can successfully make these changes, self-reflection and internal changes are necessary. The ability to reflect on their own values and beliefs, how these interact with the values and beliefs of clients, and how this interaction influences the helping process are key components of culturally competent practice and competent practice in general. Becoming culturally competent requires helping professionals to make changes so they are not imposing their own cultures and belief systems on those they serve. These changes are often difficult, and the realization that helping professionals may have acted from their own ethnocentrism is often painful. It is imperative, however, that helping professionals work toward resolving their own issues with cultural difference before they can be empowered to make a difference in others.

Cultural competence is something to strive for, not something that is ever completely achieved. Helping professionals must not become complacent in the belief that they have become culturally competent. As human beings, all helping professionals are fallible and must be constantly vigilant that they do not impose their own beliefs and values on clients. It is always possible to encounter clients from an unfamiliar culture and the professionals' learning processes must begin anew. Every client experiences his or her culture differently, and cultural identity is influenced by a host of other factors such as gender, class, age, immigration status, and sexual orientation. Helping professionals must see and relate to the individual composed of all these different influences on identity.

Helping professionals have a wide variety of resources available to them. They can seek cultural guides and consultants to help them understand cultural issues and differentiate these from other concerns. Likewise, newcomer and ethnic agencies are often available to provide information on the complex laws and policies related to benefit eligibility. A significant body of literature has been published on a wide range of cultural groups. Helping professionals have a responsibility to be informed and skilled in working with a variety of groups and to continually strive to enhance their level of cultural competence.

Working with diverse clients requires a balance of seeing the differences and seeing the similarities. The common human issues of meeting basic needs and struggling to both survive and thrive are colored by who each person is as an individual from a particular culture, class, and so on. In the long run, no single template for cultural competence can be applied to ensure appropriate work with different types of clients. Helping professionals must strive to provide quality services by balancing who the client is, who the professional is, and the context that shapes them both and their work together.

The journey to the Four Directions is one filled with challenges and rewarding experiences. Although the journey may be somewhat different for each helping professional, I offer this map based on my own journeys and reflections of those who have traveled before me.

References

Sue, D. W., Carter, R. T., Casas, J. M., Fouad, N. A., Ivey, A. E., Jensen, M., LaFromboise, T., Manese, J. E., Ponterotto, J. G., & Vazquez-Natall, E. (1998). *Multicultural Counseling Competencies: Individual and Organizational Development.* Thousand Oaks, CA: Sage.

Index

TO THE OWNER OF THIS BOOK:

I hope that you have found *Explorations in Cultural Competence* useful. So that this book can be improved in a future edition, would you take the time to complete this sheet and return it? Thank you.

School and address: _____

_____

Department: _____

Instructor's name:_____

1. What I like most about this book is:_____

_____

_____

2. What I like least about this book is: _____

_____

_____

3. My general reaction to this book is: _____

_____

_____

4. The name of the course in which I used this book is: _____

_____

5. Were all of the chapters of the book assigned for you to read? _____

   If not, which ones weren't?_____

6. In the space below, or on a separate sheet of paper, please write specific suggestions for improving this book and anything else you'd care to share about your experience in using this book.

_____

_____

TAPE HERE.
DO NOT STAPLE.

TAPE HERE.
DO NOT STAPLE.

FOLD HERE

THOMSON
™
BROOKS/COLE

BUSINESS REPLY MAIL
FIRST-CLASS MAIL   PERMIT NO. 102   MONTEREY CA

POSTAGE WILL BE PAID BY ADDRESSEE

Attn: *Lisa Gebo, Social Work Editor*

BrooksCole/Thomson Learning
60 Garden Ct Ste 205
Monterey CA 93940-9967

FOLD HERE

OPTIONAL:

Your name:_____ Date: _____

May we quote you, either in promotion for *Explorations in Cultural Competence* or in future publishing ventures?

Yes: _____ No: _____

Sincerely yours,

Hilary N. Weaver